Pro T-SQL 2022

Toward Speed, Scalability, and Standardization for SQL Server Developers

Second Edition

Elizabeth Noble

Apress®

Pro T-SQL 2022: Toward Speed, Scalability, and Standardization for SQL Server Developers

Elizabeth Noble
Roswell, GA, USA

ISBN-13 (pbk): 978-1-4842-9255-6
https://doi.org/10.1007/978-1-4842-9256-3

ISBN-13 (electronic): 978-1-4842-9256-3

Managing Director, Apress Media LLC: Welmoed Spahr
Acquisitions Editor: Jonathan Gennick
Development Editor: Laura Berendson
Editorial Project Manager: Shaul Elson
Copy Editor: Mary Behr

Cover image by Solen Feyissa from Unsplash

Distributed to the book trade worldwide by Springer Science+Business Media New York, 1 New York Plaza, Suite 4600, New York, NY 10004-1562, USA. Phone 1-800-SPRINGER, fax (201) 348-4505, e-mail orders-ny@ springer-sbm.com, or visit www.springeronline.com. Apress Media, LLC is a California LLC and the sole member (owner) is Springer Science + Business Media Finance Inc (SSBM Finance Inc). SSBM Finance Inc is a **Delaware** corporation.

For information on translations, please e-mail booktranslations@springernature.com; for reprint, paperback, or audio rights, please e-mail bookpermissions@springernature.com.

Apress titles may be purchased in bulk for academic, corporate, or promotional use. eBook versions and licenses are also available for most titles. For more information, reference our Print and eBook Bulk Sales web page at www.apress.com/bulk-sales.

Any source code or other supplementary material referenced by the author in this book is available to readers on GitHub. For more detailed information, please visit www.apress.com/source-code.

Printed on acid-free paper

To my best girl, Khari.
I miss you oodles, especially you letting me know it
was time to quit working or to go to bed.
Now I've been working on figuring that out myself.

Table of Contents

About the Author

Elizabeth Noble is a Microsoft Data Platform MVP and Director of Database Development in the metro Atlanta area. When ze was introduced to hir first database over 10 years ago, ze found the career ze wanted to pursue. Hir passion is to help others improve the quality and speed of deploying database changes through automation. When ze is not trying to automate database development, ze can be found spending time with zir dogs, painting, paddle boarding, or throwing axes.

About the Technical Reviewer

 **Eric Blinn** has been an SQL Server professional for 20 years, holding the role of DBA, developer, and architect at that time. He has learned a lot over those years, from how to write DTS packages in SQL Server 2000 to implementing read-scale availability groups in SQL Server 2022. He loves to help others on their journey by writing about and presenting on SQL Server topics. You can read his blog on MSSQLTips.com. Eric was born and raised in Ohio where he lives with his wife, Kate, and four children, Jack, Lucy, Felix, and Max.

Acknowledgments

This book would truly not be possible without the technical editing of Eric Blinn. He challenged me to make this book more organized and structured. I also want to thank the entire Apress team including Shaul Elson, Shonmirin PA, and Laura Berendson for their patience while I worked to complete this book.

I also would like to acknowledge the continued support of Mind, Eve, Danny, Mom, Dad, Kaiya, and Ares. You all played your part in helping me either destress or take a break or focus to get this book finished.

I want to thank my team at work for their support including Anthony, Helen, and Jude. I also want to thank the SQL community and the data community for being a part of this journey, and I hope you enjoy this book!

Introduction

This book was written with the intention of encouraging others to get to the next level of their T-SQL development. The goal is to not only get a better understanding of how to write better queries but also an idea of why some methods can be better than others. There is a great deal of flexibility when creating T-SQL statements. In many cases, there is more than one way to achieve the same outcome from your T-SQL. This book is designed for database developers and data professionals who have a general knowledge of T-SQL but are looking to improve their overall code quality. You should understand the T-SQL syntax and know how to write SELECT, INSERT, UPDATE, or DELETE statements before beginning this book. *Pro T-SQL 2022* will prepare you to write consistent code with improved performance. You will also learn how to protect your T-SQL code by using source control and improving your database deployment pipeline. Overall, the goal of this book is to provide you with a framework to write better T-SQL code. As data professionals, we can find ourselves in scenarios where there are high demands or short deadlines. *Pro T-SQL 2022* was written to help you write code that can save you time and energy in the future.

There are five sections in this book. The first section covers how to improve the readability of your T-SQL code. There is an overview of the various data types of T-SQL along with guidance on how to best use these data types. This first section explains the benefits and disadvantages of the various database objects in SQL Server. Additional chapters discuss standardizing and designing T-SQL code. The second section explains how to write T-SQL code that is efficient. This section includes using set-based design to write T-SQL code and how to understand the relationship between hardware and T-SQL design. You will also learn how to use execution plans and new features in SQL Server 2019 to improve the performance of your T-SQL code. The third section discusses how to manage your T-SQL code. The chapters included in this section cover developing coding standards and using source control to store your code. To further manage your T-SQL code, you will also learn some methods to test and deploy your database code. The fourth section addresses how to write T-SQL code so that it is sustainable over time. The last section gives an overview of the different options you can implement to help make your databases more secure. These chapters include methods to safely add new functionality, to log changes to data within your databases, and to manage data growth over time.

CHAPTER 1

Data Types

Data types are key to writing efficient and performant T-SQL. While many data types can be a number, string, or date/time, there are also a variety of data types that do not fit into any of these categories. When selecting a data type, it is important to understand what the data type is and when best to use it.

The most obvious use for data types is to allow users to know what type of information is stored in each column. There is also a difference in how SQL Server stores different data types, and data types can affect how SQL Server generates execution plans. In addition, columns all have a storage cost that is based on the data type and row count of the column. The effects of these storage requirements will be discussed further in Chapter 7. As you'll find later in this chapter, data types can also affect the cost of performing calculations as well as the results of those calculations.

Number Data Types

While numbers may all seem to be the same, T-SQL segments numeric data types into several different categories of data types. These segments can include whole numbers or numbers with decimal places. Numbers are also categorized by either being exact or approximate. When saving numbers there is also a variation in data types based on the range. Understanding how to work with various number data types when performing mathematical calculations is critical to ensuring that applications handle data as expected.

While it may be easiest to pick the most common data types from each category, there are times where it is best to analyze the data that will be stored and search for a more appropriate option. When choosing data types, there are various factors to consider. The most important step is to figure out what kind of data will be stored. The next logical step is to consider how the data will be used. In addition, it is important to understand how T-SQL handles calculations involving various data types. If you want to

© Elizabeth Noble 2023

E. Noble, *Pro T-SQL 2022*, https://doi.org/10.1007/978-1-4842-9256-3_1

store the day of the year, you should use a whole number that allows you to use a value between 1 and 366. When storing revenue for a large company, you need a number with multiple digits and two decimal places. However, if you need to store the price for a gallon of gas, you want a number with two digits and several decimal places. All of these situations are defined differently in SQL Server.

Exact Number Data Types

There are situations when the value of a number is definite and known. These types of numbers can be referred to as exact numbers. Some examples include 1 or 0 for true or false, quantity of units sold, discount percent, or dollars and cents. When working to select the best data type, there are often several similar data types that seem to do the job. In some cases, the categories have more than one data type available.

When considering what data type to use, you want to consider the purpose for this data type. This provides better clarity when determining which data type should be used. You want to consider both the benefits and drawbacks associated with each data type. You also want to consider if SQL Server will have to perform any implicit conversions as a result of using this data type in calculations with other data types. The final piece is to consider how the data type is stored in SQL Server. Here are a series of exact number data types. For each type, you will find some benefits, drawbacks, and common use cases.

BIT

The BIT data type is used to store a binary digit of either 1 or 0. In T-SQL, the data types can also be nullable, which indicates that the BIT data type can also store a NULL value. With only three possible values, this data type has the smallest number of values possible. Due to the small variety of values that can be stored in this data type, the BIT data type also requires the smallest amount of storage on disk. As there are 8 bits in a byte, the same holds true for storing the BIT data type in a database.

The BIT data type is great for data types where "either X or Y" is applicable. The information stored can be interpreted as true or false, on or off, and yes or no. In the case of true or false, this BIT type can be used to indicate if a data record was translated successfully. A common use of indicating on or off with the BIT data type involves indicating if a certain feature is enabled. One example of a yes or no value is recording a customer's decision to opt in to receive marketing information from a company.

One of the challenges with the BIT data type is making sure to use it in a way that promotes good database design. This means there are times when you need to consider the overall purpose when selecting the BIT data type. For instance, it may seem like indicating whether an item has specific characteristics may be a good use of the BIT data type. An example is to add a column in the Product table IsWood to indicate if a part is made of wood. However, it may be better to consider redesigning the database to record those attributes in another table.

A BIT can be used to indicate a successful status for a transaction. However, it is often better to record the state of the transaction over a period of time. If recording status changes over time is important, then using a BIT to record if a transaction is successful may not be the best option. While BIT is small and is great for yes or no values, sometimes you need more options for a column than just yes or no, so you need to consider a larger data type.

TINYINT, SMALLINT, INT, and BIGINT

SQL Server also allows you to store whole numbers, which are numbers that do not have decimals or fractional values. These numbers are known as integers. One example of data stored as integers is quantities of a given item. There are several types of integer values that can be stored within SQL Server. The first integer type is TINYINT. The TINYINT value can contain any integer value between 0 and 255. Due to the limited size of this data type, this may be useful for limited configuration types or number of locations. This data type is like the BIT data type, but this data type has a slightly wider range. This data type is also useful to configure the types of statuses in a system or categories of objects. TINYINT is good for storing these status types as many applications do not need more than 256 statuses.

Now that we've covered TINYINT, let's discuss the possibilities of SMALLINT. The range of SMALLINT covers approximately 70,000 possible values. With this range available, you want to consider what sorts of values you need to have between 256 and 65,435 unique values. The range for the SMALLINT starts at -32,768 and ends at 32,767. This data type would not be useful for a table that logs every single activity that happens. Many databases or data tables may have more than 70,000 transactions or records over the course of several years. This may cause this data type to be unsuitable for those tables. However, there may be other tables where the SMALLINT data type is ideal.

If you have data tables that do not experience high transactional activity but will be growing for some time, the SMALLINT data type may be beneficial. Understanding your business will help you determine if SMALLINT is the correct data type for that value being stored.

If you want to create a table to continue to add functionality to your applications, you may want to store a record indicating each new piece of functionality in your application. An example of this is feature flags. Your application will likely have more than 256 enhancements over the life of the application. You may also want to store configuration values for the application. Storing these configuration values in a table may benefit from the SMALLINT data type.

INT is the most frequent use of the whole number data types. Many databases use this type exclusively for any sort of whole number that is being tracked, which is not recommend. One of the reasons for this is the entire range covers about 5.3 billion records. The INT data type covers the range from −2,147,483,648 to 2,147,483,647. However, when many data tables are created, their identity column is often started, or seeded, at the integer 1. This causes the table to be limited to approximately 2.15 billion unique identities. If you believe that your table will need more than 2.15 billion unique identity records, you may want to start the identity with the lowest number possible, −2,147,483,648, or try using BIGINT. There are very few situations where you would need a value larger than INT, and I speculate there are many times the INT data type is used when TINYINT or SMALLINT would be a better choice. The BIGINT data table can store values from -9,223,372,036,854,775,808 to 9,223,372,036,854,775,808 and takes twice the storage space of INT.

This is often where you may need to perform mathematical calculations. Some businesses process a couple hundred transactions per second. Other businesses process upward of 10,000 or 20,000 transactions per second. In both cases, it's important to consider what kind of growth will be expected in the tables holding this transactional information. If your application has hundreds of transactions per second over several years, the number of records stored will be much smaller than if the application has tens of thousands of transactions per second for the same time period.

Relational databases almost always have more whole number data types than any other data type. These whole numbers do everything from incrementing tables and creating relationships between tables to storing information about various aspects of the business. One of the common temptations is to treat all whole numbers as INT, but some care should be used when selecting which data type to use.

As an example, imagine a database for the trucking industry. If you want to save the number of kilometers driven in a day, you don't need a number larger than 2,880 (120 kilometers per hour times 24 hours in a day). Storing the number of lines on an invoice will be less than 256 for most businesses. There may also be some part of the business that is storing the location of a delivery vehicle every couple of minutes. If there are 5,000 trucks updating that table every two to three minutes, over three years that table could grow to three billion records. In that case, you want to choose a BIGINT, possibly seeded at -9,223,372,036,854,775,808 instead of choosing INT seeded at 1, which would only allow you to save 2,147,483,647 records.

DECIMAL/NUMERIC

Now that we have discussed various integers, let's consider what to do with numbers that require decimals. There are various cases where you are going to want decimal places. There is no difference between DECIMAL and NUMERIC. They are the same data type in SQL Server. Some of these cases involve using dollars and cents, and other times you need decimal places for precision in measurements. There are a couple of options available in these scenarios.

First, there is the option for DECIMAL (alternatively, it is called a NUMERIC data type). This value does not save any currency information with it; however, it does record decimal places. These decimal places can be specified by indicating both the total number of digits that should be stored and the number of digits to the right of the decimal point. For instance, a DECIMAL data type of DECIMAL (10,4) indicates that you can store a number with 6, or 10 minus 4, digits to the left of the decimal point and digits to the right, such as 999999.9999. If you instead created a data type of NUMERIC (9,2), you can store numbers from -9999999.99 to 999999.99. You will find that the DECIMAL or NUMERIC data type is acceptable for almost all data types involving numbers. This includes general-purpose numbers, decimals, measurements, and money values.

Considering that the DECIMAL type can represent multiple different types of numbers, let's examine this data type. There are some specific terms for the DECIMAL data type. The values that make up a DECIMAL data type are precision and scale. Precision relates to the total number of digits that are saved in a DECIMAL data type. Scale refers to the number of digits that are stored to the right of the decimal point. Referring back to the previous examples with the trucking industry, if you want to store kilometers per liter, it may make sense to use the data type DECIMAL(3,1) as you are not likely to have kilometers per liter of 99.9.

SMALLMONEY and MONEY

The next data types to discuss are MONEY and SMALLMONEY. The MONEY and SMALLMONEY data types are like the DECIMAL or NUMERIC data type. The SMALLMONEY and MONEY data types can also be used to store values for currency. SQL Server saves the numeric value and excludes the type of currency associated with the value saved.

The largest difference between the MONEY and SMALLMONEY data types is the size and amount of storage space required. The SMALLMONEY data type covers a range from –214,000 to positive 214,000 and uses half the storage as the MONEY type, which covers a range from –922 billion to 922 billion.

The MONEY data type is accurate to store up to four decimal places. The limitation on decimal places limits the accuracy to ten thousandths of the monetary value stored. The MONEY data type saves all values to four decimal places. The fixed number of decimal places impacts how rounding affects calculations involving the MONEY data type. This is because SQL Server saves the MONEY data type as BIGINT. Similarly, the SMALLMONEY data type is saved as an INT. This explains why you may have rounding issues with MONEY or SMALLMONEY.

Choosing MONEY or DECIMAL (9,4) is mostly a matter of preference as long as you are aware of the impact the MONEY data type can have on calculations and plan accordingly. The main goal is consistency with how you are storing data relating to currency so that DBAs and developers alike can quickly understand the purpose and implications of the data field in question. While this data type will save space over a DECIMAL, there are other ways your database administrator can save space that do not involve changing the data type.

Approximate Number Data Types

Next, let's analyze the differences between exact and approximate numbers. Exact numbers exist for things that you know the exact quantity of, such as how many items you bought at the store or the exact amount in dollars and cents. Approximate numbers exist for scenarios where the measurements may not be exact. Approximate numbers can be used to store very large or very small numbers. You may also find that your application is recording a measurement that is not exact. You may cut a length of fabric that is close to but not exactly a specific value. For example, the length of fabric may be around 12 inches. Storing the value of 12 inches would be an approximate value. This measurement of 12 inches may be so close that it would be difficult to tell that the length of fabric was not exactly 12 inches.

There are some rounding issues that come into play when dealing with approximate numbers. This is because approximate numbers are known to not be the exact measurement. In SQL Server, there is one option for approximate numbers. This data type is called FLOAT. If the floating number has 24 numbers, the synonymous data type is REAL.

Caution   It may be tempting to use FLOAT or REAL because they can hold such large numbers and use only 4 or 8 bytes, respectively. However, these data types do not do well with some WHERE clauses. These data types should only be used in very limited situations where a DECIMAL or BIGINT can't be used.

When working with REAL or FLOAT numbers, there can be issues converting these data types to other data types. When you convert a FLOAT data type to an INTEGER, all the values in the decimal places get truncated. Be aware that using approximate numbers may cause unexpected results. One example is when using the DECIMAL or NUMERIC data types. When converting a FLOAT or REAL number to a DECIMAL or NUMERIC data type, you are only able to keep seven decimal places.

Converting Number Data Types

You have explored the types of numbers available and what happens in working with the various number data types. In addition to storing numbers, you also want to understand how various number data types interact with one another. First, let's consider what happens when you do calculations involving fields with the same data type. In these scenarios, if all the fields for the calculation are of the same data type, the output of the calculation is a value of the same data type. Therefore, if you multiply a quantity times the price and both values are stored as a NUMERIC data type of DECIMAL(5,2), it gives the same data type of DECIMAL as a result. SQL Server determines the result precision and scale based on the starting precision and scale as well as the type of calculation performed. You also want to consider how the precision and scale is stored in the application. The application may be expecting a value of DECIMAL(5,2). Based on the calculation performed, the data values returned may be outside the range of the data type specified. This can cause an overflow in calculation.

Things can get a little more interesting when working across various data types. To use the example of quantity times price again, let's examine what happens if you have an

INT data type for the quantity that is calculated with a DECIMAL (5,2) data type for the price. SQL Server uses the process of data type precedents. First, you should get familiar with the data type order of precedence related to the data types covered so far. The following list is ordered from highest order to lowest:

1. FLOAT

2. REAL

3. DECIMAL

4. MONEY

5. SMALLMONEY

6. BIGINT

7. INT

8. SMALLINT

9. TINYINT

10. BIT

In the preceding scenario, you are using both the INT and DECIMAL data types, shown in the preceding list as lines 8 and 3 respectively. Since INT has the lower precedence, you expect that SQL Server will internally convert the INT data type to the DECIMAL data type. This is called an implicit conversation and it adds time to the query execution. This conversion does not change the original data value, only how SQL Server uses this value as part of the calculation. Once this conversion is complete, SQL Server moves forward with the calculation. This works well unless you are performing an action like trying to concatenate number and string data types.

String Data Types

Now that you know how to work with number data types, you should spend some time on the various string data types. These data types are used to store alphabetical letters, words, or combinations or letters and numbers. In addition, string data types are used to store character values that are either non-Unicode or Unicode. The last category of string data types includes images and binary values.

Character String Data Types

There is information that will be stored in the database that is not related directly to numbers. The data stored in character strings can be ANSI or Unicode. Strings can also be created with a fixed or variable length. This data can be names, descriptions, addresses, or other character values. Determining which data type to use depends on what type of information is being stored and how much information needs to be stored. After this section, you will be prepared to choose the correct string data type for your needs.

CHAR and VARCHAR

Two of the character string data types available are CHAR and VARCHAR. These data types are similar and only vary regarding whether the string is stored as a fixed-length or variable-length character string. Both data types are used to store text data, and the characters that can be stored in these fields are the same characters allowed by the collation of the column.

CHAR is for character field, which is used to signify that the data type has a fixed length. VARCHAR is used for a variable character field. The VAR in VARCHAR indicates that the data type has a variable length. If the data will have similar lengths, like phone numbers or ZIP codes, then CHAR may be the preferred data type. However, if the column widths will vary significantly, as is the case with address lines or notes columns, then VARCHAR will be a better option.

When choosing a value for CHAR or VARCHAR, you can choose either a value between 1 and 8000 or the word MAX. Consider limiting the use of VARCHAR(MAX) for situations where you expect to save more than 8000 characters. If VARCHAR(MAX) is specified, then the maximum storage size is 2 GB. However, consider if you need this functionality or if using VARCHAR with a smaller number of characters may be more appropriate.

In order to minimize truncating data, make sure to always specify the number of bytes stored explicitly when using the CHAR or VARCHAR data types. VARCHAR defaults to 1 for data definition and 30 bytes when using the CAST or CONVERT functions.

For collations using single-byte encoding characters, such as Latin, the storage size in bytes for CHAR is equal to the number of characters. When working with VARCHAR, the string length of the field, which in the case of single-byte encoding is the same as the number of characters, plus two additional bytes is equal to the total number of bytes stored. It is also possible to save multi-byte encoding characters in the CHAR and VARCHAR data types. For both data types, the number of characters saved may be less than the total number of bytes.

Starting with SQL Server 2019, it is now possible to save Unicode values in CHAR or VARCHAR. However, this is only possible if UTF-8 encoding is enabled.

TEXT

The TEXT data types have been used to store very large strings of characters. However, this data type has been deprecated. As this data type has been deprecated, you want to avoid using the TEXT data type for new development. If you need to use the TEXT data type, use the data type VARCHAR(MAX) for new development instead.

Unicode String Data Types

Prior to SQL Server 2019, any Unicode text data needed to be saved as a special data type. This is still true for situations where UTF-8 encoding cannot be or is not enabled.

NCHAR and NVARCHAR

When using Unicode values, there are a couple of options available. These options include storing a fixed or variable-length string. In order to avoid unexpected results, you should understand how these data types work if the number of characters or collation is not specified.

Once you have determined that you need to use the NCHAR or NVARCHAR data types, choosing between them gets easy. If the data being stored will generally have similar lengths, then the NCHAR data type is the correct choice. However, if the values stored will vary significantly, then the NVARCHAR data type may be a better choice. In addition, if the number of characters to be stored is over 4000, it is recommended to use NVARCHAR(MAX).

Typically, it is best practice to specify the number of characters when declaring the NCHAR or NVARCHAR data types. The default number of characters for data definition or variable declaration is 1 character for NCHAR or NVARCHAR. However, when using the CAST or CONVERT function, the default number of characters is 30 if none are specified. If a collation is not specified for the NCHAR or NVARCHAR data type, the default database collation will be used.

Understanding the amount of space required to store this data type also allows you to make better decisions about if this is the correct data type and the number of characters that need to be stored. Storing NCHAR takes up twice as many bytes as the string length of the byte pairs; when using NVARCHAR the number of bytes stored is twice the string length in byte pairs plus 2 bytes.

NTEXT

Previously, storing very large variable-length Unicode data was accomplished using the NTEXT data type. If this data type is still in use in your systems, you can expect it to store up to 1,073,741,823 characters. However, due the size associated with Unicode values, the total length stored may be less. Going forward, it is no longer best practice to use this data type. Instead, use the NVARCHAR(MAX) data type.

Binary String Data Types

At some point, you may want to store data that is neither a number, character, nor a data or time value. Using binary strings for storing items that are strings without characters may be useful. These can include audio, video, images, or other similar items. In these cases, the use of binary strings may be appropriate. There are a couple alternatives when using binary string data types.

BINARY and VARBINARY

The options available for storing binary string data involve storing either fixed-length or variable-length character strings. Like the other string data types discussed, there are some considerations when dealing with these data types.

Two of the available data types are BINARY and VARBINARY. The best option for storing binary strings with similar lengths is the BINARY data type. Conversely, when storing binary strings with significantly varying lengths of data, the VARBINARY data type is a better choice. If the total length of the binary string is expected to exceed 4000 characters, then it is suggested to use VARBINARY(MAX).

Using the BINARY and VARBINARY data types for data definition or variable declaration has a default length of 1 if the number of characters is not specified. When converting BINARY to VARBINARY with the CAST or CONVERT function, the default

number of characters is 30. Use caution when converting to BINARY or VARBINARY
from a variable with a different length as SQL Server may pad or truncate the binary data
as necessary.

The BINARY data type stores the same number of bytes as the length of data
being stored, whereas VARBINARY uses 2 bytes plus the same number of bytes as
the length of data being stored. In both data types, the length can be up to 8000. For
VARBINARY(MAX), the maximum storage size is 2 GB.

IMAGE

The IMAGE data type has been used to store large variable-length binary data. In the
case of the IMAGE data type, you should use the VARBINARY(MAX) data type going
forward as the IMAGE data type is deprecated.

Collation for Data Types

Data can be configured to toggle case sensitivity, which determines if a lowercase c is
treated the same as an uppercase C. There is also accent sensitivity for determining if n
is treated the same as ñ. You can also indicate if Katakana and Hiragana should be sorted
the same kana sensitivity. Some other types of collation options are sensitive based
on width, variation-selector, binary, binary-code point, and UTF-8. The sensitivity that
is stored is referred to as collation. The collation of a column is the same as the database
unless there is a specific override in place.

Date and Time Data Types

Each database transaction occurs at a specific point in time. There may be a need to
reference or know when a transaction happened. Your application may record important
dates for a person including birthdays or anniversaries. Dates and times can also be used
to determine pricing and functionality. By using dates and times, you can determine
when functionality should be enabled or disabled. Dates and times can also show when
a user account is inactive or system access is enabled or expired. Pricing and billing
rates can cover multiple different date ranges. When one set of pricing becomes inactive,
another set may be active. Due to regulations, your company may need to record the
pricing over a period of time. This includes indicating when the pricing rates started and

stopped. Depending on the purpose for tracking this information, you may only need to know the date or time of the transaction. There are other situations where it is best to know both the date and time associated with a certain action.

DATE

When working with transactions, there may be a specific occasion when you want to record when something happened. In some cases, it may only matter what day the transaction happened. The DATE data type can also be used to store aggregated data for a given day. While recording the date of the activity, there may be some options available as to how that data is displayed. When choosing if the DATE data type is right for your situation, it is also important to consider not only how much data is stored for the DATE data type but any possible limitations in how the data can be stored.

There will be times when an application or a user needs to know when a specific action happened. When deciding if a DATE data type is the right choice, consider the need for the information both in terms of user and application usage. In some cases, it is easier to think about when a DATE data type is not preferable. For any action where you want to know a specific time when something happened, the DATE data type is not a good choice. However, if it is only necessary to know on what day an action occurred, then the DATE data type is a great option.

For the DATE data types, there are several options as to how a DATE can be displayed. With the date format, the default is YYYY-MM-DD. In this case, YYYY represents the four-digit year with the range of 0001 to 9999. MM represents the month number from 01 to 12, and DD stands for the day ranging from 01 to 31 per the number of days in a month. The DATE can be displayed in a variety of numeric and alphabetic formats. However, the format ydm is not supported.

The DATE values that can be stored range from 0001-01-01 to 9999-11-31. The DATE data type has a ten-digit character length with a precision of 10 and a scale of 0. The DATE data type takes up 3 bytes and is stored as an INT.

Dates can be converted to DATETIME, SMALLDATETIME, DATETIME2, or DATETIMEOFFSET. However, the time value is set to midnight. Dates cannot be converted to the TIME data type, and any attempts to perform this conversion will fail with an error. In addition, dates do not have a time zone offset and are not Daylight Saving Time (DST) aware.

TIME

Another data type related to when an action happened is the TIME data type. TIME can be used to record a specific time when a transaction or activity occurred. It is useful to understand how time is stored and formatted. When using the TIME data type, it is helpful to know the implications of converting the data type to other DATE and DATETIME data types. There are also some limitations when using the TIME data type.

TIME can be used to record a specific time when a transaction or activity occurred. When this happens, the time is recorded independently of the date and the date may not be able to be determined in the future. One way around this issue is to store the date separately from the time. The accuracy of TIME is up to 100 nanoseconds, and the default value for TIME is 00:00:00.

The default format for TIME is hh:mm:ss[.nnnnnnn]. In this format, hh stands for a two-digit hour ranging from 0 to 23, mm for a two-digit minute ranging from 0 to 59, and ss for a two-digit second from 0 to 59. The TIME data type allows for varying precision and, if specified, up to seven decimal places can be used for fractional seconds as represented by nnnnnnn. These values can range from 0 to 9999999.

Due to how AM and PM are used to differentiate between morning and evening, there are additional considerations when working with TIME. If AM or PM is not provided and the value for hour is between 00 and 11, the time will be recorded as AM. For hours 12 to 23, the time will be saved as PM. When writing TIME, if 12 AM is entered, this value will be converted to the 0 hour.

The range of TIME is 00:00:00.0000000 to 23:59:59.9999999. The character length can vary from 8 to 16 digits, depending on the precision specified for TIME. In either scenario, TIME is saved as fixed 5 bytes. If TIME is converted to any data type with a date and time, the day value is represented as 1900-01-01. If the fractional precision is higher for TIME than the new data type, the value is truncated. Any attempt to convert the TIME data type to a DATE will fail. Like DATE, TIME is neither time zone nor DST aware.

SMALLDATETIME, DATETIME, DATETIME2, and DATETIMEOFFSET

There are occasions when saving the date or time may not be enough. For these scenarios, it may be best to combine the date and time values together. Sometimes these values can be somewhat simpler, need more precision, or need to be time zone aware.

One such data type is the SMALLDATETIME. This data type is used to record both a specific date and time. It has a default value of 1900-01-01 00:00:00. This data type is accurate to one minute. While you can pass in seconds, they will always be rounded to the nearest minute.

As with the date data type, the SMALLDATETIME data type can be displayed in a variety of numeric and alphabetical formats. The range for the SMALLDATETIME is somewhat limited as compared to other DATE and DATETIME data types. The day portion of this data type can span 1900-01-01 to 2079-06-06. While the time entered can range from 00:00:00 to 23:59:59, the value saved in the database will be 00:00:00 to 23:59:00. The overall length of the SMALLDATETIME is up to 19 characters, and the storage size required is a total of 4 fixed bytes.

When converting SMALLDATETIME to other DATETIME data types, keep in mind that any additional precision needed will be recorded with 0s. While it may be tempting to use the SMALLDATETIME, this data type is not ANSI-compliant. As stated previously, the minutes for this data type will be rounded depending on the value passed for the seconds. If the seconds passed are less than or equal to 29.998, the minute will be rounded down. Otherwise, the minute will be rounded up. Like the date and time data types, SMALLDATETIME is also not time zone or DST aware.

There are more options available than just SMALLDATETIME. DATETIME is an option for a higher level of precision than the previously mentioned data types. There are also several key considerations when using this data type.

While the DATETIME data type can record a specific day and time, it may not comply with the SQL Standard. One of the key issues with this data type has to do with the limitations related to accuracy. The DATETIME data type can record three decimal places for fractional seconds; the third decimal place is always rounded to an increment ending in .000, .003, or .007.

If a value is not specified, the default for DATETIME is 1900-01-01 00:00:00. There are many numeric and alphabetical formats available when using this data type. The year range for DATETIME is 1753-01-01 to 2999-11-31, and the time can range from 00:00:00.000 to 23:59:59.997. The size of this data type is 8 bytes with a character length ranging from 19 to 26.

While it is possible to convert other data types to DATETIME, it is not recommended as this data type does not meet SQL Standards and is not ANSI-compliant. This data type is also not time zone or DST aware.

The DATETIME2 data type was added to SQL Server starting with SQL Server 2008. Many applications predate SQL Server 2008 so it is not as commonly used as DATETIME despite its obvious advantages. The DATETIME2 data type has some additional advantages over the data types previously mentioned. While some of the previously mentioned data types have a fixed size, this data type functions a little differently. You will also learn the options available for storing and formatting this data type.

The DATETIME2 data type allows for a specific date and time to be recorded with an accuracy of up to 100 nanoseconds. The default value for DATETIME2 is 1900-01-01 00:00:00. Due to this level of precision, this is a great data type to use for scenarios where the time must be known to a fraction of a second. As DATETIME2 doesn't have the same rounding issues as DATETIME, it is also more straightforward to work with this data type when writing code.

The DATETIME2 data type supports multiple numeric and alphabetical ways to display the information. The date range for DATETIME is from 1753-01-01 to 2999-11-31 and the time range is from 00:00:00 to 23:59:59.9999999. Multiple precision options are allowed, causing the character length to range from 19 for the precision to the second all the way up to 27 for the precision to 0.0000001 nanoseconds.

The variation in the precision also affects the storage size of the DATETIME2 data type. One byte is used to store the precision of DATETIME2 plus the number of bytes needed depending on the precision of time. If the precision is less than three decimal places for nanoseconds, then there are another 6 bytes used to store the DATETIME2 value. If the precision is 3 or 4, there is 1 byte to store the precision and 7 bytes to store the value, for a total of 8 bytes. However, the total is 9 bytes for any values with a precision of more than four decimal places.

Due to the high level of accuracy, the probability of converting values to DATETIME2 is highly likely. If a date is converted to DATETIME2, the time component will be recorded as 00:00:00. If time is converted to DATETIME2, the day will be 1900-01-01. In the case of SMALLDATETIME to DATETIME2, the date and time will be copied. Any additional precision will be represented with 0s. When going from DATETIME to DATETIME2, make sure to use explicit conversions to avoid unexpected results. The main limitation of using DATETIME2 is that the data type is not time zone aware or Daylight Savings Time aware.

It is common for businesses to operate across multiple time zones. The final data type for dates and times is DATETIMEOFFSET. Offset is used to refer to the concept of a time zone. When discussing DATETIMEOFFSET, there is some additional functionality that has not been presented before with the other data types. There are also things to keep in mind when formatting, storing, or converting to this data type.

The DATETIMEOFFSET data type records the specific date and time, with a high level of accuracy, for transactions or actions that have taken place. One of the key advantages of this data type is the ability to have an offset on the time, thus allowing databases from multiple geographic locations to not only be aware of when something happened in relation to their local time but also in relation to local time at another location.

The DATETIMEOFFSET is accurate to 100 nanoseconds and has a default value of 1900-01-01 00:00:00. The format of DATETIMEOFFSET is YYYY-MM-DD hh:mm:ss. nnnnnnn +|- hh:mm. The +|- hh:mm portion of this data type is related to the offset. The offset can range from +14 to –14 for the number of hours that a given time can have an offset. As with the other time and DATETIME data types, this date can be formatted or displayed numerically or alphabetically.

The dates can range from 0001-01-01 to 2999-12-31. The time that can be saved ranges from 00:00:00 to 23:59:59.9999999. When the precision is saved as YYYY-MM-DD hh:mm:ss {+|-} hh:mm, the character length is 26. The character length can go up to 34 when the precision is YYYY-MM-DD hh:mm:ss.0000000 {+|-} hh:mm. The storage space required for the DATETIMEOFFSET data type is a fixed 10 bytes. A DATETIMEOFFSET value can be very easily converted from the time zone in which it is stored to any other time zone. Going from DATETIMEOFFSET to DATETIME2 will cause the time zone to be truncated.

Other Data Types

In addition to the data types discussed, SQL Server has several other data types. Some of these data types can be used in table definition and may have special purposes, while others may only be usable as variables or inside stored procedures.

UNIQUEIDENTIFIER

The UNIQUEIDENTIFIER data type can be a column in a table or used as a variable. The UNIQUEIDENTIFIER takes up 16 bytes, and the maximum number of characters that can be stored in this data type is 36. While non-Unicode character strings can be converted to UNIQUEIDENTIFIER, if the total number of characters exceeds 36, those results will be truncated.

This data type is a GUID, or Globally Unique Identifier. The concept is that these unique values will only ever be used once. However, there have been reports of this not being true. Either way, the UNIQUEIDENTIFIER can be populated one of several ways. These include using the functions NEWID() and NEWSEQUENTIALID(). Otherwise, these values can be manually populated if the overall format of the GUID is correct and uses valid hexadecimal values of 0–9 and a–f.

While the UNIQUEIDENTIFIER can be used in place of IDENTITY, I only recommend it for scenarios where it is absolutely required. Not only does it take up significantly more space than an INT or BIGINT, but UNIQUEIDENTIFIER is limited in the types of constraints that can be used with this data type. UNIQUEIDENTIFER can be an IDENTITY but other table constraints are not allowed.

XML

Various systems and applications send, use, or store XML data. While there is the option to parse this data and save it in tables, there are also times when it may be necessary to store the XML data intact. It is important to note that XML is conceptually a NVARCHAR(MAX) data type with special rules. When storing XML data, there are other considerations that include what data is in the XML.

For the XML data type, the data must be in a valid XML format. In order to be valid, there are several requirements. All starting tags must have matching end tags. In addition, nested elements must begin and end within the same parent element. XML elements cannot have more than one attribute, and markup characters must be properly specified. If the XML data meets all the preceding requirements, then the XML data is considered well-formed. If you can't follow those rules but really want to store your XML you can use NVARCHAR(MAX).

The total amount of stored XML data allowed is limited to 2 GB. That data can have non-Unicode or Unicode data. Sometimes XML data follows a set guideline and has specified data types. In this scenario, the XML data may have a defined XML schema.

For XML data that has a schema, the XML can be considered typed. Often typed XML data will take up less space, and there may be additional functionality with the data that is stored. However, a limitation of this typed XML is that the XML must pass validation. If untyped XML data is chosen, the data does not have to be validated and may not be assigned a schema.

Spatial Geometry Types

When working with data, you may want to store various shapes in your database. While this is not a common request, there is an available data type that can be used to store shapes or drawings based on flat maps.

This data type can support several format instances including points, lines, circular lines, curves, polygons, curved polygons, multiple points, multiple strings, multiple polygons, and a collection of any or none of these objects. This data type can be used to create a map of a retail store or a map showing where delivery drivers should park to deliver or pick up goods.

Spatial Geography Types

While you may want to save shapes in SQL Server using a flat-Earth method, there are other times when it is necessary to store information based on the shape of the Earth. In these cases, using the geography data type is preferable. Use this data type for countries, roads, or maps where longitude and latitude are important.

Like the geometry data type, the geography data type supports several options. These options include all the same types as the geometry data type including points, lines, circular lines, curves, polygons, curved polygons, multiple points, multiple strings, multiple polygons, and a collection of any or none of these shapes. However, the geography data type also supports the full globe instance. The spatial geography type can allow you to create a shape that identifies when a delivery driver has arrived at the target location. This data type can also be used to identify all retail stores within a specified range of one another. This can allow customers to easily know which locations are within a set driving distance of their usual store.

SQL_VARIANT

The SQL_VARIANT data type is used internally by SQL Server, and that is where the data type should remain. While not a data type that you should use in your own databases, I do want to go over what this data type in case you want to learn more about it.

The SQL_VARIANT data type stores various data types in the same column. You can insert data directly into the column or cast the data as a specific data type. If you do not specify the data type at the time of the insert, SQL_VARIANT will try to determine the correct data type. This can cause data to be stored differently than expected. While SQL_VARIANT does seem to choose well with numbers, there are cases where dates may be stored as VARCHAR(8000) if the data type is not specified.

The way data in a SQL_VARIANT column is ordered also differs from other data types. SQL_VARIANT groups data into like types called data type families. These data type families have their own order, and values with data types in higher families are considered greater than values in lower families. If a data that is being compared exists in same family, SQL_VARIANT will implicitly convert the data type that is lower to the data type that is higher and then complete the comparison.

ROWVERSION

There are instances when you may want to know when an action happened to a table. While there are some methods that can be used to track database changes, there is also a specific data type that can be used to record when a record has been updated.

The ROWVERSION data type allows you to get a relative idea of when a specific record or set of records was updated. This value neither has a date nor a time component but is a binary value. ROWVERSION can be compared to other rowversion values or to the current rowversion value in the database. You can create a table that has a column named RowVersion with the type ROWVERSION. Upon inserting a record, the ROWVERSION column may be updated to have the value 0x00000000000007D1. You can update one of the columns in the same row, and the ROWVERSION column may be updated to 0x00000000000007D2. While you can tell a change has happened, you cannot determine when the change happened or determine what was changed.

Note   The ROWVERSION value is incremented at the database level. Any insert or update associated with a row having a ROWVERSION data type will increment the rowversion value for the database.

Therefore, the rowversion values for a given table may appear to be missing records in the sequence. However, these records may be saved in a different table.

When storing the rowversion value, the total storage space required is 8 bytes. You can specify if ROWVERSION should be either non-nullable or nullable. If the column is not nullable, then the column will act similarly to BINARY(8). Otherwise, the column will behave similarly to VARBINARY(8). Only one ROWVERSION column can be added per table. This column is updated systematically any time one or more rows is inserted or updated.

HIERARCHYID

Sometimes data has an ordered relationship to a different data record in the same table. Oftentimes this has to do with data that is a parent or child of other data. A very common scenario is a table that stores all employees for an organization. A HIERARCHYID column can be added, allowing the organizational structure between employees to be saved and accessible to an application. Another possibility is a product table where some products in the table are components of other products.

For these scenarios, the HIERARCHYID may be useful to help categorize how data is interrelated. The data type HIERARCHYID is limited to 892 bytes. However, this data type is a system data type with a variable length. Even though this data type is a system data type, the application using this data type is responsible for determining the correct hierarchy that should be stored.

Table

A special data type is the table data type. This data type is not part of a CREATE TABLE definition. Rather, this data type is either used as a variable, which is commonly referred to as a table variable, or is used to store values returned from a table-valued function. When you find yourself wanting to store data for later use, this may be a good data type to consider. However, there are some caveats and limitations to keep in mind with using tables as a data type.

Usually, it is preferable to limit the use of table variables to scenarios where there will not be a significant amount of data returned. Historically, SQL Server has not accurately estimated the total number of rows in a table variable. In the past, it would estimate low. When your row count is low, you're good to go. But if you put a lot of rows and the estimate is a few rows, the query plan can be poor. SQL Server 2019 made some updates to improve this fault in the query optimizer. Therefore, starting with SQL Server 2019 the database engine should give a better estimation when dealing with table variables going forward.

While table variables can be used in stored procedures, batches, or functions, the table variable only exists for the duration of that object.

Note   Batches are one or more SQL statements that are executed as a group. A single statement, like a stored procedure, can be considered a batch if there are multiple queries within the stored procedure. This is similar to when you have multiple queries in the SQL Server Management Studio (SSMS) and you select F5 to have all queries execute at the same time. Adding semicolons after each query will also create a batch if there are two or more statements.

In the case of functions or stored procedures, the table variable no longer exists after the function or stored procedure has completed executing. In the case of batches, the table will exist for the entirety of the batch. As table variables only persist for the entirety of an update, using them may decrease the locks required as part of an update.

Another limitation of tables as data types is that there are no statistics generated on the table variable. This also means that using indexes with table variables is very limited. Some indexes can be included when creating a table variable.

Cursor

Another data type that cannot be used as a column in a table is cursor. Overall, this data type can be very limited, but there are occasions when this is the best data type for the task. When considering this data type, it is best to understand the potential performance impact associated with using the cursor data type.

The cursor data type is usually used as a variable. However, this data type can also be used as an output from a stored procedure. In either case, the cursor data type takes a set of data and interacts with each record row by row. Since the cursor data type can hold a set of data, it is also possible for this data type to have no data. This indicates that the cursor data type is nullable.

This data type is most commonly created using T-SQL. Cursors can also be implemented using API (application programming interface) server cursors and client cursors, but both of these are outside the scope of this book. In order to create a cursor, a local variable must be declared as a cursor. Like other local variables, it is possible to either declare the cursor and populate values or declare the cursor and populate values using a set statement. Other functions used to create cursors can be used with this data type. They include open, fetch, close, deallocate, and cursor_status. In addition, there are system stored procedures that have cursor data types.

One of the key factors in understanding the various data types available is knowing which data type to use. In some cases, using the correct data type may come down to saving space. Other times, using an incorrect data type can lead to significant performance issues. You also want to be consistent in how you use and reference your data types both in your T-SQL code and database objects. If SQL Server needs to compare two different types, it will need to convert at least one of the data types so that both data types are the same. This process is known as implicit conversion. The CPU cost associated with implicit conversion can be significant and should be avoided if possible. The best way to avoid implicit conversion is to use the same data types for fields that will be compared. The biggest challenge is that sometimes it takes several years to realize how an incorrect data type may be negatively impacting application performance.

CHAPTER 2

Database Objects

You need to know more than just the right data types to write T-SQL that performs quickly and uses hardware efficiently. Data types will help you determine how your data should be stored, but the next step is to design the process to access that data. One of the largest benefits and drawbacks of using T-SQL is the number of options available to access data. This chapter was written with the expectation that you are already familiar with how to write T-SQL to read, insert, update, and delete data.

In this chapter, I will discuss various methods that can be used to interact with your data. There are objects that allow you to pull information together consistently and quickly. You may also want a database object that performs small, quick actions and can reuse that code for multiple purposes. Some database objects can store information temporarily for reusability within the same batch or connection. Other database objects can perform actions as the result of activities on server or database objects. While T-SQL performs best with set-based activities, you may also find yourself needing to loop through data one record at a time.

Depending on your purpose, one or more database objects may meet your needs. While each of these database objects has its place, there are pros and cons for when and how to use each of these objects. Throughout this chapter, I will walk through various scenarios showing both the positive and negative consequences of using each of these database objects. First, I will start by discussing views in T-SQL.

Views

What is a view? Like the definition of the word *view*, a view in T-SQL is a means of taking several different items and putting them together to form one cohesive image. A view is a select query that is saved with a new name called the view name. Users can query that view name and SQL Server will actually use the underlying predefined query. In this

© Elizabeth Noble 2023

E. Noble, *Pro T-SQL 2022*, https://doi.org/10.1007/978-1-4842-9256-3_2

section, I will discuss some of the options available when using views. As with any tool, there are advantages to using views, and there are risks associated with views if they are used incorrectly.

User-Defined Views

The term *user-defined view* is the full name for the basic version of a view. One of the results of a view is simplicity. It is one way for applications and users to access complex sets of information without needing to understand all the relationships in a database. There is some additional functionality for protection and security that is available when using views. I will go through examples of views that help performance as well as some situations where views may not be the right option.

For standard user-defined views, SQL Server does not store the actual data returned by a view physically. Therefore, each time a view is called, it will use the statement inside the view to pull back the data that currently exists in the underlying table(s). One of the advantages for this method is it allows users accessing these views to have code that is cleaner and easier to read. Another feature of views is that users can be granted permission to the view but not to the associated tables. This can allow users to have access to some but not all the data from the tables that make up the view.

Let's start by comparing the performance of a view to the performance of the same query as an ad hoc query or a stored procedure. Listing 2-1 shows the query that will be used as the basis for the comparison.

Listing 2-1. Query for Analysis

```
SELECT cus.FirstName,
       cus.LastName,
       cus.FirstName + ' ' + cus.LastName AS FullName,
       ord.OrderNumber,
       ord.OrderDate,
       ord.ShipDate
FROM dbo.CustomerOrder ord
       INNER JOIN dbo.Customer cus
       ON ord.CustomerID = cus.CustomerID;
```

In the case of this query, the logic is simple. In Listing 2-2, the query shows how to make a view using T-SQL code.

Listing 2-2. Creating a View

```
CREATE VIEW dbo.vwCustomerOrder
AS
SELECT cus.FirstName,
      cus.LastName,
      cus.FirstName + ' ' + cus.LastName AS FullName,
      ord.OrderNumber,
      ord.OrderDate,
      ord.ShipDate
FROM dbo.CustomerOrder ord
      INNER JOIN dbo.Customer cus
      ON ord.CustomerID = cus.CustomerID;
```

Once the view has been created, it becomes much simpler to use the view to pull back the same information as the original query. Listing 2-3 shows how the view can be used to simplify pulling back data from SQL Server.

Listing 2-3. Calling the View

```
SELECT FullName, OrderNumber, OrderDate
FROM dbo.vwCustomerOrder
WHERE FirstName = 'Karim';
```

While having a simplified way to access data is nice, another consideration is how querying the view performs vs. running the query as an ad-hoc statement. In general, you can expect the view to perform the same as the query that exists inside the view. I will give you a visual comparison between how SQL Server executes the query for the ad hoc statement as well as the view. The images below are called *execution plans*. If you want to learn more about them, refer to Chapter 7. For the time being, it is not important to understand the details of the execution plan, only to compare the shape of the images in Figure 2-1 and Figure 2-2. Figure 2-1 shows the actual query execution plan for the ad hoc query in Listing 2-2.

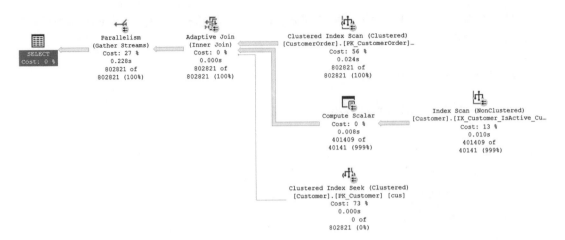

Figure 2-1. *Ad hoc query execution plan*

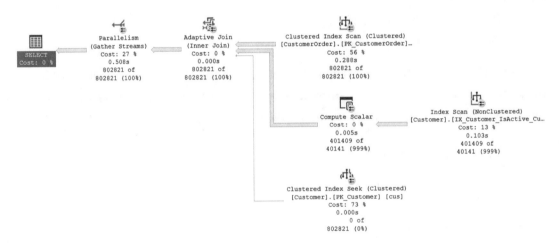

Figure 2-2. *Execution plan for the view*

Comparing this to the query execution plan for the view from Listing 2-3 in Figure 2-2, you can confirm there is no difference between the execution plans.

As stated, the execution plan for both is the same. One of the issues that can occur when using views is that the execution plan does not identify that you are using a view to access this data. While views can make things simpler to use, there are other ways you may want to use views. Since views make interacting with complex queries simpler, they may also make modifying data easier. However, there are some caveats that you need to consider when updating data through views. In Listing 2-4, you can find the query to update data based upon the view.

Listing 2-4. Updating Data in a View

```
UPDATE dbo.vwCustomerOrder
SET OrderNumber = '76871-1'
WHERE OrderDate = '2022-08-30 23:20:08.86'
      AND FirstName = 'Karim'
      AND LastName = 'Khalil';
```

Through a view you can update data from the base table. If a view is used to modify data from more than one base table, then the update will fail. The same is true for inserts as it is for updates. In Listing 2-5, you can determine what happens when you attempt to insert a record for data in more than one table.

Listing 2-5. Inserting Data Through a View

```
INSERT INTO dbo.vwCustomerOrder
(
      FirstName,
      LastName,
      OrderNumber,
      OrderDate,
      ShipDate
)
VALUES
(
      'Abeba',
      'Kidana',
      '1324-9',
      GETDATE(),
      NULL
);
```

When trying to execute the preceding query, SQL Server returns the error "View or function 'dbo.vwCustomerOrder' is not updatable because the modification affects multiple base tables."

There are other features available when using views. There is a way to prevent an underlying table from being modified when it is referenced by a view. If you want to make sure that users cannot accidentally drop a table, having a view reference table with SCHEMABINDING is an available option. You can implement this additional level of security using a query like the one in Listing 2-6.

Listing 2-6. Creating a View with Schema Binding

```
CREATE VIEW dbo.vwCustomerOrderBound
WITH SCHEMABINDING
AS
SELECT cus.FirstName,
       cus.LastName,
       cus.FirstName + ' ' + cus.LastName AS FullName,
       ord.CustomerOrderID,
       ord.OrderNumber,
,
       ord.ShipDate
FROM dbo.CustomerOrder ord
       INNER JOIN dbo.Customer cus
       ON ord.CustomerID = cus.CustomerID;
```

Here, when adding SCHEMABINDING to a view, I change how SQL Server handles changes to the columns contained within the view. Specifically, I can't modify columns in the dbo.Customer or dbo.CustomerOrder tables in a way that would impact the view dbo.vwCustomerOrderBound. Listing 2-7 shows a query where I try to drop a column in the dbo.CustomerOrder table that is referenced by the dbo. vwCustomerOrderBound schema.

Listing 2-7. Removing a Column in a Schemabound View

```
ALTER TABLE dbo.CustomerOrder
DROP COLUMN ShipDate;
```

When trying to execute the preceding query, I get the following error "The object 'vwCustomerOrderBound' is dependent on column 'ShipDate'. ALTER TABLE DROP COLUMN ShipDate failed because one or more objects access this column."

However, there is also a potential loophole regarding protecting data. Once a view is created with SCHEMABINDING, a user can change what data is returned as long as the column names returned in the SELECT statement remain the same.

As an example, let's assume a user wants to view the OrderDate instead of the ShipDate. In Listing 2-8, the last column shows the values for OrderDate, but the column name is called ShipDate. Even though the view is schemabound, the view can be altered so that the OrderDate is the last column returned instead of ShipDate. However, unless someone reviews the code, the applications using the view will have no way of knowing the data being returned is no longer the ShipDate! This can create a scenario where users can access data that they should not be able to access. In Listing 2-8, I alter the original dbo.vwCustomerOrder view.

Listing 2-8. Altering the View to Change the Column

```
ALTER VIEW dbo.vwCustomerOrder
AS
SELECT cus.FirstName,
       cus.LastName,
       cus.FirstName + ' ' + cus.LastName AS FullName,
       ord.OrderNumber,
       ord.OrderDate AS ShipDate
FROM dbo.CustomerOrder ord
       INNER JOIN dbo.Customer cus
       ON ord.CustomerID = cus.CustomerID;
```

Previously, I had a user that only had permission to access the data within the view dbo.vwCustomerOrder. My intention was to allow this user to only have access to the original columns in the view. If this same user attempts to query the view at a later date, this view no longer returns the data in the ShipDate column.

With all these features, one of the largest issues with views remains around nested views. In typical software development, there is a desire to reuse the same software code in multiple scenarios. To get an idea of how nested views can affect performance, let's use a view as part of a join condition inside of another view. First, I create a view that returns the CustomerID, FirstName, LastName, FullName, and LastOrderDate in Listing 2-9.

Listing 2-9. View for Customer Information

```
CREATE VIEW dbo.vwCustomer
AS
SELECT cus.CustomerID,
      cus.FirstName,
      cus.LastName,
      cus.FirstName + ' ' + cus.LastName AS FullName,
      MAX(ord.OrderDate) AS LastOrderDate
FROM dbo.CustomerOrder ord
      INNER JOIN dbo.Customer cus
      ON ord.CustomerID = cus.CustomerID
GROUP BY cus.CustomerID,
      cus.FirstName,
      cus.LastName;
```

Now I have an easy way to find some general information about my customers. If I still want to view order detail information, I can join dbo.Customer to the view dbo.vwCustomer. Listing 2-10 contains the create statement for the nested view.

Listing 2-10. Nested View for Customer Orders

```
CREATE VIEW dbo.vwCustomerOrderNest
AS
SELECT cus.FirstName,
      cus.LastName,
      cus.FullName AS FullName,
      ord.OrderNumber,
      ord.OrderDate ,
      ord.ShipDate
FROM dbo.CustomerOrder ord
      INNER JOIN dbo.vwCustomer cus
      ON ord.CustomerID = cus.CustomerID;
```

This view returns the same results as the original view, dbo.vwCustomerOrder. The view above is not recommended and has only been created as an example of what not to do and why. The next steps are to compare the relative performance of these views. The queries in Listing 2-11 return all customer orders that aren't for order number 76871.

Listing 2-11. Query to Compare Views

```
SELECT FullName, OrderDate
FROM dbo.vwCustomerOrder
WHERE OrderNumber <> '76871';

SELECT FullName, OrderDate
FROM dbo.vwCustomerOrderNest
WHERE OrderNumber <> '76871';
```

The first query uses the view that is not nested, and the second query used the nested view. They both return the results in Table 2-1.

Table 2-1. *Customers with Order Number 78871*

FullName	OrderDate
Karim Khalil	2022-08-30 23:20:08.86
Myra Acharya	2022-10-31 00:00:00.00
Myra Acharya	2022-10-31 00:00:00.00

While the results returned are the same, how SQL Server executed these two queries is very different. I will be using images of execution plans, but you will only need to compare the shape of the two execution plans. Figure 2-3 shows the execution plan for the original view.

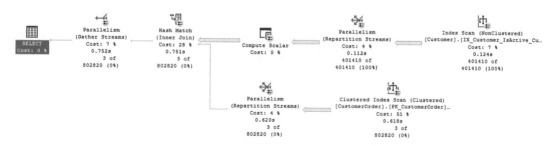

Figure 2-3. *Execution plan for the original view*

For a comparison, the execution plan for the nested view is in Figure 2-4.

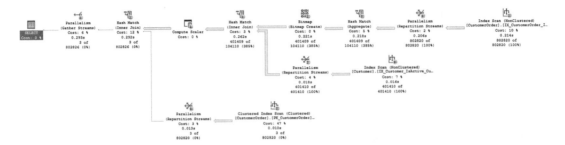

Figure 2-4. *Execution plan for the nested view*

How SQL Server executes the query for the nested view is more complex, and this is a basic example! Comparing the relative percentage for execution time, the execution of the nest view was three times as long as the original view. Imagine what would happen with many more nested views, especially if they are complex. Why does the execution plan seem different for the nested view?

One factor affecting the performance of nested views involves the process of acquiring data. When SQL Server joins to a view, it must determine what values match the join criteria. This means that each nested view, depending on the join criteria, needs to access the data for the view to determine if the data meets the join criteria. The added complexity of joining layers of tables together within the nested views also makes it difficult for SQL Server to get a good execution plan. Instead, the query optimizer may have to choose an execution plan before it can determine the best execution plan. All of this can contribute to the performance issues that can happen when using nested view.

When creating views, it can be tempting to reuse those views to create other views. Unfortunately, this can create a situation where one view can start performing poorly. Once the view is performing poorly, it can take considerable effort to weave through the various layers of nested views to find the root cause.

Indexed View

I covered how views can be used to simplify writing queries, to modify data, and to protect database schemas. I also covered how reusing views to create other views can cause significant performance issues. As you saw in the previous section, views can help make T-SQL simpler, but the execution plan is the same for both the ad hoc query and the view. In some instances, there are joins that do not perform well either as a query or a view.

If you have a view that is misbehaving, your first step should always be to tune the view by fixing bad joins and such. If that's off limits or doesn't work, step 2 should be adding indexes to the underlying tables. Only if these steps fail (or aren't allowed because of some rules) should you explore indexed views. When adding indexes to a view, the view is then considered an indexed view. The first index added to a view must be a unique clustered index. After a clustered index has been added, non-clustered indexes can also be added to the view. However, there is a cost associated with adding indexes to a view. Each time data is modified, the indexes on any related table and the indexed view must also be updated.

The first step in creating an indexed view is to create a view with schema binding. In this example, I will be using the view created in Listing 2-2. The next step is to add an index to this view. In Listing 2-12, I add a clustered index to this view.

Listing 2-12. Adding a Clustered Index to a View

```
CREATE UNIQUE CLUSTERED INDEX CX_vwCustomerOrderBound_
FullNameCustomerOrderID
    ON dbo.vwCustomerOrderBound (FullName, CustomerOrderID);
```

Comparing the performance between the view before adding a clustered index and after shows an improvement in performance overall. Remember that while there are situations where indexed views can help performance when pulling back the data, there can still be performance issues that happen when data is inserted, updated, or deleted on the affected tables. In Figure 2-5, the execution plan is displayed for when data is inserted into the base table.

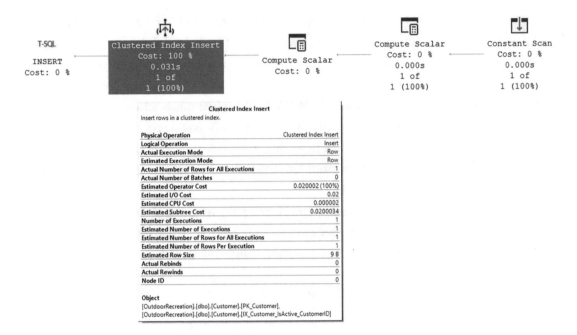

Figure 2-5. Execution plan for an insert into the base table

As shown above, there is an extra step where the index on the view is updated as part of the insert into the base table.

Functions

In many applications, there are core parts of the functionality that may be recalculated or reused several times. Sometimes you may want to write some simple piece of code once and reuse that code throughout various other database objects. There are other situations where you may want to take complex logic and create a database object that encompasses that logic and returns the required results. This could be done to make T-SQL code appear less complex and therefore less overwhelming. Either way, functions can help you simplify your T-SQL code.

Scalar Functions

You may find yourself in a situation where you need to rerun the same portion of code in many different scenarios. You may be finding a configuration value, or you may want to rerun the same basic logic in many different parts of your code where only one value is returned. When you want to pass zero or more parameters and you only want to return a single value, you may be able to use a scalar function. However, consider the potential cost of using a scalar function.

Prior to SQL Server 2019, scalar functions were optimized very differently. Historically, SQL Server did not include cost-based optimization on scalar functions. This often meant that scalar functions were not included as part of the execution plan. Now that SQL Server 2019 has implemented additional features as part of the intelligent query processing, including scalar user-defined function (UDF) inlining, the queries that reference functions are improved because the estimates are better.

An inline function is one that can be included as part of the execution plan. One of the largest advantages of inlining scalar UDFs is the significantly improved performance when it comes to using scalar UDFs. When wanting to simplify complex processes and reuse code, scalar UDFs are the ideal option when the function only needs to return one result.

The difference between scalar UDFs between prior versions of SQL Server and SQL Server 2019 in terms of performance is significant. To compare these execution plans, let's change the compatibility mode at the database level to match that of SQL Server 2017 and SQL Server 2019. By using compatibility mode 140 as the optimizer, it works like SQL Server 2017. Putting the compatibility mode of the data to 160 uses the optimizer available in SQL Server 2022. Listing 2-13 shows the code necessary to create a scalar UDF in T-SQL.

Listing 2-13. Creating a Scalar UDF

```
CREATE FUNCTION dbo.ProductTotal
(
    @Quantity     SMALLINT,
    @ProductPrice DECIMAL(6,2)
)
RETURNS DECIMAL (8,2) AS
BEGIN
        RETURN @Quantity * @ProductPrice;
END;
```

When executing the preceding function in compatibility mode 140, the execution plan ends up appearing to be simpler than the execution plan generated in compatibility mode 160. Listing 2-14 shows the code in compatibility modes 140 and 160.

Listing 2-14. Code to Execute Function

```
SELECT ord.CustomerID,
     ord.CustomerOrderID,
     SUM(dbo.ProductTotal(dtl.QuantitySold, dtl.ProductPrice)) AS
     LineItemTotal
FROM dbo.CustomerOrder ord
     INNER JOIN dbo.OrderDetail dtl
     ON ord.CustomerOrderID = dtl.CustomerOrderID
GROUP BY ord.CustomerID,
     ord.CustomerOrderID;
```

In order to simulate the behavior of SQL Server 2017, change the compatibility mode of the database to 140. The T-SQL code needed to change the compatibility mode is in Listing 2-15.

Listing 2-15. Change Database Compatibility Mode to SQL Server 2014

```
ALTER DATABASE OutdoorRecreation
SET COMPATIBILITY_LEVEL = 120;
```

The query in Listing 2-16 allows us to force SQL Server to generate new execution plans for all queries using compatibility level 140.

Listing 2-16. Clear Execution Plan for Query from Listing 2-14

```
DBCC FREEPROCCACHE;
```

It is important to note that the preceding T-SQL code should not be run in your Production environments. This code will cause SQL Server to use additional resources to determine how every query should be run the first time the query is called. I saved the actual execution plan from running the preceding query using compatibility mode 140. You can find this actual execution plan in Figure 2-6.

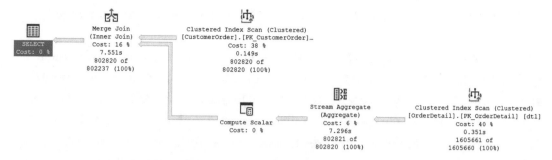

Figure 2-6. *Execution plan for compatibility mode 140*

Analyzing at the actual execution plan for compatibility mode 160, you can ascertain that it appears more complex. However, you may notice that the scalar function now includes a number of rows below the Scalar Operator in the execution plan in Figure 2-7.

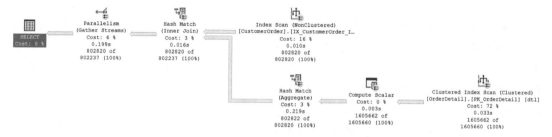

Figure 2-7. *Execution plan for compatibility mode 160*

While the execution plan for SQL Server 2019 may be more complex, the execution time between these two versions of SQL Server is relatively significant because using scalar UDF inlining causes the query to complete almost 50% faster. You can also compare the CPU and elapsed times for compatibility modes 140 and 160. In Table 2-2, you can find the average CPU and elapsed times for both queries after executing each 10 times.

Table 2-2. *Elapsed and CPU Times for Query Execution*

Compatibility Mode	CPU Time	Elapsed Time
140	8,206 milliseconds	9,225 milliseconds
160	1,866 milliseconds	3,877 milliseconds

The speed for CPU time is decreased when this function is used in compatibility mode 160 vs. 140.

The ability to inline scalar UDFs in SQL Server 2019 does not apply only to single query scalar UDFs. There is also improved functionality when it comes to using multi-statement scalar UDFs. Multi-statement scalar UDFs return a single value, similar to the scalar UDF created in Listing 2-10. The difference with a multi-statement scalar UDF is that additional logic can exist within the function. Let's improve the function created in Listing 2-10 so that the function can handle a divide-by-zero error. Listing 2-17 shows the T-SQL code to enhance Listing 2-13 by using a multi-statement scalar UDF.

Listing 2-17. Creating a Multi-Statement Scalar UDF

```
CREATE OR ALTER FUNCTION dbo.ProductAverage
(
    @Quantity      SMALLINT,
    @ProductPrice DECIMAL(6,2)
)
RETURNS DECIMAL (6,2) AS
BEGIN
    DECLARE @ProductAvg DECIMAL (6,2);
    IF @Quantity = 0
        BEGIN
            SET @ProductAvg =  0.00;
        END
    ELSE
        BEGIN
            SET @ProductAvg = @ProductPrice / @Quantity;
        END
    RETURN @ProductAvg;
END;
```

The multi-statement scalar UDF created in Listing 2-17 benefits from the same scalar inlining as the scalar UDF created in Listing 2-13. Regardless of the scalar UDF you decide to use, SQL Server 2019 has been improved so that you may have improved performance with these functions.

Table-Valued Functions

There will be times when you find yourself needing to perform complex logic, but you need to return more than one value. When these situations come up, you may want to consider using a table-valued function. A table-valued function returns a table. Unlike a UDF that often appears in SELECT or WHERE clauses, you put it in a FROM clause and treat its output like any other table or view. It can be alone in a FROM clause or you can join to it. Prior to SQL Server 2019, the only function that could run inline was a variation of table-valued functions.

Table-valued functions are useful for those times when you need a table as a result. This could be anything from one row with multiple columns to one column with the potential for multiple rows or many rows and many columns. No matter your purpose, if you want a reusable piece of code that can give you a table output, then table-valued functions may be what you want. Keep in mind that there are two main types of table-valued functions, and while the output can seem the same, the performance of each of these types can be incredibly different.

Inline Table-Valued Functions

If you're using a function to perform some complex logic, but you can survive only using a select statement, then you may want to learn more about how inline table-valued user-defined functions can work for you. It is important to note that you do not specifically indicate that a function is inline or multi-statement. It is how you create and declare the function that will determine which type of function you have created.

Like the inline scalar user-defined functions (UDFs) available in SQL Server 2019, table-valued functions can also be inlined. Also be aware that table-valued functions have been able to be inlined for quite some time, while inlining scalar UDFs is quite new. Either way, the advantage is clear. When a table-valued function can be run inline with the rest of the query, the optimizer can provide a better execution plan for the function and the T-SQL code overall.

Historically, the most popular use for inline table-valued functions is to operate similarly to views, except that in the case of inline table-valued functions, parameters can be used to limit the data returned, whereas views will return all data available to the view for each execution. Let's determine the steps necessary to create an inline table-valued function in Listing 2-18.

Listing 2-18. Creating an Inline Table-Valued Function

```
CREATE FUNCTION dbo.CustomerOrderSummaryForCustomer (@CustomerID INT)
RETURNS TABLE
AS
RETURN
(
    SELECT cus.FirstName,
              cus.LastName,
              ord.CustomerOrderID,
              ord.OrderNumber,
              ord.OrderDate,
              prd.ProductName,
              SUM(dtl.QuantitySold) AS QuantitySold,
              dtl.ProductPrice,
              SUM(dtl.QuantitySold) * dtl.ProductPrice AS
              ProductRevenue
    FROM dbo.CustomerOrder ord
              INNER JOIN dbo.OrderDetail dtl
              ON ord.CustomerOrderID = dtl.CustomerOrderID
              INNER JOIN dbo.Customer cus
              ON ord.CustomerID = cus.CustomerID
              INNER JOIN dbo.Product prd
              ON dtl.ProductID = prd.ProductID
    WHERE cus.CustomerID = @CustomerID
      GROUP BY cus.FirstName,
              cus.LastName,
              ord.CustomerOrderID,
              ord.OrderNumber,
              ord.OrderDate,
              prd.ProductName,
              dtl.ProductPrice
);
```

The process to create an inline table-valued function is straightforward. There may be concerns about the impact functions have on performance. You can determine how an inline table-valued function performs; let's run a query using this function so you can verify what happens in the execution plan. Listing 2-19 shows the script to determine the effectiveness of an execution plan.

Listing 2-19. Query to Call an Inline Table-Valued Function

```
SELECT FirstName,
       LastName,
       CustomerOrderID,
       OrderNumber,
       OrderDate,
       ProductName,
       QuantitySold,
       ProductPrice,
       ProductRevenue
FROM dbo.CustomerOrderSummaryForCustomer (234);
```

Figure 2-8 shows the execution plan generated from the code in Listing 2-19 as it was returned in SQL Server 2022.

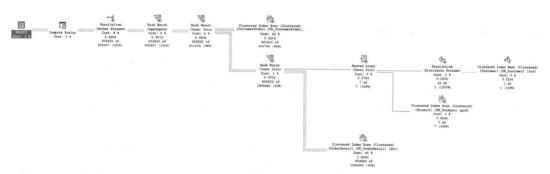

Figure 2-8. *Inline table-valued function execution plan*

Upon close investigation, you can confirm the function does not appear in the execution plan. While inline table-valued UDFs can be used like a table and can accept parameters, there are still limitations associated with using inline table-valued UDFs. These types of functions can only allow for one select statement and one result set. In addition, the data that is returned in these functions cannot be modified in the database.

However, you can modify the output of the select statement for inline table-valued. For instance, if you want to create an output of what CustomerID 234's sales could be if you raise the price of all products by 0.05%, you can execute the query in Listing 2-20.

Listing 2-20. Modifying the Output from an Inline Table-Valued Function

```
SELECT FirstName,
       LastName,
       CustomerOrderID,
       OrderNumber,
       OrderDate,
       ProductName,
       QuantitySold,
       ROUND(ProductPrice * 1.05, 2) AS ProductPrice,
       QuantitySold * (ROUND(ProductPrice * 1.05, 2)) AS TotalRevenue
FROM dbo.CustomerOrderSummaryForCustomer (234);
```

This query takes the `ProductPrice` and adds an addition 5%. In addition, the query also shows what the total revenue would be if Customer 234 purchased the same items when the 5% price increase was in place. This change to the data is cosmetic and does not affect the data that is stored in the database.

Multi-Statement Table-Valued Functions

When you must have both code reuse and the ability to update SQL Server, it may be time to consider using multi-statement table-valued functions. I caution you to carefully consider whether this approach is necessary because these types of functions can end up having a tremendous performance impact.

Multi-statement table-valued functions are not just inline table-valued functions that can do more. They also can't be inlined with the query execution. This signifies that the query optimizer does not attempt a best guess when using these types of functions. As a matter of fact, prior to SQL Server 2014, multi-statement table-valued functions were estimated to have one row. For SQL Server 2014 and SQL Server 2016, the estimated number of rows was 100. However, as of SQL Server 2017, there is a possibility that SQL Server will get a proper estimate for the rows returned by using interleaved execution.

What happens is that the optimization process will pause to allow execution so that the cardinality estimator can determine the actual number of rows that should be returned by the multi-statement table-valued function. While interleaved execution is part of the new adaptive query processing, there are some limitations to keep in mind. If there is a CROSS APPLY used in conjunction with a multi-statement table-valued function, then the interleaved functionality will not work. It has also been reported that if there is a WHERE clause inside the multi-statement table-valued function that depends on an input parameter, then interleaved execution may also not apply.

To get a better idea of how this all works, refer to the multi-statement table-valued function in Listing 2-21.

Listing 2-21. Multi-Statement Table-Valued Function

```
CREATE FUNCTION dbo.GetTopCustomersByCountry (@Country VARCHAR(75),
@TopN INT)
RETURNS @TopCustomer TABLE
(
    CustomerRank        INT,
    FirstName           VARCHAR(40),
    LastName            VARCHAR(100),
    CustomerOrderID     INT,
    TotalProductSales DECIMAL(12,2)
)
AS

BEGIN
    WITH cte_TopCust (FirstName, LastName, CustomerOrderID,
    TotalProductSales) AS
    (
        SELECT cus.FirstName,
               cus.LastName,
               ord.CustomerOrderID,
               SUM(dtl.QuantitySold * dtl.ProductPrice) AS
               TotalProductSales
        FROM dbo.Customer cus
               INNER JOIN dbo.CustomerOrder ord
               ON cus.CustomerID = ord.CustomerID
```

```
            INNER JOIN dbo.OrderDetail dtl
            ON ord.CustomerOrderID = dtl.CustomerOrderID
        WHERE (cus.Country = @Country OR @Country IS NULL)
        GROUP BY ord.CustomerOrderID,
            cus.FirstName,
            cus.LastName
    )

    INSERT INTO @TopCustomer
    (
        CustomerRank,
        FirstName,
        LastName,
        CustomerOrderID,
        TotalProductSales
    )
    SELECT TOP(@TopN) ROW_NUMBER() OVER(ORDER BY TotalProductSales DESC)
    AS CustomerRank,
        FirstName,
        LastName,
        CustomerOrderID,
        TotalProductSales
    FROM cte_TopCust
    ORDER BY 5 DESC, CustomerOrderID DESC;

    RETURN
END;
```

Let's execute this function in compatibility mode for SQL Server 2017 and SQL Server 2022. When analyzing sales for a company, it is very common to compare customer purchasing behavior. Sometimes this can cause the logic within queries to get quite complex. Now that this function has been created, you can write a script to test the performance of this function in the various versions of SQL Server; refer to Listing 2-22.

Listing 2-22. Code to Execute Function

```
SELECT cty.CustomerRank,
       cty.FirstName,
       cty.LastName,
       COUNT(cty.CustomerOrderID) AS NumberOfOrders,
       cty.TotalProductSales
FROM dbo.GetTopCustomersByCountry (NULL, 5999) AS cty
GROUP BY cty.CustomerRank,
       cty.FirstName,
       cty.LastName,
       cty.TotalProductSales;
```

Next, let's test the execution plans and relative performance across the various versions of SQL Server. Figure 2-9 show the execution plan in SQL Server 2012 by using the compatibility mode 110.

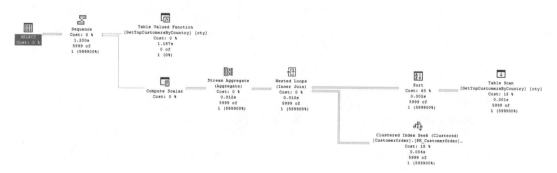

Figure 2-9. *Execution plan for compatibility mode 110*

The execution plan does not appear to have too many different operators. The table-valued function is represented as a single operator. The properties for the table-valued function are shown in Figure 2-10.

Table Valued Function

Table valued function.

Physical Operation	Table Valued Function
Logical Operation	Table Valued Function
Actual Execution Mode	Row
Estimated Execution Mode	Row
Actual Number of Rows for All Executions	0
Actual Number of Batches	0
Estimated Operator Cost	0.0000012 (0%)
Estimated I/O Cost	0
Estimated CPU Cost	0.0000012
Estimated Subtree Cost	0.0000012
Number of Executions	1
Estimated Number of Executions	1
Estimated Number of Rows for All Executions	1
Estimated Number of Rows Per Execution	1
Estimated Row Size	9 B
Actual Rebinds	1
Actual Rewinds	0
Node ID	1

Object
[OutdoorRecreation].[dbo].[GetTopCustomersByCountry] [cty]

Figure 2-10. *Properties for table-valued function in compatibility mode 110*

Figure 2-10 shows the estimated number of rows as 1. Additional enhancements were made to the database engine in SQL Server 2014. The estimation for the number of rows for a table-valued function was improved. Using the compatibility mode 120 for SQL Server 2014, you can refer to the execution plan generated in Figure 2-11.

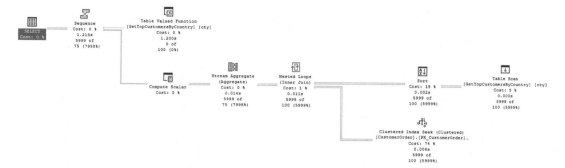

Figure 2-11. *Execution plan for compatibility mode 120*

Figure 2-11 seems the same as Figure 2-9. The only visible differences are in the percentages displayed for some of the operators. The percentage variance is not significant enough to affect the performance of the execution of this query in both compatibility modes 110 and 120. You can find the execution times in Table 2-3.

Table 2-3. *Comparing Execution Time for s Multi-Statement Table-Valued Function in Compatibility Modes 110 and 120*

Compatibility Mode	CPU Time	Elapsed Time
110	1,357 milliseconds	4,343 milliseconds
120	1,414 milliseconds	2,685 milliseconds

The times displayed here indicate that while the CPU time for SQL Server 2014 is 4% slower, the elapsed time is about 37% faster than SQL Server 2012. While the execution plans and times are similar, you can also check if the properties on the table-valued function are the same. In Figure 2-12, you can ascertain the properties associated with the table-valued function.

Table Valued Function

Table valued function.

Physical Operation	Table Valued Function
Logical Operation	Table Valued Function
Actual Execution Mode	Row
Estimated Execution Mode	Row
Actual Number of Rows for All Executions	0
Actual Number of Batches	0
Estimated Operator Cost	0.0001002 (0%)
Estimated I/O Cost	0
Estimated CPU Cost	0.0001002
Estimated Subtree Cost	0.0001002
Number of Executions	1
Estimated Number of Executions	1
Estimated Number of Rows for All Executions	100
Estimated Number of Rows Per Execution	100
Estimated Row Size	9 B
Actual Rebinds	1
Actual Rewinds	0
Node ID	1

Object
[OutdoorRecreation].[dbo].[GetTopCustomersByCountry] [cty]

Figure 2-12. *Properties for a table-valued function in compatibility mode 120*

You can verify that the estimated number rows in Figure 2-12 is 100. This is different from the estimated number of rows of 1 as shown in Figure 2-10. You can also confirm that the estimated operator cost and estimated subtree cost have all changed slightly.

Now that you have run the query from Listing 2-22, you can run the same query using the optimizer from SQL Server 2019. Before you do this, you need to change the compatibility level back to 160. While changing the compatibility level should clear the plan cache, you can use T-SQL to ensure the execution plan cache has been cleared. Once this has been done and you execute the query from Listing 2-22, you get an execution plan like the one in Figure 2-13.

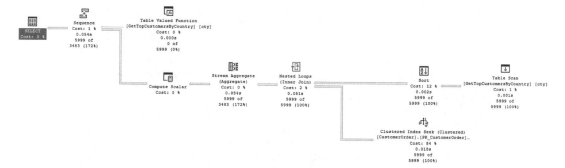

Figure 2-13. *Execution plan for compatibility mode 160*

The execution plan in Figure 2-13 is different from either of the execution plans in Figure 2-9 and Figure 2-11. You can also determine that the Index Scan on one of the non-clustered indexes from the dbo.OrderDetail table takes the majority of time to execute. As expected, this is the same operator that takes the majority of time in the execution plans for Figures 2-5, 2-11, and 2-13. You can also compare the elapsed and CPU times across compatibility levels 110, 120, and 160. This allows you to compare the expected execution times from the SQL Server optimizer from SQL Server 2012, SQL Server 2014, and SQL Server 2019. Table 2-4 shows all three compatibility levels and their associated times.

Table 2-4. *Comparing Execution Time for a Multi-Statement Table-Valued Function in Compatibility Modes 110, 120, and 160*

Compatibility Mode	CPU Time	Elapsed Time
110	1,357 milliseconds	4,343 milliseconds
120	1,414 milliseconds	2,685 milliseconds
160	910 milliseconds	1,620 milliseconds

Comparing times in Table 2-4, the CPU time is 30% faster in SQL Server 2022 than in SQL Server 2014 or SQL Server 2012. Additionally, the elapsed time for SQL Server 2022 is about 40% faster than SQL Server 2014 and about 60% faster than SQL Server 2012! You can also compare the table-valued function properties from Listing 2-12, which represented the compatibility level associated with SQL Server 2017, to those of compatibility level 160. Figure 2-14 shows the properties for the table-valued function in compatibility mode 160.

Table Valued Function	
Table valued function.	
Physical Operation	Table Valued Function
Logical Operation	Table Valued Function
Actual Execution Mode	Row
IsInterleavedExecuted	True
Estimated Execution Mode	Row
Actual Number of Rows for All Executions	0
Actual Number of Batches	0
Estimated Operator Cost	0.0059992 (0%)
Estimated I/O Cost	0
Estimated Subtree Cost	0.0059992
Estimated CPU Cost	0.0059992
Number of Executions	1
Estimated Number of Executions	1
Estimated Number of Rows Per Execution	5999
Estimated Number of Rows for All Executions	5999
Estimated Row Size	9 B
Actual Rebinds	1
Actual Rewinds	0
Node ID	1
Object	
[OutdoorRecreation].[dbo].[GetTopCustomersByCountry] [cty]	

Figure 2-14. *Properties for a table-valued function in compatibility mode 160*

Referring to Figure 2-14, there are several values that match those of Figure 2-12. They include the more accurate estimated number of rows in both Figure 2-12 and Figure 2-14. The estimated operator cost, estimated CPU cost, and estimated subtree cost are also the same in both Figure 2-12 and Figure 2-14.

The performance of the multi-statement table-valued function improves in the newer versions of SQL Server. In addition, you can verify that both SQL Server 2017 and SQL Server 2022 have the most accurate estimated and actual rows returned in the execution plan. While there still are performance concerns to keep in mind with multi-statement table-valued functions, there are scenarios where the performance is improved enough that it may be beneficial to use these functions starting with SQL Server 2017.

Other User-Defined Objects

There are many ways of working with complex data and breaking data up into sections that can be easily managed and analyzed. In some cases, data can be saved to temporary tables or table variables. However, there are other options available depending on your needs. SQL Server 2016 introduced the concept of external tables. This is a feature where external data sources, that is data not within the current SQL Server instance, can be treated as a table within SQL Server. In SQL Server 2022, this feature has been expanded to include s3-compatible object storage as an external data source. This will allow you to use data files, such as CSV or parquet files, as tables within SQL Server. In order to add external data source, you will need create a master key for the database. To create the external data source, use the authentication of Shared Access Signature (SAS) along with the SAS token for the associated storage account. You will then be able to create an external data table to s3-compatible object storage, generic ODBC connections, Oracle, Teradata, and other options supported by SQL Server. Another option in SQL Server is using table-valued parameters. This allows for similar performance as a temporary table, but it also works similarly to table variables. There is also a method where a temporary result set is created for use in the next statement in a batch.

User-Defined Table Types

When working with databases and stored procedures, you may find yourself needing to pass many values for one or more fields into a stored procedure as a parameter. There is an option to create a user-defined table type that will allow you to specify multiple columns and data types. The user-defined table type can be used to pass in a single column with many rows. As an example, you can allow users to pick multiple days of the week and save those values into a table type. When the parameter is passed into the stored procedure, it can be used to join to other tables thus allowing you to filter queries based on multiple values at one.

One advantage of creating a user-defined table type is that this table type can be reused. For instance, you can use three separate user-defined tables, one each for the INT, DATE, and VARCHAR(30) data types. Then these requests can be put into the proper user-defined table type and sent to the correct stored procedures. You can add code that verifies if there is any data in the user-defined table type. You can have the stored procedure count the number of rows. If the count is zero, ignore it. Otherwise, you can select the column from the user-defined table type. You can find an example of creating a user-defined table type in Listing 2-23.

Listing 2-23. Creating a User-Defined Table Type

```
CREATE TYPE dbo.CustomerOrderNumber AS TABLE
(
    CustomerOrderID INT,
    OrderNumber     VARCHAR(15)
);
```

Once a user-defined table type has been created, it can be used as a parameter for a stored procedure or be used for variable declaration. The reusability and consistency that is created with user-defined table types comes with a cost. As the stored procedures now use a single parameter to represent all of the columns and rows stored in this object, it becomes difficult to determine what parameters in a stored procedure represent a single value and what parameters represent a user-defined table type. This object can make code easier to read; it can also make it harder to troubleshoot performance issues in the future.

Table-Valued Parameters

A high percentage of stored procedures can be used to insert, update, or delete data from tables. In some cases, the application may need to send one parameter per column of a table to various stored procedures. While using one parameter per field is straightforward and easy to debug, some contend that it's cleaner and simpler to send multiple fields in one parameter. I understand wanting to simplify the code, but I also believe that too much simplification can make it difficult to troubleshoot code in the future.

However, you may want to use an array type format in a stored procedure or other code. In this case, it's beneficial to use this data to perform a set-based operation. When doing so, you must remember that the user-defined table type that is passed in as a parameter cannot be modified. When this parameter is passed in, the data passed can be treated like a temporary table and used to join to the base table and make any necessary modifications.

As SQL Server is designed to perform best for set-based operations, you may get to the point where you want to take advantage of SQL Server's inherent ability to work best with sets. You may want to consider using table-valued parameters if you want to pass in a table to a stored procedure and use that table relationally with other tables within the same stored procedure.

Since a table-valued parameter is ultimately a variable, SQL Server will not necessarily optimize the execution plan for the actual estimated number of rows. If you find yourself in this situation, you may need to take the values from the parameter and save them into a table variable within the stored procedure. I advise against using table-valued parameters solely to improve readability of the code. Listing 2-24 shows an example of using a table-valued parameter in a stored procedure.

Listing 2-24. Using a Table-Valued Parameter

```
CREATE PROCEDURE dbo.UpdateCustomerOrderNumber
    @CustomerOrder CustomerOrderNumber READONLY
AS
SET NOCOUNT ON;

UPDATE co
SET OrderNumber = fco.OrderNumber,
    DateModified = GETDATE()
FROM dbo.CustomerOrder co
    INNER JOIN @CustomerOrder fco
    ON co.CustomerOrderID = fco.CustomerOrderID;
```

The table-valued parameter in Listing 2-24 uses the user-defined table type created in Listing 2-23. When you want to execute the stored procedure using the table-valued parameter, you can run the code in Listing 2-25.

Listing 2-25. Executing a Stored Procedure with a Table-Valued Parameter

```
DECLARE @CustomerOrder AS CustomerOrderNumber;

INSERT INTO @CustomerOrder (CustomerOrderID, OrderNumber)
VALUES
(802818, 'AZ-72834'),
(802819, 'AZ-98341');

EXECUTE dbo.UpdateCustomerOrderNumber @CustomerOrder;
```

The execution plan from this code is in Figure 2-15. Notice the Table Scan on the table-valued parameter.

Figure 2-15. *Execution plan for a stored procedure with a table-valued parameter*

If you keep the indexed view created in Listing 2-12, the execution plan returned gets even more complex. Figure 2-16 shows the resulting execution plan if the indexed view still exists.

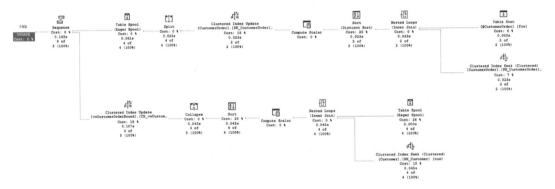

Figure 2-16. *Execution plan for a table-valued parameter with an indexed view*

While table-valued parameters can streamline your code, keep in mind that there can be a hidden performance impact. One of the best practices when developing new code is to check the execution plan and confirm that SQL Server is processing the code in a method that aligns with the shape of the data.

Common Table Expressions

Although not a user-defined database object, I include common table expressions in this section because they are often used for similar purposes as temporary tables, table variables, and table-valued parameters. A common table expression is a transitory result from a SQL statement that only exists long enough to be used in the SELECT, INSERT,

UPDATE, or DELETE statement immediately following the creation of the result set. Their purpose is to help break up complex logic or get a subset of data to be used later in the T-SQL code, batch, or stored procedure.

The primary reason for using basic common table expressions is to improve overall readability of code. Listing 2-26 shows a common table expression using the same logic as the view that was created in Listing 2-2. The expectation is that when this code is executed, it will perform the same as the view created earlier.

Listing 2-26. Creating a Basic Common Table Expression

```
DECLARE @CustomerID INT = 234;

WITH cte_orderavg AS
(
        SELECT ord.CustomerOrderID,
            AVG(dtl.QuantitySold * dtl.ProductPrice)
            AS OrderAverage
        FROM dbo.CustomerOrder ord
            INNER JOIN dbo.OrderDetail dtl
            ON ord.CustomerOrderID = dtl.CustomerOrderID
        WHERE ord.CustomerID = @CustomerID
        GROUP BY ord.CustomerOrderID
)

SELECT cag.CustomerOrderID, cag.OrderAverage
FROM cte_orderavg cag;
```

In Figure 2-17, you can confirm that the execution plan generated from Listing 2-26 matches the execution in Figure 2-6. If you recall, the execution plan in Figure 2-8 was generated from the view created in Listing 2-20.

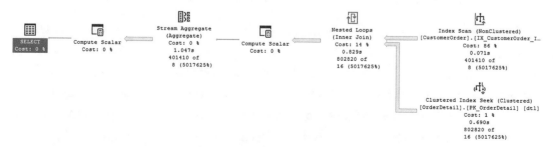

Figure 2-17. *Execution plan for a basic common table expression*

When you use a common table expression, you can also join the common table
expression (CTE) to other tables as you would do for a view or a temporary table. You
also get the ability to use CTEs to not only SELECT but also INSERT, UPDATE, and
DELETE data based on the CTE. Listing 2-27 shows a query with more complex logic
when using common table expressions.

Listing 2-27. Using Joins with Common Table Expressions

```
DECLARE @CustomerID INT = 234;

WITH cte_orderavg AS
(
        SELECT ord.CustomerOrderID,
            AVG(dtl.QuantitySold * dtl.ProductPrice)
            AS OrderAverage
        FROM dbo.CustomerOrder ord
            INNER JOIN dbo.OrderDetail dtl
            ON ord.CustomerOrderID = dtl.CustomerOrderID
        WHERE ord.CustomerID = @CustomerID
        GROUP BY ord.CustomerOrderID
)
SELECT cus.FirstName, cus.LastName, cag.OrderAverage
FROM    dbo.Customer cus
        INNER JOIN dbo.CustomerOrder ord
        ON cus.CustomerID = ord.CustomerID
        INNER JOIN dbo.OrderDetail dtl
        ON ord.CustomerOrderID = dtl.CustomerOrderID
        INNER JOIN cte_orderavg cag
        ON ord.CustomerOrderID = cag.CustomerOrderID;
```

There is one final piece of functionality related to common table expressions that
makes them somewhat unique. You can create recursive common table expressions.
In this scenario, a CTE will reference itself to help generate hierarchical data. It may be
tempting to try to get recursive CTEs to solve many different issues. I advise caution
when implementing recursive CTEs. They can be the correct tool when needed, but they
can also cause significant performance challenges. Listing 2-28 is an example of creating
a recursive CTE to find products that are components of other products.

Listing 2-28. Recursive CTE to Find All Products and Their Components

```
WITH cte_product (ProductID, ProductName, ProductPrice,
ProductComponentLevel) AS
(
     SELECT prd.ProductID, prd.ProductName, prd.ProductPrice, 1 AS
     ProductComponentLevel
     FROM dbo.Product prd
          LEFT JOIN dbo.ProductComponent cmp
          ON prd.ProductID = cmp.ProductID
     WHERE cmp.ProductComponentID IS NULL
     UNION ALL
     SELECT prd.ProductID, prd.ProductName, prd.ProductPrice,
          (cpd.ProductComponentLevel + 1) AS ProductComponentLevel
     FROM cte_product cpd   --References the cte created above
          INNER JOIN dbo.ProductComponent cmp
          ON cpd.ProductID = cmp.ProductComponentID
          INNER JOIN dbo.Product prd
          ON cmp.ProductID = prd.ProductID
)
SELECT ProductID, ProductName, ProductPrice, ProductComponentLevel
FROM cte_product;
```

As you can find the partial execution plan in Figure 2-18, the steps SQL Server needs to take to execute this query get considerably more complex.

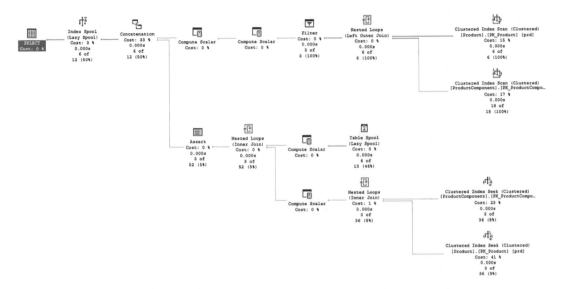

Figure 2-18. *Partial execution plan for a recursive CTE*

I have found very few times where I have absolutely needed to use a recursive CTE. However, when I have had to use a common table expression, I have found them very helpful.

Temporary Objects

You may find yourself in a situation where you need to create an object but only for a short period of time. Sometimes these objects are created so that you can work with a subset of data when dealing with complex logic. Other times it is easier to break some of the code out to create a temporary object to improve readability or make it easier for others to understand what you are doing. Regardless of the scenario, it is possible to create temporary objects in SQL Server.

Temporary Tables

Temporary tables are exactly what they sound like. They take the same shape as tables where they have columns and data types and stored data. The main difference is that temporary tables do not persist in the database. Depending on what you want to do with your temporary tables and how long you need them to last will determine which type of temporary table you end up creating. This section will cover local temporary tables, global temporary tables, and persistent temporary tables. Most temporary tables are created as local temporary tables, and these tables are only accessible through the connection that created the table. The global temporary table is like the local temporary table but is available to all connections. However, both of these temporary tables will be dropped if SQL Server is restarted. The persistent temporary table is a standard table created within the `tempdb` database.

There are other advantages to using temporary tables. These include the ability to use primary keys and indexes for improved performance. Statistics can also be created on temporary tables, further improving their performance. One thing to consider is that statistics may not be automatically updated on the temporary table if additional modifications are performed after the temporary table is first created.

Local Temporary Tables

If you find yourself needing to put data aside for additional analysis or processing, then you can consider using a local temporary table. This type of temporary table can also be useful inside of stored procedures. Local temporary tables are only available within the same session or connection as they were created. Once the session is closed or the connection is terminated, you can't access the local temporary table.

While local temporary tables can be used for many different scenarios, it is often recommended to not use temporary tables as the first option when needing to store data temporarily. There is nothing inherently wrong with local temporary tables, but you may find other objects can store data temporarily with less potential performance impact. As with all things related to SQL Server, it is best to implement a solution and test your solution including load testing before pushing the T-SQL code to Production.

Creating temporary tables is easy. While you can use SELECT statement to create a temporary table by using the code `SELECT <column list> INTO #<temp table name>...`, it is considered best practice to create the temporary table with a defined data type before inserting records. Listing 2-29 shows code to generate a local temporary table. For comparison, this code used to populate this table is the same as the code used in Listing 2-2.

Listing 2-29. Creating a Temporary Table

```
CREATE TABLE #TempOrderAverage
(
        CustomerID      INT,
        CustomerOrderID INT,
        OrderAverage    DECIMAL(6,2)
);
```

Once the temporary table has been created, run the query in Listing 2-30 to populate the data in the table.

Listing 2-30. Populating the Temporary Table

```
DECLARE @CustomerID INT = 234;

INSERT INTO #TempOrder
(
      CustomerID,
      CustomerOrderID,
      OrderAverage
)
SELECT ord.CustomerID,
       ord.CustomerOrderID,
       AVG(dtl.QuantitySold * dtl.ProductPrice) AS OrderAverage
FROM dbo.CustomerOrder ord
INNER JOIN dbo.OrderDetail dtl
ON ord.CustomerOrderID = dtl.CustomerOrderID
WHERE ord.CustomerID = @CustomerID
GROUP BY ord.CustomerID,
       ord.CustomerOrderID;
```

When I ran the process to populate the temporary table, I also got the execution plan for this process. In Figure 2-19, you will determine that the execution plan seems like the ones generated for the view and the common table expression. While the shape is similar, some of the activities that are happening and the percent distribution are different.

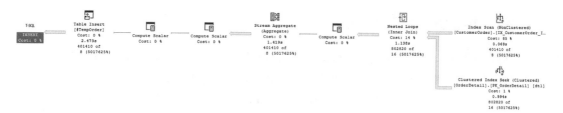

Figure 2-19. *Execution plan to create a temporary table*

Now that you have determined the execution plan to create the temporary table, how does the execution plan seem after you query from the temporary table? Listing 2-31 shows how to query the existing temporary table.

Listing 2-31. Querying the Temporary Table

```
SELECT cus.FirstName, cus.LastName, AVG(OrderAverage) AS AverageOrder
FROM dbo.Customer cus
      INNER JOIN #TempOrder ord
      ON cus.CustomerID = ord.CustomerID
GROUP BY cus.FirstName, cus.LastName;
```

So far, you have determined where most of the work for a query happens: the same time as when the data is originally selected. In this case, the insert and the select have been separated into two separate steps. Figure 2-20 is the execution that was generated when the data in the temporary table was queried.

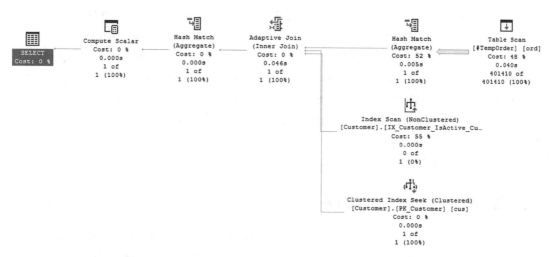

Figure 2-20. *Querying the temporary table*

While this query used a Table Scan, it is possible to add indexes to a temporary table.

Global Temporary Tables

You may find yourself wanting to create a temporary table that is available to other connections besides the connection that created the temporary table. Maybe you want a temporary table that can be accessed by more than one user. In this case, you may want to create a global temporary table. This global temporary table can exist after the original session but only when all other tasks that use the global temporary table have been completed.

Creating a global temporary table is straightforward. If you want to recreate the temporary table in Listing 2-26 but make sure that the table is global, you can run the code in Listing 2-32 to create the global temporary table.

Listing 2-32. Creating a Global Temporary Table

```
-- The use of ## make this a global temporary table
CREATE TABLE ##TempOrder
(
    CustomerID      INT,
    CustomerOrderID INT,
    OrderAverage    DECIMAL(6,2)
);
```

The only change between creating a local and global temporary table is with the table name used during creation. Comparing the code in Listing 2-30 for a local temporary table and Listing 2-32 for a global temporary table, you can confirm the difference in the table names. In Listing 2-30, the table name is #TempOrder, while the temporary table name is ##TempOrder in Listing 2-32. The addition of the second # character at the beginning of the table name indicates that this temporary table is a global temporary table. In addition, global temporary tables operate similarly to local temporary tables. The key difference is global temporary tables can be accessed outside of the specific connection that created the temporary table.

Persistent Temporary Table

When working with temporary tables, you may want a table that can last beyond the closure of the session that created it. One thing to consider is if you plan on creating a temporary table that exists within tempdb, the table and the data will not be saved when

SQL Server is restarted. In order to ensure that the persistent temporary table remains in tempdb, you need to use the techniques shown below. You can create a persistent temporary table by using the same sort of T-SQL as you would to create a table in a user database. An example of this database code is in Listing 2-33.

Listing 2-33. Creating a Persistent Temporary Table

```
USE tempdb;
GO

CREATE TABLE TempOrder
(
    CustomerID      INT,
    CustomerOrderID INT,
    OrderAverage    DECIMAL(6,2)
);
```

You can use the T-SQL code in Listing 2-33 to create a persistent table, but I recommend a method that is more consistent with the use of tempdb. Instead, you can create a stored procedure that executes when SQL Server starts. This stored procedure then creates any global temporary tables that you may need. You can use the T-SQL in Listing 2-34 to create a stored procedure to create global temporary tables.

Listing 2-34. Creating a Stored Procedure for Recreating a Persistent Temporary Tables

```
USE tempdb;
GO

CREATE PROCEDURE dbo.CreateGlobalTempOrder
AS
    CREATE TABLE TempOrder
    (
        CustomerID      INT,
        CustomerOrderID INT,
        OrderAverage    DECIMAL(6,2)
    );
```

Once the stored procedure in Listing 2-34 is created, you modify the stored procedure options so that the stored procedure is executed when SQL Server restarts. The T-SQL in Listing 2-35 allows you to modify the stored procedure to execute on startup.

Listing 2-35. Updating a Stored Procedure to Execute on Startup

```
EXECUTE sp_procoption 'CreateGlobalTempOrder', 'startup', 'true';
```

If you find yourself in a situation where you are considering a persistent temporary table, consider your environment and what potential difficulty is being added in terms of maintenance and knowledge sharing so that everyone is aware a mission critical table may exist on the `tempdb` database.

Table Variables

There are instances when you want to store data locally, but you know that the number of records you will be storing is limited. If you do not need to have the data available to other connections and it is acceptable to only have the data persist within the batch, then you may want to try using table variables. When it comes to using table variables, you also have the option to reuse the table variable as many times as you like if you are willing to keep everything in the same batch.

Prior to SQL Server 2019, the estimated number of rows for a table variable was one record. Like other objects discussed previously in this chapter, SQL Server has made significant strides to improve general performance related to table variables. SQL Server is now capable of generating a more accurate estimated number of rows when it comes to using table variables. Part of executing a query involves SQL Server determining how to execute the query. SQL Server saves the method of how to execute the query in what is called an execution plan. Now that SQL Server estimates the number of rows more accurately, it also saves that logic in the execution plan.

When the execution plan is first created, it is calculated using the original values provided in the parameters. However, some data tables may have an uneven distribution of number of records per value. If you find yourself in this situation where the data that will be pulled back with the table variable can be highly skewed, you may find that the T-SQL code will perform inconsistently. This concept is referred to as *parameter sniffing*. Now that the information about the table variable is getting stored in the execution plan, there is a higher probability of coming across parameter sniffing. While this may be troublesome, remember that SQL Server also generates an execution plan that can be highly efficient for at least some data values.

Like temporary tables, table variables can be straightforward to create and use. Listing 2-36 shows the method to declare and populate a table variable.

Listing 2-36. Declaring and Populating a Table Variable

```
DECLARE @CustomerID INT = 234;
DECLARE @TempOrder TABLE
(
      CustomerID      INT,
      CustomerOrderID INT,
      OrderAverage    DECIMAL(6,2)
);

INSERT INTO @TempOrder
(
      CustomerID,
      CustomerOrderID,
      OrderAverage
)
SELECT ord.CustomerID,
      ord.CustomerOrderID,
   AVG(dtl.QuantitySold * dtl.ProductPrice)
     AS OrderAverage
FROM dbo.CustomerOrder ord
INNER JOIN dbo.OrderDetail dtl
ON ord.CustomerOrderID = dtl.CustomerOrderID
WHERE ord.CustomerID = @CustomerID
GROUP BY ord.CustomerID,
      ord.CustomerOrderID;

SELECT cus.FirstName,
     cus.LastName,
     AVG(OrderAverage) AS AverageOrder
```

```
FROM dbo.Customer cus
     INNER JOIN @TempOrder ord
     ON cus.CustomerID = ord.CustomerID
GROUP BY cus.FirstName, cus.LastName;
```

The execution plan for this query appears very similar to the one generated in Figure 2-18 when populating the local temporary table. Figure 2-21 shows the execution plan created when populating the table variable.

Figure 2-21. *Populating the table variable*

Now that SQL Server 2019 has been updated to allow for better estimates when using table variables, I expect the execution plans to get a more accurate number of rows in the table variable when creating the execution plan. This improved accuracy will help SQL Server create a more performant execution plan. However, double-check the query performance especially if you are planning on adding large quantities of data to the table variable.

Temporary Stored Procedures

If a stored procedure is created in the tempdb database, then this stored procedure is a temporary stored procedure. SQL Server may have made this functionality possible, but keep in mind how developers and applications will interact with this database object. At the very least, having a temporary stored procedure in the tempdb database will make it more difficult to troubleshoot or maintain code related to these stored procedures.

Triggers

SQL Server provides the ability to have specific actions occur as a result or instead of an insert, update, or delete. The reactions can occur as a result of a user logging into the system. There are other reactions that can happen after or prevent changes to the existing database. When dealing with applications and data, the most common type of reaction is in response to changing data in the database. Regardless of the reason, these reactions are defined as triggers. Triggers are a special type of stored procedure that responds to a specific action on the server, database(s), or table(s).

Logon Triggers

When users log onto the server, you may want to record that specific activity. In other instances, you may want to limit user activity upon login or implement additional security functionality as a result of a server login. The logon trigger gives you the ability to allow SQL Server to initiate reactions in response to some or all logins onto the server.

There are not many scenarios where logon triggers are needed for application development. However, there are some things that can be done with logon triggers that can help protect or monitor connections to your applications. They include using a logon trigger to store login activity including who and when a connection was made to the database. A logon trigger can limit the number of connections allowed by a login or prevent users from connecting to the server entirely. In the case of a breach, this can ensure the database does not get flooded with excess connections. Conversely, limiting the number of connections allowed per login can also limit scalability and futureproofing. The number of acceptable connections today may be much lower than the number of logins needed in the future.

Data Definition Language Triggers

When applications or users change the overall database schema, they use data definition language (DDL). In the case of SQL Server, it is possible to react to specific scenarios resulting from changes to the database. While I do not expect this to be a standard part of application development, it may be helpful to be aware of this type of trigger. DDL triggers can be configured to respond to various CREATE, ALTER, DROP, GRANT, DENY, REVOKE, and UPDATE STATISTICS statements.

If you are concerned about SQL injection causing issues on your server, DDL triggers can help mitigate the damage. There are options to prevent or control all sorts of changes to database objects including creating, altering, or dropping various object. You can also use DDL triggers to do things like generate an error in response to users trying to modify database objects. In addition, it is possible to log or record when database objects are created or altered. While you may want to use triggers to set up all sorts of triggers to monitor every activity on the server and the databases, there may be better options available. There are alternatives available for tracking this type of behavior, including SQL Server Audit for both server and database activity. Typically, applications are not concerned with logging changes to the server or database schemas.

Data Manipulation Language Triggers

If you find yourself needing to implement auditing or logging as a part of your application development, you may find using data manipulation language (DML) triggers quite helpful. These triggers can be executed in response to the completion of an INSERT, UPDATE, or DELETE statement or instead of the SQL statement entirely. In some cases, you may just want to record when the change happened and what changed. In other instances, it may be more important to change or verify the functionality of the request.

One method for triggers is to have an action performed after something happens. Say you want to successfully modify a record in the dbo.Product table, but you also want to keep a history of that item's cost changes over time. Listing 2-37 shows some T-SQL that will add an entry to a history table after a change is made.

Listing 2-37. Creating After Insert or Deleting a DML Trigger

```
CREATE TRIGGER dbo.LogProductPriceHistory
ON dbo.Product
AFTER INSERT, DELETE
AS
      IF (ROWCOUNT_BIG() = 0)
      RETURN;

      INSERT INTO dbo.ProductPriceHistory
        (
            ProductID,
            ProductPrice,
            UserName,
            DateCreated
        )
```

```
SELECT
        ProductID,
        ProductPrice,
        SYSTEM_USER,
        SYSDATETIME()
FROM inserted;
```

When a record is inserted or deleted in the dbo.Product table, the new product price and the date the price was changed will be recorded in the dbo.ProductPriceHistory table. To determine the performance of this trigger, test this trigger by running the code in Listing 2-38.

Listing 2-38. Query to Insert Record into Product

```
INSERT INTO dbo.Product (ProductName, ProductPrice)
VALUES ('Disk Golf Disk - Small', 7.99);
```

When executing the preceding code, the execution plan includes two steps. The first is to run the code to insert the record into dbo.Product. The second execution plan shows the plan for the insert that occurs due to the trigger. The execution plans generated from Listing 2-38 are in Figure 2-22.

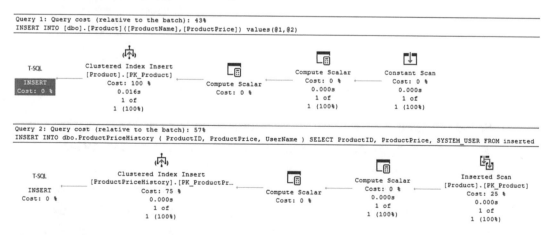

Figure 2-22. *Execution plans to insert a record with a trigger*

The execution plans in Figure 2-22 shows what happens when a record is modified in a way to fire the trigger. However, the T-SQL code IF (ROWCOUNT_BIG() = 0) RETURN; from Listing 2-35 prevents the DML trigger from firing if no records were updated.

This is considered a best practice to minimize resource utilization on the server when no actions are needed. Listing 2-39 shows an update query where no records will be updated.

Listing 2-39. Delete Statement That Will Not Update Any Records

```
DELETE FROM dbo.Product
WHERE ProductID = 500;
```

As shown in Figure 2-23, the execution plan only has one step. That is the execution plan for the deletion of the data. There is no T-SQL code execution from the trigger.

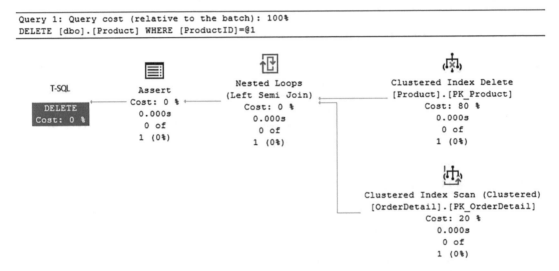

```
Query 1: Query cost (relative to the batch): 100%
DELETE [dbo].[Product] WHERE [ProductID]=@1
```

Figure 2-23. *Execution plan where no records are updated*

SQL Server was aware that there were no records to update returned from the trigger. Without attempting to insert any records into the dbo.ProductPriceHistory table, the only action was to generate an execution plan for the delete.

Having a trigger execute after an activity is not the only option for data manipulation triggers. There is also the possibility of having a trigger perform an action instead of the original action that was requested. Listing 2-40 shows a trigger that will disable a record when a user issues a delete.

Listing 2-40. Instead of a Trigger

```
CREATE TRIGGER dbo.DisableProduct
ON dbo.Product
INSTEAD OF DELETE
AS
      UPDATE prd
      SET IsActive = 0,
            DateDisabled = GETDATE()
        FROM dbo.Product prd
            INNER JOIN deleted del
            ON prd.ProductID = del.ProductID;
```

There is more than one option available when using DML triggers in SQL Server. There is also the possibility of having multiple triggers per database object. You can have up to one INSTEAD OF trigger per INSERT, UPDATE, and DELETE. You can have multiple AFTER triggers on the same table or view as well. Due to the number of triggers allowed, you can also specify which trigger should be run first and last per INSERT, UPDATE, or DELETE. If you have more than one type of AFTER trigger per action type, any of the triggers will be run in a random order.

Since there can be so many layers of triggers on a given database object, testing the functionality of these triggers is important. Like many other concepts discussed in this chapter, understanding how triggers will perform under load helps prepare for how the application will perform. It is worth mentioning that triggers should be used sparingly. They should be short like my examples. You should not start writing 2,000 line triggers with 3 cursors in them.

Cursors

In order to use relational databases effectively, it is often critical to think of processes and data in large chunks or sets. The goal in almost all scenarios is to write T-SQL that takes advantage of this set-based logic. While this is the ideal method, you may find yourself in a situation where you feel handling data in large sections is not possible. In some of these scenarios, it may mean that it is time to handle the data by each row individually. In order to do this in SQL Server, you use a cursor. The cursor is an object that takes a query and allows you to loop through each row of the resulting data set.

If you consider this route, it is imperative to acknowledge that SQL Server is designed to perform best when dealing with one large section of data vs. dealing with lots of individual records one at a time. In cases where it is tempting to use something that handles row-by-row logic, it may be time to find another tool to handle your needs better. Such is the case when creating a cursor to connect to several instances of SQL Server one at a time and perform a task. While it is outside the scope of this book, this specific situation may be best resolved by creating an SQL Server Integration Services (SSIS) package to handle connecting to the various SQL Server instances.

There are other times when you may need to use T-SQL to generate a result set where the data returned is the same, but the data must be segmented by location or vendor information. In this example, SQL Server Reporting Services (SSRS) could be used to achieve the same goal. However, your business may decide not to use SSRS. Therefore, using a cursor may be the right choice. I have also had situations when data needed to be updated with a calculation using a specific, calculated value per record. In this case, it was almost impossible to perform the updates using set-based logic.

While SQL Server can handle this task, it's preferable for the application to handle these changes. A major factor of writing T-SQL is being aware of the effects your code can have on SQL Server. This is just as true for cursors as it is for triggers. Triggers may seem like a quick fix to a variety of issues, but triggers also come with a cost on the server. Imagine SQL Server having to evaluate each insert into a table to determine if it meets the criteria for the trigger and, if the insert meets the criteria, then SQL Server has to perform another action. That's quite a bit of extra work for SQL Server to manage.

Cursors can help make a repeatable process that touches one record at a time. While cursors can be used to address a variety of issues, it is important to remember that there may be a different way to achieve the same outcome without using cursors. If you have decided that you must really use a cursor, the next step is to determine which type of cursor to use. While the concept of a cursor is the same regardless of which type is used, the type of cursor will determine the functionality and accessibility of the data within the cursor.

When choosing the right type of cursor for your needs, choose the one with the least amount of functionality that will meet your needs. This will help reduce negative performance as compared to cursor types with more functionality. Whenever you handle records in SQL Server one at a time, they will almost always perform worse than handling data in groups.

A cursor selects a set of data, fetches one record at a time, and then modifies the current record. Once the required actions have been taken, the next record can be fetched. This is where knowing the various types of cursors available will allow you to choose the correct type.

Forward-Only Cursors

The default type of cursor is called the forward-only cursor. For this type of cursor, the data can only be fetched in one direction. Records fetched in forward-only cursors can insert, update, and delete records that are fetched within the cursor. If a record has been updated previously, it will not be fetched again unless the cursor is closed and reopened. There are also limited cases where you can return the same record within the cursor after it has already been updated. Listing 2-41 shows an example of forward-only cursor.

Listing 2-41. Example of a Forward-Only Cursor

```
SET NOCOUNT ON;
DECLARE
        @CustomerID       INT = 1,
        @CustomerOrderID INT,
        @CustomerName     VARCHAR(140),
        @message          VARCHAR(50);

SELECT @CustomerName =
        FirstName + ' ' + LastName
        FROM dbo.Customer
        WHERE CustomerID = @CustomerID;

PRINT '------- Order History for ' + @CustomerName + ' -------';

DECLARE customer_cursor CURSOR FORWARD_ONLY
FOR

        SELECT CustomerOrderID
        FROM dbo.CustomerOrder
        WHERE CustomerID = @CustomerID
        ORDER BY CustomerOrderID;
```

```
    OPEN customer_cursor;
        FETCH NEXT FROM customer_cursor
        INTO @CustomerOrderID;

            WHILE @@FETCH_STATUS = 0
            BEGIN
                PRINT ' ';
                SELECT @message = '----- Order Number:' +
                    CAST(@CustomerOrderID AS VARCHAR(8)) +
                    '-----';
                PRINT @message;
                  SELECT prd.ProductName,
                      dtl.QuantitySold,
                      dtl.ProductPrice
                  FROM dbo.OrderDetail dtl
                      INNER JOIN dbo.Product prd
                      ON dtl.ProductID = prd.ProductID
                  WHERE dtl.CustomerOrderID =
                      @CustomerOrderID;

                  FETCH NEXT FROM customer_cursor INTO
                      @CustomerOrderID;
            END;

    CLOSE customer_cursor;
DEALLOCATE customer_cursor;
```

This forward-only cursor generates a list of all customer orders with all the products per order. In Figure 2-24, you can find what this result is when using the output to text window.

```
------- Order History for Myra Acharya -------


----- Order Number:401508-----
ProductName                      QuantitySold ProductPrice
------------------------         ------------ ----------------------------------------

Telescope                        1            249.99
Telescope                        3            599.00




----- Order Number:802819-----
ProductName                      QuantitySold ProductPrice
------------------------         ------------ ----------------------------------------

Telescope                        1            599.00
```

Figure 2-24. *Output from the forward-only cursor*

While this produced the output wanted, keep in mind the performance impact. In Figure 2-25, you can review part of the execution plan for this cursor.

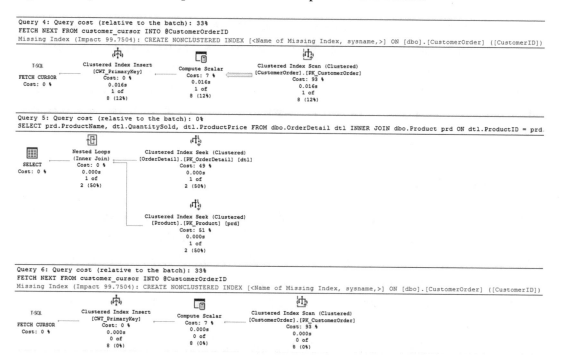

Figure 2-25. *Execution plan for a forward-only cursor*

It is important to remember that the second and third sections of this figure will rerun for each row processed in this cursor. When the underlying queries are quick and perform efficiently, that may not be an issue. However, if the queries inside the cursor have any performance issues at all, a cursor can severely exacerbate any of these performance issues.

Static Cursors

Sometimes you want to be able to move backward and forward when running the cursor. When using a static cursor, the available result set does not change from when the cursor is first opened. The static cursor has the option to be read only or allow reads and writes. When the cursor is read only, data cannot be modified. If the data is modified, there is no guarantee that the cursor will pull back the modified data.

Keyset Cursors

When defining a cursor, there may be a set of columns that create a unique entry. If that set of unique data can be found and you need to be able to interact with records that have changed, using the keyset cursor may be an option. The keyset is a set of keys from a unique set of columns. The cursor can move backward and forward, but the only way to detect changes to the order are the records that belong in the cursor to close and reopen the cursor.

Dynamic Cursors

If the other cursors don't work for your situation, there is a final type of cursor available. This type of cursor should be used as infrequently as possible due to the potential performance implications. The dynamic cursor allows you to move forward and backward through the result set. In addition, it will be aware of changes made to the data. While dealing with transaction levels is outside the scope of this book, there are some additional caveats for dynamic cursors when related to transaction levels. All changes from committed transactions will be visible. However, the only way uncommitted transactions can be found if the transaction level of the cursor is set to uncommitted.

Earlier in this section, I showed how to create a forward-only cursor. The interesting thing about creating cursors is that the code does not change significantly when switching between the various types of cursor. The largest difference between the cursor types is what data modifications each cursor can access and how the data is fetched. One of the largest temptations is that cursors work very similarly to application code. Instead of handling large quantities all at once, the cursors loop through data. In application code, this is the preferred method of accessing data, which makes using cursors even more tempting.

Where I have had cursors most used is to handle processes that could be better handled by applications. You may find yourself in a situation where a cursor seems like one of the only solutions available. Referring to Listing 2-42, you can get an idea of what a dynamic cursor can be.

Listing 2-42. Creating a Dynamic Cursor

```
SET NOCOUNT ON;
DECLARE
        @CustomerID       INT = 1,
        @CustomerOrderID INT,
        @CustomerName     VARCHAR(140),
        @message          VARCHAR(50);

SELECT @CustomerName =
        FirstName + ' ' + LastName
        FROM dbo.Customer
        WHERE CustomerID = @CustomerID;

PRINT '------- Order History for ' + @CustomerName + ' -------';

DECLARE customer_cursor CURSOR DYNAMIC
FOR

        SELECT CustomerOrderID
        FROM dbo.CustomerOrder
        WHERE CustomerID = @CustomerID
        ORDER BY CustomerOrderID;
```

```
    OPEN customer_cursor;
        FETCH NEXT FROM customer_cursor
        INTO @CustomerOrderID;

            WHILE @@FETCH_STATUS = 0
            BEGIN
                PRINT ' ';
                SELECT @message = '----- Order Number:' +
                CAST(@CustomerOrderID AS VARCHAR(8)) + '-----';
                PRINT @message;
                  SELECT prd.ProductName, dtl.QuantitySold, dtl.
                  ProductPrice
                  FROM dbo.OrderDetail dtl
                            INNER JOIN dbo.Product prd
                            ON dtl.ProductID = prd.ProductID
                  WHERE dtl.CustomerOrderID = @CustomerOrderID;

                FETCH NEXT FROM customer_cursor INTO
                @CustomerOrderID;
            END;

    CLOSE customer_cursor;
DEALLOCATE customer_cursor;
```

Changing the cursor type from FORWARD_ONLY to DYNAMIC is as easy as swapping out the phrases for one another. The output of these cursors is also the same. The real difference that could have happened is behind the scenes. If a record changed while the cursor was running, the forward-only cursor may not have been aware of that change, whereas the dynamic cursor may have been able to scroll to access that change or in certain scenarios the dynamic cursor may have found the change before it was committed.

Throughout this chapter, I covered several different types of database objects that are available to use when writing T-SQL. These objects can help make code more readable. While some of these database objects can improve performance in the right circumstances, none of these database objects are designed to resolve every technical challenge. There are situations where using the wrong database objects can have a negative performance impact on the database and your application code. Now that you know when to use each database object, it is time to start considering the quality of code you write.

CHAPTER 3

Standardizing T-SQL

Creating a method for how you write your code can help increase the speed at which you and others can understand the purpose of the code. How many times have you written code and come back to it later and not understood what it was doing? The goal is that if you follow good practices for formatting, naming, and commenting your T-SQL, it will be easier and faster to understand the purpose of the T-SQL. While determining these standards can take some extra time upfront, the cost savings in the long run will be worth it.

Writing T-SQL that is understandable helps you and your company. Many other coding languages have standards or best practices, and I believe that T-SQL should be no different. While the primary goal of writing T-SQL may be to implement a piece of functionality, no less important is the secondary goal of making sure that your T-SQL makes sense. Over time, code changes or bugs are found. The more readable and understandable your T-SQL code is, the easier it is to modify or troubleshoot.

Formatting T-SQL

How T-SQL looks when it is written can be as significant as what is written. Like other application code, there is always a chance that someone will need to look at your code in the future or you will need to look at theirs. If I am not writing new code, I am looking at pre-existing code to understand its purpose, to debug the code, to performance tune the query, or to update the business logic. Depending on why I am reviewing the code, I generally determine what is important to me at the time.

If I am looking at the T-SQL code to understand what the code does, I review any comments and the tables involved to understand what application may be using this T-SQL code. I am not concerned with how tables are joined together as I expect that to be functioning correctly, although incorrect logic on table joins can be a cause of queries returning very unexpected results. Next, I look at the criteria used to filter the results of

81

© Elizabeth Noble 2023
E. Noble, *Pro T-SQL 2022*, https://doi.org/10.1007/978-1-4842-9256-3_3

the T-SQL code. Only at the very end of my analysis will I review the columns returned in the query. Oftentimes I am only concerned with the columns if there is special business logic involved. Applying this thought pattern to writing simple queries, you can see that I list the column names on one line in Listing 3-1.

Listing 3-1. Basic Query

```sql
SELECT ProductID, ProductName, DateCreated, DateModified
FROM dbo.Product;
```

I format my code this way because I want to be able to quickly see all the action items that are happening through the FROM clause and the WHERE criteria. If I were to create one line per column, it would be harder for me to see how tables were related and what conditions were being applied to those relationships. In Listing 3-2, I altered how the columns in the SELECT clause are displayed.

Listing 3-2. Queries with Joins

```sql
SELECT cus.FirstName,
    cus.LastName,
    prd.ProductName,
    dtl.QuantitySold AS QuantitySold
FROM dbo.CustomerOrder ord
    INNER JOIN dbo.OrderDetail dtl
    ON ord.CustomerOrderID = dtl.CustomerOrderID
    INNER JOIN dbo.Product prd
    ON dtl.ProductID = prd.ProductID
    INNER JOIN dbo.Customer cus
    ON ord.CustomerID = cus.CustomerID
        AND cus.Country = 'India';
```

For this query, the columns are listed line by line. This is because I altered something about the actual column being pulled back. If I am ever aliasing a column or adding special logic to a column, I change how I format the columns in the SELECT statement. For these scenarios, I create one line or more per column depending on the complexity of the logic. Notice the two join conditions on the last two lines of the query. I usually indent any join condition after the first one because I want it to be immediately obvious there has been more than one condition applied to a join.

Often I am reviewing T-SQL code to troubleshoot why it is returning incorrect results. When there are issues with the results being returned, I start with a user story indicating what is happening that is incorrect. In these cases, I go immediately to the WHERE clause to double-check the logic and confirm that it is correct. Once I have confirmed that logic, I look at the join criteria to confirm that the tables are joined correctly. I use the same process to troubleshoot the code as I use to understand T-SQL code; I look at the SELECT statement last, focusing on any primarily columns with any special logic. Looking at the query in Listing 3-3, I can scan first the WHERE clause and then the FROM clause.

Listing 3-3. Queries with Subqueries

```
SELECT
    (
        SELECT prd.ProductName
        FROM dbo.CustomerOrder ord
            INNER JOIN dbo.OrderDetail dtl
            ON ord.CustomerOrderID = dtl.CustomerOrderID
            INNER JOIN dbo.Product prd
            ON dtl.ProductID = prd.ProductID
        WHERE ord.CustomerID = bord.CustomerID
        GROUP BY prd.ProductName
    ) AS ProductName,
    bord.CustomerOrderID,
    bord.OrderNumber,
    bord.OrderDate,
    bdtl.QuantitySold,
    bprd.ProductPrice
FROM dbo.CustomerOrder bord
    INNER JOIN dbo.OrderDetail bdtl
    ON bord.CustomerOrderID = bdtl.CustomerOrderID
    INNER JOIN dbo.Product bprd
    ON bdtl.ProductID = bprd.ProductID
WHERE bprd.ProductName LIKE '%board%';
```

This allows me to immediately determine that this query is dealing with products that contain the word board. With the columns in the SELECT statement listed on individual lines, I am immediately aware that there is some special logic involved in the part of the SELECT statement. I also indented the subquery portion of the logic, which helps that subquery stand out even further. Now that I am trying to troubleshoot potentially inaccurate results, I can quickly identify what may be causing the issue. Depending on the bug reported, there is a very high possibility the issue is either with the WHERE clause or the first column returned in the SELECT statement. Analyzing the view created in Listing 3-4 shows a different conclusion.

Listing 3-4. Create a View

```
CREATE OR ALTER VIEW dbo.CustomerProduct
AS
SELECT cus.FirstName,
    cus.LastName,
    prd.ProductName,
    SUM(dtl.QuantitySold) AS QuantitySold
FROM dbo.CustomerOrder ord
    INNER JOIN dbo.OrderDetail dtl
    ON ord.CustomerOrderID = dtl.CustomerOrderID
    INNER JOIN dbo.Product prd
    ON dtl.ProductID = prd.ProductID
    INNER JOIN dbo.Customer cus
    ON ord.CustomerID = cus.CustomerID
GROUP BY cus.FirstName, cus.LastName, prd.ProductName;
```

In the T-SQL code for this view, I still go first to the FROM clause. I immediately identify that there are several joins. In addition, there is no WHERE clause, and I can also quickly determine there is no special logic in the SELECT statement as all columns are not on their own line(s). Matching the information about this view to any potential bug I am researching, I know the most complex part of this query is the join logic. If the joins are correct, I can quickly rule out the SELECT statement if the view is returning too many results. A similar pattern can be followed when creating a function, as shown in Listing 3-5.

Listing 3-5. Create a Function

```
CREATE FUNCTION dbo.ProductsByCustomer (@CustomerID INT)
RETURNS TABLE
AS
RETURN
(
    SELECT cus.CustomerID, dtl.ProductID
    FROM dbo.Customer cus
        INNER JOIN dbo.CustomerOrder ord
        ON cus.CustomerID = ord.CustomerID
        INNER JOIN dbo.OrderDetail dtl
        ON ord.CustomerOrderID = dtl.CustomerOrderID
    WHERE cus.CustomerID = @CustomerID
    GROUP BY cus.CustomerID, dtl.ProductID
);
```

In the preceding function, I can quickly identify several joins in the FROM statement and one criterion in the WHERE clause. If the function is returning only results for the customer provided, it is highly likely that any bug that has been found is related to the join conditions.

My process for performance tuning queries is handled differently, and I will discuss those differences further in Part II of this book. When it comes to reviewing the T-SQL as part of performance tuning, I focus on what tables are used. If there is more than one table, I also look at how those tables are joined together. My final focus is on what columns are being used and how they relate to indexes that already exist.

I also review T-SQL code when updating logic inside the T-SQL code. Either new functionality has been added, changed, or removed so I need to modify the T-SQL code to mirror those modifications. Depending on the modifications, it may be as simple as looking at the fields in the SELECT clause and changing what fields are displayed or how calculations are performed. Other times, I may need to look at the FROM clause and add or remove tables from join conditions. In some cases, I may need to update criteria in the WHERE clause to handle the new business requirements. Such is the case in Listing 3-6, which shows the creation of a table-valued parameter.

Listing 3-6. Creating a Table-Valued Parameter

```
CREATE PROCEDURE dbo.UpdateProductPricing
    @ProductList ProductPricing READONLY
AS
SET NOCOUNT ON

UPDATE prd
SET ProductName = pr.ProductName,
    ProductPrice = pr.ProductPrice
FROM dbo.Product prd
    INNER JOIN @ProductList pr
    ON prd.ProductID = pr.ProductID;
```

One of the first things I notice is the lack of a WHERE clause in the this stored procedure. This is also where some complexity is added when dealing with user-defined table types. It is very likely that the user-defined table is being used to filter the data on the join. However, just looking at the code, it is very difficult to tell how the application uses this stored procedure. Because of the user-defined table type, the amount of work required to enhance the logic on this stored procedure is significantly increased. I need to be aware of how data is being passed in the table-valued parameter, but I also need to consider how the data being passed to this table-valued parameter can change over time. As database administrators are often the ones managing the T-SQL code long after the application has been deployed, I find it best to design T-SQL code so that it can be easily supported going forward. As you can see in Listing 3-7, when creating a common table expression, I use the same method, but I indent the query inside of the common table expression. Once again, I use this indent to help signify that special logic is happening in a given section.

Listing 3-7. Creating a Common Table Expression

```
WITH cte_customer AS
(
    SELECT cus.CustomerID,
        cus.FirstName,
        cus.LastName,
        dtl.ProductID,
        MIN(ord.OrderDate) AS FirstOrder
```

```
    FROM dbo.CustomerOrder ord
        INNER JOIN dbo.OrderDetail dtl
        ON ord.CustomerOrderID = dtl.CustomerOrderID
        INNER JOIN dbo.Customer cus
        ON ord.CustomerID = cus.CustomerID
    GROUP BY cus.CustomerID, cus.FirstName, cus.LastName, dtl.ProductID
)
SELECT cus.CustomerID,
    cus.FirstName,
    cus.LastName,
    cus.FirstOrder,
    SUM(dtl.QuantitySold) AS QuantitySold
FROM cte_customer cus
    INNER JOIN dbo.CustomerOrder ord
    ON cus.CustomerID = ord.CustomerID
    INNER JOIN dbo.OrderDetail dtl
    ON ord.CustomerOrderID = dtl.CustomerOrderID
        AND cus.ProductID = dtl.ProductID
GROUP BY cus.CustomerID,
    cus.FirstName,
    cus.LastName,
    cus.FirstOrder
HAVING SUM(dtl.QuantitySold) > 5;
```

When defining my own personal style, I have learned that my overall objective is to have a query fit in a small enough area that I can quickly and efficiently find the part of T-SQL code that I am trying to review. When it comes to designing your own standard, you will want to think about your overall objective.

In many companies, junior team members will be hired. Some of these junior team members will be new to SQL Server, and it will take any new hire some time to understand how the applications in your business work. When designing an internal T-SQL coding standard, you want to take into consideration what formatting conventions should be followed that will help new employees quickly learn your company's systems and data flows.

Another factor in developing a T-SQL formatting standard is creating a standard that employees can easily remember or reference. You want your team members to be able to succeed when implementing a new standard and not be overwhelmed by all the nuances when writing the code. This is especially important if all T-SQL code must be written manually and your company does not have software that can automatically format the T-SQL code for you.

There are also some formatting considerations for inserts, updates, and deletes. Listing 3-8 contains a sample INSERT statement. In this example, I listed all the column names for an INSERT.

Listing 3-8. Query to Insert Data

```
INSERT INTO dbo.Product (ProductName, ProductPrice) VALUES
('Telescope', 599.00);
```

While listing the column names may seem unnecessary, this formatting standard makes what data is being inserted easily identifiable, but this format also protects the application code from future issues if columns are added or the column order changes. The format to update data is simple, as you can see in Listing 3-9. I am still following the same formatting for reserved words and referencing user-defined database objects.

Listing 3-9. Simple Query to Update Data

```
UPDATE dbo.Customer
SET Address = '123 Main Street'
WHERE CustomerID = 1;
```

You can also see that I consistently pad the operator. I have done this in several examples. Like other decisions I have made for formatting, I believe adding a space before and after the equal sign improves the readability of the T-SQL code. I have also included Listing 3-10 to show how to format deleting data in T-SQL.

Listing 3-10. Query to Delete Data

```
DELETE FROM dbo.Product
WHERE ProductName = 'Electric surfboard';
```

This example is for a simple delete, and when joins are involved, the format to delete data can become even more involved. Deleting data often seems more significant than other data manipulation activities in SQL Server. There are times where you may want to write a query to systematically delete data from a table. When I first started writing queries to delete data from tables, I would start with writing the SELECT statement. This would help with several factors. I could clearly see what data would be affected. I could also get a row count for the number of records I expected to be affected. Once I had the SELECT statement written, I could easily modify the code to delete the necessary records. The query in Listing 3-11 shows the SELECT statement I use to prepare for deleting data records.

Listing 3-11. Select Orders with ProductID of 2

```
SELECT ord.CustomerOrderID, ord.OrderNumber
FROM dbo.CustomerOrder ord
     INNER JOIN dbo.OrderDetail dtl
     ON ord.CustomerOrderID = dtl.CustomerOrderID
WHERE dtl.ProductID = 2;
```

In this case, I am preparing to delete records from the dbo.Customer table that have a ProductID of 2. Using the result from Listing 3-11, I can confirm what data I am deleting and how many records I can expect to delete. After I review the results from Listing 3-11, I can update my T-SQL code to delete the records. In Listing 3-12, I replaced the SELECT statement with a DELETE FROM referencing the table alias for dbo.Customer.

Listing 3-12. Delete Orders with Product of 2

```
BEGIN TRAN
DELETE FROM ord
FROM dbo.CustomerOrder ord
     INNER JOIN dbo.OrderDetail dtl
     ON ord.CustomerOrderID = dtl.CustomerOrderID
WHERE dtl.ProductID = 2;
COMMIT
```

Over the years, I have found it best to wrap complex DELETE statements in an explicit transaction. By default, when we execute T-SQL code on SQL Server, we are using an implicit transaction. That means that SQL Server knows to commit the transaction automatically after we execute the transaction. We also have the option of specifying an explicit transaction. This is where SQL Server will not complete the execution of the T-SQL code until we send the COMMIT to SQL Server. Particularly with deletes, but often with any complex code, I have found that it is best to always be careful. I have two options. I could run the BEGIN TRAN and DELETE statements by themselves. If I like what I see, I can run a commit. If I don't like what I see, I can roll back and start over. If you use this method, you must make sure to ROLLBACK or COMMIT the explicit transaction properly. The other option is to run the whole script of BEGIN TRAN and DELETE statements, but with a ROLLBACK. If the row count looks correct, I can change the ROLLBACK to a COMMIT and re-execute.

This allows me to verify the number of records affected. This is my last chance to confirm that my query is working as expected. If I get a different number of records returned than the one I expected, I could issue a ROLLBACK and SQL Server would undo the code that I attempted to run. This is only possible while using explicit transactions. It is also worth mentioning that if you are using multiple levels of transactions, referred to as nested transactions, the functionality of the ROLLBACK may work differently than expected as it will rollback all nested open transactions.

This leads to another consideration when designing your T-SQL formatting. You will need to know how your T-SQL code will be written and stored. If all T-SQL code will be written manually and cannot be formatted by a third-party tool, then you may need to keep the coding standard very simple and limit criteria for special situations. However, if you have a third-party tool available, you can create a format that is as complex as that tool can handle.

One of the factors that makes a good developer or engineer is discipline. The same is true when writing T-SQL. To a certain extent, it does not matter what specific style of formatting you use. What does matter is being consistent with that formatting. Ideally, you should try to get your entire team to agree to a standard method of formatting T-SQL.

When your whole team writes T-SQL code the same way, it makes it much easier to look at someone else's code. You no longer need to translate both the format and the coding style, which can lead to quicker analysis and quicker problem resolution. Formatting your T-SQL code to make it more readable is all about how the code looks.

You should move toward having consistent formatting for all T-SQL code written at your company. Since the formatting will be the same regardless of who writes the code, it also means that everyone reading the code will become more and more familiar with quickly interpreting their code. In Listing 3-13, I create a user-defined table type.

Listing 3-13. Create User-Defined Table Type

```
CREATE TYPE ProductPricing AS TABLE
(
    ProductName  VARCHAR(25),
    ProductPrice DECIMAL(6,2)
);
```

I also use a consistent format in Listing 3-14 when creating a temporary table.

Listing 3-14. Create a Temporary Table

```
CREATE TABLE #TempCustomerFirstOrder
(
    CustomerID    INT,
    FirstName     VARCHAR(40),
    LastName      VARCHAR(100),
    FirstOrder    DATETIME2(2),
    QuantityOrder SMALLINT
);
```

You can also see I use the same format when creating a table variable in Listing 3-15.

Listing 3-15. Create a Table Variable

```
DECLARE @TempCustomerFirstOrder TABLE
(
    CustomerID    INT,
    FirstName     VARCHAR(40),
    LastName      VARCHAR(100),
    FirstOrder    DATETIME2(2),
    QuantityOrder SMALLINT
);
```

Comparing Listings 3-13, 3-14, and 3-15, you can quickly see that I use a consistent format when creating tables and declaring variables. This will allow anyone else to see code in this format and quickly know that this code is creating a table.

There are at least two things to consider when it comes to capitalization. There is capitalization related to keywords and capitalization for all other terms. I prefer to uppercase all reserved words. The list of T-SQL reserved words can be quite lengthy. I chose to consider any word that is not part of the database schema as a reserved word. I capitalize database objects and column names as they were created. When I create table aliases, I use lowercase. You can see in Listing 3-16 how the reserved words are uppercased and the first letter of each word for a database object name is capitalized.

Listing 3-16. Create a DML Trigger

```
CREATE TRIGGER dbo.ArchiveProduct
ON dbo.Product
AFTER INSERT, UPDATE
AS
      IF (ROWCOUNT_BIG() = 0)
      RETURN;
      INSERT INTO dbo.ProductArchive (ProductID, ProductPrice, DateCreated)
      SELECT inserted.ProductID, inserted.ProductPrice, GETDATE()
      FROM inserted;
```

One of the other factors to consider when determining formatting standards for T-SQL is if and how to use aliasing. Aliasing is a method that allows you to create a shortened name to reference a table. It is also possible to alias column names in your select statements when writing queries. How the aliased values can be used depends on whether a table or a column is being aliased. However, the overall concept is the same. If an alias is created for a table name, the alias must be used in place of the table name for the entirety of the given query. For columns, aliases are often used to rename a column or make the output more user-friendly. Often the column aliases are not referenced.

The only time I will reference a column alias when writing my queries is if I must order by a column that has been aliased, particularly if that column has more logic than only renaming the original column name. It is possible to provide a numeric representation of the column order in the ORDER BY statement instead of proving a column name. While this is a quick method to sort data, this is not recommended to be used as part of permanent application code because the order of columns in the SELECT statement can be changed without the ORDER BY clause getting updated. This would cause the data returned to potentially be ordered differently than intended.

Another debated topic when it comes to T-SQL code formatting is how to format commas when writing code. There are those who prefer to put the commas at the beginning of each line. This can improve readability and help others quickly identify that this is one of multiple lines. Adding the commas at the front of each line does simplify debugging as it is easy to comment out a single line that begins with a comma and the rest of the query will parse correctly. I prefer adding my commas at the end so that I can ignore the commas and focus on the columns being returned in a query.

When it comes to multiple criteria in the WHERE clause, I do prefer to precede each criteria with the operator. For many types of criteria, this is either an OR or an AND. This allows me to quickly review the logic in the WHERE clause without having to scan the entire WHERE clause to determine how all the criteria works together. You can choose to have each line end with the operator, but you may find that this complicates debugging.

There are times when working with T-SQL code that you will write complex code. This code may include subqueries or logic in the WHERE clause involving ANDs or ORs. If there is logic like a subquery or a mixture of ANDs and ORs in the WHERE clause, I wrap those in parentheses. I indent all the code inside the parentheses so that it is easy to identify what logic is wrapped together. There are also times where there are multiple join conditions between two tables. If there is more than one join condition between two tables, I indent every join condition except the first one so that others can easily tell there are multiple join conditions between two tables.

You will also want to consider how to format T-SQL code when adding additional levels of logic to your code. There are various reasons for T-SQL code blocks including TRY... CATCH blocks, IF... ELSE statements, BEGIN...END, or other reasons to segment code. For these scenarios, I indent the interior of the code block. If code blocks end up being nested, I indent each subsequent code block. I prefer to indent my code blocks so that others reviewing my code can see the parent activity such as the WHILE loop in Listing 3-17. Once you see the first level of indentation, you know that all the logic that has been indented belongs to the same code block.

Listing 3-17. Create a Cursor

```
SET NOCOUNT ON;
DECLARE @ProductID INT,
    @ProductName VARCHAR(25),
    @message VARCHAR(50);
PRINT '-------- Product Listing --------';
DECLARE product_cursor CURSOR DYNAMIC
FOR
SELECT ProductID, ProductName
FROM dbo.Product;
OPEN product_cursor;
FETCH NEXT FROM product_cursor
INTO @ProductID, @ProductName;
```

```
WHILE @@FETCH_STATUS = 0
BEGIN
    PRINT ' ';
    SELECT @message = '----- Customers For Products: ' + @ProductName +
    '-----';
    PRINT @message;
      SELECT LEFT(cus.FirstName, 25), LEFT(cus.LastName, 25), SUM(dtl.
      QuantitySold) AS QuantitySold
      FROM dbo.CustomerOrder ord
            INNER JOIN dbo.OrderDetail dtl
            ON ord.CustomerOrderID = dtl.CustomerOrderID
            INNER JOIN dbo.Product prd
            ON dtl.ProductID = prd.ProductID
            INNER JOIN dbo.Customer cus
            ON ord.CustomerID = cus.CustomerID
        WHERE prd.ProductID = @ProductID
        GROUP BY cus.FirstName, cus.LastName, prd.ProductName;
      FETCH NEXT FROM product_cursor INTO @ProductID, @ProductName;
END;
CLOSE product_cursor;
DEALLOCATE product_cursor;
```

Formatting T-SQL code consistently improves readability for yourself and anyone in the future who will need to review your code. Well-formatted code can help provide clarity when troubleshooting, performance tuning, and code enhancing. Creating a T-SQL formatting standard in your organization can also help when onboarding new employees or training junior database developers. Once T-SQL formatting standards have been determined, you will want to consider what steps need to be taken to create naming conventions for your T-SQL code.

Naming T-SQL

When you write T-SQL, you have options on how to write that code. As covered in Chapter 2, you will most likely create persistent objects in T-SQL. Regardless of your purpose, following a good naming policy makes it easier for others to understand the purpose of your T-SQL code. Ideally, your team members should be able to determine the purpose of your code based on the object name where the code lives. This is particularly helpful for new or less experienced employees.

The practices for a naming convention are similar to those for formatting T-SQL. One of the aspects that comes with naming conventions is look and feel. This can involve the capitalization used for objects. There are various options available when providing a case for database objects. The main choices are camel case or pascal case. Camel case is where the first letter of the first word is not capitalized, but the first letter of all of the other words is capitalized. Pascal case is where the first letter of every word is capitalized. The primary difference between these casing styles is the first letter of the first work of the database object. Listing 3-18 shows a query using camel case.

Listing 3-18. Query with Camel Case

```
SELECT productID, productName, dateCreated, dateModified
FROM dbo.product;
```

Conversely, you can see in Listing 3-19 what pascal case looks like when writing the same query.

Listing 3-19. Query with Pascal Case

```
SELECT ProductID, ProductName, DateCreated, DateModified
FROM dbo.Product;
```

In addition, there is also an option where the first letter is not capitalized and there is an underscore between words. I am generally not a fan of non-alphabetic characters in database names, but I do know some people that prefer underscores. If you want another alternative, Listing 3-20 shows how tables and columns are named in what is called snake case.

Listing 3-20. Query with Snake Case

```
SELECT productID, product_name, date_created, date_modified
FROM dbo.product;
```

When determining which case to use for your naming convention, make sure to also be aware of the collation for your database and if any tables have a special collation. Being aware of case sensitivity will help you ensure that your naming conventions and your formatting standards line up.

This can also involve where objects appear in Object Explorer. Some of this has to do with what type of object is being named and who will be looking for these objects. If you want to find objects by their use, you may want to specify schema names that group those objects together. This can be particularly useful for applications or services. Depending on what type of troubleshooting is expected, database objects, particularly stored procedures, can be named with the action they are taking. This allows for an easy search of stored procedures that are selecting data vs. inserting data. However, there is another option where the main table affected could be the first word in the stored procedure name. This allows someone to search in Object Explorer by affected table to see all the stored procedures that exist.

Another consideration is whether reserved words can be used when naming database objects. If reserved words are used in database object names, you will want to add another word to the object name so that brackets are not needed when referencing the object name.

When determining naming conventions, you may also want to consider if there are columns in tables that will have the same names as columns in other tables. Some of these types of columns include specifying the date a record was created, the date a record was last updated, and if the record has been soft deleted. For tables that are specifying status or types, these tables can have columns with a status or type name and an associated description. You may decide that you want all these columns to have the exact same name in all tables with these columns.

When writing my queries, I prefer not to alias my column names, if possible. I also don't display more than one date created or updated. Therefore, I use the exact same name for creation date, modified date, and the soft delete flag. However, I also usually return the name or description field from multiple tables when I write my queries. Therefore, I prefer those columns to include the table name as part of the column name. For instance, instead of using the column name `Description` in the tables `Customer` and `Product`, I prefer to name the columns `CustomerDescription` in the `Customer` table and `ProductDescription` in the `Product` table. This allows others to view the select statement and easily identify which table is being referenced. It also means I alias less columns when I write my queries.

Naming persistent database objects can get tricky as well. Naming tables can be different than naming indexes or views or triggers or functions. Once again, naming these objects is more than just giving them a descriptive name. It may also be about giving them a name that makes it clear what type of object it is. This is because many database engineers and developers use Object Explorer as their primary tool for finding objects. As discussed, if table names begin with nouns and stored procedures begin with verbs, I next need to figure out how to differentiate other database objects from tables and stored procedures.

One of the options is to precede the object name with an abbreviation for the object type. In the case of indexes, you can use IX_ for non-clustered indexes and CX_ for clustered indexes. When naming indexes, once you specify the IX_ or CX_, the next item should be the table name where the index exists. After the table name should be the list of columns in the index. The columns should be listed in the same order that they are specified when the index is created. In Listing 3-21, you can see a clustered index. The clustered index name begins with CX followed by the table name and then the column name. Each section is separated by an underscore.

Listing 3-21. Create a Clustered Index

```
CREATE CLUSTERED INDEX CX_Product_ProductName
     ON dbo.Product (ProductName);
```

Creating a non-clustered index follows the same pattern. In Listing 3-22, you see the non-clustered index also includes multiple columns.

Listing 3-22. Create a Non-clustered Index with Multiple Columns

```
CREATE NONCLUSTERED INDEX IX_Customer_DateCreated_FirstName_
LastName_Country
    ON dbo.Customer
    (
        DateCreated ASC,
        FirstName ASC,
        LastName ASC,
        Country ASC
    );
```

The same is true when creating primary and foreign keys. If you do not specify a name when you create a primary or foreign key in T-SQL, SQL Server will assign a name at random. Therefore, it is best practice to explicitly name the primary or foreign key. When naming the primary key, you want the primary key to begin with PK_ which stands for primary key. Similarly, you want to precede the foreign key with FK_ and then name the rest of the key. The next part of the name is the table name where the primary or foreign key is assigned. This is followed by the column or columns used to define the primary or foreign key. If there is more than one column specified, the columns listed in the primary or foreign key should be listed in order. Listing 3-23 shows an example of how to create and name a primary key after table has been created.

Listing 3-23. Add a Primary Key

```
ALTER TABLE dbo.Product
ADD CONSTRAINT PK_Product_ProductID
    PRIMARY KEY (ProductID);
```

As you can see, the primary key name begins with PK followed by the table name and then the column name used for the creation of the primary key.

Similarly, you want to precede the foreign key with FK_ and then name the rest of the key. The next part of the name is the table name where the primary or foreign key is assigned. This is followed by the column or columns used to define the primary or foreign key. If there is more than one column specified, the columns listed in the primary or foreign key should be listed in order. When creating a foreign key after the table has been created, you can refer to Listing 3-24.

Listing 3-24. Add a Foreign Key

```
ALTER TABLE dbo.CustomerOrder
ADD CONSTRAINT FK_Order_CustomerID
    FOREIGN KEY (CustomerID)
    REFERENCES dbo.Customer(CustomerID);
```

Like creating the primary key, the foreign key follows a similar naming structure. The foreign key begins with FK followed by the table name and then the column name.

I also precede views with vw_ and triggers with tr_. There are other options available that can be less obvious. For instance, you can define a list of nouns or verbs that will be reserved for only views or triggers. This will give you more flexibility, and it will also keep Object Explorer from having all items in the list begin with the same three characters. This will allow anyone to easily be able to tell these objects are neither tables nor stored procedures. This is particularly true when it comes to views and triggers.

One of the biggest challenges is that if they are not named to make it obvious that they are views or triggers, people can spend a significant amount of time looking for these objects without being able to find them. Views are used in joins like tables, whereas triggers change objects similar to stored procedures. Triggers are even trickier because they can cause you to spend a significant amount of time researching stored procedures trying to determine why values are changing.

When naming tables, you want to use only nouns. This helps signify that these objects are for storage and not for performing any specific activity. When naming objects, one of the naming conventions that is often overlooked until it is too late is whether objects are singular or plural. It is not really an issue until the first time where an object is pluralized. Once a plural database object is in the overall schema, it becomes obvious very quickly the issues with a plural object. This is because once a plural object exists in the database, it becomes increasingly difficult to write queries without specifically remembering which tables are plural and which are singular.

You also want to make sure that you choose a descriptive name when naming a table. You want to describe your table in a way that other database engineers and developers will easily know what type of information is stored in the table. Naming tables with nouns also indicates that the object is for storage and not performing any specific activities.

Most users become easily familiar with tables and stored procedures. It is easy to choose a naming convention that differentiates these objects either by having stored procedure preceded with a verb or having additional high-level criteria as part of the stored procedure name. Listing 3-25 shows a stored procedure that has a verb at the beginning of a stored procedure name.

Listing 3-25. Stored Procedure Beginning with a Verb

```
EXECUTE dbo.GetCustomer;
```

If I see that stored procedure name, I expect it to retrieve all customers. The stored procedure in Listing 3-26 returns all the customer information for a specific customer.

Listing 3-26. Stored Procedure with Selection Criteria

```
EXECUTE dbo.GetCustomerByCustomerID 1;
```

As you can see, there are many considerations when it comes to naming your T-SQL database objects. In many of these cases, a good name helps you easily determine the purpose of the database object. In special circumstances, it can also help you identify the type of object. While you normally name your objects after formatting and commenting the T-SQL, I saved the commenting for last as it covers both the creation of the database object and the T-SQL code that goes inside the database object.

Commenting T-SQL

While the primary goal of writing T-SQL is to allow an application to do a specific action regarding data, almost equally important is ensuring that others will understand your T-SQL code going forward. At the very least, this makes sure that you are not the only one responsible for a certain piece of code or business logic going forward. It also helps all your other team members build confidence in their ability to do their job and improve their understanding of the code behind the scenes.

In many cases, quickly scanning the T-SQL code or looking at the name of a database object is not enough to understand the purpose of the T-SQL code. Listing 3-27 shows sample T-SQL code for creating a header section at the top of database objects.

Listing 3-27. Comment for Header of Persistent Database Object

```
/*-----------------------------------------------------------*\
Name:               <name of database object>
Author:             <original author name>
Created Date:       <original creation date>
Description:        <Brief description of database object>
Sample Usage:
        <Example of how this database object will be called>
Change Log:
        Update on <date> by <user>: <Brief summary of changes>
        Update on <date> by <user>: <Brief summary of changes>
\*-----------------------------------------------------------*/
```

The purpose of this heading is to give other users a summary of this database object at a glance. Depending on the purpose for reviewing this T-SQL will determine what is important to the user. For those who are not familiar with all the details of the business applications, the description segment will provide a high-level idea of the purpose of the T-SQL database object. Likewise, the sample usage allows those looking into performance issues to understand how the applications are using this piece of T-SQL code. The author-of-the-database object can be useful to determine if the original creator is still with the company to answer more specific questions about the database object. If your databases are in source control, you may decide to omit some of these fields. I discuss source control further in Chapter 11. In Listing 3-28, you can see how the header information looks while creating the view originally found in Listing 3-4.

Listing 3-28. Create a View with a Commented Header

```
/*-------------------------------------------------------------------*\
Name:              dbo.CustomerProduct
Author:            Elizabeth Noble
Created Date:      2022-10-31
Description:       Simple view to display all customer purchases
Sample Usage:
      SELECT FirstName, LastName, ProductName, QuantitySold
      FROM dbo.CustomerProduct;
Change Log:
      Update on 2022-10-31 by enoble: Added header to view
\*-------------------------------------------------------------------*/
CREATE OR ALTER VIEW dbo.CustomerProduct
AS
SELECT cus.FirstName, cus.LastName, prd.ProductName, SUM(dtl.QuantitySold)
AS QuantitySold
FROM dbo.CustomerOrder ord
    INNER JOIN dbo.OrderDetail dtl
    ON ord.CustomerOrderID = dtl.CustomerOrderID
    INNER JOIN dbo.Product prd
    ON dtl.ProductID = prd.ProductID
    INNER JOIN dbo.Customer cus
    ON ord.CustomerID = cus.CustomerID
GROUP BY cus.FirstName, cus.LastName, prd.ProductName;
```

Sometimes it may be enough to write simple T-SQL that is easily readable. However, there are other times where a database object may have T-SQL code that is difficult to understand at a quick glance. I often find one of the challenges in commenting after

I've written my code is that my comments are too technical to easily describe what I am trying to accomplish. You want to make sure that someone unfamiliar with your code can easily understand the purpose of your T-SQL code.

If there is any complex logic, you want to clearly explain how the complex logic works. This is especially true if you are using T-SQL coding practices that are not best practices. Any explanation as to why non-standard practices were chosen helps save other people's valuable time. This can also save your team members' time if you have already determined that standard best practices will not perform well enough in the given situation. Looking back to Listing 3-3, there is a subquery in the SELECT statement. When first writing this code, it may be obvious why a subquery was used, but you may forget the reason in the future. In addition, it is probably not obvious to others who read my code why I chose to include a subquery for that column. In Listing 3-29, I show how to add comments so that it is easier to quickly understand the purpose or logic of the code that is written.

Listing 3-29. Queries with Subqueries

```
-- The outer query shows all customers that bought products that contain
the word "board"
SELECT
-- The subquery below is used to show all parts purchased
---- by customers that also bought parts like "board"
    (
        SELECT prd.ProductName
        FROM dbo.CustomerOrder ord
            INNER JOIN dbo.OrderDetail dtl
            ON ord.CustomerOrderID = dtl.CustomerOrderID
            INNER JOIN dbo.Product prd
            ON dtl.ProductID = prd.ProductID
        WHERE ord.CustomerID = bord.CustomerID
        GROUP BY prd.ProductName
    ) AS ProductName
FROM dbo.CustomerOrder bord
    INNER JOIN dbo.OrderDetail bdtl
    ON bord.CustomerOrderID = bdtl.CustomerOrderID
    INNER JOIN dbo.Product bprd
```

```
   ON bdtl.ProductID = bprd.ProductID
WHERE bprd.ProductName LIKE '%board%';
```

It is often easiest to include comments in your code if you start commenting your
T-SQL code even before you begin writing any T-SQL. In Listing 3-30, you can see the
header information and the beginning comments. The comments indicate the concept
behind writing the stored procedure.

Listing 3-30. Create New Stored Procedure

```
/*------------------------------------------------------------*\
Name:                dbo.GetCustomerPurchase
Author:              Elizabeth Noble
Created Date:        2022-10-30
Description:         Lookup customer information for a given product
Sample Usage:
      DECLARE @ProductID INT;
      SET @ProductID = 1;
      EXECUTE dbo. GetCustomerPurchase @ProductID;
\*------------------------------------------------------------*/
-- Get the product sold to a customer
-- Show total number sold as well as most recent purchase date
-- Show details for quantity purchased by product price
---- at time of purchase
```

Once you specify the general logic for the query, you can move forward with writing
the T-SQL so that these requirements are met. This is often helpful if you usually find
yourself rephrasing the code you have already written instead of explaining the overall
purpose of the code.

Writing these comments before writing any T-SQL code ensures the comments
explain the purpose of the stored procedure instead of how the code executes.

You should now be prepared to start defining SQL formatting standards for yourself
and in your own organization. This will allow you and other members of your team to
quickly review your organization's T-SQL code. In addition, I discussed strategies to use
when providing additional documentation about your T-SQL code. Commenting your
T-SQL code allows others to understand what the T-SQL code should be doing both
regarding business logic and advanced technical logic. I also covered options available

when defining naming conventions for your organization. Well-defined naming conventions should make it easier for anyone accessing the database schema to know where to find database objects.

You should now be familiar with SQL Server data types from Chapter 1 and the best time to use them. You should also be comfortable with some of the various database objects that are available when writing your T-SQL. Now that you are also more familiar with how to style your code to improve readability and understanding, you are ready to learn more about designing T-SQL code using parameters, complex logic, and stored procedures as covered in the next section.

CHAPTER 4

Designing T-SQL

The focus of building understandable T-SQL is to increase the speed at which you can understand code that you have not seen before or seen in a while. As discussed in Chapter 1, choosing the right data type can increase the speed of your T-SQL code because smaller amounts of data need to be retrieved. As important as formatting and data types can be, choosing the correct database objects for your T-SQL code can also have an impact on the speed of your applications. This chapter will discuss how your query design can affect the speed of your queries.

When writing T-SQL for your applications, stored procedures are usually the most desirable option when it comes to performance. There are many advantages to using stored procedures including the possibility of making your code more adaptable and reusable. Similarly, using parameters with your code can increase the flexibility of your T-SQL code. You can use stored procedures and parameters when designing solutions for more complex queries. In addition, you may want to consider other techniques when it comes to solving complex issues. There are several items to consider when designing T-SQL code including stored procedures, parameters, and complex query logic.

Using Stored Procedures

When writing T-SQL code, there are several ways the code can be written, and this can affect how quickly the query executes. The relative speed of the query will be slower if there is no execution plan in the plan cache. Being able to use a cached execution plan will increase the speed of your queries since SQL Server will not have to spend additional resources to determine how to retrieve the data. The method SQL Server uses to retrieve the data is called an execution plan and it is discussed in more detail in Chapter 8.

There are several aspects to consider when writing T-SQL code for applications. In order to better understand how you want your applications to use T-SQL, it may be best to understand how SQL Server handles each of the T-SQL options available. When SQL

© Elizabeth Noble 2023
E. Noble, *Pro T-SQL 2022*, https://doi.org/10.1007/978-1-4842-9256-3_4

Server executes a query, it must determine how it will go about executing that query. Before doing this, SQL Server will check to see if there is already an execution plan for this query. How the T-SQL is designed will have some impact on how SQL Server verifies that the execution plan is already in place.

To show how stored procedures, ad hoc queries, and prepared statements affect the plan cache, let's walk through some examples. Using stored procedures will allow your T-SQL code to be repeatable, potentially allowing the query plan to stay in the cache longer and improving the speed of your query execution. In Listing 4-1, you can see a statement to create the stored procedure.

Listing 4-1. Creating a Stored Procedure

```
/*-------------------------------------------------------------*\
Name:              dbo.GetCustomer
Author:            Elizabeth Noble
Created Date:      2022-04-20
Description:       Get a list of all customers in the databases
Sample Usage:
       EXECUTE dbo.GetCustomer;
\*-------------------------------------------------------------*/
CREATE PROCEDURE dbo.GetCustomer
AS
       SELECT
           CustomerID,
           FirstName,
           LastName,
           Address,
           City,
           PostalCode,
           Country,
           IsActive,
           DateCreated,
           DateModified,
           DateDisabled
       FROM dbo.Customer;
```

In this example, you create a stored procedure that is not parameterized and will execute the exact same T-SQL each time. This stored procedure returns results for the requested columns in the SELECT statement for all customers that have been entered into the database. If you want to see the results for this stored procedure, you can execute the stored procedure as shown in Listing 4-2.

Listing 4-2. Executing the Stored Procedure

```
EXECUTE dbo.GetCustomer;
```

SQL Server creates the execution plan in Figure 4-1 and, in most cases, saves the execution plan to the query plan cache. It is possible this plan may be deemed trivial and will not be saved in the cache at all. If this stored procedure is run again in the future, SQL Server will check the plan cache to see if this stored procedure already exists in the cache. This plan will sit in the plan cache for as long as SQL Server deems the plan relevant. Chapter 8 will go into more detail as to how SQL Server calculates the relevance of an execution plan. In Figure 4-1, you can see the execution plan associated with the stored procedure in Listing 4-2.

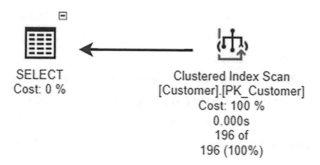

Figure 4-1. *Execution plan for a stored procedure*

If the plan is in the cache, SQL Server will continue to reuse the same execution plan. This works well for stored procedures. However, there are other ways of accessing data in SQL Server. One of these methods is to write ad hoc queries. When writing ad hoc queries, you have the option to hard code the values or parameterize them. The example of the type of query shown in Listing 4-3 has the same logic as the stored procedure in Listing 4-1.

Listing 4-3. Adhoc Query Logic

```
SELECT
      CustomerID,
      FirstName,
      LastName,
      Address,
      City,
      PostalCode,
      Country,
      IsActive,
      DateCreated,
      DateModified,
      DateDisabled
FROM dbo.Customer;
```

The logic in Listings 4-1 and 4-3 is the same. The largest difference is in how SQL Server handles the two different T-SQL queries. However, what happens is SQL Server checks the plan cache to see if the same plan exists. The plans that are stored in the plan cache are not based on the core logic but are based on how the actual ad hoc query or stored procedure execution is written.

As you can see in Table 4-1, the ad hoc query is even stored as an ad hoc object type, whereas SQL Server can properly tell that the second row is a stored procedure. In Table 4-1, you can see the results in the plan cache from running the stored procedure and the same code as an ad hoc query.

Table 4-1. *Plan Cache for Ad Hoc Query and Stored Procedure*

Use Count	Object Type	Query Text
1	Adhoc	SELECT CustomerID, FirstName, LastName, Address, City, PostalCode, Country, IsActive, DateCreated, DateModified, DateDisabled FROM dbo.Customer;
1	Proc	/*-- -----------*\ Name: dbo.GetCustomer Author: Elizabeth Noble Created Date: 2022-10-30 Description: Get a list of all customers in the databases Sample Usage: EXECUTE dbo.GetCustomer *----------------------------------- --------------------------*/ CREATE PROCEDURE dbo.GetCustomer AS SELECT CustomerID, FirstName, LastName, Address, City, PostalCode, Country, IsActive, DateCreated, DateModified, DateDisabled FROM dbo.Customer;

Where this all can become important is when users or applications write code inconsistently. The query is modified from Listing 4-3 by moving the first column in the select statement to the same row as the SELECT clause. Listing 4-4 shows the updated query.

Listing 4-4. Adhoc Query Modified

```
SELECT CustomerID,
    FirstName,
    LastName,
    Address,
    City,
    PostalCode,
    Country,
    IsActive,
    DateCreated,
```

```
    DateModified,
    DateDisabled
FROM dbo.Customer;
```

The only thing that has really changed is the formatting of the query itself. While you may be able to see that the query is using the same logic, you should run the query in Listing 4-5 to see how SQL Server handles this query in relation to the plan cache. After running the query in Listing 4-4, the plan cache will show the results in Table 4-2.

Table 4-2. *Plan Cache for Modified Ad Hoc Query*

Use Count	Object Type	Query Text
1	Ad hoc	SELECT CustomerID, FirstName, LastName, Address, City, PostalCode, Country, IsActive, DateCreated, DateModified, DateDisabled FROM dbo.Customer;
1	Ad hoc	SELECT CustomerID, FirstName, LastName, Address, City, PostalCode, Country, IsActive, DateCreated, DateModified, DateDisabled FROM dbo.Customer;
1	Proc	/*-- ---------*\ Name: dbo. GetCustomer Author: Elizabeth Noble Created Date: 2022-10-30 Description: Get a list of all customers in the databases Sample Usage: EXECUTE dbo.GetCustomer *---------------------------- --------------------------------*/ CREATE PROCEDURE dbo.GetCustomer AS SELECT CustomerID, FirstName, LastName, Address, City, PostalCode, Country, IsActive, DateCreated, DateModified, DateDisabled FROM dbo.Customer;

You can see in Table 4-2 that there are now three entries in the plan cache. Instead of SQL Server reusing the execution plan from the first time the ad hoc query was called, SQL Server generated an entirely new execution plan. Each time SQL Server creates a new execution plan, it uses additional resources to create and store the plan. Needing to generate an execution plan can delay the speed of the query by a couple of seconds.

Each query plan executed is saved in the plan cache. Having multiple execution plans saved for each query can fill up the execution plan cache. This can cause other query execution plans to be removed from the plan cache prematurely. The removal of a query plan from the cache will cause SQL Server to expend additional resources to create a new execution for that other query. Chapter 7 will have a more information about how memory usage can affect the speed of the query performance. This is something to consider when determining how your applications will call T-SQL code.

While a stored procedure gives you a consistent way to call that same type of code more than once, generic stored procedures may not give you the flexibility you need in your applications. If that is the case, you want to see how using parameters can help increase the scalability of your T-SQL code.

Using Parameters

In addition to using stored procedures to help T-SQL code be more reusable, you can use parameters with your T-SQL code. Parameters can be used with ad hoc queries, prepared statements, or stored procedures. It is also possible to use parameters as an input or output. Regardless of where parameters are used, parameters are what allow you to write queries that can be reused in a variety of situations. Listing 4-5 shows a stored procedure that returns customer information based on the CustomerID provided in the stored procedure.

Listing 4-5. Creating a Stored Procedure with a Parameter

```
/*--------------------------------------------------------------*\
Name:              dbo.GetCustomerByCustomerID
Author:            Elizabeth Noble
Created Date:      2022-10-30
Description:       Get Customer information when a Customer ID is provided
Sample Usage:
    DECLARE @CustomerID INT;
```

```
    SET @CustomerID = 1;
    EXECUTE dbo.GetCustomerByCustomerID @CustomerID;
\*-----------------------------------------------------------------*/
CREATE PROCEDURE dbo.GetCustomerByCustomerID
    @CustomerID    INT
AS
    SELECT
        CustomerID,
        FirstName,
        LastName,
        Address,
        City,
        PostalCode,
        Country,
        IsActive,
        DateCreated,
        DateModified,
        DateDisabled
    FROM dbo.Customer
    WHERE CustomerID = @CustomerID;
```

This stored procedure allows you to pass in any CustomerID and the stored procedure will return a predefined set of customer information based on that CustomerID. This also allows the T-SQL code to be called in a much simpler method. Listing 4-6 contains code to execute the stored procedure, passing a hard-coded value as part of the execution.

Listing 4-6. Executing a Stored Procedure with a Hard-Coded Value

```
EXECUTE dbo.GetCustomerByCustomerID 1;
```

While it is possible to use this method to call the stored procedure, using variables is a much more dynamic way to execute this stored procedure. One such method is to declare a variable with a specific data type and then set that variable to a specific value. This more closely simulates how an application might call a stored procedure. The application code generally has a variable already declared and uses the same variable when executing the stored procedure. The process of declaring a variable, setting that variable to a value, and executing the stored procedure using that variable can be seen in Listing 4-7.

Listing 4-7. Executing a Stored Procedure with a Variable

```
DECLARE @CustomerID INT;
SET @CustomerID = 1;
EXECUTE dbo.GetCustomerByCustomerID @CustomerID;
```

To get a comparison of the plan cache for the stored procedure in Listing 4-6 vs. an ad hoc query, execute the ad hoc query that will use the same overall logic as Listing 4-5. However, this value will not be parameterized. In Listing 4-8, the query below has a hard-coded value for the CustomerID.

Listing 4-8. Running an Adhoc Query with a Hard-Coded Value

```
SELECT CustomerID,
       FirstName,
       LastName,
       Address,
       City,
       PostalCode,
       Country,
       IsActive,
       DateCreated,
       DateModified,
       DateDisabled
FROM dbo.Customer
WHERE CustomerID = 1;
```

Another method for executing the same stored procedure is to use a query like the one in Listing 4-8 but to use a parameter as part of the where clause. This will perform that same overall logic as Listings 4-6, 4-7, and 4-8. The code in Listing 4-9 uses the same code by declaring a variable and parameterized the query overall.

Listing 4-9. Running an Adhoc Query with a Parameter

```
DECLARE @CustomerID INT;
SET @CustomerID = 1;
SELECT CustomerID,
     FirstName,
     LastName,
     Address,
     City,
     PostalCode,
     Country,
     IsActive,
     DateCreated,
     DateModified,
     DateDisabled
FROM dbo.Customer
WHERE @CustomerID = @CustomerID;
```

While all these queries return the same data, the way SQL Server handles these four queries can be surprisingly different. In my test case, I cleared the plan cache by executing the code DBCC FREEPROCCACHE.

Caution   Do not run this stored procedure on a Production system because it can negatively impact the performance of SQL Server.

Then I executed the T-SQL code in Listings 4-7, 4-8, 4-9, and 4-10. Even though each of these queries returns the same results, you will see in Table 4-3 how SQL Server has calculated or used execution plans for each of these queries.

Table 4-3. *Comparison of Plan Cache for Variables and Hard-Coded Values*

Use Counts	Object Type	Text
2	Proc	/*---*\ Name: dbo.GetCustomerByCustomerID Author: Elizabeth Noble Created Date: 2022-10-30 Description: Get Customer information when a Customer ID is provided Sample Usage: DECLARE @CustomerID INT; SET @CustomerID = 1; EXECUTE dbo.GetCustomerByCustomerID @CustomerID *---*/ CREATE PROCEDURE dbo.GetCustomerByCustomerID @CustomerID SELECT CustomerID, FirstName, LastName, Address, City, PostalCode, Country, IsActive, DateCreated, DateModified, DateDisabled FROM dbo.Customer WHERE CustomerID = @CustomerID;
1	Adhoc	DECLARE @CustomerID INT; SET @CustomerID = 1 SELECT CustomerID, FirstName, LastName, Address, City, PostalCode, Country, IsActive, DateCreated, DateModified, DateDisabled FROM dbo.Customer WHERE @CustomerID = 1;
1	Adhoc	SELECT CustomerID, FirstName, LastName, Address, City, PostalCode, Country, IsActive, DateCreated, DateModified, DateDisabled FROM dbo.Customer WHERE CustomerID = 1;
1	Prepared	(@1 tinyint)SELECT [CustomerID],[FirstName], [LastName],[Address],[City],[PostalCode],[Country], [IsActive],[DateCreated],[DateModified],[DateDisabl ed] FROM [dbo].[Customer] WHERE [CustomerID]=@1

In Table 4-3, you can see that the stored procedure has been executed twice. The SELECT statement with the hard-coded value and the SELECT statement with the parameter value each have their own execution plan. This may not have a large impact when you are discussing only a handful of queries. However, if your entire environment has a significant number of queries that are not stored procedures or prepared statements, you may want to check your plan cache to determine how they are being handled.

This is not the only topic you need to consider when writing your queries. Another potential option has to do with what is commonly referred to as parameter sniffing. Parameter sniffing does not sound as dangerous as it can be. PSP!! The key takeaway when understanding what parameter sniffing is and how it affects you is to consider how your data is shaped. For many companies, not all data stored in a data table is evenly distributed.

A query plan for a query where SQL Server expects many rows to be returned due to column statistics can look very different than a plan for that very same query if it now expects very few rows due to a different parameter bringing back different statistics. All this parameterization is trying to get both of versions of these queries to share a single plan that is saved in the plan cache. This problem of sharing plans when the queries may do better without sharing is called parameter sniffing. In Listing 4-10, you can see the stored procedure to test for parameter sniffing.

Listing 4-10. Stored Procedure to Find Customer and Order by Product

```
/*----------------------------------------------------------------*\
Name:              dbo.GetCustomerAndOrderNumberByProductID
Author:            Elizabeth Noble
Created Date:      2022-10-30
Description:       Get customer and products ordered for an order number
Sample Usage:
      EXECUTE dbo.GetCustomerAndOrderNumberByProductID 1
\*----------------------------------------------------------------*/
CREATE PROCEDURE dbo.GetCustomerAndOrderNumberByProductID
      @ProductID      INT
WITH RECOMPILE
AS
      SELECT
            cus.FirstName,
            cus.LastName,
```

```
        ord.OrderNumber,
        ord.OrderDate,
        prd.ProductName,
        SUM(dtl.QuantitySold),
        dtl.ProductPrice
    FROM dbo.Customer cus
        INNER JOIN dbo.CustomerOrder ord
        ON cus.CustomerID = ord.CustomerID
        INNER JOIN dbo.OrderDetail dtl
        ON ord.CustomerOrderID = dtl.CustomerOrderID
        INNER JOIN dbo.Product prd
        ON prd.ProductID = dtl.ProductID
    WHERE prd.ProductID = @ProductID
    GROUP BY cus.FirstName,
        cus.LastName,
        ord.OrderNumber,
        ord.OrderDate,
        prd.ProductName,
        dtl.ProductPrice
    ORDER BY cus.FirstName, cus.LastName;
```

In the case of products, you may have a significant difference in the quantity of the types of products that are stored in the tables. If you have hundreds or thousands of telescopes sold but only a handful of paddleboards sold, you may find yourself in a scenario where parameter sniffing will affect your application performance. In this scenario, you may execute a stored procedure wanting telescopes. The first time you call your stored procedure, SQL Server will use the parameter provided to generate an execution plan. That execution plan will end up stored in the plan cache. To test for parameter sniffing, you may want to execute the stored procedure with a given parameter, as shown in Listing 4-11.

Listing 4-11. Executing a Stored Procedure with a Parameter with Many Records

```
EXECUTE dbo.GetCustomerAndOrderNumberByProductID 1;
```

This stored procedure execution results in the partial execution plan in Figure 4-2 for retrieving the customer order and order detail information.

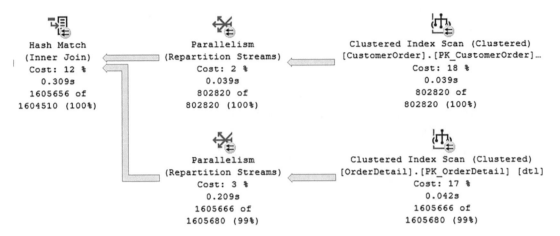

Figure 4-2. *Execution plan for a stored procedure with a parameter that has many records*

If you come back later and want to rerun the stored procedure for paddleboards, SQL Server will reuse the original execution plan that was generated when you ran the query for telescopes, of which there are many. However, the first execution plan that SQL Server created may perform worse when trying to find customers with the product of paddleboards. If you clear the plan cache and rerun the stored procedure in a different order, you can verify that the issue is related to parameter sniffing. In Listing 4-12, you can see the T-SQL code used to generate a different execution plan based on the fact that there are far fewer rows expected now.

Listing 4-12. Executing a Stored Procedure with a Parameter with Few Records

```
EXECUTE dbo.GetCustomerAndOrderNumberByProductID 4;
```

When you execute this stored procedure, a different plan cache is created. You can see the execution plan that is created in Figure 4-3.

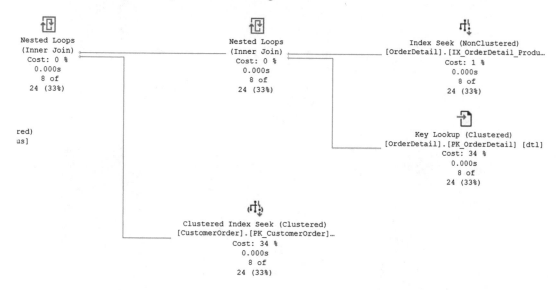

Figure 4-3. Execution plan for a stored procedure with a parameter that has few records

There is a new join that allows the execution plan to handle different shapes of data with the same execution plan. This is the use of the adaptive join operator. For now, the important thing to understand is that the adaptive join operator in the execution plan gives SQL Server the option to choose one of two different operators for the query execution, as shown in Figure 4-4.

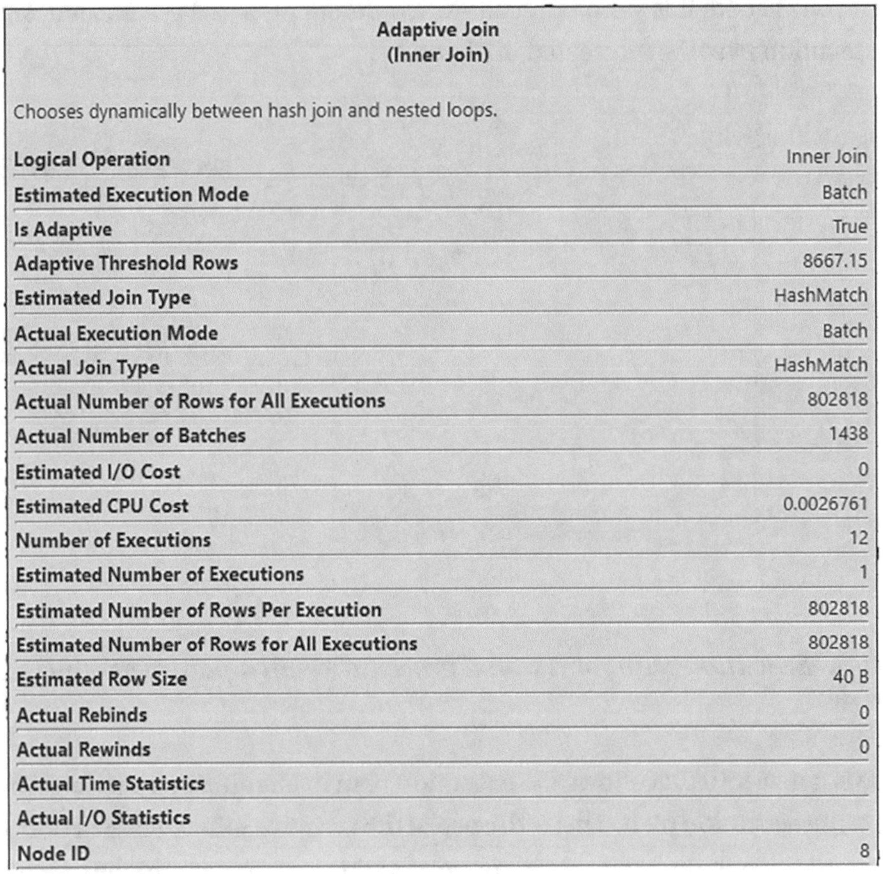

Adaptive Join (Inner Join)	
Chooses dynamically between hash join and nested loops.	
Logical Operation	Inner Join
Estimated Execution Mode	Batch
Is Adaptive	True
Adaptive Threshold Rows	8667.15
Estimated Join Type	HashMatch
Actual Execution Mode	Batch
Actual Join Type	HashMatch
Actual Number of Rows for All Executions	802818
Actual Number of Batches	1438
Estimated I/O Cost	0
Estimated CPU Cost	0.0026761
Number of Executions	12
Estimated Number of Executions	1
Estimated Number of Rows Per Execution	802818
Estimated Number of Rows for All Executions	802818
Estimated Row Size	40 B
Actual Rebinds	0
Actual Rewinds	0
Actual Time Statistics	
Actual I/O Statistics	
Node ID	8

Figure 4-4. *Adaptive join operator properties*

As you can see, the adaptive join allows SQL Server to choose dynamically between either a hash join operator or a nested loop. The ability for this operator to switch between the hash join and nest loop operators helps alleviate many of the performance issues experienced with parameter sniffing. The batch mode named Adaptive Join was introduced in SQL Server 2017 and is available as long as your database is in compatibility mode 140 or greater. I will discuss adaptive joins in more detail in Chapter 8.

Using Complex Logic

There are some basic operations in SQL Server that are not significantly complex. These basic operations can include inserting, reading, updating, and deleting tables from single tables and may be referred to as CRUD (create, read, update, and delete) operations. Some of these operations may involve a couple of joins, but at some point in time, there may be a need for more complex logic. One of the challenges that happens while working with T-SQL is dealing with complex logic.

When dealing with complex logic, it is important to keep a couple of things in mind. The first step in dealing with complex logic is breaking down the request into smaller parts. Part of this logic is to figure out what data you need to start with and how to whittle that data down into a smaller data set. You also want to focus on taking all the requirements and breaking them down into simplified steps.

Many of these query requests can involve either dealing with databases that were not designed to take advantage of the strengths of relational databases and systems that were not designed to be integrated or interacting with legacy applications. Oftentimes, we do not have control over what we are requested to do, and we are lucky if we get to design how the data is stored in the database.

These types of scenarios can also involve various types of coding methodologies that do not necessarily coincide with best practices. This includes needing to loop through data including recursion. There are also times when you may want to use correlated subqueries or work with various strings such as XML or JSON. While many of these options may seem like they are the perfect solution, many are overly complex. This is where the balancing act between making T-SQL code easy to understand and having T-SQL code that performs well can be tricky. The goal is to show how using what seems like more advanced query techniques may be contributing to poor performance in your applications.

It is often tempting to write your code in a way that matches the specific acceptance criteria or business request. Sometimes this will work well, and you will end up with code that performs very well. In other instances, not only can trying to write to solve complex problem be difficult and frustrating, but if the T-SQL code is not written in a way that works best for SQL Server, you have the potential for significant performance issues. I have found that SQL Server generally works best if I keep my code simple and straightforward. This also means that using new functionality in SQL Server may not always yield the best results in terms of performance, even if the code is easier to write.

The most common case I see where the T-SQL code does not always consider how SQL Server performs best is involving loops. SQL Server allows many options for looping through data, and while the code will return the correct results, I often find the cost on SQL Server more significant than figuring out a different way of interacting with the same data. I've taken the code from Listing 2-29 from Chapter 2 and repeated the same logic in Listing 4-13.

Listing 4-13. Creating a Dynamic Cursor

```
SET NOCOUNT ON;
DECLARE @ProductID INT,
    @ProductName VARCHAR(25),
    @message VARCHAR(50);
PRINT '-------- Product Listing --------';
DECLARE product_cursor CURSOR DYNAMIC
FOR
SELECT ProductID, ProductName
FROM dbo.Product;
OPEN product_cursor;
FETCH NEXT FROM product_cursor
INTO @ProductID, @ProductName;
WHILE @@FETCH_STATUS = 0
BEGIN
    PRINT ' ';
    SELECT @message = '----- Customers For Products: ' + @ProductName +
    '-----';
    PRINT @message;
      SELECT LEFT(cus.FirstName, 25), LEFT(cus.LastName, 25), SUM(dtl.
      QuantitySold) AS QuantitySold
      FROM dbo.CustomerOrder ord
            INNER JOIN dbo.OrderDetail dtl
            ON ord.CustomerOrderID = dtl.CustomerOrderID
            INNER JOIN dbo.Product prd
            ON dtl.ProductID = prd.ProductID
            INNER JOIN dbo.Customer cus
            ON ord.CustomerID = cus.CustomerID
        WHERE prd.ProductID = @ProductID
        GROUP BY cus.FirstName, cus.LastName, prd.ProductName;
      FETCH NEXT FROM product_cursor INTO @ProductID, @ProductName;
END
CLOSE product_cursor;
DEALLOCATE product_cursor;
```

This query will give us the exact results we want, but SQL Server will have to repeat the logic inside the cursor for each row that the cursor is analyzing. When the query logic inside the cursor is written well, there can be minimal impact. However, the real challenges happen when the T-SQL code inside the query either performs slowly or uses a significant amount of hardware. Then the server may use more resources, causing the speed of the query to slow down and potentially causing issues with your applications if the query takes longer than your application timeout period. While it is easy to blame cursors specifically, other scenarios like WHILE loops, not cursors, may still cause performance issues.

Another of the larger struggles is that even if the code performs well when it is first created, there is the potential for the performance of this code to decrease over time as the database grows or the shape of the data changes. In these situations, what once appeared to be a great solution can quickly become one of the largest headaches. There are some options to get the same output by writing the T-SQL code in a manner that is more efficient and less resource intensive.

When working through complex logic, it may be beneficial to take notes and try to break the problem into smaller steps. In Listing 4-14, you will see comments that outline the steps needed to get the same data output as would be returned in Listing 4-13.

Listing 4-14. Simplifying T-SQL Code Logic with Comments

```
-- Create Report Heading for All Products
-- Repeat the following per product
---- Create Section Subheading per Product
---- List All Customers with Quantity Sold Per Product
```

Ideally, the process of breaking the acceptance criteria down allows you to focus on where to start minimizing data accessed. Look at the query from two different perspectives. The first is to determine how to start paring the data down to only the data needed in the result. I usually try to do that as early as possible in my query design. I also try to look for the sections where I know the T-SQL code needed will be simple.

When referring to Listing 4-15, the acceptance criteria shows all customers that bought a product. An additional requirement is to show a header with the receipt name for each product. It is important to note that this example has been created to show how to improve performance using different coding techniques with T-SQL. If you have received a request to write T-SQL code like this, you may want to work with your internal teams to see if this can be handled differently. It is better to focus on the easiest part of the query first. In this case, getting a list of all customers per product is the simplest code set of requirements, so see Listing 4-15.

Listing 4-15. Getting All Parts for All Customers

```
-- Create Report Heading for All Products
-- Repeat the following per product
---- Create Section Subheading per Product
---- List All Customers with Quantity Sold Per Product
     SELECT cus.FirstName, cus.LastName, prd.ProductName, SUM(dtl.
QuantitySold) AS QuantitySold
     FROM dbo.CustomerOrder ord
               INNER JOIN dbo.OrderDetail dtl
               ON ord.CustomerOrderID = dtl.CustomerOrderID
               INNER JOIN dbo.Product prd
               ON dtl.ProductID = prd.ProductID
               INNER JOIN dbo.Customer cus
               ON ord.CustomerID = cus.CustomerID
          GROUP BY cus.FirstName, cus.LastName, prd.ProductName;
```

Now that you know how to get all customers who bought certain products, you can continue to add pieces of logic. The next challenge is to figure out how you can create a header for each product. Listing 4-16 shows one way you can start adding header information.

Listing 4-16. Getting All the Data Pulled Together

```
-- Create Report Heading for All Products
PRINT '-------- Product Listing --------';
-- Repeat the following per product
     SELECT
             '----- Customers For Products: ' + ProductName + '-----'
     FROM  dbo.Product
---- Create Section Subheading per Product
---- List All Customers with Quantity Sold Per Product
     SELECT cus.FirstName, cus.LastName, prd.ProductName, SUM(dtl.
     QuantitySold) AS QuantitySold
```

```
FROM dbo.CustomerOrder ord
            INNER JOIN dbo.OrderDetail dtl
            ON ord.CustomerOrderID = dtl.CustomerOrderID
            INNER JOIN dbo.Product prd
            ON dtl.ProductID = prd.ProductID
            INNER JOIN dbo.Customer cus
            ON ord.CustomerID = cus.CustomerID
    GROUP BY cus.FirstName, cus.LastName, prd.ProductName;
```

After adding some header information, you are ready to start getting the output to match the output that was returned in the cursor in Listing 4-13. In Listing 4-17, you can see all the code required to match the original output.

Listing 4-17. Rewritten Query to Avoid Using a Cursor

```
SET NOCOUNT ON;

-- Create a temporary table to store the product information
    CREATE TABLE #ProductList
    (
            OrderedList             INT,
            ProductID               INT,
            SectionHeader           VARCHAR(100)
    );
-- Repeat the following per product
---- Create Section Spacing per product
    INSERT INTO #ProductList (OrderedList, ProductID, SectionHeader)
    SELECT
            0 AS OrderedList,
            ProductID,
            '' AS SectionHeader
    FROM  dbo.Product;

---- Create Section Subheading per Product
    INSERT INTO #ProductList (OrderedList, ProductID, SectionHeader)
    SELECT
            10 AS OrderedList,
            ProductID,
```

```
                '----- Customers For Products: ' + ProductName + ' -----' AS
                SectionHeader
        FROM   Product;

---- Add the column headings for customers per product
        INSERT INTO #ProductList (OrderedList, ProductID, SectionHeader)
        SELECT
                15 AS OrderedList,
                ProductID,
                CAST('FirstName' AS CHAR(25)) + ' ' +
                        CAST('LastName' AS CHAR(22)) + ' ' +
                        CAST('QuantitySold' AS CHAR(19)) AS SectionHeader
        FROM   dbo.Product;

        INSERT INTO #ProductList (OrderedList, ProductID, SectionHeader)
        SELECT
                20 AS 'OrderedList',
                ProductID,
                '---------------------- ---------------------- ----------------
                ' AS SectionHeader
        FROM   dbo.Product;

---- List All Customers per Product
        INSERT INTO #ProductList
        (
                OrderedList,
                ProductID,
                SectionHeader
        )
        SELECT
                25 AS 'OrderedList',
                grp.ProductID,
                CAST(grp.FirstName AS CHAR(25)) + ' ' +
                        CAST(grp.LastName AS CHAR(22)) + ' ' +
                        CAST(CAST(grp.QuantitySold AS VARCHAR) AS CHAR(19)) AS
                          SectionHeader
```

```
FROM
(
        SELECT cus.FirstName, cus.LastName, prd.ProductID, SUM(dtl.
        QuantitySold) AS QuantitySold
        FROM dbo.CustomerOrder ord
                    INNER JOIN dbo.OrderDetail dtl
                    ON ord.CustomerOrderID = dtl.CustomerOrderID
                    INNER JOIN dbo.Product prd
                    ON dtl.ProductID = prd.ProductID
                    INNER JOIN dbo.Customer cus
                    ON ord.CustomerID = cus.CustomerID
        GROUP BY cus.FirstName, cus.LastName, prd.ProductID
) AS grp;

SELECT SectionHeader AS '-------- Product Listing --------'
FROM #ProductList
ORDER BY ProductID, OrderedList;

DROP TABLE #ProductList;
```

The original cursor gave the output shown in Figure 4-5 when the results were written to text.

```
-------- Product Listing --------


----- Customers For Products: Telescope-----
                                                    QuantitySold
------------------------  ------------------------  ------------
Jose                      Gomez                     2408452
Stacy                     Alexander                 4
Myra                      Acharya                   802816




----- Customers For Products: Disk Golf Disk-----
                                                    QuantitySold
------------------------  ------------------------  ------------




----- Customers For Products: Inflatable Paddleboa
                                                    QuantitySold
------------------------  ------------------------  ------------
```

Figure 4-5. *Output from the cursor*

To confirm that the rewrite from Listing 4-17 is correct, I captured the results to text when executing the same query. The output in Figure 4-6 appears to be the same.

```
-------- Product Listing --------
------------------------------------------------------------------

----- Customers For Products: Telescope -----
FirstName                    LastName                QuantitySold
-------------------------    -------------------     ----------------
Jose                         Gomez                   2408452
Stacy                        Alexander               4
Myra                         Acharya                 802816

----- Customers For Products: Disk Golf Disk -----
FirstName                    LastName                QuantitySold
-------------------------    -------------------     ----------------

----- Customers For Products: Inflatable Paddleboard -----
FirstName                    LastName                QuantitySold
-------------------------    -------------------     ----------------
```

Figure 4-6. *Output from modified query*

However, these outputs are only similar when they are exported to text. When dealing with small sets of data, the extra code and level of work may not seem to be required. As is usually the case, most performance issues do not become apparent until the performance is significantly and negatively impacting application performance. In the case of these two methods, when working with two records, the performance appears the same. However, when handling over 10,000 products sold, it becomes immediately clear that the query from Listing 4-17 performs significantly better.

This chapter covered how and why you want to use stored procedures. This includes creating code that is reusable and consistent. You also saw how parameters can improve code scalability. Parameters can help make your code more adaptable and dynamic. Parameters are helpful for many different scenarios. While parameters are very useful in many different situations, you also need to make sure your T-SQL is not being negatively affected by parameter sniffing. You explored common situations where you may need to solve complex problems using T-SQL. T-SQL performs better when you keep the code more straightforward. This may mean that the code is not as readable or clean, but SQL Server will have a better idea how to get an optimal execution plan.

This also concludes the current section on writing understandable T-SQL. This is T-SQL that uses the best data type for each scenario. This is usually a data type that takes up the least amount of space possible and provides the necessary accuracy. You also want to understand the various SQL Server database objects available to build your T-SQL. You must determine the benefits vs. the challenges of using one database object over another. In some cases, you need to decide if code readability or database performance is more important. Another aspect of writing understandable T-SQL is formatting, naming, and commenting your T-SQL so that others can quickly understand what you have written.

When working with T-SQL, there will be times when you want to write T-SQL that can be called consistently more than once. This T-SQL code may become more flexible using parameters. When faced with writing T-SQL that is not straightforward, break the code into segments to simplify what needs to be written. Once you feel comfortable writing T-SQL that is understandable, you're ready to write T-SQL that is efficient and minimizes performance impact on SQL Server.

CHAPTER 5

Set-Based Design

Knowing how to design T-SQL is part of the foundation of writing professional code. Once you can write T-SQL code that can be easily understood, you can focus on improving the performance of your T-SQL code. If you learned T-SQL informally as part of your job or your primary function is writing code for software applications, you may not consciously consider set-based design when writing your T-SQL code. Or you may be an experienced database developer and want to learn more about set-based design.

In this chapter, I will discuss how to work with your data. The first step is to get familiar with the various ways to interact with your data. Once you understand the different ways you can interact with your data, you can start thinking about how to put the data in the best format for your queries. Then you should be able to write those queries in a way that takes advantages of SQL Server's natural strengths.

Introducing Set-Based Design

The concept of set-based design is making sure the processing takes place as close to the data as possible. Doing so minimizes network round trips. It can also minimize context switches within the database engine.

Row-by-row processing is slow because part of the logic is in some program that is external to the database engine. Or in the case of a T-SQL cursor loop, the logic is in procedural code that requires a context switch for each row, and for each row to be passed back from whatever part of the database engine accesses the actual data to whatever part of the database engine runs the T-SQL.

Set-based processing pushes everything as deeply into the database engine as possible. Each row is not individually returned to a calling program, nor is there a context switch occurring for each row. The database engine spins through at full speed making whatever changes you have specified be made.

© Elizabeth Noble 2023
E. Noble, *Pro T-SQL 2022*, https://doi.org/10.1007/978-1-4842-9256-3_5

Data is created in almost every aspect of our lives, and much of that data is stored for various purposes. To increase the speed of data retrieval, it is often important to consider how data will be stored and accessed. Using SQL Server will allow you to take advantage of the relationships between data. This is because SQL Server is a relational database management system (RDBMS). While the focus of this book is writing T-SQL, understanding how data is stored will also help you write queries that return values with increased speed.

This book uses a sample database called OutdoorRecreation for a company that specializes in selling environmentally conscious, ethically sourced gear for the outdoors. To get an idea of various ways data can be stored, let's first look at various types of information that may be useful:

- Customer Name

- Customer Address

- Product

- Product Cost

- Product Price

- Order Date

- Order Status

- Current Product Price

- Quantity Sold

Looking at the above columns, you can start grouping the data into similar categories. For instance, you can group information about customers as shown in Table 5-1.

Table 5-1. *General Information for OutdoorRecreation*

Customer	Product	Order
Customer Name	Product	Order Date
Customer Address	Product Price	Order Status
	Product Cost	Current Product Price
		Quantity Sold

Once that information is grouped, the data can be stored by the groups. Within a database, the groups are referred to as *tables*. If you start populating data for customers, the data can be stored in a table like Table 5-2.

Table 5-2. *Customer Information*

First Name	Last Name	Address	City	Postal Code	Country
Myra	Acharya	30 Magrath Road	Bengaluru	560025	India
Josè	Gomez	790 Calle Cinco de Mayo	Cancun	53778	Mexico
Stacy	Parks	123 Rua de Santa Catarina	Porto	1234-567	Portugal
Karim	Khalil	153 Road Mit Rahina Al Shabab	Memphis	3364932	Egypt
Marty`	Bethel	750 Cherry Rd	Memphis	38117	United States

The data organized in the table is a *data set*. Looking at the data in the fourth column, City, there are two records with the city of Memphis. There are also two rows contain "de" in the Address column. You can create a set of data for all customers in the city of Memphis. Alternatively, you can create a different set of data for all customers where the address contains "de". You will use these two sets of data later in the chapter.

One of the things that can be difficult when working with SQL Server is the use of set-based transactions. You are using set-based transactions when you apply a single operation, such as a SQL statement, to all rows in a group of data. In SQL Server, the group of rows must be the additional threshold of meeting the conditions of any joins between tables as well as criteria in the WHERE clause. As an example, if you modify all addresses that end in Rd to end in Road using a single query, you are using a set-based transaction. Set-based operations look at data in terms of chunks or segments instead of looking at records or data row by row. While using set-based transactions is not inherently difficult, it is not always apparent how much using set-based transactions can improve the speed of many queries. In addition, SQL Server will return results for any query that has the correct syntax. Therefore, it might seem easier to interact with data one record at a time instead as a set.

This can lead to a very natural line of questions asking about the purpose and benefits for set-based operations. To better explain set-based operations, let's go through an example of what the output of a query will be if you access the data individually or as a set. To show you a comparison, Table 5-3, Table 5-4, and Table 5-5 each show an individual data record.

Table 5-3. *First Customer as Individual Record*

First Name	Last Name
Myra	Acharya

Table 5-4. *Second Customer as Individual Record*

First Name	Last Name
Josè	Gomez

Table 5-5. *Third Customer as Individual Record*

First Name	Last Name
Stacy	Parks

If you select the data from Table 5-3, Table 5-4, and Table 5-5 in this manner, it is far less efficient than trying to select the data as a set. Think of Tables 5-3 through 5-5 as representing three distinct select operations or three different round trips to the database. Table 5-6 shows what it looks like to select the data as a set, making a single round trip to retrieve all three rows in a single operation.

Table 5-6. *Customers as One Data Set*

First Name	Last Name
Myra	Acharya
Josè	Gomez
Stacy	Parks

Viewing the data like this allows you to also see the similarities between the data.

When you write T-SQL code, you want to return the data you need with fewer individual queries run against SQL Server. The goal is to consider doing the same thing to all the rows at the same time. In the preceding example, you can quickly determine which records have the same city name. The data provides a hint that if you want to look at or change something about customers with the same city, there may be more than one way to accomplish this goal. This type of scenario may indicate your logic should be structured in a way that it can function correctly by using relationships or variables instead of hard-coded or static values.

Understanding Data Retrieval

Procedural code is described as not only telling a system what to do but how to do it. In many companies, the software developers or software engineers are the ones responsible for writing the T-SQL code. One of the things I have learned from interacting with developers is that writing application code is procedural in nature. Many application developers spend most of their day working with code in a procedural context. This means that the mental cost of context switching between procedural application code and database T-SQL code can be significant. The process of writing set-based code can use a very different thought process than dealing with the code iteratively.

Why are we even interested in using set-based design? Why is it worth the trouble? This has to do with how the SQL Server engine works and how data is retrieved for queries. When a query is issued, SQL Server needs to retrieve one or more data records. When SQL Server retrieves data for a query result, the data page must be in memory. This memory set aside to hold the data pages is referred to as the *buffer cache*, also known as the *buffer pool*. SQL Server goes to the buffer cache to see if this data is available. Figure 5-1 shows the process SQL Server goes through to retrieve data as part of a query request if the data is cached in the buffer pool.

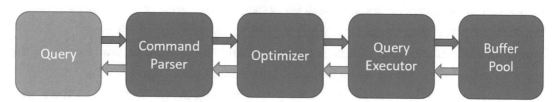

Figure 5-1. *Data retrieval from a single query*

Whether the data is retrieved row by row or as a set is dependent on the procedural logic or program code. If the T-SQL is written using cursor-based logic, it will use row-by-row processing, which will cause SQL Server to go to the buffer cache for each record. The process of retrieving a single row at a time can increase the workload on SQL Server. Since each query is its own set, and that can be a set of one, the goal is to design queries that will process the highest number of available records with the least amount of unique queries. Designing queries to work with larger data sets will prevent SQL Server from having to iterate through the same query multiple times. In Figure 5-2, you can see the additional workload required to retrieve one row at a time.

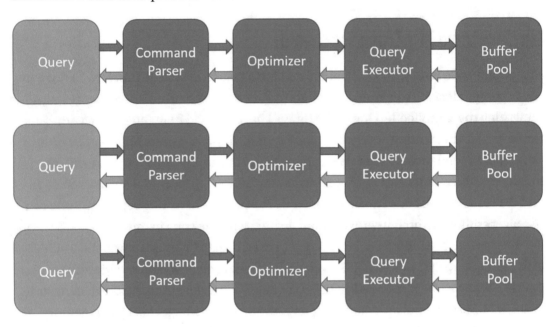

Figure 5-2. *Data retrieval when the query retrieves one row at a time*

Figure 5-2 shows the query process to retrieve a single record at a time with the data stored in the buffer pool. However, if the query is written for set-based design, there will be one call to the buffer pool. On a small set of data, this may not be a very large impact. When dealing with data sets of thousands or millions of records, the difference in execution time can be drastic. There is also something else to consider with how the data is stored in the buffer cache. When SQL Server executes a query and pulls back data, it only pulls back data that exists in the buffer cache. Starting in SQL Server 2019, there is a feature called the hybrid buffer pool. The hybrid buffer pool allows both data stored on RAM and in persistent memory (PMEM) to be treated as being part of the buffer cache. Otherwise, if the data is not available in RAM or PMEM, SQL Server will need to go to disk to retrieve the data. The data retrieved will then be stored in memory. Figure 5-3 shows how this data is retrieved from disk and stored in the buffer cache.

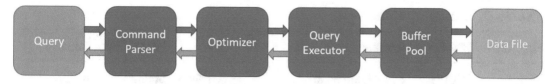

Figure 5-3. *Data retrieval from disk to the buffer cache*

When the query is executed, that data may not even be in the buffer cache at that point in time. SQL Server must go to the disk subsystem to find that data. Once that data is found, that data is stored in the buffer cache.

If each row is pulled individually, that call to the disk I/O will have to happen individually for each record. Pulling data from the buffer cache is not instantaneous. Getting data from the disk I/O and putting it in the buffer cache to then be retrieved by the query is even more resource intensive. Ultimately this creates a scenario where you want to focus on set-based design to have the best possible speed and performance for the queries that you are executing.

Thinking in Data Sets

Now that I have discussed what data sets are, I want you to be comfortable thinking about data in a way that embraces data sets. Before you start writing T-SQL code, it may save you time and energy to first understand what information is stored, how the data is stored, and selecting or using that data in groups of similar characteristics. Working with data sets is also easier to accomplish when the underlying tables are designed to work best with data sets.

Your goal is to learn to think in terms of data sets. This means thinking about handling multiple records at once instead of a single record. As an example, you may have a task like generating a report. Challenge yourself to generate a report from a single query. This won't be optimal for performance in all cases, but it will get you accustomed to thinking through how to describe the set of rows that will go into the report. This really requires an approach that is less arithmetic and more algebraic. In general, performing SELECT statements is the easiest way to get comfortable with set-based transactions. Consider the data shown in Table 5-7.

Table 5-7. *Customer Data*

First Name	Last Name	Address	City	Postal Code	Country
Myra	Acharya	30 Magrath Road	Bengaluru	560025	India
Josè	Gomez	790 Calle Cinco de Mayo	Cancun	53778	Mexico
Karim	Khalil	153 Road Mit Rahina Al Shabab	Memphis	3364932	Egypt
Marty`	Bethel	750 Cherry Rd	Memphis	38117	United States
Stacy	Alexander	123 Rua de Santa Catarina	Porto	1234-567	Portugal

This is a partial list of customers with their address. You can write the T-SQL query in Listing 5-1 to get the data set above.

Listing 5-1. Partial Customer List

```
SELECT FirstName,
       LastName,
       [Address],
       City,
       PostalCode,
       Country
FROM dbo.Customer
WHERE CustomerID BETWEEN 401405 AND 401409
ORDER BY City,
         Country;
```

By looking at the preceding data, you can find similarities between the data in some of the columns.

You can create a data set that gets all orders for customers in the city of Memphis. These records are shown in Table 5-8.

Table 5-8. *Customers in the City of Memphis*

First Name	Last Name	Address	City	Postal Code	Country
Karim	Khalil	153 Road Mit Rahina Al Shabab	Memphis	3364932	Egypt
Marty`	Bethel	750 Cherry Rd	Memphis	38117	United States

If you want to use T-SQL to find this same information, you can write the query in Listing 5-2.

Listing 5-2. Customers in Memphis

```
SELECT FirstName, LastName
FROM dbo.Customer
WHERE City = 'Memphis';
```

You can instead get the data set for all orders where the price per product is greater than or equal to $500 as shown in Table 5-9.

Table 5-9. *Customer Orders with a Products Equal to $500*

First Name	Last Name	CustomerOrderID	Quantity Sold
Karim	Khalil	802818	2
Marty`	Bethel	802817	1
Myra	Acharya	802816	1

Listing 5-3 is the query needed to retrieve the data in Table 5-9.

Listing 5-3. Query to Identify Customer Orders with Products Equal to $500

```
SELECT cus.FirstName,
    cus.LastName,
    ord.CustomerOrderID,
    SUM(dtl.QuantitySold) AS QuantitySold
FROM dbo.Customer cus
    INNER JOIN dbo.CustomerOrder ord
    ON cus.CustomerID = ord.CustomerID
    INNER JOIN dbo.OrderDetail dtl
    ON ord.CustomerOrderID = dtl.CustomerOrderID
WHERE dtl.ProductPrice = 249.99
GROUP BY cus.FirstName,
    cus.LastName,
    ord.CustomerOrderID;
```

Now that you have a set of data, you can consider how you want to interact with that data set. Knowing that you can group like data together and perform an action on that entire set of data is the key to using T-SQL code effectively. If you want to find out the average amount of products purchased, you can divide the order total by the number of units. To calculate the average amount purchased for each record, you can calculate the cost manually for each record. In this case, the order total for CustomerOrderID 802817 is $2,295. The total number of units sold on this invoice is 5: three telescopes and two inflatable paddleboards. This gives the result of $459 per unit sold. Alternatively, you can use the columns in the data sets to do the same calculation. To calculate the cost per unit as a data set, you can specify Average Unit Price. The result of handling the data in this fashion is shown in Table 5-10.

Table 5-10. *Calculated Average Unit Price*

CustomerOrderID	Average Unit Price
802817	$459.00
802924	$249.00

One of the greatest challenges working with SQL Server is learning how to think in data sets. The simplest way to think of data sets is to view the process of retrieving data as performing an action on a column or a subset of a column. If you can find some sort of pattern on how to perform that action on a subset of the data, then you are thinking in terms of data sets.

Identifying Data Sets

Looking at the Customer table, you can create a data set where all cities have the word Memphis in the name. All the available values in the Customer table are in Table 5-11.

Table 5-11. *General Listing of Customers*

First Name	Last Name	Address	City	Postal Code	Country
Myra	Acharya	30 Magrath Road	Bengaluru	560025	India
Josè	Gomez	790 Calle Cinco de Mayo	Cancun	53778	Mexico
Stacy	Parks	123 Rua de Santa Catarina	Porto	1234-567	Portugal
Karim	Khalil	153 Road Mit Rahina Al Shabab	Memphis	3364932	Egypt
Marty`	Bethel	750 Cherry Rd	Memphis	38117	United States

There are a couple different ways to do this. You can write a query that looks for the CustomerID of 401407 or 401405. You can see the results of this logic in Table 5-12.

Table 5-12. *Customers in the City of Memphis*

First Name	Last Name	Address	City	Postal Code	Country
Karim	Khalil	153 Road Mit Rahina Al Shabab	Memphis	3364932	Egypt
Marty`	Bethel	750 Cherry Rd	Memphis	38117	United States

Going back to the preceding table, add a new customer for Memphis. Table 5-13 shows the new record added

Table 5-13. *Adding New Memphis Customer*

First Name	Last Name	Address	City	Postal Code	Country
Karim	Khalil	153 Road Mit Rahina Al Shabab	Memphis	3364932	Egypt
Marty`	Bethel	750 Cherry Rd	Memphis	38117	United States
Ruth	Johnson	4711 Ponce de Leon	Memphis	38110	United States

If you want to still show all records that have the city of Memphis and you use the same logic as earlier, which is to use the CustomerID to display the desired values, you will not get the results you expect. If you don't change how the data is accessed and use the same logic to get the results as in Table 5-13, you will get the result set shown in Table 5-14.

Table 5-14. *Customers in Memphis using CustomerID*

CustomerID	First Name	Last Name	City	Postal Code	Country
401407	Karim	Khalil	Memphis	3364932	Egypt
401405	Marty`	Bethel	Memphis	38117	United States

Table 5-15 shows the expected results by changing the logic to look at the city name to find all cities equal to Memphis.

Table 5-15. *Customers with Memphis as City Name*

CustomerID	First Name	Last Name	City	Postal Code	Country
401407	Karim	Khalil	Memphis	3364932	Egypt
401405	Marty`	Bethel	Memphis	38117	United States
401408	Ruth	Johnson	Memphis	38110	United States

In that case, I would want to run a query where the city name was equal to Memphis. As you can see in this example, there are not only limitations with regard to data sets that affect performance but can also affect functionality.

One of the largest challenges in using data sets has to do with inserting data records. In most cases, when you insert a data record, you are inserting a single record at a time. This can cause it to become a habit to only deal with inserting one individual record at a time. When you are designing new table or moving data, you may have situations where you can think of an insert in terms of a data set. This will often happen when you are creating a query to insert data into another table.

While it does not seem like these situations will come up very often, I frequently use data sets when I populate temporary tables, table variables, and common table expressions.

Inserting data as a set uses the foundation of selecting data as data set. Once you select data as a set, you can insert data as a set. I have used inserting data into an object like a temporary table for a couple of different reasons. One of the more common situations when I insert data sets is when I join several different tables and implement criteria that make complicated calculations or functions. Looking at Table 5-16 and Table 5-17, you can see some examples of data inserted into dbo.Customer.

Table 5-16. *Marty` Added As a Record*

CustomerID	First Name	Last Name	City	Postal Code	Country
401405	Marty`	Bethel	Memphis	38117	United States

Table 5-17. *Ruth Added As a Record*

CustomerID	First Name	Last Name	City	Postal Code	Country
401408	Ruth	Johnson	Memphis	38110	United States

While all these entries can be inserted individually, it is also possible to insert multiple records at once. In this case, it may look something like Table 5-18.

Table 5-18. *Adding Customers As a Data Set*

CustomerID	First Name	Last Name	City	Postal Code	Country
401405	Marty`	Bethel	Memphis	38117	United States
401408	Ruth	Johnson	Memphis	38110	United States

Another scenario where I have used bulk inserts into temporary objects is when those records may require additional modifications by joining to other queries that include multiple table joins.

Using Data Sets

If you are changing how your application code works and inserting new tables or changing how the value should be populated, you may find yourself needing to perform bulk updates. While you can perform bulk updates by updating one record at a time with hard-coded values, let's see if there is a way to update all the records in the data set by using the same code logic. This can be where data sets really help you out.

You can write one query to find all the records that you need to update and systematically perform all those updates. In addition to the advantages in terms of performance and functionality, this type of process also ensures that your data is being handled consistently.

Overall, the process for updating data as a data set is very much like the methods discussed for selecting and inserting data. In Table 5-19, you can see information stored in the dbo.Customer table.

Table 5-19. *Customers and Address Information*

First Name	Last Name	Address	City	Postal Code	Country
Myra	Acharya	30 Magrath Road	Bengaluru	560025	India
Josè	Gomez	790 Calle Cinco de Mayo	Cancun	53778	Mexico
Stacy	Parks	123 Rua de Santa Catarina	Porto	1234-567	Portugal
Karim	Khalil	153 Road Mit Rahina Al Shabab	Memphis	3364932	Egypt

While this is how the customers are currently saved, you may decide that you want to change how address information is saved. You may want to change the country to use a country code abbreviation instead of the full county name. In this case, you can update the records one at a time as shown in Table 5-20, Table 5-21, Table 5-22, and Table 5-23.

Table 5-20. *Update Country for Myra*

First Name	Last Name	Address	City	Postal Code	Country
Myra	Acharya	30 Magrath Road	Bengaluru	560025	IND

Table 5-21. *Update Country for Josè*

First Name	Last Name	Address	City	Postal Code	Country
Josè	Gomez	790 Calle Cinco de Mayo	Cancun	53778	MEX

Table 5-22. *Update Country for Stacy*

First Name	Last Name	Address	City	Postal Code	Country
Stacy	Parks	123 Rua de Santa Catarina	Porto	1234-567	PRT

Table 5-23. *Update Country for Josè*

First Name	Last Name	Address	City	Postal Code	Country
Karim	Khalil	153 Road Mit Rahina Al Shabab	Memphis	3364932	EGY

To use T-SQL to perform these updates one at a time, execute the code in Listing 5-4 below.

Listing 5-4. Updating the Country Code Individually

```
UPDATE dbo.Customer
SET Country = 'IND'
WHERE CustomerID = 401408;

UPDATE dbo.Customer
SET Country = 'MEX'
WHERE CustomerID = 401406;

UPDATE dbo.Customer
SET Country = 'PRT'
WHERE CustomerID = 401409;

UPDATE dbo.Customer
SET Country = 'EGY'
WHERE CustomerID = 401407;
```

You can create a handful of queries that can update all records with the country of either India, Mexico, Egypt, or Portugal. Listing 5-5 shows these queries.

Listing 5-5. Updating the Country Code by Country

```
UPDATE dbo.Customer
SET Country = 'IND'
WHERE Country = 'India';

UPDATE dbo.Customer
SET Country = 'MEX'
WHERE CustomerID = 'Mexico';

UPDATE dbo.Customer
SET Country = 'PRT'
WHERE CustomerID = 'Portugal';

UPDATE dbo.Customer
SET Country = 'EGY'
WHERE CustomerID = 'Egypt';
```

This code will work, and it creates some sets. There are still more efficient ways to update this data, especially if you don't want to create one query per country. You can create a reference table with the full country name and three-digit country abbreviation. You can write a simple query and update all the records at the same time as shown in Table 5-24.

Table 5-24. *Customers as Data Sets by Country*

First Name	Last Name	Address	City	Postal Code	Country
Myra	Acharya	30 Magrath Road	Bengaluru	560025	IND
Josè	Gomez	790 Calle Cinco de Mayo	Cancun	53778	MEX
Stacy	Parks	123 Rua de Santa Catarina	Porto	1234-567	PRT
Karim	Khalil	153 Road Mit Rahina Al Shabab	Memphis	3364932	EGY

This table shows the entire data set you want to update using a single query. Before you perform the update, you should create the reference table. The SQL to create this table is in Listing 5-6.

Listing 5-6. Creating the Country Reference Table

```
CREATE TABLE dbo.Country
(
      CountryCode VARCHAR(3),
      Country     VARCHAR(75)
);

INSERT INTO dbo.Country (CountryCode, Country)
VALUES
('EGY','Egypt'),
('IND','India'),
('MEX','Mexico'),
('PRT','Portugal');
```

Now that the country table has been created, you can write a single query that will update all the country names, as long as they exist in the reference table, to the country codes you've specified. The SQL in Listing 5-7 updates all customer records to use a country code if the country name exists in dbo.Country.

Listing 5-7. Updating the Customer Country to Country Code

```
UPDATE cus
SET Country = cty.CountryCode,
    DateModified = GETDATE()
FROM dbo.Customer cus
    INNER JOIN dbo.Country cty
    ON cus.Country = cty.Country;
```

While these updates can be done in a with hard-coded values, there are times when it may be better to join the table you are updating to other related tables. This type of interaction between the tables may make it easier to perform your updates.

You can use the addresses for the customers to determine how to update the country codes. It helps to think about the logic you want to use. If you want to add the continent to the address, you first need to determine the country for each customer. The next step is to get a table for countries and their associated continent. Once you have both pieces of information, you can create a temporary table to map the country to a specific continent. While it may seem like this is a significant amount of work for just a few changes, the power comes when you need to maintain this data over time and may need to make updates like these on a more regular basis.

In general, I found anytime that I am dealing with data one record of the time, I often have to perform some type of manual interaction. I have found that manual interactions are the most likely to have issues or errors where data is inserted, updated, or deleted incorrectly. I much prefer writing code in data sets, so that I can be more assured that my logic is consistent.

Writing Code for Data Sets

Previously, I discussed how to start thinking about your data as data sets instead of individual records. I frequently use data sets when selecting, updating, or deleting data. While most application code inserts single records at a time, there are many common scenarios where inserting data as a data set may be helpful. In this next section, I will walk through various scenarios where you may want to think about your data as sets instead of individual records.

The most frequent use for data sets is when you want to view a portion of data. Ideally, these data sets are selected based upon specific criteria. This is not only good for performance but can also help make sure you are only looking at the specific data that you want. For most scenarios, it does not even make sense to retrieve and display one individual record at a time. Oftentimes, if you find yourself in a situation where you are selecting one record at a time, it is a good indication that you may want to see if that T-SQL code can be rewritten to use set-based logic.

There are more complex ways that queries can be selected. In some cases, you may find yourself wanting to combine or compare two different data sets. If you want to join two data sets together, you have the option of UNION or UNION ALL. There is only one small but important difference between them. Referring back to Table 5-2, I identified two different sets of data, one based on the city name and the other based on part of the address. In the following example, I will show one method you can use to find results that contain both of these data sets. When you UNION data, each record returned will be distinct between the SELECT statements that are joined together. Listing 5-8 shows a UNION between two queries.

Listing 5-8. Union of Two Queries

```
SELECT FirstName, LastName
FROM dbo.Customer
WHERE City = 'Memphis'
UNION
SELECT FirstName, LastName
FROM dbo.Customer
WHERE [Address] LIKE '%de%';
```

Table 5-25 shows the data currently stored for all customers. There are six customers.

Table 5-25. *All Customers*

First Name	Last Name	Address	City	Postal Code	Country
Myra	Acharya	30 Magrath Road	Bengaluru	560025	India
Josè	Gomez	790 Calle Cinco de Mayo	Cancun	53778	Mexico
Stacy	Parks	123 Rua de Santa Catarina	Porto	1234-567	Portugal
Karim	Khalil	153 Road Mit Rahina Al Shabab	Memphis	3364932	Egypt
Marty`	Bethel	750 Cherry Rd	Memphis	38117	United States
Ruth	Johnson	4711 Ponce de Leon	Memphis	38110	United States

Table 5-26 shows the values from the first query.

Table 5-26. *Customers in Memphis*

First Name	Last Name	Address	City	Postal Code	Country
Karim	Khalil	153 Road Mit Rahina Al Shabab	Memphis	3364932	Egypt
Marty`	Bethel	750 Cherry Rd	Memphis	38117	United States
Ruth	Johnson	4711 Ponce de Leon	Memphis	38110	United States

The data from the second query is shown in Table 5-27.

Table 5-27. *Customer with Address Containing de*

First Name	Last Name	Address	City	Postal Code	Country
Josè	Gomez	790 Calle Cinco de Mayo	Cancun	53778	Mexico
Stacy	Parks	123 Rua de Santa Catarina	Porto	1234-567	Portugal
Ruth	Johnson	4711 Ponce de Leon	Memphis	38110	United States

A union provides the result set shown in Table 5-28.

Table 5-28. *Union of Results from Tables 5-26 and 5-27*

First Name	Last Name	Address	City	Postal Code	Country
Josè	Gomez	790 Calle Cinco de Mayo	Cancun	53778	Mexico
Stacy	Parks	123 Rua de Santa Catarina	Porto	1234-567	Portugal
Karim	Khalil	153 Road Mit Rahina Al Shabab	Memphis	3364932	Egypt
Marty`	Bethel	750 Cherry Rd	Memphis	38117	United States
Ruth	Johnson	4711 Ponce de Leon	Memphis	38110	United States

However, for a UNION ALL, every record returned in both queries will be returned regardless of whether there are duplicate values in the multiple queries. If you run the same query but use a UNION ALL, the T-SQL code looks like Listing 5-9.

Listing 5-9. Union All of Two Queries

```
SELECT FirstName, LastName
FROM dbo.Customer
WHERE City = 'Memphis'
UNION ALL
SELECT FirstName, LastName
FROM dbo.Customer
WHERE [Address] LIKE '%de%';
```

You are returning all data, even if it is a duplicate. The result for a UNION ALL is shown in Table 5-29.

Table 5-29. *Union All of Results from Tables 5-26 and 5-27*

First Name	Last Name	Address	City	Postal Code	Country
Josè	Gomez	790 Calle Cinco de Mayo	Cancun	53778	Mexico
Stacy	Parks	123 Rua de Santa Catarina	Porto	1234-567	Portugal
Ruth	Johnson	4711 Ponce de Leon	Memphis	38110	United States
Karim	Khalil	153 Road Mit Rahina Al Shabab	Memphis	3364932	Egypt
Marty`	Bethel	750 Cherry Rd	Memphis	38117	United States
Ruth	Johnson	4711 Ponce de Leon	Memphis	38110	United States

As you can see, the UNION ALL returns two rows that are identical. There are times where each of these scenarios may be desirable.

There are times where the query logic is complex enough that I may not quickly understand all the T-SQL code or other times where I am troubleshooting very large data sets. If I write a simpler query that returns all the data that I want, I will often write an INTERSECT between those two queries to find where the records match. Using the same general query as earlier, I want to show you what the data returned will look like when using INTERSECT as compared to the other options. In Listing 5-10, you can see the query to find the intersection between the two queries.

Listing 5-10. Intersect of Two Queries

```
SELECT FirstName, LastName
FROM dbo.Customer
WHERE City = 'Memphis'
INTERSECT
SELECT FirstName, LastName
FROM dbo.Customer
WHERE [Address] LIKE '%de%';
```

You already know the results returned for each query individually from the preceding figures. The actual results for the preceding T-SQL code are shown in Table 5-30.

Table 5-30. *Intersect of Results from Tables 5-26 and 5-27*

First Name	Last Name	Address	City	Postal Code	Country
Ruth	Johnson	4711 Ponce de Leon	Memphis	38110	United States

In addition, if you are trying to find missing records or verify that there are matching records, you can use an EXCEPT between two queries. Listing 5-11 shows the T-SQL code if you exclude the results from one query from the results of the other query.

Listing 5-11. Except of Two Queries

```
SELECT FirstName, LastName
FROM dbo.Customer
WHERE City = 'Memphis'
EXCEPT
SELECT FirstName, LastName
FROM dbo.Customer
WHERE [Address] LIKE '%de%';
```

In this case, the first query returns all results where the city name includes the word Memphis. However, the except statement indicates that if a record is returned in both the first and second query, the record will be excluded from the result set. The results of this query are in Table 5-31.

Table 5-31. *Except of Results from Tables 5-26 and 5-27*

First Name	Last Name	Address	City	Postal Code	Country
Josè	Gomez	790 Calle Cinco de Mayo	Cancun	53778	Mexico
Stacy	Parks	123 Rua de Santa Catarina	Porto	1234-567	Portugal

Using an EXCEPT statement may not be the preferred method to exclude results from a data set, but it is the method that I am more accustomed to using. Therein lies the benefits and challenges of T-SQL code: for almost any scenario there is almost certainly more than one way to write T-SQL code. The reason you are writing the database code will determine the level of flexibility you have in writing your code. If you are executing a query for a single time, you may be able to use a less efficient method to access this data. However, if you are writing your code for an application, you want to balance writing T-SQL code that is readable and improves the speed at which the data is returned.

Listing 5-12 is an example of how to use data sets when inserting data.

Listing 5-12. Inserting Data as a Set

```
CREATE TABLE #TempProductArchive
(
        ProductID       INT             NOT NULL,
        ProductName     VARCHAR(25)     NOT NULL,
        ProductPrice    DECIMAL(6,2)    NOT NULL,
        IsActive        BIT             NOT NULL,
        DateCreated     DATETIME2(2)    NOT NULL,
        DateModified    DATETIME2(2)    NOT NULL,
        DateDisabled    DATETIME2(2)    NULL,
        DateInserted    DATETIME2(2)    NOT NULL
);

INSERT INTO #TempProductArchive
(
        ProductID,
        ProductName,
        ProductPrice,
        IsActive,
```

```
        DateCreated,
        DateModified,
        DateDisabled,
        DateInserted
)
SELECT
        ProductID,
        ProductName,
        ProductPrice,
        IsActive,
        DateCreated,
        DateModified,
        DateDisabled,
        GETDATE()
FROM dbo.Product
WHERE DateDisabled < '2022-08-01';
```

Listing 5-13 shows what the insert statements look like if they are inserted record by record.

Listing 5-13. Inserting Data Record by Record

```
CREATE TABLE #TempProductArchive
(
        ProductID        INT              NOT NULL,
        ProductName      VARCHAR(25)      NOT NULL,
        ProductPrice     DECIMAL(6,2)     NOT NULL,
        IsActive         BIT              NOT NULL,
        DateCreated      DATETIME2(2)     NOT NULL,
        DateModified     DATETIME2(2)     NOT NULL,
        DateDisabled     DATETIME2(2)     NULL,
        DateInserted     DATETIME2(2)     NOT NULL,
);
```

```
INSERT INTO #TempProductArchive
(
        ProductID,
        ProductName,
        ProductPrice,
        IsActive,
        DateCreated,
        DateModified,
        DateDisabled,
        DateInserted
)
VALUES
(
        14,
        'Water shoes - Large',
        25.00,
        0,
        '2018-01-01',
        '2022-07-29',
        '2022-07-29',
        GETDATE()
);
INSERT INTO #TempProductArchive
(
        ProductID,
        ProductName,
        ProductPrice,
        IsActive,
        DateCreated,
        DateModified,
        DateDisabled,
        DateInserted
)
```

```
VALUES
(
    15,
    'Water shoes - Medium',
    25.00,
    0,
    '2018-01-01',
    '2022-07-29',
    '2022-07-29',
    GETDATE()
);

INSERT INTO #TempProductArchive
(
    ProductID,
    ProductName,
    ProductPrice,
    IsActive,
    DateCreated,
    DateModified,
    DateDisabled,
    DateInserted
)
VALUES
(
    16,
    'Water shoes - Small',
    25.00,
    0,
    '2018-01-01',
    '2022-07-29',
    '2022-07-29',
    GETDATE()
);
```

```
INSERT INTO #TempProductArchive
(
        ProductID,
        ProductName,
        ProductPrice,
        IsActive,
        DateCreated,
        DateModified,
        DateDisabled,
        DateInserted
)
VALUES
(
        17,
        'Water shoes - Child',
        15.00,
        0,
        '2018-01-01',
        '2022-07-29',
        '2022-07-29',
        GETDATE()
);
```

As you can see, inserting data record by record takes up considerably more code and can be quite a bit more tedious.

One of my favorite uses for data sets is to update data. In many situations, I am not updating a specific record, but I am updating multiple records that share the same characteristics. If I want to make all the products inactive from the table, I have a couple different ways I can do this. For instance, I can write one update statement per record to set the IsActive value to zero as shown in Listing 5-14.

Listing 5-14. Updating Data Record by Record

```
UPDATE dbo.Product
SET IsActive = 0,
    DateModified = GETDATE(),
    DateDisabled = GETDATE()
WHERE ProductID = 1;

UPDATE dbo.Product
SET IsActive = 0,
    DateModified = GETDATE(),
    DateDisabled = GETDATE()
WHERE ProductID = 2;

UPDATE dbo.Product
SET IsActive = 0,
    DateModified = GETDATE(),
    DateDisabled = GETDATE()
WHERE ProductID = 3;
```

This requires three unique transactions. In addition, SQL Server must access the data page that each of these records is on three times. As shown in Listing 5-15, I can also write a query that allows me to update all three records at once.

Listing 5-15. Updating Data as a Range

```
UPDATE dbo.Product
SET IsActive = 0,
    DateModified = GETDATE(),
    DateDisabled = GETDATE()
WHERE ProductID BETWEEN 1 AND 3;
```

In fact, if all three of these records live on the same data page, I only need to access that page once. A much more likely scenario is a request to deactivate all products that contained the word water in the product name. This is type of pattern you want to find. If there is a pattern like this, you can write a query like the one in Listing 5-16.

Listing 5-16. Updating Data as a Data Set

```
UPDATE dbo.CustomerOrder
SET IsActive = 0,
     DateDisabled = GETDATE()
WHERE IsActive = 1
     AND CustomerID = 234;
```

This query accomplishes two goals. It lets you update more than one record in a given query. The WHERE clause has the `IsActive` and `CustomerID` columns allowing the query to use the index `IX_CustomerOrder_IsActive_CustomerID_OrderID_DateCreated`.

There is no limit to using data sets for updating multiple records. I have often needed to update hundreds or thousands of records. While I could write a query to identify each record individually and then manually pull those IDs to update all those records individually or in a set, there are easier ways to update those multiple records and minimize the risk of errors due to human intervention. The query in Listing 5-17 shows how you can update data while joining tables together.

Listing 5-17. Updating Data with Joins to Create a Data Set

```
UPDATE prd
SET DateModified = GETDATE(),
     IsActive = 0
FROM dbo.Product prd
     INNER JOIN dbo.ProductArchive pch
     ON prd.ProductID = pch.ProductID
WHERE pch.DateInserted >= CAST(GETDATE() AS DATE);
```

When using joins during your updates, I recommend that you confirm what data you are updating. This can be done by converting the update statement to a select statement as shown in Listing 5-18.

Listing 5-18. Verifying the Data Set with a Select Statement

```
SELECT
      ProductID,
      ProductName,
      ProductPrice,
      IsActive,
      DateCreated,
      DateModified,
      DateDisabled
FROM dbo.Product prd
      INNER JOIN dbo.ProductArchive pch
      ON prd.ProductID = pch.ProductID
WHERE pch.DateInserted >= CAST(GETDATE() AS DATE);
```

You can check the records and verify the record count. Before performing the update, I suggest wrapping the UPDATE statement in a BEGIN TRAN... ROLLBACK to verify the record count.

Just like working with updates, you can also use data sets when deleting data. I have found that deleting data using data sets can be significantly more efficient, but it can also be somewhat risky if the data is not verified prior to deleting.

One of the largest problems overall in writing T-SQL code is not taking advantage of data sets. Often, this is a result of being more comfortable writing procedural code or not having developed the ability to think in terms of data sets. My goal throughout this book is to guide you through various ways to write code that embraces using data sets.

CHAPTER 6

Hardware Usage

You have learned about the elements of set-based design when considering how to design your queries. There are other things to take into consideration when working with SQL Server. You are working with a system that involves more than its pieces. There are many aspects to SQL Server. There is the data that is stored. There is accessing the data. There is also the process of how to access the data. SQL Server is not only software; it's also how that software interacts with your computer's or server's hardware.

When it comes to working with hardware, there are several different parts that SQL Server uses. Some may seem straightforward and others may be surprising at first. SQL Server is known as a relational database management system (RDBMS). As part of a relational database management system, SQL Server's purpose is to allow for efficient storage and retrieval of data. This implies that one of the most important pieces of hardware is the memory on the system that is running SQL Server. When it comes to long-term storage of data, the hard drives become the most significant. I will refer to them as *storage* for the purposes of this chapter as storage is not only limited to hard disks. However, there are other elements that are less obvious such as the CPU.

In this chapter, you will go over at coding patterns and anti-patterns that can cause server resources to be allocated effectively or ineffectively. For the anti-patterns, you will explore alternate methods to achieve the same outcome without overtaxing these limited hardware resources.

Considering Memory with T-SQL Design

When you first start working with data in SQL Server, it may come as a surprise that memory is one of the most important factors. Much of this has to do with what memory is used for within SQL Server. SQL Server is designed to take advantage of memory. There is a process called *caching* that keeps information in memory. There are two types of caching that are important when it comes to SQL Server. The first has to do with

161

caching execution plans. This is where SQL Server saves directions on how it will execute a stored procedure or ad hoc query again in the future. The goal is to take advantage of the knowledge SQL Server already has calculated when it comes to the best way to execute a specific query. The second form of cache that has to do with query design can almost be more important. It has to do with how information is stored in memory. This is called the *buffer pool*.

In this section, I talk about data being stored in the buffer pool. What happens if we need data that is not in the buffer pool? This can be where things within SQL Server get a little more complex. SQL Server only interacts with data that is inside the buffer pool. Therefore, if data is needed that is not in the buffer pool, the first step is to determine what data has been used less frequently. Then you remove this data from the buffer pool. These first steps already give us a hint into the memory usage. If there is something that fills up the buffer pool unnecessarily, you now know that critical data may be cleared out of the buffer pool to make room for this new data.

The real key is to limit the amount of data SQL Server must process. When writing your queries, this can be handled based on your join logic; this can also be handled with your where clause criteria. You want to make sure that you are accessing as little data as possible. Accessing the smallest amounts of data needed allows you to minimize your use of memory when it comes to your T-SQL. Listing 6-1 provides a query where there are not included in the SELECT statement.

Listing 6-1. Query to Get Only Customer and Products

```
SELECT cus.FirstName,
       cus.LastName,
       prd.ProductName
FROM dbo.Customer cus
       INNER JOIN dbo.CustomerOrder ord
       ON cus.CustomerID = ord.CustomerID
       INNER JOIN dbo.OrderDetail dtl
       ON ord.CustomerOrderID = dtl.CustomerOrderID
       INNER JOIN dbo.Product prd
       ON dtl.ProductID = prd.ProductID
```

```
WHERE prd.ProductName LIKE 'Tel%'
    AND cus.LastName LIKE 'G%'
    AND ord.IsActive = 1;
```

While it did not affect the original performance of the query, now that the data table has more data, there is an obvious performance impact.

The speed and versatility of memory is an important part of SQL Server. Another factor is related to the cost of memory vs. the cost of storage. This difference in costs increases the importance of using memory effectively. There are many different types of things that are stored in memory. The process SQL Server uses to access the data needed to meet a query's criteria is saved in memory as an execution plan. The data retrieved for a query's results is also stored in memory. You can also have database objects that exist in memory such as table variables or temporary tables. You often hear the term *OLTP* (online transaction processing). What this really means is you want a system that can perform a high volume of write and update activity. These are the types of activities that happen frequently within our applications. When referring to write and update activity, using the database for recipes involves each time a recipe is accessed, each change that is made to a recipe, or every new ingredient that is added to the system.

While there is a significant amount of data being stored within the system, often someone only wants to deal with a very small subset of that data. The skill comes when trying to determine what data should remain readily available. This will increase the speed required to add new entries, to update existing entries, or to access pre-existing entries. This is where a better understanding of hardware can assist you.

We most commonly think of memory as the RAM available on our servers or in our machines. However, there are other types of memory available. Memory is the most common hardware that SQL Server uses to access data quickly.

While both the execution plan and the data can be saved in cache, certain calculations are performed by SQL Server to determine how much should be allocated in memory to either the plan cache or the buffer pool. In addition, complex calculations are used to determine how long to keep something in the plan cache or the buffer pool. The real goal is to make certain that stored procedures or queries that are not frequently accessed are dropped from the plan cache so they do not take up unnecessary space. In the same way, when it comes to the buffer pool, the goal is to only keep data in the buffer pool that is being actively used and to clear out data that is no longer needed by the application. In both scenarios, items are not cleared from cache until the cache is full and space is needed for new execution plans or data.

Another solution is the buffer pool extension. While the buffer pool only exists on RAM, the buffer pool extension allows you to extend the buffer pool to use RAM and solid state drives (SSDs). However, not all of the data pages in the buffer pool can reside on the SSD. Only data pages in the buffer pool that match the data pages written to storage can be on the SSD. This means all changes to the page have been written to disk. This process is called *hardening* when changes are written to disk. Before the changes are written to disk, the pages are called *dirty pages*. After the pages are written to disk, they are called *clean pages*. Considering that SSDs can be more cost-effective than purchasing additional RAM, this can help to reduce I/O bottlenecks that occur when SQL Server frequently moves pages out of the buffer pool due to lack of available memory for the data being accessed by business applications.

When it comes to the plan cache, there are some specific considerations that need to be remembered. By default, SQL Server is optimized to deal with stored procedures and prepared statements. This optimization for stored procedures is also a factor when using the plan cache. In a perfect world, your plan cache would have a significant amount of stored procedures in the cache and very few ad hoc queries. However, this is not always the case for every business. Your company may use ORM (object relational mapping) or other technologies like LINQ to write ad hoc queries inside application code. While they are convenient for the developers to write, they put an additional cost on SQL Server. Often times the ORM software writes T-SQL code that is functional but may not be better optimized for performance than a query written by a developer. In addition, ORM software also tends to create ad-hoc queries that can fill the plan cache. When the plan cache is full of ad hoc queries, it can create multiple versions of the same query in the cache, wasting the allocation of queries in the plan cache and causing other valuable plans to be dropped from the plan cache. This can be especially true if those queries are not converted into prepared statements.

If stored procedures are dropped out of the plan cache by the application, then when the stored procedure is called the next time, SQL Server will need to recalculate its execution plan. This will require an additional CPU cost to generate a new execution plan. There are various ways to handle situations where there are a high number of ad hoc queries in your plan cache. However, this is outside the scope of this book.

One of the other issues I have seen when interacting with SQL Server has to do with the buffer pool and the data that is being held in the buffer pool. I have heard more than once that when dealing with very large tables, you will always be stuck having to deal with accessing large quantities of data. When the table design, indexes, queries, or any combination of the preceding are not optimized, this exact scenario can happen. However, there are ways to prevent this.

The main aspect to consider when working with memory and with SQL Server is when you write queries, they must return the correct results and complete in an acceptable amount of time for your applications. However, depending on the overall table design or how the queries are written, these queries may be accessing far greater amounts of data than is necessary. This may not seem like a significant issue at first. It typically will not be an issue when the data tables are new and not full of data. The query in Listing 6-2 is used to return some data in the application.

Listing 6-2. Query to Get Customer Order Information

```
SELECT cus.FirstName,
       cus.LastName,
       cus.Country,
       ord.OrderNumber,
       prd.ProductName,
       dtl.QuantitySold,
       prd.ProductPrice
FROM dbo.Customer cus
       INNER JOIN dbo.CustomerOrder ord
       ON cus.CustomerID = ord.CustomerID
       INNER JOIN dbo.OrderDetail dtl
       ON ord.CustomerOrderID = dtl.CustomerOrderID
       INNER JOIN dbo.Product prd
       ON dtl.ProductID = prd.ProductID
WHERE prd.ProductName LIKE 'Tel%'
       AND cus.LastName LIKE 'G%'
       AND ord.IsActive = 1;
```

When the tables are new and there is not much data, you will see logical reads as shown in Table 6-1.

Table 6-1. *Logical Reads When Data Table Is Small*

Number of Customers	Number of Orders	Number of Recipe Order Details	Records Returned	Logical Reads
401,409	4	8	4	54

The logical reads of 54 refers to the number of data pages read in order to execute this query. As your tables grow and SQL Server must sift through more and more data, you may start seeing a significant performance impact related to this behavior. When this happens, the number of logical reads can increase significantly, as shown in Table 6-2.

Table 6-2. *Logical Reads When Data Table Is Larger*

Number of Customers	Number of Orders	Number of Order Details	Records Returned	Logical Reads
401,409	802,820	1,605,638	1,204,224	20,755

As you can see, a query that originally seemed to perform well may start experiencing performance issues as the application matures and acquires more data.

In these situations, the data that is frequently accessed by the application may be getting cleared out of the buffer pool. When a stored procedure must sift through a significant amount of data, you can usually see this when you look at the logical reads associated with the query. You may be working with a query that only returns five results; however, it must go through two million logical reads to return the results. This is a sign that you are potentially using more of your buffer pool than you intended.

This type of behavior can cause a significant amount of data in the buffer pool to be cleared out. There is value called *page life expectancy* in SQL Server that shows the amount of time on average that data pages stay in the buffer pool. I have come to use page life expectancy as an indicator that there are queries that may be reading far more data in SQL Server than are returned in the result set. This can cause those same queries to use more memory than the query needs. When I work with queries that work with the application, they normally do not involve more than ten records at a time. If the query is used for some form of report, it is still usually not more than a couple thousand records at a time. Even if I look at 200,000 records at a time, I still don't want to be handling tens of millions of logical reads in order to get those results. I can add some indexes to help minimize the number of logical reads for the query. Listing 6-3 shows the added indexes.

Listing 6-3. NonClustered Indexes to Reduce Logical Reads

```
CREATE NONCLUSTERED INDEX IX_Customer_CustomerNameName
    ON dbo.Customer(LastName ASC, FirstName ASC);

CREATE NONCLUSTERED INDEX IX_CustomerOrder_CustomerID_IsActive
    ON dbo.CustomerOrder(CustomerID ASC, IsActive ASC);

CREATE NONCLUSTERED INDEX IX_OrderDetail_CustomerOrderID_ProductID
    ON dbo.OrderDetail(CustomerOrderID ASC, ProductID ASC);
```

Even though I expect the query to involve less logical reads, I should verify this hypothesis by executing the query. In Table 6-3, you can see by the logical reads that the query has been modified.

Table 6-3. *Logical Reads with Only Necessary Columns*

Number of Recipes	Number of Ingredients	Number of Recipe Ingredients	Records Returned	Logical Reads
401,409	802,820	1,605,638	1,204,224	5,899

Comparing the results from Table 6-2 to Table 6-3, you can see that the logical reads have decreased. The index has organized the data within itself, making it easier and faster for SQL Server to find data pages. As a result, SQL Server needs to access less data pages in the buffer pool to perform this query. In this case, an index should help other applications using this instance of SQL Server perform better.

However, you want to be mindful of making an index for every unique scenario. Creating an index for every slow query can have a negative impact on performance due to increased disk activity to maintain each index. In addition, SQL Server does allocate memory when the index is created to allow the data to be sorted. Using indexes can be a powerful way to make sure you're only accessing the data you need. You also want to understand the data and associated T-SQL to effectively create indexes without overburdening SQL Server.

There are queries you can execute to determine how many logic reads stored procedures are using. As shown, logical reads are an indicator of if a query is affecting memory. If the stored procedure exists in the plan cache, you can find which ones have the higher logic reads. Listing 6-4 shows the query to find stored procedures and their logical reads.

Listing 6-4. Finding Logical Reads for Stored Procedures in the Plan Cache

```
USE OutdoorRecreation;
GO

SELECT db.[name] AS name_database,
       obj.[name] AS name_stored_procedure,
       sts.execution_count,
       sts.total_logical_reads
FROM sys.objects obj
       INNER JOIN sys.dm_exec_procedure_stats sts
       ON obj.[object_id] = sts.[object_id]
       LEFT JOIN sys.databases db
       ON sts.database_id = db.database_id;
```

This query gives you the stored procedures that are currently in your plan cache for the OutdoorRecreation database. The number of times this stored procedure has been executed is included as well as the sum of all logic reads for all executions. To analyze the average logic reads per stored procedure, you divide the total_local_reads by the execution_count. Once you identify the queries with the highest logical reads, you may want to review Chapter 8 to learn how optimize logical reads for these queries.

While memory can be considered the most powerful and beneficial hardware available to SQL Server, there are monetary costs associated with memory. Memory can make up for T-SQL that has not been optimized. However, there often comes a point where tables are significantly large and the queries are not fully optimized. At that time, it is tempting to get more memory to solve the performance issues. In many cases, this ends up being a short-term solution to a long-term problem. On top of that, the cost associated with purchasing additional memory is not always an option for the business. One way to prevent this or resolve this issue is to look at the stored procedures and prepared statements in your system and identify queries that can be improved by reducing the logical reads associated with those queries.

Considering Storage with T-SQL Design

I have covered how to interact with the data that you plan on accessing frequently; you also want to consider how the bulk of your data is stored. When it comes to working with storage, it is important to consider what activities cause you to have to access data on disk. These are the types of activities that you want to minimize or improve. In some cases, when I see a significant amount of disk I/O, it may be a sign that there is some other part of the T-SQL design that needs to be improved. This may be the symptom instead of the cause.

SQL Server uses indexes to organize data and allow data to be retrieved easily and quickly. When it comes to tables that are larger than a couple of data pages, SQL Server tries to use indexes to traverse the various data pages and find the data it needs quickly. However, there can be scenarios where the necessary indexes do not exist. This causes SQL Server to have to read more data pages, sometimes all the data in a table, to determine which rows are needed in order to satisfy the query requirements.

Once the data has been deemed to not be a priority, SQL Server can then go to disk and get the data that it needs. This data will be stored in the buffer pool until a future point when it is deemed that this data is no longer needed. In terms of the speed of hardware, there is already a slowness introduced with this process. If the data does not exist in the buffer pool, there is also the time associated with determining what records need to be dropped from the buffer pool. Dropping those records from the buffer pool and going to disk incurs additional cost in terms of time to retrieve that data from disk.

If this data is only needed for a job that runs once every four to six hours, most of this data may be deemed irrelevant for every other process. This introduces a high churn of data that is being removed from the buffer pool. New data can be grabbed from disk and saved to the buffer pool. Then this new data may be removed from the buffer pool and be replaced with even newer data that has been retrieved from disk.

In addition to this overhead associated with dealing with significant amount of data, there are other activities that interact with the disk or storage. When new data is being written to the system, that data will get stored in the transaction log. Data will continue to be added to the transaction log until the transaction log is cleared. Flushing the log can occur when the transaction is committed and the information is written to disk. In cases where a significant amount of data is being added, updated, or deleted from the system, this can cause a significant amount of disk activity to modify the table and an increase of disk storage due to log growth and data saved in the case of an insert.

Knowing how this data is stored and how SQL Server can easily find that data through indexes and other data pages stored on disk is important. When information is added to an index or an index needs to be updated, this information will also incur storage cost. This is not only in terms of the time needed to store the data but also the time involved to go to disk and make these additions or changes.

When working with T-SQL, you want to consider how your queries affect your data storage. This can mean multiple things, as you saw in the previous section. You want to make sure that you are not accessing, inserting, updating, or deleting more data than you need at a given time. That is not the only factor that comes into play when writing T-SQL. There are some things you can do to monitor storage use associated with your queries. Most of these things involve looking at the number of physical reads, read-ahead reads, or the I/O cost associated with the query.

If you have confirmed that you are dealing with the minimal amount of data that you want to interact with, there may be nothing you can do to decrease the storage cost associated with your T-SQL queries. In some cases, just like with memory, finding large storage usage may point to other issues. These issues can include things like how the data is saved on disk and how the indexes are designed.

In some cases, you may find that frequent index updates are causing a significant amount of storage cost. This may be due to indexes constantly needing to be reorganized based on how the index is designed. If a non-clustered index is created on the ShipDate in the dbo.CustomerOrder table, then the index will need to be updated if the ShipDate is populated or changed. When this happens, the ShipDate may need to be moved to a different page. If that page is full, SQL Server will create a new page. That new page may have some data transferred over from the old page, and the new data will be added to the page. There will also be a pointer created so that SQL Server knows where to look for the next data page in the logical sequence. When this happens, it is referred to as *index fragmentation*. This can cause queries using this index to perform poorly as the index information is not stored in sequence. While this is less of an issue with SSDs, index fragmentation can still cause the index to take up more space than it would if the index was properly organized.

There are also cases involving page splits where you may see a significant storage cost associated with this activity. The way that your tables are ordered or your indexes are designed may cause a significant number of page splits. For instance, I can create the table using the ShipDate as the clustered index in the dbo.CustomerOrder table. If the application does not populate a ship date for every order, or if a ship date gets changed, then the data record could get moved to a different page. In some cases, the record may be moved to a page that is already full. If so, then the page will split, allowing the record to be added to a data page with available space. You may see an increase in disk activity associated with maintaining some of these indexes.

For additional information regarding how storage costs work, it may help to understand how the SQL Server storage engine operates. When dealing with T-SQL queries, there is one aspect that depends on the storage engine more frequently. This has to do with accessing data that is currently not in the buffer pool.

The storage engine has several different functions. These functions involve accessing data that is not in the buffer pool. Another function of the storage engine has to do with how data is handled when locks are required. The third function of the storage engine involves commands that are not related to running T-SQL that is used by applications.

The storage engine can experience performance bottlenecks when accessing data. These bottlenecks can in turn cause performance issues when it comes to accessing the data that is stored. One example is when queries access rows in data tables or interact with indexes. At other times, the storage engine may need to handle page allocations related to retrieving data for the buffer pool. If your company has decided to implement row versioning, this could cause performance issues with storage. While this is outside the scope of this book, if you are using row versioning and you experience issues related to storage performance, you may want to do additional research to confirm that row versioning is not the cause.

When accessing data rows or indexes, SQL Server will utilize the storage engine. The data being accessed may be stored in the buffer pool. It is up to the storage engine to keep track of where these rows live in the B-Tree. A B-tree is a type of self-balancing binary search tree that creates a hierarchal structure for data to be stored. This specific design for this structure allows for many branches causing the children (called *nodes* or *levels*) to be flatter than with typical binary search tree. The B-Tree was specifically designed to work with large amounts of data such as databases. The same process happens with regard to managing, adding, updating, or removing entries from indexes within SQL Server. This is collectively called *row and index operations maintenance* within the storage engine.

When writing queries to access data, SQL Server keeps track of the data that needs to be accessed by a query using a metric called a *read*, which is pronounced like the verb ("to read"). If the data is available in memory, the act of accessing that data is referred to as a *logical read*. There are also times when accessing data may require SQL Server to go to disk or storage to access the data pages. Data pages are the smallest amount of data SQL Server will store, which is 8 kb of data. If the data is accessed from disk, the data is referred to as a *physical read*. If the pages are moved to the buffer pool, that action is referred to as a *read-ahead read*. In either case, SQL Server will need to go to disk to access the requested records. When you write a query and it needs to retrieve records that do not exist in the buffer pool, SQL Server will need to access those records on disk. This can be a very normal process for SQL Server. However, in cases where the query requires more records to be read than are needed for the query results, this can cause more activity on disk than is required. One way to monitor the amount of time spent retrieving data from disk is with latch waits. This is the amount of time SQL Server spends accessing data that does not exist in the buffer pool.

In addition to SQL Server managing data access within the storage engine, the storage engine also manages activities relating to locking data. This type of activity can be affected by the isolation level configured on the server, application, or transaction. The isolation level determines how SQL Server will handle locks and row versions between transactions. In many cases, the isolation level configuration is managed by a different team than the team that is responsible for writing the T-SQL code. The storage engine is also responsible for handling locks in SQL Server.

Additional factors that can contribute to performance issues related to storage have to do with other areas of query design that may interact with the hard drive, such as database actions that require a large amount of activity to get recorded to the transaction log. This can include inserting, updating, or deleting a large quantity of data. SQL Server is designed to record these changes to the transaction log promptly. However, these modifications need to be recorded to disk as well. Depending on fragmentation or other processes utilizing the hard disk, this may cause additional performance issues.

tempdb is another part of SQL Server that can have a noticeable amount of overhead related to storage. There may be queries that are causing quite a bit of activity to happen within tempdb . This can occur if you are creating large temporary tables as this information can be stored in tempdb . It is also possible that SQL Server has not estimated the execution plan correctly. This is often due to out-of-date statistics, which are histograms of the data within a table. If these statistics are incorrect, SQL Server may not allocate enough resources to execute the query. If tempdb is put on the same drive as the data or log files, there may be issues with disk latency. To avoid this, it is often recommended to move tempdb to a separate drive from the data and log files. In those causes, any storage overhead on tempdb should only affect other queries also relying on tempdb .

Writing T-SQL queries is fundamentally linked to how SQL Server interacts with data that has been stored. There are some aspects of this interaction that can be controlled, like making sure that you are accessing the least amount of data possible. There are other factors such as how SQL Server accesses data or manages locking that may be outside of your control. Either way, it is important to be aware of how all these pieces come together and may affect your query performance.

Considering CPU with T-SQL Design

SQL Server not only works with memory and storage; it also interacts with the server CPU. This is one of the final pieces to consider when designing your queries. When it comes to licensing SQL Server, the CPU can be a significant cost. Some of this may be due to not understanding the best CPU needed for SQL Server. SQL Server has licensing limits. If you don't fit into them, you may buy CPU cores that SQL will never see or use. Because most people pay by the core, it makes sense to make sure each individual core is as powerful as possible. You may even be able to save money on SQL licensing that overcomes the increased cost of the higher-powered CPU. There is the matter of performing calculations as part of your T-SQL code.

As discussed, there are times where a significant use of memory can cause I/O issues. The same can be said when there is a significant amount of I/O activity; this can lead to CPU issues. When considering memory in your overall T-SQL design, there are two types of caching. In that section, I mainly focused on buffer caching or the buffer pool. In this section, I'm coming full circle to discuss how caching of execution plans can contribute to CPU performance issues.

When you run a query, SQL Server has to review at all the tables involved, all the indexes on those tables, and all join predicates and where clauses to figure out which combination of tables, indexes, and join types will bring about acceptable and accurate performance of the query. The result of this calculation is called a *query execution plan*.

While sometimes queries are simple and that process is quick and easy, other times it can be much more resource intensive. Especially for this second scenario, we would very much like SQL Server to be able to reuse that plan rather than have to recalculate it should a similar query be executed.

For SQL Server to know how to execute a query, it must utilize the CPU. This is considered a CPU cost. The expectation is that this type of cost should not cause performance issues because frequently executed prepared statements and stored procedures will already have their plans saved in the cache and do not need to have these execution plans recreated with any amount of significant frequency.

This leads to what causes SQL Server to determine that a new execution plan is needed. This is directly related to understanding what SQL Server does when it creates an execution plan. Part of creating an execution plan is making a value that allows SQL Server to quickly find a previously created execution plan. This value is known as the plan hash. The goal is to create execution plans when necessary and reuse those execution plans as much as possible. All of these plans are stored in the plan cache. Only queries that look the same have the same plan hash and will use the same execution plan. While you may have several queries that look similar or return the same results, SQL Server may not give them the same plan hash. If SQL Server doesn't identify an existing plan in the plan cache, it will need to create a new execution plan. This dependency on the plan hash helps determine if a new execution plan needs to be created.

This causes us to become dependent on using parameters. These parameters can exist either in stored procedures or prepared statements. If the query that is being executed has the same plan hash as one in the plan cache, SQL Server will not recreate a new execution plan. This process of creating an execution plan is called *compilation*. This can be one of the many reasons that your queries may be using more CPU resources than you expected.

It is also possible that SQL Server may determine it needs to create a new execution plan for a query where there is already an associated plan hash in the execution cache. Introduced in SQL Server 2016, the statistics on database tables are updated based on a dynamic threshold for the number of rows in the table. If the statistics are updated, SQL Server may opt to generate a new execution plan. This can be the result of frequent data changes or it can be the result of parameter sniffing. For more information about parameter sniffing, see Chapter 2 and Chapter 8. Either way, it will lead to something that SQL Server identifies as a recompilation. Just like there is a cost associated with a query compilation, there is also a cost on the CPU associated with recompilations.

If there is a significant amount of I/O being handled for a query, this may spill over into causing CPU performance issues. While it is possible that a query may be accessing more data than is necessary, it may not be due to the overall T-SQL query design. It could be due to out-of-date statistics. While the concept of managing statistics is outside the scope of this book, you want to be aware of the effect that statistics have on your execution plans. Statistics are what give SQL Server a quick glance at the overall distribution of data within a specific data table or index. The concept is that proper statistics help SQL Server make a best guess as to how to create an execution plan. If these values are out of date or stale, SQL Server may decide on an execution plan that is would not be as efficient as it could be if SQL Server had up-to-date statistics. Due to the out-of-date statistics, there can be a significant difference between the estimated and actual number of reads. This can have a performance impact on the CPU. You can see that the statistics have been updated and the estimated and actual number of rows returned remains relatively consistent.

There is also the possibility that SQL Server is having to traverse more of the hard disk or storage than it originally anticipated. This can be due to situations involving fragmentation. In the case of higher-than-normal CPU activity, it could be due to index fragmentation. This means that SQL Server may have only estimated a certain amount of work required to retrieve data by assuming that the index was not fragmented. However, since the index is fragmented, SQL Server must do potentially more work than it anticipated to access the requested data.

Another common issue that can happen with your T-SQL query design involves data types. There are many different places in SQL Server where you will define data types. They can be defined in tables, temporary tables, parameters, stored procedure, variables, and even the data types that are specified through your application code. As discussed in Chapter 1, SQL Server can convert one data type to another in the background; this process is called *implicit conversion*. While SQL Server can handle implicit conversion and has a structured process to do so, forcing SQL Server to perform an implicit conversion can also have a CPU cost associated with that activity. The code in Listing 6-5 is an example of an implicit conversion.

Listing 6-5. Query with Implicit Conversion

```
DECLARE @IsActive NVARCHAR(1);
SET @IsActive = 1;
SELECT CustomerID,
       FirstName,
       LastName,
        [Address],
       City,
       PostalCode,
       IsActive,
       DateCreated,
       DateModified,
       DateDisabled
FROM dbo.Customer
WHERE IsActive = @IsActive;
```

The implicit conversion is created in Listing 6-4 because the data type for the variable @IsActive is set to an NVARCHAR. The data type for the field IsActive in the dbo.Customer table is a BIT. Therefore, SQL Server will have to perform an implicit conversion to compare these two values. In Figure 6-1, you can see the impact of an implicit conversion on an execution plan.

Clustered Index Scan (Clustered)

Scanning a clustered index, entirely or only a range.

Physical Operation	Clustered Index Scan
Logical Operation	Clustered Index Scan
Actual Execution Mode	Row
Estimated Execution Mode	Row
Storage	RowStore
Number of Rows Read	401409
Actual Number of Rows for All Executions	401407
Actual Number of Batches	0
Estimated I/O Cost	3.5009
Estimated Operator Cost	3.94261 (100%)
Estimated Subtree Cost	3.94261
Estimated CPU Cost	0.441707
Estimated Number of Executions	1
Number of Executions	1
Estimated Number of Rows for All Executions	401409
Estimated Number of Rows Per Execution	401409
Estimated Number of Rows to be Read	401409
Estimated Row Size	223 B
Actual Rebinds	0
Actual Rewinds	0
Ordered	False
Node ID	0

Predicate

[OutdoorRecreation].[dbo].[Customer].[IsActive]=CONVERT_IMPLICIT(bit, [@IsActive],0)

Object

[OutdoorRecreation].[dbo].[Customer].[PK_Customer]

Output List

[OutdoorRecreation].[dbo].[Customer].CustomerID, [OutdoorRecreation].
[dbo].[Customer].FirstName, [OutdoorRecreation].[dbo].
[Customer].LastName, [OutdoorRecreation].[dbo].[Customer].Address,
[OutdoorRecreation].[dbo].[Customer].City, [OutdoorRecreation].[dbo].
[Customer].PostalCode, [OutdoorRecreation].[dbo].[Customer].IsActive,
[OutdoorRecreation].[dbo].[Customer].DateCreated, [OutdoorRecreation].
[dbo].[Customer].DateModified, [OutdoorRecreation].[dbo].
[Customer].DateDisabled

Figure 6-1. *Index scan in an execution plan showing implicit conversion*

An implicit conversion can have a significant and negative overall performance impact on the query. Make sure you avoid implicit conversions when writing your T-SQL queries.

Some companies may also utilize data compression. One of the benefits of data compression is the ability to keep more data in memory because the amount of data that is taken up by the compressed data is smaller than the uncompressed data. There are some drawbacks to using data compression in SQL Server. One of these drawbacks has to do with the CPU cost incurred as part of the overall data compression process. This does not mean that you should not use data compression. I only mention this so that you can be aware of any potential issues should they arise.

That brings us to the overall concept of parallelism. The most common way that you can easily see CPU usage is when it comes to parallelism with your queries. Parallelism is a concept where instead of a query executing on a single thread, a query can execute on more than one thread. If your CPU has four cores, and each core has two threads, you have eight total threads available. A single-threaded query that only runs on one thread runs on one-half of one core, or an eighth of your overall CPU. However, if the query is running in parallelism, it may be able to run on more than one thread. For instance, if it runs on four threads, this query can use two threads per core. While the time CPU may use may increase, the query should take less time than if the query were to execute single-threaded.

There are many factors involved for SQL Server to determine whether parallelism should be used when executing a query. Much of this involves how SQL Server is configured. While configuring SQL Server is outside the scope of this book, I want you to be aware of how it works when SQL Server creates an execution plan. SQL Server gives the execution plan and overall cost. SQL Server also has a configured value that indicates a minimum cost that should exist before it decides to implement parallelism. This cost is referred to as the *cost threshold for parallelism*. If the execution plan has a cost that is greater than the cost threshold of parallelism, SQL Server can determine if there is a better execution plan that runs in parallel.

If SQL Server does decide to create an execution plan using parallelism, it will also need to determine the maximum number of threads that are allowed for a given execution plan. There is also a configured value that indicates the maximum number of threads that can be used for parallelism. This value is referred to as the *maximum degree of parallelism*. MAXDOP is the abbreviation for maximum degrees of parallelism.

This does not mean that SQL Server must use the same number of threads as specified in the maximum degrees of parallelism. It only means that this is the maximum amount of threads that can be allowed for an execution plan to run in parallelism.

SQL Server will determine the number of threads to use for an execution plan that will run in parallelism at the time of execution. This will be done based on the number of threads that are not utilized at the beginning of the execution of the query. One factor that can affect CPU performance when it comes to parallelism can occur if more threads come into use while the query is running in parallelism. The general idea for parallelism is that more CPU process will be used overall but for a much shorter duration. If there are more queries that come into the queue and need to be run, requiring more threads to be active, it may cause the CPU to operate at a higher-than-normal level for a longer period.

One of the main reasons you want to make sure your T-SQL is not negatively impacting CPU usage has to do with the monetary cost related to CPUs. Since SQL Server 2012, the licensing for SQL Server has been related to the number of cores using SQL Server. In later versions of SQL Server, this has been modified to be the number of cores available to the server even if they are not explicitly allocated to SQL Server. One of the common solutions when companies start experiencing performance issues is to add more hardware. While this may solve performance issues in the short term, it can also be a very expensive solution depending on what hardware needs to be added. As the license per core can be over $1000, it is ideal to minimize the need for additional CPUs by reducing performance bottlenecks related to CPU usage.

There are many aspects to consider when designing your T-SQL queries. Some of these factors include being aware of the impact T-SQL can have on the physical hardware that runs SQL Server. When writing your T-SQL queries, you want to be mindful of the amount of data being accessed in order to make the best use of the memory available. Another added benefit to minimizing the data is decreasing storage resources. Making sure that your statistics are up to date and that proper indexes are in place will benefit the CPU usage. Being aware of how your queries are affecting your hardware will not only minimize the need for additional hardware but also allow your current hardware to better support your applications.

CHAPTER 7

Execution Plans

As you become more familiar with writing T-SQL, you will progress from focusing on syntax to accuracy to performance. In this chapter, you will learn how to view and understand SQL Server execution plans. This chapter will include demonstrations of how your existing and new indexes can affect your execution plans. You will learn how SQL Server joins data together in the execution plan. By the end of this chapter, you will know how to use execution plans to improve the performance of your T-SQL.

Introducing Execution Plans

In order to generate results for a T-SQL query, SQL Server needs to decide how to run the query. It needs to decide things like what index to use and what join type to use when running the query. The result of these decisions is the execution plan. Learning how to read and understand an execution plan will help you to better form your queries for performance.

Execution plans are stored in XML in the database. SSMS provides a visual representation tool for these plans and this is where you'll be spending the bulk of your time in this chapter. There are different kinds of plans like estimated and actual, which you'll cover during this section. An example of a graphical execution plan can be found in Figure 7-1.

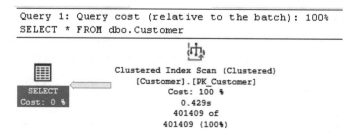

Figure 7-1. Graphical execution plan

Figure 7-1 has several elements that we will discuss in this chapter. The icons are called *operators*. The arrows are used to show the order of operations. There are different kinds of plans like estimated and actual. Most importantly, while this image doesn't make a ton of sense right now, by the end of the chapter you'll be able to turn back a few pages and read this entire image!

Reading Execution Plans

This section will cover the basics of reading execution plans. This includes discussing the difference between estimated execution plans, actual executions plans, and live query statistics. I will go over the graphical execution plan showing the operators and how to read them. In addition, this section will cover how to view operator details and properties in the execution plan. Finally, this section will go over the details of an execution plan including multiple steps, arrows, warnings, operators, estimated, and actual values.

Your goal when writing T-SQL is to make sure that you get accurate results. In some cases, the queries you write may be simple and straightforward. You may find yourself needing to performance tune queries related to reporting or to write new queries for reporting. If you need to write queries to provide reports on transactional data, you may need to incorporate more joins and more logic than you would need if you were to write queries for an application. While this is not ideal, this is a very common scenario for many companies.

Many companies have begun to realize the importance of the data in their systems, or they want additional monitoring to ensure the applications are working as intended. In either case, it is highly likely that you will come across a query in your environment that is negatively affecting your applications. At that time, you will want to know what you can do to resolve the issue. In this section, you will learn why execution plans are important and when you need to use them. You will learn how to read execution plans including commonly used symbols. You will also learn about properties and warnings in execution plans.

My first mentor once told me that in order to write good T-SQL, I needed to understand how SQL Server worked. It was some of the wisest advice I have received, and I am still working to understand SQL Server internals better each day. Using this advice, one way that you can have a better understanding of SQL Server is to understand how SQL Server executes any queries that you have written. Some of the internals related to executing a query are in Chapter 1. In this chapter, I will show you the instructions that SQL Server has determined should be used to execute your T-SQL code. These instructions can be found in the execution plan for as long as the plan is still in the plan cache. If you have Query Store enabled for your database, you can check Chapter 9 to determine how to access the query plans saved in Query Store.

Once you have decided that you want to start investigating an execution plan for some T-SQL code, you should confirm that you have access in SQL Server to view execution plans. When reviewing execution plans, you can view estimated, actual, or live query statistics. The estimated execution plan will show the best guess as to how the plan *would* be executed. However, since the query has not been executed, the estimated execution plan may not represent what will happen if the query is run. The actual execution plan executes the query, returns the results, and shows what steps SQL Server took to execute the query. The live query statistics is the same as the actual execution plan, except it also shows how the query moves through the execution plan in real time. This can be helpful when trying to debug poorly performing queries. However, if your query is very fast, it may end up looking exactly like the actual execution plan.

If you are getting the actual execution plan when the T-SQL code is executed, you need to make sure you have permissions to execute that code and that you have SHOWPLAN access for the databases that exist in the T-SQL code. Managing the user permissions for execution plans is outside the scope of this book. However, if you want to verify user access to execution plans, you can execute the query in Listing 7-1.

Listing 7-1. Viewing SHOWPLAN Permissions

```
USE OutdoorRecreation;
GO

SELECT prn.[name] AS UserName, prm.state_desc, prm.[permission_name]
FROM sys.database_permissions prm
     INNER JOIN sys.database_principals prn
     ON prm.grantee_principal_id = prn.principal_id
WHERE prm.[permission_name] = 'SHOWPLAN';
```

This query shows all users who have been granted or denied SHOWPLAN permissions.

You can also get the execution plan from the plan cache, but you need to be able to query the dynamic management view `sys.dm_exec_cached_plans`.

When you troubleshoot performance issues, you can usually retrieve the execution plan from `sys.dm_exec_cached_plans`. This is the method you want to use if you want the execution plan that was used previously. You may not be able to find the query or stored procedure here if the execution plan has been cleared from the plan cache.

In addition, depending on when the performance issue happened, the plan that was in cache may have been cleared. This may mean you can find an execution plan, but it may not be the same one used previously. In this case, see Chapter 9 for information about troubleshooting performance issues using Query Store.

If you find that the execution plan has been changed since the performance issue, you can try to find the current execution plan. There are two options available when using this method. One option is to get a hypothetical idea of what SQL Server would use as an execution plan. This can be done without running the actual T-SQL code on the server. This is called the *estimated execution plan*. The largest challenge when using this method is since SQL Server has estimated an execution, there is no guarantee that this will be the actual execution plan that SQL Server will use when the query is run. I have used estimated execution plans only a handful of times, and that was when I was hesitant to run the T-SQL code for fear of causing an outage in Production or wanted a quick guess at how the query would run without waiting for the query to finish.

If you can't find the execution plan in the plan cache, you may want to look at the execution plan that is generated if the T-SQL runs now. When using SQL Server Management Studio (SSMS) or Azure Data Studio (ADS), requesting an actual execution plan when you execute your T-SQL code will cause the execution plan to be available after the query execution completes. There is also the ability to see the flow of data through the execution plan as the query is executing. Instead of viewing the actual execution plan, you ask SQL Server to show you the live query statistics. While this option may be helpful in slower queries where there is one specific pain point, I often find that many queries complete too quickly to use this method to effectively diagnose many issues I am trying to resolve.

How and when you retrieve an execution plan are factors that you can control when it comes to working with execution plans. There is also the option of what the execution plan should look like once you retrieve it. My usual method is to look at the graphical output for the execution plan. The process of reviewing execution plans for T-SQL code is the same regardless of whether you are writing new T-SQL or performance tuning existing code.

The graphical execution gives a high-level view of how a query is executed. This makes the execution plan easier to read at a glance, but it also means that there is additional information that needs to be accessed when getting into the details in the execution plan. Included in an execution plan are operators, which are descriptors of how SQL Server will execute a query. Each of these operators has a distinct name, which is available in the execution plan. When using a graphical execution plan, these operators have a distinct icon. Figure 7-2 shows some details that can be viewed when you mouse over the Clustered Index Scan operator in the execution plan.

Clustered Index Scan (Clustered)

Scanning a clustered index, entirely or only a range.

Physical Operation	Clustered Index Scan
Logical Operation	Clustered Index Scan
Actual Execution Mode	Row
Estimated Execution Mode	Row
Storage	RowStore
Number of Rows Read	401409
Actual Number of Rows for All Executions	401409
Actual Number of Batches	0
Estimated I/O Cost	3.5009
Estimated Operator Cost	3.94261 (100%)
Estimated CPU Cost	0.441707
Estimated Subtree Cost	3.94261
Number of Executions	1
Estimated Number of Executions	1
Estimated Number of Rows for All Executions	401409
Estimated Number of Rows Per Execution	401409
Estimated Number of Rows to be Read	401409
Estimated Row Size	262 B
Actual Rebinds	0
Actual Rewinds	0
Ordered	False
Node ID	0

Object

[OutdoorRecreation].[dbo].[Customer].[PK_Customer]

Output List

[OutdoorRecreation].[dbo].[Customer].CustomerID, [OutdoorRecreation].
[dbo].[Customer].FirstName, [OutdoorRecreation].[dbo].
[Customer].LastName, [OutdoorRecreation].[dbo].[Customer].Address,
[OutdoorRecreation].[dbo].[Customer].City, [OutdoorRecreation].[dbo].
[Customer].PostalCode, [OutdoorRecreation].[dbo].[Customer].Country,
[OutdoorRecreation].[dbo].[Customer].IsActive, [OutdoorRecreation].
[dbo].[Customer].DateCreated, [OutdoorRecreation].[dbo].
[Customer].DateModified, [OutdoorRecreation].[...

Figure 7-2. *Operator details from a graphical execution plan*

185

In addition to the properties in this tool tip, in newer versions of SQL Server Management Studio, you have access to extended properties as shown in Figure 7-3.

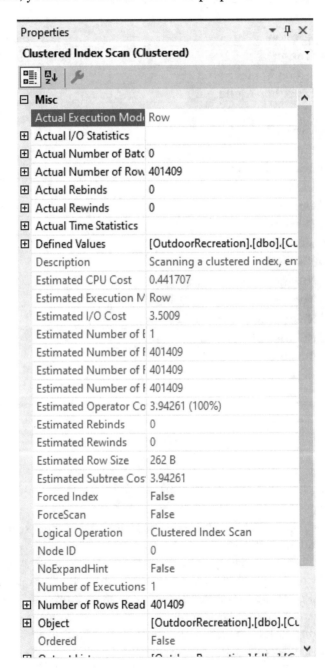

Figure 7-3. *Additional properties for execution plans*

There is an option to interact with the execution plan in an XML format. You can see an example of this in Listing 7-2.

Listing 7-2. XML Execution Plan

```
<?xml version="1.0" encoding="utf-16"?>
<ShowPlanXML xmlns:xsi="http://www.w3.org/2001/XMLSchema-instance"
xmlns:xsd="http://www.w3.org/2001/XMLSchema" Version="1.564"
Build="16.0.700.4" xmlns="http://schemas.microsoft.com/sqlserver/2004/07/
showplan">
  <BatchSequence>
    <Batch>
      <Statements>
        <StmtSimple StatementCompId="1" StatementEstRows="401409"
        StatementId="1" StatementOptmLevel="TRIVIAL"
        CardinalityEstimationModelVersion="160"
        StatementSubTreeCost="3.94261" StatementText="SELECT * FROM dbo.
        Customer" StatementType="SELECT" QueryHash="0xFD0D147390ABD5EC"
        QueryPlanHash="0x31540AC4CB8F96C9" RetrievedFromCache="true"
        SecurityPolicyApplied="false">
          <StatementSetOptions ANSI_NULLS="true" ANSI_PADDING="true" ANSI_
          WARNINGS="true" ARITHABORT="true" CONCAT_NULL_YIELDS_NULL="true"
          NUMERIC_ROUNDABORT="false" QUOTED_IDENTIFIER="true" />
          <QueryPlan DegreeOfParallelism="1" CachedPlanSize="24"
          CompileTime="0" CompileCPU="0" CompileMemory="104">
            <MemoryGrantInfo SerialRequiredMemory="0"
            SerialDesiredMemory="0" GrantedMemory="0" MaxUsedMemory="0" />
            <OptimizerHardwareDependentProperties
            EstimatedAvailableMemoryGrant="138117"
            EstimatedPagesCached="103588"
            EstimatedAvailableDegreeOfParallelism="6"
            MaxCompileMemory="1839456" />
            <WaitStats>
              <Wait WaitType="ASYNC_NETWORK_IO" WaitTimeMs="2822"
              WaitCount="8482" />
```

```
      <Wait WaitType="PAGEIOLATCH_SH" WaitTimeMs="220"
      WaitCount="11" />
      <Wait WaitType="MEMORY_ALLOCATION_EXT" WaitTimeMs="7"
      WaitCount="4763" />
    </WaitStats>
    <QueryTimeStats CpuTime="315" ElapsedTime="3339" />
    <RelOp AvgRowSize="262" EstimateCPU="0.441707"
    EstimateIO="3.5009" EstimateRebinds="0" EstimateRewinds="0"
    EstimatedExecutionMode="Row" EstimateRows="401409"
    EstimatedRowsRead="401409" LogicalOp="Clustered Index Scan"
    NodeId="0" Parallel="false" PhysicalOp="Clustered Index Scan"
    EstimatedTotalSubtreeCost="3.94261" TableCardinality="401409">
      <OutputList>
        <ColumnReference Database="[OutdoorRecreation]"
        Schema="[dbo]" Table="[Customer]" Column="CustomerID" />
        <ColumnReference Database="[OutdoorRecreation]"
        Schema="[dbo]" Table="[Customer]" Column="FirstName" />
        <ColumnReference Database="[OutdoorRecreation]"
        Schema="[dbo]" Table="[Customer]" Column="LastName" />
        <ColumnReference Database="[OutdoorRecreation]"
        Schema="[dbo]" Table="[Customer]" Column="Address" />
        <ColumnReference Database="[OutdoorRecreation]"
        Schema="[dbo]" Table="[Customer]" Column="City" />
        <ColumnReference Database="[OutdoorRecreation]"
        Schema="[dbo]" Table="[Customer]" Column="PostalCode" />
        <ColumnReference Database="[OutdoorRecreation]"
        Schema="[dbo]" Table="[Customer]" Column="Country" />
        <ColumnReference Database="[OutdoorRecreation]"
        Schema="[dbo]" Table="[Customer]" Column="IsActive" />
        <ColumnReference Database="[OutdoorRecreation]"
        Schema="[dbo]" Table="[Customer]" Column="DateCreated" />
        <ColumnReference Database="[OutdoorRecreation]"
        Schema="[dbo]" Table="[Customer]" Column="DateModified" />
        <ColumnReference Database="[OutdoorRecreation]"
        Schema="[dbo]" Table="[Customer]" Column="DateDisabled" />
```

```
</OutputList>
<RunTimeInformation>
  <RunTimeCountersPerThread Thread="0" ActualRows="401409"
  ActualRowsRead="401409" Batches="0" ActualEndOfScans="1"
  ActualExecutions="1" ActualExecutionMode="Row"
  ActualElapsedms="429" ActualCPUms="210" ActualScans="1"
  ActualLogicalReads="4742" ActualPhysicalReads="3"
  ActualReadAheads="4731" ActualLobLogicalReads="0"
  ActualLobPhysicalReads="0" ActualLobReadAheads="0" />
</RunTimeInformation>
<IndexScan Ordered="false" ForcedIndex="false"
ForceScan="false" NoExpandHint="false" Storage="RowStore">
  <DefinedValues>
    <DefinedValue>
      <ColumnReference Database="[OutdoorRecreation]"
      Schema="[dbo]" Table="[Customer]"
      Column="CustomerID" />
    </DefinedValue>
    <DefinedValue>
      <ColumnReference Database="[OutdoorRecreation]"
      Schema="[dbo]" Table="[Customer]" Column="FirstName" />
    </DefinedValue>
    <DefinedValue>
      <ColumnReference Database="[OutdoorRecreation]"
      Schema="[dbo]" Table="[Customer]" Column="LastName" />
    </DefinedValue>
    <DefinedValue>
      <ColumnReference Database="[OutdoorRecreation]"
      Schema="[dbo]" Table="[Customer]" Column="Address" />
    </DefinedValue>
    <DefinedValue>
      <ColumnReference Database="[OutdoorRecreation]"
      Schema="[dbo]" Table="[Customer]" Column="City" />
    </DefinedValue>
```

```
            <DefinedValue>
              <ColumnReference Database="[OutdoorRecreation]"
              Schema="[dbo]" Table="[Customer]"
              Column="PostalCode" />
            </DefinedValue>
            <DefinedValue>
              <ColumnReference Database="[OutdoorRecreation]"
              Schema="[dbo]" Table="[Customer]" Column="Country" />
            </DefinedValue>
            <DefinedValue>
              <ColumnReference Database="[OutdoorRecreation]"
              Schema="[dbo]" Table="[Customer]" Column="IsActive" />
            </DefinedValue>
            <DefinedValue>
              <ColumnReference Database="[OutdoorRecreation]"
              Schema="[dbo]" Table="[Customer]"
              Column="DateCreated" />
            </DefinedValue>
            <DefinedValue>
              <ColumnReference Database="[OutdoorRecreation]"
              Schema="[dbo]" Table="[Customer]"
              Column="DateModified" />
            </DefinedValue>
            <DefinedValue>
              <ColumnReference Database="[OutdoorRecreation]"
              Schema="[dbo]" Table="[Customer]"
              Column="DateDisabled" />
            </DefinedValue>
          </DefinedValues>
          <Object Database="[OutdoorRecreation]" Schema="[dbo]"
          Table="[Customer]" Index="[PK_Customer]"
          IndexKind="Clustered" Storage="RowStore" />
        </IndexScan>
      </RelOp>
    </QueryPlan>
```

```
        </StmtSimple>
      </Statements>
    </Batch>
  </BatchSequence>
</ShowPlanXML>
```

While this method may be more difficult to read, it does contain all information related to the execution plan. The query that generated this table was a SELECT statement on one table. Having the execution plan in XML gives quite a bit of code that needs to be reviewed.

When you want to access an execution plan in SSMS, you use the GUI (graphical user interface) to choose which one. Figure 7-4 shows the icons for the different ways to access execution plans.

Figure 7-4. *Execution plan icons in SSMS*

The first icon generates an estimated execution plan of the T-SQL code selected. The fourth icon allows you to generate an actual execution plan from the T-SQL code executed. The fifth icon allows you to view active operators as the SQL Engine processes the data through the actual execution plan. You can select any of these icons to use execution plans in SQL Server Management Studio.

You can use Azure Data Studio to view execution plans also. In ADS, you can select either the actual or estimated execution plan in the GUI as shown in Figure 7-5.

⊹ Estimated Plan ⁝⁝⁙ Enable Actual Plan

Figure 7-5. *Execution plan icons in ADS*

You can toggle either of these options on the top bar of the query window in ADS. The first option shows an estimated execution plan for the code selected. The second option provides an actual execution plan when you execute T-SQL code.

There is also an option to use T-SQL to get execution plan information instead of executing a query. This T-SQL code will provide an output without pictures. If you want to get the information about how SQL Server will execute a query as well as estimates, you should use the T-SQL in Listing 7-3.

Listing 7-3. Showing an Execution Plan and Estimates in Text

```
SET SHOWPLAN_ALL <ON/OFF>;
```

If you find this is too much information, you can instead execute T-SQL to only retrieve how SQL Server would execute a query. The <ON/OFF> indicates that you can enable and disable this functionality. Listing 7-4 has the T-SQL to only see how SQL Server would execute a query.

Listing 7-4. Showing an Execution Plan in Text

```
SET SHOWPLAN_TEXT <ON/OFF>;
```

You may find that you prefer the information about how SQL Server would execute a query in XML instead of text. If so, you can run the query in Listing 7-5 to see the execution plan in well-formed SQL.

Listing 7-5. Showing the Execution Plan in XML

```
SET SHOWPLAN_XML <ON/OFF>;
```

Choosing any of the above options allows you to start interacting with execution plans for your queries. When using any of these T-SQL methods to enable an execution plan, remember to turn the functionality off once you are finished reviewing the execution plans.

Once you have set up SQL Server Management Studio to give you an execution plan, you want to identify items of significance in the execution plan. You need to know how to interpret the flow in the execution plan to better understand how SQL Server will execute the query. There are also some general shapes you need to be familiar with as they may help increase the speed to find potential issues. In the execution plan you may find additional text that quickly shows issues that have been determined to be negatively affecting the execution of your query, including causing the speed of results to be returned slowly. Having a better understanding of all these elements will help you figure out the pain points for your queries so that you can determine where to focus your efforts.

Once you have an execution plan, you can get a better idea of exactly how SQL Server will execute that query. When we read English, we are accustomed to reading from left to right and from top to bottom. To compare this to execution plans, the uppermost left corner represents the result of the query. If we compare this to reading a book, as you move from left to right, you are drilling down into steps that SQL Server took to get the result set. The same is true when moving from top to bottom. Looking at the example in Figure 7-6, you can see an execution plan with multiple steps.

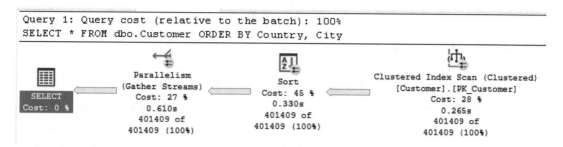

Figure 7-6. *Execution plan with multiple steps*

If you read from left to right, you can see the representation for the results returned with the SELECT. When you move to the right, you can see that SQL Server used parallelism immediately before getting the result set. This means that if you move to the right-most object, this is the first action SQL Server took when executing the query. In this case, the first step SQL Server performed when executing this query was a Clustered Index Scan. This is important to know because you may hear references to reading execution plans right to left. In these cases, the person is referring to reading the execution plan in the same way SQL Server executes the query.

When I first started working with execution plans, I was quickly overwhelmed with the amount of information available in them. I wanted to understand everything from the beginning. However, there is so much information in an execution plan that it is best to start with some basics. Through my years of troubleshooting, I learned to start my analysis by finding differences. With the execution plans, it did not take long to identify the issues right away. The first thing I check when analyzing an execution plan is the percentage associated with each operator. Going back to Figure 7-6, the operator with the highest percentage is the Sort operator with 45%. This percentage represents how long SQL Server expects to spend on each step of the query execution relative to the other steps. One of the quick wins can be to identify the operator or operators with the largest percentage and determine if there are ways to rewrite the query or add indexes that will improve performance. In the case of the example from Figure 7-6, removing the ORDER BY can improve the performance of the query and would be a good choice if we do not need to order the data.

I also try to identify any places where the arrows between two operators are not the same size relative to one another. There are two different arrows side by side in Figure 7-7 for comparison.

Figure 7-7. *Arrows from execution plans*

I learned that the difference in the thickness of the lines indicated the relative amount of records SQL Server was accessing for each step. While there are some queries that are going to return more records than others and therefore have thicker lines, you will find execution plans where one step has a very thick line and the next step will have a thin line. This usually indicates that the step with the thicker line could be written more efficiently to only get the data needed by the query. Looking at the thickness of the lines is one of the things you can check when you look at execution plans.

There are times when you want your data ordered in a specific way. For instance, you may want to show a list of customers alphabetically or by creation date. The customers can either be sorted within the application code or within SQL Server. If you choose to order the data within SQL Server, you may see a sort operator in your execution plan. You can see an example of what the sort operator looks like in Figure 7-8.

Sort

Figure 7-8. *Sort operator*

You may see sort operators in your execution plans. While there are occasions where the sort operator is necessary, you may want to review your T-SQL code for instances where the sort operator may not be needed. For instance, sort operations can be needed when returning data in query that is ordered in a particular manner. However, there are other occasions when the sort operator is present even if the results are not ordered. For instance, this can happen when comparing two tables and at least one of them is not sorted. These sorts are required for merge joins and may negatively impact the performance of a query. This chapter will discuss merge joins in the next section. In these cases, see if there is an index that can be used for the join that already has the data sorted. Even more significant performance gains can be made when there is a warning related to the sort operator.

One of the most helpful features of execution plans is when they return a warning. Ideally, you want to write T-SQL that performs well. This also means the T-SQL should not return execution plans with warnings. There will be times when you get a warning as part of your execution plan. The warning will look like Figure 7-9.

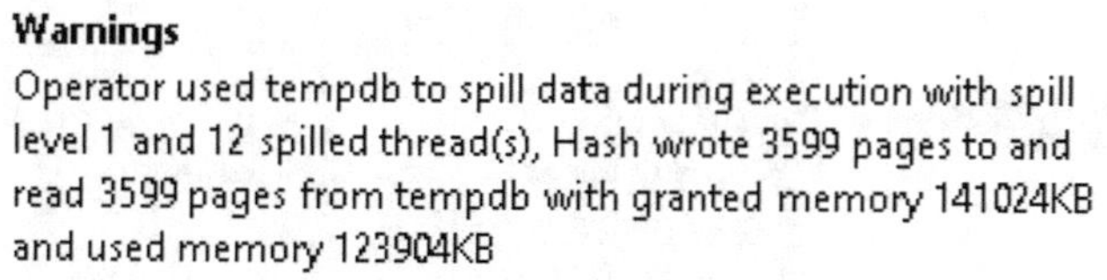

Warnings
Operator used tempdb to spill data during execution with spill
level 1 and 12 spilled thread(s), Hash wrote 3599 pages to and
read 3599 pages from tempdb with granted memory 141024KB
and used memory 123904KB

Figure 7-9. *Warning in an execution plan*

The main advantage of seeing a warning is that SQL Server has identified a potential issue with your T-SQL code. You should investigate any warnings that are returned and see if you can take steps to resolve them. While not all warnings are the same, the warning above is referencing spills to tempdb. This type of warning usually means there is a bad estimate and the number of rows returned in a query. This can cause the memory grant for the query to be incorrect, causing SQL Server to use tempdb. To resolve this warning, you may want to confirm that statistics are up to date and your tables are properly indexed.

Execution plans have other elements that will alert you to potential performance issues. While warnings can give you specific advice about issues with your T-SQL, there are other items in your execution plan that do not provide the same level of guidance. When creating an execution plan, SQL Server uses statistics to make a guess as to the number of rows that will be returned. SQL Server also keeps track of the actual number of rows returned in each step of the execution plan. If you mouse over the operators, you can see something like Figure 7-10.

Clustered Index Scan (Clustered)

Scanning a clustered index, entirely or only a range.

Physical Operation	Clustered Index Scan
Logical Operation	Clustered Index Scan
Actual Execution Mode	Batch
Estimated Execution Mode	Batch
Storage	RowStore
Number of Rows Read	401409
Actual Number of Rows for All Executions	200702
Actual Number of Batches	232
Estimated I/O Cost	3.5009
Estimated Operator Cost	3.57452 (34%)
Estimated Subtree Cost	3.57452
Estimated CPU Cost	0.0736178
Estimated Number of Executions	1
Number of Executions	12
Estimated Number of Rows for All Executions	202343
Estimated Number of Rows Per Execution	202343
Estimated Number of Rows to be Read	401409
Estimated Row Size	230 B
Actual Rebinds	0
Actual Rewinds	0
Ordered	False
Node ID	2

Figure 7-10. *Estimated vs. actual number of rows*

The first arrow points to the actual number of rows returned for this step of the
execution plan. The second arrow points to the estimated number of rows returned.
In this case, the numbers of rows match. If the numbers of rows match or are close in
range, you will not have performance issues related to estimates. If the two numbers
are significantly different, you may get an execution plan that does not perform as well
as it could. This could be happening because the statistics are out of date, and SQL
Server cannot accurately determine the number of rows that will be returned. Another
possibility is that SQL Server may have created the execution plan for a different set of
values. Regardless of the reason, if you see a large variation between the estimated and
actual number of rows returned, this is something that you should investigate.

By reading execution plans, you can quickly identify where there are performance
issues in your queries and what steps you can take to solve those issues. This includes
knowing how to access execution plans and knowing the difference between estimated
and actual execution plans. Execution plans also have several features that help you
quickly identify possible performance issues. By looking at the size of the arrows, you can
tell the relative amount of data passing through each step in an execution plan. The sort

operator may provide insights into data that is sorted for more reasons than returning an ordered result set. You can also look at the estimated and actual number of rows returned to help determine if SQL Server has enough information to give you a good execution plan. Once you have gotten familiar with these aspects of execution plans, you may want to investigate how SQL Server is using your indexes.

Index Usage in Execution Plans

Now that you are familiar with the basics of using execution plans, this section will discuss how to view index usage (or lack thereof) within an execution plan. This will include the different operators SQL Server uses when accessing the data depending on how much data in an index SQL Server must access to find all relevant data. There are also different operators showing if the execution plan is using a clustered index, non-clustered index, or a heap. Another aspect of index usage in execution plans is how SQL Server looks up additional information that is not contained in an index. This can differ based on whether there is a clustered index in the table or not, or if the index contains all columns needed for the query.

In terms of managing T-SQL, one of the largest differences I have seen across companies is how indexes are managed. In some cases, the development teams own writing all the T-SQL code including index creation. There are also companies where the database team handles all index creation and maintenance. Since database administrators usually have less access to development than the developers, I believe it may be most helpful to have the two teams work together. The database administrators can find indexes that are performing poorly and may have more experience designing indexes for multiple T-SQL queries. On the other hand, the developers may have a better idea of how the tables are designed and how the T-SQL code uses those tables.

There are many queries, health checks, and monitoring tools that can help you identify issues with your indexes. You can either use queries to find what stored procedures use the same database objects or you may have a specific query in mind to improve performance. Once you get the execution plan from the cache or generate the current actual execution plan, you can start looking into potential performance issues. As discussed in the previous section, you know that you can check the relative amount of data records for each step, look at various operators and warnings, and verify the estimated and actual number of rows returned. You can also look at how indexes are being used as part of your execution plan.

When working with data in SQL Server, the preference is that data is found as quickly as possible. When data is saved in a clustered index, the data is sorted based on the columns of the index. This means that when SQL Server searches through a clustered index, the data is stored in order. In the best scenario, SQL Server looks through the data and finds the data quickly. If this happens, you will see a clustered index seek in the execution plan. The clustered index seek in the execution plan will look like Figure 7-11.

Clustered Index Seek (Clustered)
[Customer].[PK_Customer] [cus]

Figure 7-11. *Clustered Index Seek icon*

Seeing a clustered index seek lets you know that your T-SQL code is written well enough to find the data quickly. If you do not see a clustered index seek in your execution plan, you may want to see if there is a way to rewrite your T-SQL to use one.

While it is ideal for your data to use a clustered index seek, you may see something in your execution plan that looks similar but not the same. It is possible for SQL Server to use the clustered index but not find the data quickly. In this case, SQL Server may need to look through a significant percentage of the index. If this happens, you may see a clustered index scan in the execution plan as shown in Figure 7-12.

Clustered Index Scan (Clustered)
[CustomerOrder].[PK_CustomerOrder]…

Figure 7-12. *Clustered Index Scan icon*

This mean that SQL Server looked through the data as sorted by the clustered index but had to scan through the table to find all the records needed to satisfy the query requirements.

SQL Server uses the term *seek* to indicate that the requested data could be found without searching a significant portion of the reference index. When more records are accessed that the matching records in the table t, SQL Server refers to this as a scan. While seeks or scans can apply to clustered indexes, they can also apply to non-clustered indexes. Non-clustered indexes are not sorted in the same order as the clustered index or the table, if the table is a heap. The non-clustered index is sorted in the order of key columns specified in the index. If there is a clustered index on the table, the non-clustered index will have a pointer back to the clustered index. If there is no clustered index, then the non-clustered index will point back to the row ID in the table.

If the execution plan uses a non-clustered index, there are a couple of different ways the SQL Server can search through the data records. If SQL Server knows where to find the data in the non-clustered index, you will see an index seek in the execution plan. The index seek will look like Figure 7-13.

```
Index Seek (NonClustered)
[Customer].[IX_Customer_DateCreated]
```

Figure 7-13. *Index Seek icon*

If a clustered index seek cannot be used based on the T-SQL code that is written, the next best option is an index seek, where a there is a seek on a non-clustered index. If a seek is not possible, SQL Server will end up using an index scan. Like the clustered index scan, this means that SQL Server needed to go through the index to find the necessary data records. If the execution plan uses an index scan, Figure 7-14 shows how it will appear in your execution plan.

```
Index Scan (NonClustered)
[Customer].[IX_Customer_DateCreated]
```

Figure 7-14. *Index Scan icon*

Also, like clustered index scans, if you see an index scan, you may want to see what can be done in terms of rewriting T-SQL to use an index seek instead.

Keep in mind what kind of data is needed when writing your T-SQL queries. While including additional data fields can have additional hardware overhead, it can also affect how SQL Server searches the data records. If SQL Server needs to use an index seek or an index scan to find the required data records, that does not mean that all the data fields need to exist in the non-clustered index. If additional data columns are required, SQL Server may need the non-clustered index to get the additional data columns from the clustered index. When this happens, you will see a key lookup in your execution plan like the one in Figure 7-15.

```
Key Lookup (Clustered)
[Customer].[PK_Customer]
```

Figure 7-15. *Key Lookup icon*

When you see a key lookup, that lets you know that not all the columns needed for your query existed in the non-clustered index. In these scenarios, it signifies that the index may need to be modified to include those columns. Before deciding to add these data fields as included columns, you should be aware that including the columns in the index may have an additional cost associated with writing or updating the index.

A table that does not have a clustered index is also known as a heap. If there are no other indexes on the table, SQL Server will have to search row by row to find the data records it needs for query results. There are many other factors that can be involved, but this can cause SQL Server to scan the entire table. This can be seen in the execution plan in Figure 7-16.

```
Table Scan
[ProductPriceHistory]
```

Figure 7-16. *Table Scan icon*

Some tables that are very small may not need to have indexes and using a table scan may be acceptable. If there are many records in the table, then a table scan is not ideal. When this is the case, you may want to investigate if there are any possible indexes that can be added to the table.

If there is a non-clustered index on the heap, it is possible that SQL Server can use the non-clustered index as part of the execution plan. If this is the case, you will see an index seek or an index scan. When either an index seek or index scan is in the execution plan, it is possible that the columns used in the query do not exist in the non-clustered index. If additional columns need to be looked up in the table, you will see a RID lookup in the execution plan. You can see this in Figure 7-17.

RID Lookup (Heap)

Figure 7-17. *RID Lookup icon*

Like the key lookup, you want to see if you can alter any non-clustered indexes to include the necessary columns from the T-SQL code. It is also possible that the query can be modified to exclude the columns that are causing the RID lookup.

As an example, Listing 7-6 shows a query to retrieve all customers that have a first name that begins with the letter S.

Listing 7-6. Query to Get Customers

```
SELECT FirstName, DateCreated
FROM dbo.Customer
WHERE FirstName LIKE 'S%';
```

The first time I ran this query, there was only a primary clustered index on CustomerID in this table. The execution plan from the T-SQL code in Listing 7-6 is shown in Figure 7-18.

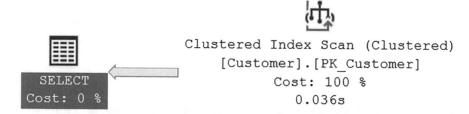

Figure 7-18. *Execution plan with only a clustered index*

There are no non-clustered index on the table. The only option SQL Server has is to search through the entire clustered index to find the requested records. You can see this by looking over the properties associated with the clustered index scan. The properties for this query execution can be found in Figure 7-19.

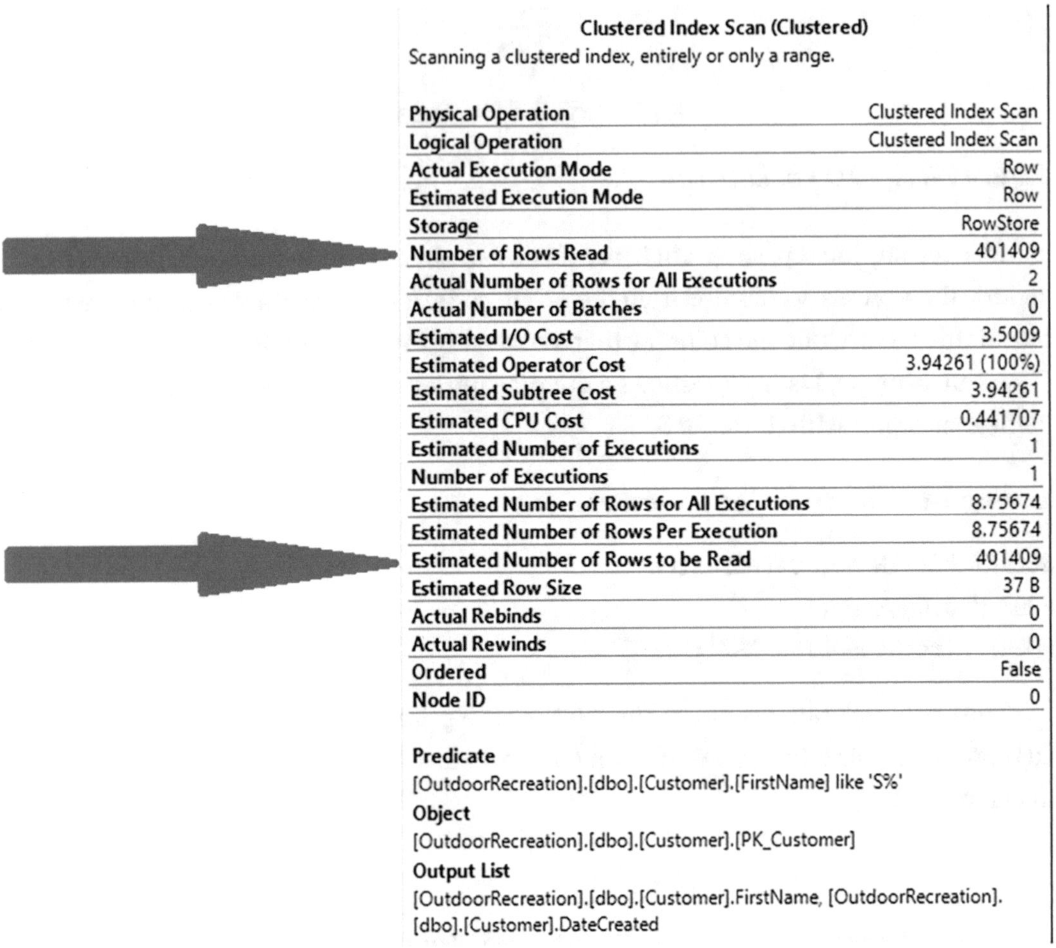

Clustered Index Scan (Clustered)

Scanning a clustered index, entirely or only a range.

Physical Operation	Clustered Index Scan
Logical Operation	Clustered Index Scan
Actual Execution Mode	Row
Estimated Execution Mode	Row
Storage	RowStore
Number of Rows Read	401409
Actual Number of Rows for All Executions	2
Actual Number of Batches	0
Estimated I/O Cost	3.5009
Estimated Operator Cost	3.94261 (100%)
Estimated Subtree Cost	3.94261
Estimated CPU Cost	0.441707
Estimated Number of Executions	1
Number of Executions	1
Estimated Number of Rows for All Executions	8.75674
Estimated Number of Rows Per Execution	8.75674
Estimated Number of Rows to be Read	401409
Estimated Row Size	37 B
Actual Rebinds	0
Actual Rewinds	0
Ordered	False
Node ID	0

Predicate
[OutdoorRecreation].[dbo].[Customer].[FirstName] like 'S%'
Object
[OutdoorRecreation].[dbo].[Customer].[PK_Customer]
Output List
[OutdoorRecreation].[dbo].[Customer].FirstName, [OutdoorRecreation].[dbo].[Customer].DateCreated

Figure 7-19. *Reads with a clustered index*

Looking at the estimated and actual number of rows to be read, they are the same. The total for each is 401,409 rows read. The actual number of rows is 2. SQL Server must search 401,409 rows to find the 2 rows that matched the criteria.

This scenario has a query that is reading significantly more rows than the number of rows returned. You cannot rewrite the query to use a non-clustered index since none exist. The best option is to write a non-clustered index to improve performance. The new non-clustered index is Listing 7-7.

Listing 7-7. Creating a Non-clustered Index

```
CREATE NONCLUSTERED INDEX IX_Customer_FirstName
      ON dbo.Customer (FirstName ASC);
```

Now that I have created the non-clustered index, I can run the query again to see if I get a new execution plan. The new execution plan is in Figure 7-20.

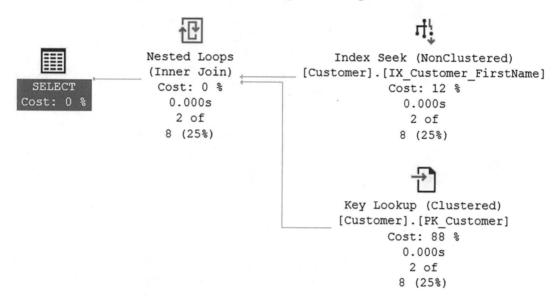

Figure 7-20. *Execution plan with a non-clustered index*

In Figure 7-18, the clustered index scan has been replaced with an index seek and a key lookup. While this may seem like I have decreased the performance of the execution plan, you can verify this by looking at the number of rows read. In Figure 7-21, you can see the properties associated with the Index Seek.

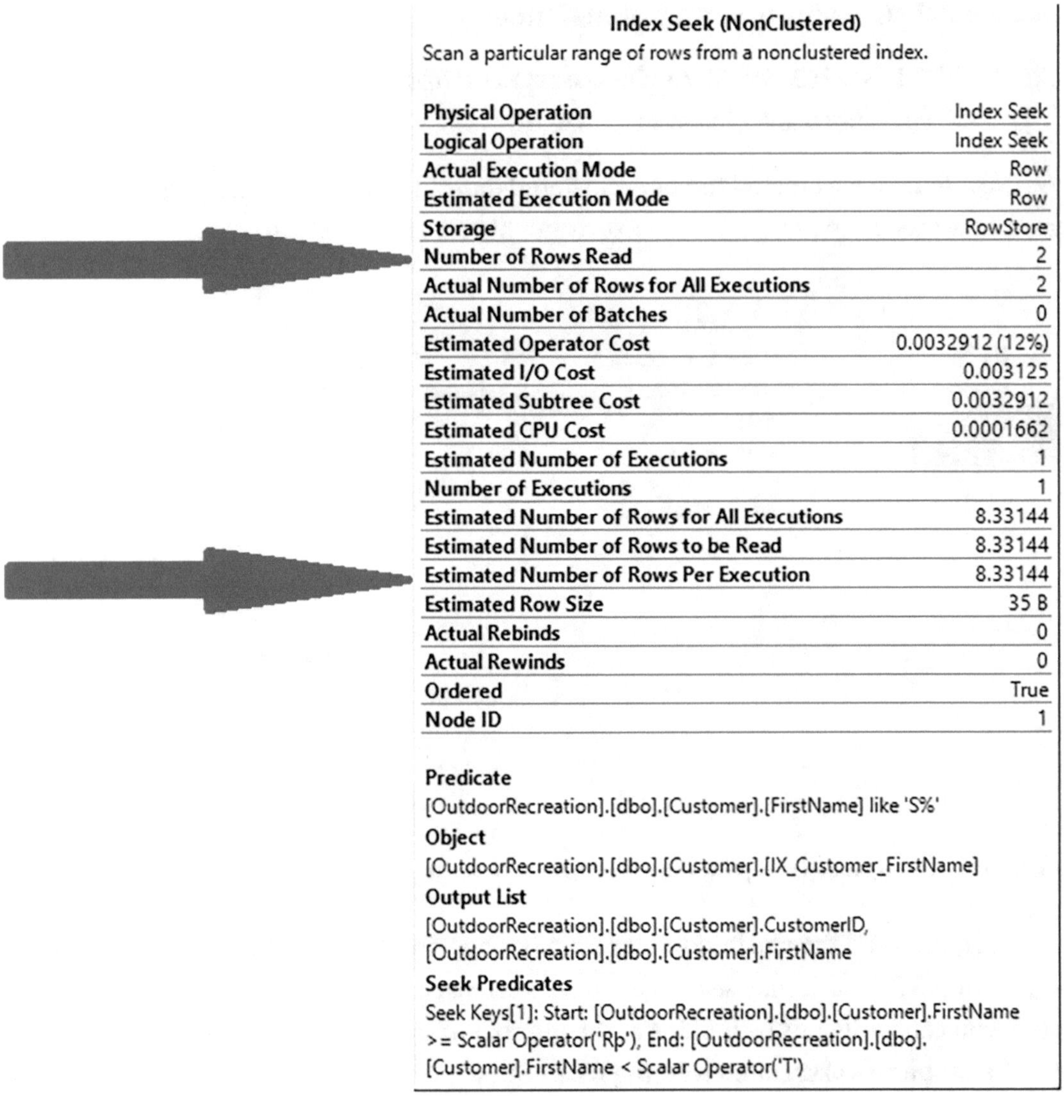

Index Seek (NonClustered)

Scan a particular range of rows from a nonclustered index.

Physical Operation	Index Seek
Logical Operation	Index Seek
Actual Execution Mode	Row
Estimated Execution Mode	Row
Storage	RowStore
Number of Rows Read	2
Actual Number of Rows for All Executions	2
Actual Number of Batches	0
Estimated Operator Cost	0.0032912 (12%)
Estimated I/O Cost	0.003125
Estimated Subtree Cost	0.0032912
Estimated CPU Cost	0.0001662
Estimated Number of Executions	1
Number of Executions	1
Estimated Number of Rows for All Executions	8.33144
Estimated Number of Rows to be Read	8.33144
Estimated Number of Rows Per Execution	8.33144
Estimated Row Size	35 B
Actual Rebinds	0
Actual Rewinds	0
Ordered	True
Node ID	1

Predicate

[OutdoorRecreation].[dbo].[Customer].[FirstName] like 'S%'

Object

[OutdoorRecreation].[dbo].[Customer].[IX_Customer_FirstName]

Output List

[OutdoorRecreation].[dbo].[Customer].CustomerID,
[OutdoorRecreation].[dbo].[Customer].FirstName

Seek Predicates

Seek Keys[1]: Start: [OutdoorRecreation].[dbo].[Customer].FirstName
>= Scalar Operator('Rþ'), End: [OutdoorRecreation].[dbo].
[Customer].FirstName < Scalar Operator('T')

Figure 7-21. *Properties for index seek*

Now that the non-clustered index has been created, you can see that the actual number of rows read has decreased from 401,409 to 2. You would expect that the key lookup would have the same number of reads, but you can look at the properties to confirm. In Figure 7-22, you can see the properties returned.

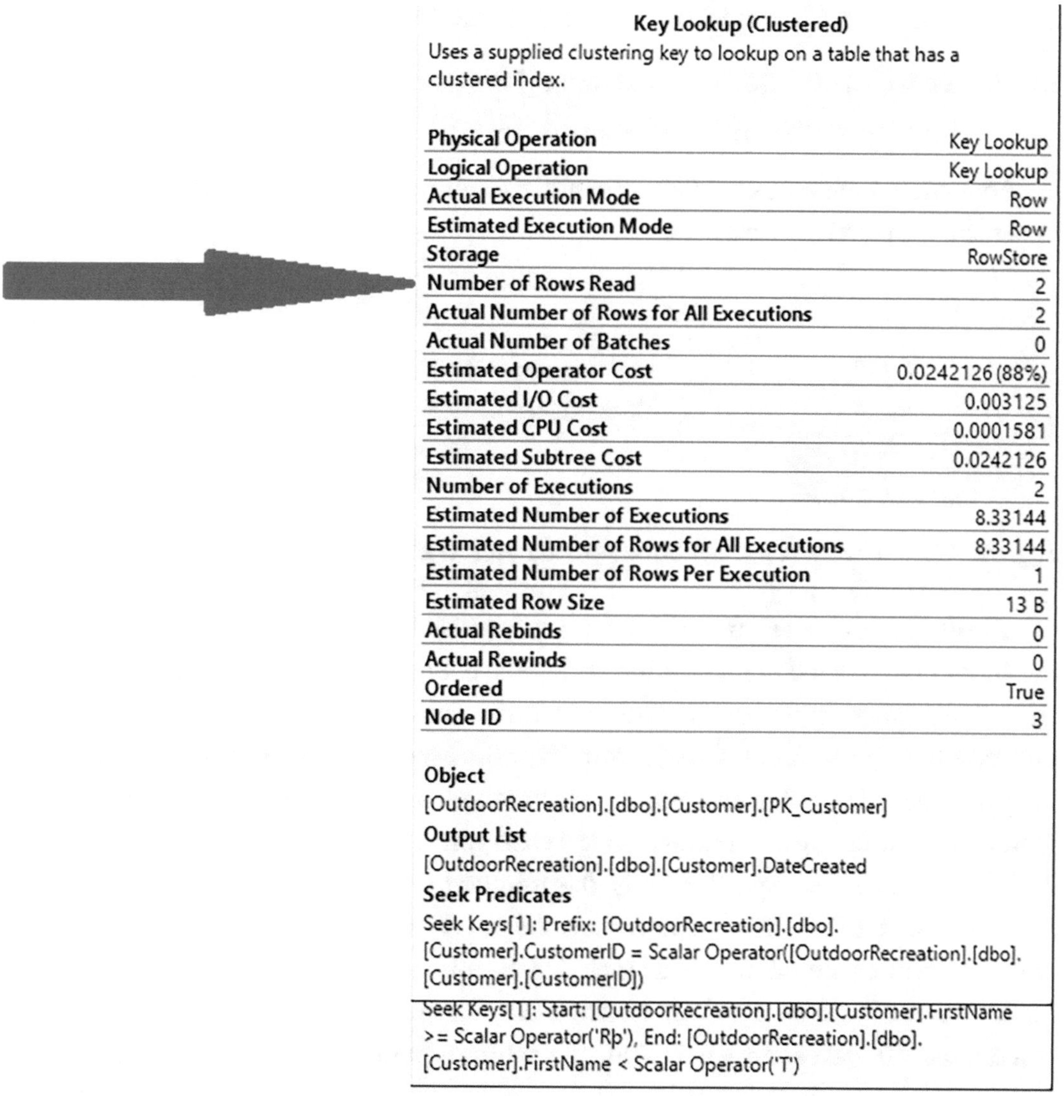

Key Lookup (Clustered)

Uses a supplied clustering key to lookup on a table that has a clustered index.

Physical Operation	Key Lookup
Logical Operation	Key Lookup
Actual Execution Mode	Row
Estimated Execution Mode	Row
Storage	RowStore
Number of Rows Read	2
Actual Number of Rows for All Executions	2
Actual Number of Batches	0
Estimated Operator Cost	0.0242126 (88%)
Estimated I/O Cost	0.003125
Estimated CPU Cost	0.0001581
Estimated Subtree Cost	0.0242126
Number of Executions	2
Estimated Number of Executions	8.33144
Estimated Number of Rows for All Executions	8.33144
Estimated Number of Rows Per Execution	1
Estimated Row Size	13 B
Actual Rebinds	0
Actual Rewinds	0
Ordered	True
Node ID	3

Object
[OutdoorRecreation].[dbo].[Customer].[PK_Customer]
Output List
[OutdoorRecreation].[dbo].[Customer].DateCreated
Seek Predicates
Seek Keys[1]: Prefix: [OutdoorRecreation].[dbo].
[Customer].CustomerID = Scalar Operator([OutdoorRecreation].[dbo].
[Customer].[CustomerID])

Seek Keys[1]: Start: [OutdoorRecreation].[dbo].[Customer].FirstName
>= Scalar Operator('Rþ'), End: [OutdoorRecreation].[dbo].
[Customer].FirstName < Scalar Operator('T')

Figure 7-22. *Properties of the key lookup*

Reviewing the key lookup, there were also 2 rows read in it. The T-SQL code without the non-clustered index had rows of 401,409. The total number of rows read with the non-clustered index is 4: 2 rows for the index seek and 2 for the key lookup.

You could get rid of the key lookup by including the DateCreated column as part of the non-clustered index or remove the column from the original query. Listing 7-8 shows an example of a non-clustered index with an included column.

Listing 7-8. Non-Clustered Index with Included Column

```
CREATE NONCLUSTERED INDEX IX_Customer_FirstName
       ON dbo.Customer (FirstName ASC) INCLUDE (DateCreated);
```

After adding the index in Listing 7-8 and running the query from Listing 7-6, look at the execution plan in Figure 7-23.

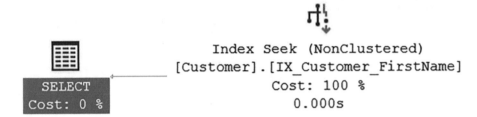

Figure 7-23. *Execution plan with non-clustered index and included column*

The execution plan shows that the query is still using the non-clustered index. Since this index has changed to include the additional column in the select statement, the execution plan has changed. Previously, with the non-clustered index, the execution plan had an index seek and a key lookup. Now the execution plan is using an index seek.

Once you get familiar with reading execution plans, you can start using them to determine how to improve performance. When you look at your execution plan, you may find a clustered index scan. Generally, this implies that SQL Server had to look through the entire table to find the data that meets the query criteria. As shown in this section, creating a non-clustered index that includes the join criteria can help improve the performance of your query. If you find that SQL Server is having to perform a key lookup, you can see if it makes sense to include the columns being selected as part of the non-clustered index. Understanding how SQL Server uses indexes can help improve your query performance. Understanding how SQL Server compares data from more than one data set can also help you improve query performance.

Logical Join Types in Execution Plans

This last section of the chapter goes into detail about the several different logical join operators within SQL Server including INNER JOIN, LEFT or RIGHT OUTER JOIN, and FULL OUTER JOIN. The type of logical join operator, how the data is sorted, the size of the data being compared, and how the data is being compared can determine the physical operators that SQL Server can use in an execution plan. There are examples of T-SQL as well as physical operators so that you can see the correlation between logical and physical operators.

In addition to reading execution plans and understanding indexes, your T-SQL code can also be used to determine how an execution plan will be generated. In some cases, how tables are joined together is just as important as how data is stored in the tables. There are times when how you are joining your columns together may also affect your execution plan. Some T-SQL in the WHERE clause can impact what types of logical joins are used in the query execution. If multiple queries are combined, it is also possible that it may change how the query is executed. Ultimately, there is a relationship between how the T-SQL code is written and how SQL Server decides to execute the query.

There are several different logical joins in SQL Server. Some of these logical joins are easily visible in T-SQL. They include the INNER JOIN, LEFT OUTER JOIN, RIGHT OUTER JOIN, and FULL OUTER JOIN. These are not the only logical joins that exist in SQL Server. With some T-SQL commands, SQL Server will compare one table to another looking for records that match or not. In these scenarios, SQL Server does not perform a full join but a SEMI JOIN. This type of join is not specified as a T-SQL command, but some T-SQL commands like EXISTS or NOT EXISTS will indicate a SEMI JOIN. Available SEMI JOINs include the LEFT SEMI JOIN, LEFT ANTI-SEMI JOIN, RIGHT SEMI JOIN, and RIGHT ANTI-SEMI JOIN. Finally, there are some logical joins that are related by combining two or more query results in the same transaction. They include CONCATENATION, which is often associated with a UNION ALL, or the UNION logical join, which can happen with a UNION in T-SQL. Based on the logical join, SQL Server will determine what physical joins can be used. In this way, logical joins can be used to affect query performance.

There are physical join operators that can be associated with logical joins. The four physical join operators are called merge join, hash join, nested loop, and adaptive join. When using an INNER JOIN, any of these four types of physical join operators can be used as part of the execution plan. How the data is stored in the table and the relative sizes of the tables may affect which physical operator is used. If the data from both tables being compared is sorted, the records from the two tables can be compared side by side. This lets SQL Server quickly find the records that do or do not match, depending on the query requirements. When this happens, it is called a merge join. A merge join physical operator appears in the execution plan shown in Figure 7-24.

Merge Join
(Left Outer Join)

Figure 7-24. *Merge join icon*

There are times where the tables being joined together are not sorted. If that is the case, SQL Server can still compare the rows between each of the tables. However, SQL Server will need to convert the records to something that can be compared easily. This can be done by hashing. If SQL Server hashes the columns being compared in both tables and compares them, the physical operator will be a hash match. If you see the icon in Figure 7-25 in your execution plan, you know SQL Server is performing a hash match physical join.

Hash Match
(Inner Join)

Figure 7-25. *Hash match icon*

If there are two tables where one table is smaller than another, then SQL Server may decide to compare the values or one table one row at a time to all rows of the other table. When this happens, SQL Server will use a nested loop as shown in Figure 7-26.

Nested Loops
(Inner Join)

Figure 7-26. *Nested loop icon*

Starting in SQL Server 2017, a new physical join operator can be used when SQL Server determines an execution plan for a query. This new physical join operator is intended to help in situations when the data stored in a given table may vary significantly based on the criteria in the WHERE clause. This type of physical join allows SQL Server to determine if a hash match or nested loop should be used depending on the data selected for the query. This is referred to as an adaptive join. In SQL Server 2017, adaptive joins were only available with columnstore indexes. Starting in SQL Server 2019, adaptive joins can be used in other scenarios.

Going through the logical joins that are available, the next ones are the LEFT OUTER JOIN and the RIGHT OUTER JOIN. In some ways, these two types of logical joins are the same but also different. For instance, nested loops can only use a LEFT OUTER JOIN. If a query is written using a RIGHT OUTER JOIN, SQL Server will incur an additional cost to convert a RIGHT OUTER JOIN to a LEFT OUTER JOIN. Except this specific scenario, all physical join types support the use of LEFT OUTER JOIN. In previous versions of SQL Server, it was possible for SQL Server to generate two different execution plans depending on whether a LEFT OUTER JOIN or a RIGHT OUTER JOIN was used in the query. This was due to the limitations around how joins can be reordered.

The LEFT OUTER JOIN has several specifics about when one physical join type may be used over another. Listing 7-9 shows ordering the table by the identifier.

Listing 7-9. Primary Key to Sort Data by OrderDetailID

```
ALTER TABLE [dbo].[OrderDetail]
    ADD CONSTRAINT [PK_OrderDetail]
    PRIMARY KEY CLUSTERED ([OrderDetailID] ASC);
```

Once the table has been ordered by the OrderDetailID, you can join the CustomerOrder table to the OrderDetail table. The T-SQL code for this join is shown in Listing 7-10.

Listing 7-10. Outer Join Between CustomerOrder and OrderDetail

```
SELECT ord.OrderNumber
FROM dbo.CustomerOrder ord
    LEFT OUTER JOIN dbo.OrderDetail dtl
    ON ord.CustomerOrderID = dtl.CustomerOrderID
WHERE ord.CustomerOrderID < 80000;
```

In this scenario, the two tables are not ordered in the same way. The CustomerOrder table is sorted by the CustomerOrderID, whereas the OrderDetail table is sorted by the OrderDetailID. You can see in Figure 7-27 that the physical operator is a hash match.

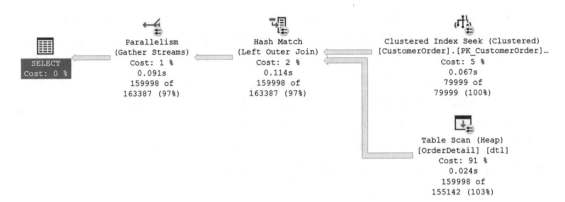

Figure 7-27. *Execution plan using a hash match*

You have seen what happens when the tables are ordered differently. If you run the T-SQL code in Listing 7-11, both tables will be ordered by the same column, CustomerOrderID.

Listing 7-11. Changing the Primary Key to Sort Data by CustomerOrderID

```
ALTER TABLE dbo.OrderDetail
    ADD CONSTRAINT PK_OrderDetail
    PRIMARY KEY CLUSTERED (CustomerOrderID ASC, OrderDetailID ASC);
```

Looking at Figure 7-28, you can see that the execution plan has changed and now uses a merge join.

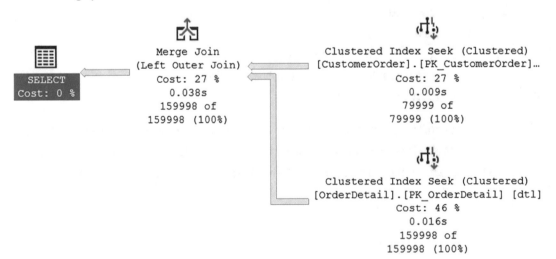

Figure 7-28. *Execution plan using a merge join*

210

Now that these two tables are ordered in the same manner, SQL Server has determined that it is more cost-effective to use a merge join. In the preceding example, SQL Server took the two ordered data sets and compared the records to determine which records match. All the preceding examples assume equality between the columns being compared. As a general guide, SQL Server will always use a nested loop for LEFT OUTER JOINs if none of the joins in the query are equal. You can see an example of a query that meets this criterion in Listing 7-12.

Listing 7-12. Left Outer Join with Inequality

```
SELECT TOP(500) ord.OrderNumber
FROM dbo.CustomerOrder ord
        LEFT OUTER JOIN dbo.OrderDetail dtl
        ON ord.CustomerOrderID <> dtl.CustomerOrderID;
```

If I recreate the primary key referenced in Listing 7-8, the data between the two tables will be sorted differently. Due to the amount of data that will be compared between the two tables, I limit the result to the first 500 records. After running this query, I get the execution plan returned in Figure 7-29.

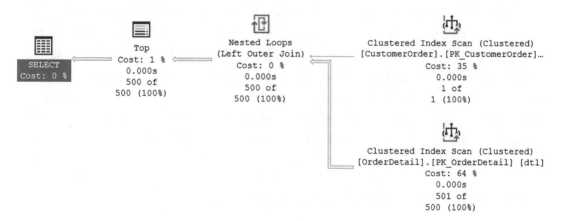

Figure 7-29. *Execution plan using a nested loop*

Now that the only join in the T-SQL code is an inequality, SQL Server uses a nested loop physical join. Almost every query where there are no joins that are equal must use a nested loop except one specific scenario. If the data being compared is sorted and there is an inequality, SQL Server can use a merge join. Creating the primary key from Listing 7-10 will order the data the same between the two tables. The execution plan in Figure 7-30 is returned when executing the query from Listing 7-9.

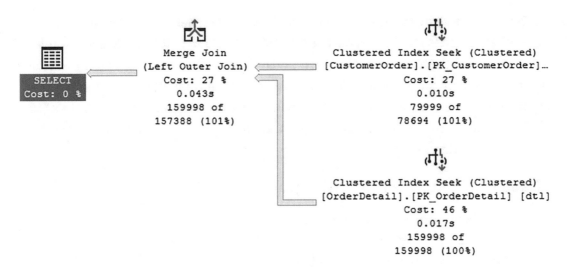

Figure 7-30. *Execution plan using a merge join*

Figure 7-30 shows that it is possible to have a merge join when there is an inequality. However, only when the tables are sorted and there is an inequality will you see a merge join with a LEFT OUTER JOIN. In addition to T-SQL joins that relate to logical joins, there are other logical join types that SQL Server can use.

Another logical join type involves situations when SQL Server compares data between two tables but without doing a full join between the tables. Depending on the T-SQL code used, this can be referred to as a SEMI JOIN or an ANTI SEMI JOIN. Like the LEFT OUTER JOIN and RIGHT OUTER JOIN, SQL Server has some of the same limitations matching the SEMI JOIN and ANTI SEMI JOIN to physical join operators. When working with either a SEMI JOIN or an ANTI SEMI JOIN, there is the concept of left or right. This left or right has to do with which side is being compared. Listing 7-13 finds all orders for the customer with an ID of 234.

Listing 7-13. All Orders For CustomerID 234

```
SELECT ord.OrderNumber
FROM dbo.CustomerOrder ord
WHERE NOT EXISTS
      (
            SELECT *
            FROM dbo.OrderDetail dtl
```

```
        WHERE dtl.CustomerOrderID = ord.CustomerOrderID
            AND ord.CustomerID = 234
);
```

When this query is run, the data in OrderDetail is sorted by CustomerOrderID and then OrderDetailID. In Figure 7-31, the execution plan shows a RIGHT ANTI SEMI JOIN.

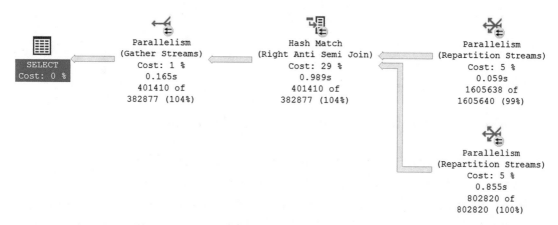

Figure 7-31. *Partial execution plan with RIGHT ANTI SEMI JOIN*

The ANTI SEMI JOIN is due to the NOT EXISTS in the query from Listing 7-11. In the preceding scenario, SQL Server has chosen a right join. The query in Listing 7-14 looks for all orders that have products other than ProductID of 2.

Listing 7-14. All Orders Except Those with Only ProductID 2

```
SELECT ord.*
FROM dbo.CustomerOrder ord
WHERE EXISTS
    (
        SELECT dtl.ProductID
        FROM dbo.OrderDetail dtl
        WHERE ord.CustomerOrderID = dtl.CustomerOrderID
            AND dtl.ProductID <> 2
    );
```

As shown in execution plan in Figure 7-32, you can see a RIGHT SEMI JOIN.

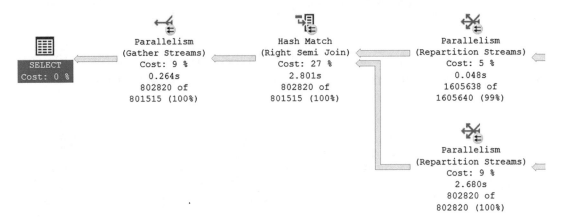

Figure 7-32. *Partial execution plan with RIGHT SEMI JOIN*

The use of the RIGHT SEMI JOIN is due to the EXISTS in the T-SQL from Listing 7-10. The use of right is stating that SQL Server is evaluating the results returned from the EXISTS statement to the list of customer orders. While the use of EXISTS or NOT EXISTS can indicate that there will be a SEMI JOIN or an ANTI SEMI join, that may not always be what happens. This is also true for a ANTI JOINs, as the database engine can convert a RIGHT SEMI JOIN to a LEFT ANTI JOIN. Listing 7-15 shows a query that will return all orders that exist for the product with an ID of 2.

Listing 7-15. All Orders with ProductID 2

```
SELECT ord.OrderNumber
FROM dbo.CustomerOrder ord
WHERE EXISTS
    (
        SELECT *
        FROM dbo.OrderDetail dtl
        WHERE dtl.CustomerOrderID = ord.CustomerOrderID
            AND dtl.ProductID = 2
    );
```

The execution plan in Figure 7-33 shows how SQL Server has determined to execute this query.

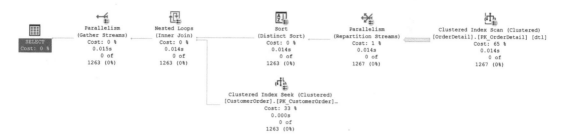

Figure 7-33. *ExecutionpPlan with No SEMI JOINs*

For this execution, SQL Server has decided to convert this T-SQL to act like an INNER JOIN instead of a SEMI JOIN. This is because SQL Server has calculated that this will give the best execution out of those evaluated.

There are ways to combine data that consist of comparing values between two data sets and selecting items that match or do not match between them. There is also the possibility of combining entire data sets as part of the logical join types. This can include the use of UNION or UNION ALL in your T-SQL code. The query shown in Listing 7-16 shows the use of a UNION between the two tables.

Listing 7-16. All Products with Tele

```
SELECT prd.ProductName
FROM dbo.Product prd
WHERE prd.ProductName LIKE '%scope'
UNION
SELECT prd.ProductName
FROM dbo.Product prd
WHERE prd.ProductName = 'Telescope';
```

In this query, the list of products that begin with Tele or the product name is equal to Telescope will be returned for the current data in the database, but the first and second SELECT statements will return identical results. Using UNION ensures that the results are not cumulative between the first and second SELECT statements. If there was a product microscope as well as telescope, the query would only return a single record for each product that matches either criteria. However, if you used a UNION ALL instead of UNION, you would get the full results from each SELECT statement returned in the result set. When this query is executed in the SQL Server, the execution plan in Figure 7-34 is returned.

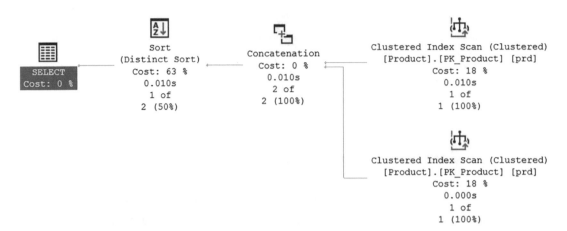

Figure 7-34. Execution plan with concatenation

In this query, SQL Server does not join the data together as it has in the other examples from this chapter. Instead, there is only one operator, concatenation, that indicates how SQL Server is combining this data.

Overall, the goal is to use the physical join that is the most effective for the data that is being joined. Merge joins can perform very well, but they are limited to data that has been ordered by indexes or ORDER BY or GROUP BY statements. As expected, index merge joins will perform even better than merge joins that do not use an index. When data is not sorted and particularly if one of the two sides of the data being joined is small, SQL Server may use a nested loop. You will want to confirm that looping through the other table does not incur a significant cost. Just as a merge join using an index performs better than a merge join without an index, the same is true for a nested loop. For both a merge join and nested loop, see if you can alter your T-SQL code to use an index. This does not mean creating an index if one does not exist; instead, you can check the indexes on the table and see if any will apply for your specific query. If the tables are not sorted and particularly if the numbers of records being joined on either side are both large, the hash match can be the ideal solution.

Throughout this chapter, I have gone over various aspects of working with execution plans. I started with some of the ways you can access and view execution plans. I also discussed how estimated execution plans, actual execution plans, and executions in the plan cache differed. When looking at execution plans, there are some items such as arrow sizes, estimated number of rows, and actual number of rows that can give you some hints regarding the next steps you can take to improve the performance of your T-SQL code. After looking into these items, you may also be able to check how the execution is using indexes. It is helpful to not only focus on what indexes are being used but how SQL Server is searching through those indexes. When joining tables, use T-SQL code that can reference certain logical join type behavior. These logical join types can affect what types of physical join types will be used as part of the execution plan. By writing your T-SQL code differently, you may be able to impact the execution plan generated by SQL Server. The information covered in this chapter should help you get more comfortable with reviewing your T-SQL code and improving the speed and hardware usage associated with your T-SQL.

CHAPTER 8

Optimizing Databases for T-SQL

In this part of the book, I have gone over many aspects of writing T-SQL code. I started by going over the use of set-based design in queries. When designing queries, it is also be important to design queries that use hardware effectively. One way to check the performance of your queries is by using execution plans. Once you have the execution plan of the query you want to improve, you can start focusing on how to optimize the query. There are some options available when it comes to optimizing T-SQL.

You have many options available to you when you start working on performance tuning your queries. In the past, one option was to manually identify poorly performing queries and improve them. When identifying queries that need to be optimized, there are many different factors that you can take into consideration. Starting in SQL Server 2017, additional functionality allows SQL Server to automatically improve the performance of certain aspects of executing T-SQL. With SQL Server 2019, there have been even more enhancements to help queries run better and faster without changing the underlying T-SQL code. This chapter will show recent changes to SQL Server, including SQL Server 2022, and how you can use them to improve the performance of your code without needed to rewrite your T-SQL.

Using Query Store

When executing queries in SQL Server, one of the key benefits is the use of execution plans. In Chapter 7, I briefly discussed how memory is used in SQL Server, and in Chapter 8, I explained how execution plans are saved in their own plan cache. One of the challenges with execution plans happens when an execution plan gets cleared from the plan cache. Not only is there a cost associated with generating a new execution plan, but there is also the risk that the new execution plan may perform poorly compared to the original.

© Elizabeth Noble 2023
E. Noble, *Pro T-SQL 2022*, https://doi.org/10.1007/978-1-4842-9256-3_8

Starting with SQL Server 2016, there is new functionality for how execution plans can be managed. Instead of only having execution plans available in the plan cache, there is the option to save historical information about the execution plans that have been generated. The big win here is that the performance information that is saved alongside the plans themselves. This new feature is called Query Store. In order to use Query Store, you must enable it as shown in Listing 8-1.

Listing 8-1. Query to Enable Query Store

```
ALTER DATABASE Menu
SET QUERY_STORE (OPERATION_MODE = READ_WRITE);
```

Enabling Query Store allows SQL Server to keep track of the execution plans over time. SQL Server 2022 also introduces the ability to compile Query Store data for replicas in an availability group. This can be very helpful, particularly if you are using a read-only replica to offload reporting tasks. In addition to keeping track of execution plans, Query Store also records execution statistics. Starting in SQL Server 2017 and Azure SQL Database, Query Store also tracks information regarding wait statistics for specific query executions. You can use query store to identify one query that has been compiled or optimized into different plans. You can also use query store to force the optimizer to consistently pick a specific, better performing plan.

In SQL Server 2016, you had to manually manage the Query Store to determine if there were better execution plans for your T-SQL code. If you found a query that would benefit from an execution plan in the Query Store, you needed to manually force a plan for that query. This caused additional maintenance over time because you needed to go back and undo forced plans as the data in your database changed over time.

Optimizing Logical Reads

You may have seen T-SQL code that appears to run well. The code executes in a timely fashion and returns the correct results. When you look at one of your SQL Server monitoring tools, however, you may notice some unexpected behavior that indicates there is a performance issue on your system. In some cases, you may find queries that are reading pages from memory that are not included in the result set. Reading the data pages can be identified as logical reads. You should look at the execution plan for the

T-SQL code to figure out what could be causing this discrepancy. This involves looking at what T-SQL code is executing and also trying to determine what can be done to improve performance.

The advantage of optimizing this query to use less reads is that this should decrease the number of data pages that are read into memory as part of this query execution. Put another way, the downside of reading more data than is needed for the query result is that pages that are used more frequently by the applications may be cleared from memory too soon. Unfortunately, we often are only aware of performance issues when we find out that an application is running slowly or is crashing. At these times, it can be difficult to diagnose the specific query causing the issues. If you do not have access to monitoring software, this situation can become even more difficult to troubleshoot. When I first started investigating performance issues, I would check SQL Server Agent's job history. Sometimes you will find a process running at the same time as the Production issue. While this does not confirm that the SQL Server Agent job is the cause, it may be worth investigating.

For these situations, it's preferable to know the exact stored procedure or prepared statement that is causing performance issues. Aside from third-party software, Query Store, or extended events that were previously set up, you may have very few options available. In addition, I prefer to identify queries that may cause performance issues before there is an outage. If I do not have access to third-party tools, I use DMVs to find queries before they become an issue. I often use any combination of the preceding actions with Performance Monitor to help track SQL Server over time and confirm if my performance tuning is effective.

If you do not have third-party tools or you want to get more familiar with DMVs to find T-SQL that needs performance tuning, you can query `sys.dm_exec_query_stats`. This DMV tracks statistics about T-SQL code that is executed and is still part of the plan cache. This will only return results for queries that have not been cleared out of the plan cache. If you believe that this DMV is missing some stored procedures that you expect to see, you may want to do some research on your plan cache and determine if the cache is getting filled with ad hoc queries. You need to join this data to `sys.dm_exec_sql_text` to find the T-SQL code associated with the statistics.

When trying to find queries with high logical reads, you want to look at T-SQL code based on various criteria. Looking at the average logical reads is usually my main target when looking for queries to performance tune. I prefer this metric because it often identifies T-SQL code that runs frequently on the server and probably has more reads than I expect. If there is a process that runs frequently on the server, I would not expect the average number of reads to be very high as a frequent process would imply the T-SQL code is directly related to an application. There are also some queries that do not run very often but use a high number of logical reads when they do run. In my experience, if the total logical reads are high and the overall execution count is low, I prioritize these queries below T-SQL code that has a higher average logical read value and a high number of executions.

Once you have identified the T-SQL code that needs to be performance tuned, look at both the code and the execution plan to get familiar with what data the query is retrieving and how SQL Server is retrieving the data. Listing 8-2 shows a query that you will be optimizing.

Listing 8-2. Original Query for Customer Orders

```
DECLARE @CustomerID        INT = 1;
DECLARE @CustomerOrderID   INT = 401508;
DECLARE @ProductID         INT = 1;

-- Get all orders for a specific customer and product
SELECT cus.CustomerID,
       ord.CustomerOrderID,
       prd.ProductID
INTO #TmpOrder
FROM dbo.Customer cus
       INNER JOIN dbo.CustomerOrder ord
       ON cus.CustomerID = ord.CustomerID
       INNER JOIN dbo.OrderDetail dtl
       ON ord.CustomerOrderID = dtl.CustomerOrderID
       INNER JOIN dbo.Product prd
       ON dtl.ProductID = prd.ProductID
WHERE (cus.CustomerID = @CustomerID OR @CustomerID = -1)
       AND (ord.CustomerOrderID = @CustomerOrderID OR @CustomerID = -1)
       AND (dtl.ProductID = @ProductID OR @ProductID = -1)
       AND prd.IsActive = 1;
```

```
SELECT ProductID
INTO #HistPriceCost
FROM dbo.ProductPriceHistory
GROUP BY ProductID
HAVING COUNT(*)>3;

SELECT cus.CustomerID,
      cus.FirstName,
      cus.LastName,
      ord.CustomerOrderID,
      ord.OrderNumber,
      prd.ProductName,
      dtl.QuantitySold,
      dtl.ProductPrice
FROM #TmpOrder tor
      INNER JOIN #HistPriceCost hpc
      ON tor.ProductID = hpc.ProductID
      LEFT JOIN dbo.Customer cus
      ON tor.CustomerID = cus.CustomerID
      INNER JOIN dbo.CustomerOrder ord
      ON tor.CustomerOrderID = ord.CustomerOrderID
      INNER JOIN dbo.OrderDetail dtl
      ON tor.CustomerOrderID = dtl.CustomerOrderID
            AND tor.ProductID = dtl.ProductID
      INNER JOIN dbo.Product prd
      ON tor.ProductID = prd.ProductID
WHERE cus.IsActive = 1
ORDER BY
      cus.CustomerID,
      CASE WHEN
      (
            cus.CustomerID = @CustomerID
            AND ord.CustomerOrderID = @CustomerOrderID
      )
            THEN 0
            ELSE 1
```

```
    END,
    ord.CustomerOrderID DESC,
    cus.LastName ASC;

DROP TABLE #TmpOrder;
DROP TABLE #HistPriceCost;
```

You will also want to get the execution plan from the plan cache so that you can see how SQL Server is executing the T-SQL code. The partial execution plan in Figure 8-1 shows one part of the execution plan that may benefit from optimization.

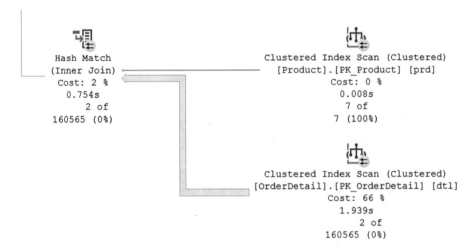

Figure 8-1. *Partial execution plan for Listing 8-2*

The execution plan has one thick line that results in a thin line after the hash match. This is a good indication that the query may be able to be optimized to use less reads overall. Based on this information, you need to investigate how the data from dbo.OrderDetail is combined with the results of dbo.Customer and dbo.CustomerOrder. Looking at either the T-SQL code or the output of the T-SQL code, you can get a better idea of the purpose of this query. This query is returning all customer orders where the product price has changed three times along with information about what customers place these orders.

Knowing this helps you begin the process of optimizing the logical reads on this query. You know that this query is based on products that have had their price changed more than three times. It may be possible to reduce the number of reads if you focus on trying to find only orders that contain products where the price has been changed more than three times. While the table dbo.OrderDetail is ordered by CustomerOrderID and then by OrderDetailID, this does not help when the T-SQL code in Listing 8-2 is only looking for customer orders that have specific products. The execution plan indicates that there is a non-clustered index that SQL Server is using to retrieve the data. The T-SQL code to create this index is in Listing 8-3.

Listing 8-3. Query for Index on OrderDetail

```
CREATE NONCLUSTERED INDEX [IX_OrderDetail_ProductID_CustomerOrderID]
    ON [dbo].[OrderDetail]([ProductID] ASC, [CustomerOrderID] ASC);
```

The non-clustered index does not change the order of the data in the table, but the index does keep the data for the index ordered. In this case, the index orders all the data first by the value of the ProductID column and then by the CustomerOrderID. The non-clustered index also must be able to reference back to the clustered index for situations where SQL Server decides to use this non-clustered index but also may need some additional data from the table. SQL Server does this by including the columns for the clustered index as part of this index. This helps you because this means the OrderDetailID from this index can be used to find all order details with this product.

This all sounds great, but it does not look like this index is currently providing the best performance. While you could work on tuning the indexes, I have found that on very large tables and on highly transactional systems, you may not be able to add or alter indexes as they exist. Sometimes those indexes are there doing exactly what they need to be doing, making sure a critical part of the application performs well. Modifying these indexes may cause even more headaches. You are fortunate that in this scenario you can add one line of the code to the T-SQL from Listing 8-1 and decrease the number of reads. The index is ordered by the ProductID and then CustomerOrderID. If you remove (... AND @IsActive = 1) from the query, you may be able to get the index to work more efficiently. See Listing 8-4.

Listing 8-4. Optimized Query for Customer Orders

```
DECLARE @CustomerID          INT = 1;
DECLARE @CustomerOrderID     INT = 401508;
DECLARE @ProductID           INT = 1;

-- Get all orders for a specific customer and product
SELECT cus.CustomerID,
      ord.CustomerOrderID,
      prd.ProductID
INTO #TmpOrder
FROM dbo.Customer cus
      INNER JOIN dbo.CustomerOrder ord
      ON cus.CustomerID = ord.CustomerID
      INNER JOIN dbo.OrderDetail dtl
      ON ord.CustomerOrderID = dtl.CustomerOrderID
      INNER JOIN dbo.Product prd
      ON dtl.ProductID = prd.ProductID
WHERE (cus.CustomerID = @CustomerID OR @CustomerID = -1)
      AND (ord.CustomerOrderID = @CustomerOrderID)
      AND (dtl.ProductID = @ProductID OR @ProductID = -1)
      AND prd.IsActive = 1;

SELECT ProductID
INTO #HistPriceCost
FROM dbo.ProductPriceHistory
GROUP BY ProductID
HAVING COUNT(*)>3;

SELECT cus.CustomerID,
      cus.FirstName,
      cus.LastName,
      ord.CustomerOrderID,
      ord.OrderNumber,
      prd.ProductName,
      dtl.QuantitySold,
      dtl.ProductPrice
```

```
FROM #TmpOrder tor
     LEFT JOIN #HistPriceCost hpc
     ON tor.ProductID = hpc.ProductID
     LEFT JOIN dbo.Customer cus
     ON tor.CustomerID = cus.CustomerID
     INNER JOIN dbo.CustomerOrder ord
     ON tor.CustomerOrderID = ord.CustomerOrderID
     INNER JOIN dbo.OrderDetail dtl
     ON tor.CustomerOrderID = dtl.CustomerOrderID
          AND tor.ProductID = dtl.ProductID
     INNER JOIN dbo.Product prd
     ON tor.ProductID = prd.ProductID
WHERE hpc.ProductID IS NOT NULL
ORDER BY
     cus.CustomerID,
     CASE WHEN
     (
          cus.CustomerID = @CustomerID
          AND ord.CustomerOrderID = @CustomerOrderID
     )
          THEN 0
          ELSE 1
     END,
     ord.CustomerOrderID DESC,
     cus.LastName ASC;

DROP TABLE #TmpOrder;
DROP TABLE #HistPriceCost;
```

Now that you have changed the code, you need to get a new execution plan to confirm that these changes worked as you intended. Figure 8-2 shows that same general area of the execution plan, but this is what it looks like after the T-SQL code change.

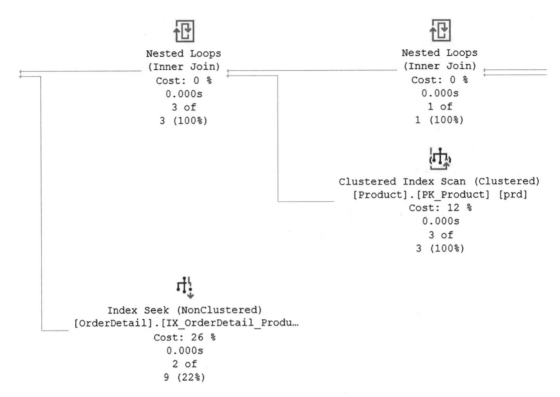

Figure 8-2. *Partial execution plan for Listing 8-4*

There are a couple of changes that happened. Looking at the execution plan overall, you can see that all the lines are much thinner than they were before. While the order of some steps has changed, the largest difference is related to the non-clustered index. In Figure 8-1, SQL Server was performing an index scan on this index. Now that you have created an index that is sorted differently, SQL Server is using an index seek on this same non-clustered index. Not all attempts to optimize your T-SQL code are this simple. However, it is possible for you to make dramatic improvements in your T-SQL code when you understand how your data is stored and how the indexes on your tables reference that data.

Optimizing Duration

My goal when working with SQL Server is to have the queries executing T-SQL code run as quickly as possible. I tend to focus on logical reads because I want to minimize the number of data pages going into the cache that are not needed by the query that is being executed. However, there are other issues that can happen in SQL Server that can have negative effects downstream.

Prior to SQL Server 2019, one of the most common reasons for slow queries was parameter sniffing. The adaptive join in SQL Server 2019 has helped minimize issues associated with parameter sniffing. If an execution plan has an adaptive join, SQL Server will determine at execution time whether to use a merge join or a nested loop. The flexibility of the adaptive join allows the execution of T-SQL code to execute one way if there is a small set of data and use a different physical join if there is a larger set of data. This will cause the execution of the query to perform well regardless of the data being retrieved.

Working to find the queries that have the slowest durations can be challenging especially if you are trying to find real-time data regarding query performance. Thankfully, SQL Server does keep track of query performance for T-SQL code that exists in the query plan cache. You can use the same DMV from the previous section, `sys.dm_exec_query_stats`, but instead of looking for records with the highest total logical reads or average logical reads, you want to look at worker time. You can either start with total worker time or average worker time. The time of day your queries are running may help you decide which to focus on first. If one of the queries with the highest worker time is running during the most active time for your business, I would address that query first. However, if you have T-SQL code with the highest average worker time running frequently throughout the busy time of your day, you may see more benefit by working on this code first. Either way, you want to look up the query plan in `sys.dm_exec_sql_text` that matches the query hash from `sys.dm_exec_query_stats` to find the associated query text.

One of the challenges with SQL Server is that the same solution does not always work for every situation. I have come across some queries where breaking the data up into smaller segments will improve performance. There are other times where it may be more efficient to combine several steps into a single T-SQL statement. The query in Listing 8-5 shows a series of T-SQL statements.

Listing 8-5. Original Query for Order Information for All Customers

```
DECLARE @CustomerID       INT = NULL;
DECLARE @CustomerOrderID  INT = NULL;
DECLARE @ProductID        INT = NULL;

-- Get all orders for a specific customer and product
SELECT cus.CustomerID,
    cus.FirstName,
```

```
        cus.LastName,
        ord.CustomerOrderID,
        prd.ProductID
INTO #TmpOrder
FROM dbo.Customer cus
        INNER JOIN dbo.CustomerOrder ord
        ON cus.CustomerID = ord.CustomerID
        INNER JOIN dbo.OrderDetail dtl
        ON ord.CustomerOrderID = dtl.CustomerOrderID
        INNER JOIN dbo.Product prd
        ON dtl.ProductID = prd.ProductID
WHERE prd.IsActive = 1
        AND EXISTS
          (
                SELECT *
                FROM dbo.ProductPriceHistory hist
                WHERE prd.ProductID = hist.ProductID
                GROUP BY hist.ProductID
                HAVING COUNT(*) > 3
        );

SELECT ord.CustomerID,
        tor.FirstName,
        tor.LastName,
        ord.CustomerOrderID,
        ord.OrderNumber,
        prd.ProductName,
        dtl.QuantitySold,
        dtl.ProductPrice
FROM #TmpOrder tor
        INNER JOIN dbo.CustomerOrder ord
        ON tor.CustomerOrderID = ord.CustomerOrderID
        INNER JOIN dbo.OrderDetail dtl
        ON tor.CustomerOrderID = dtl.CustomerOrderID
                AND tor.ProductID = dtl.ProductID
```

```
        INNER JOIN dbo.Product prd
        ON tor.ProductID = prd.ProductID
WHERE (tor.CustomerID = @CustomerID OR @CustomerID IS NULL)
        AND (ord.CustomerOrderID = @CustomerOrderID OR @CustomerOrderID
        IS NULL)
        AND (dtl.ProductID = @ProductID OR @ProductID IS NULL)
ORDER BY
        ord.CustomerID,
        CASE WHEN
        (
            ord.CustomerID = @CustomerID
            AND ord.CustomerOrderID = @CustomerOrderID
        )
            THEN 0
            ELSE 1
        END,
        ord.CustomerOrderID DESC,
        tor.LastName ASC;

DROP TABLE #TmpOrder;
```

Overall, the goal of Listing 8-5 is to return the customer and order information for any combination of customers, orders, and products. The cost percentage indicates the percent of time the SQL Server Engine expects to spend on that step in the execution plan. When reviewing the execution plan, you want to investigate the specific part of the execution plan with the highest cost percentage, as shown in Figure 8-3.

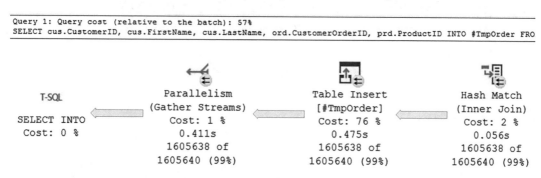

Figure 8-3. Partial execution plan for Listing 8-5

The insert into the temporary table is the most significant part of the first T-SQL statement. The same statement also took up a higher percentage of the overall execution plan. Therefore, the highest cost associated with this query is inserting data into the temporary table. You can rewrite this query to the one shown in Listing 8-6.

Listing 8-6. Optimized Query for Order Information for All Customers

```
DECLARE @CustomerID        INT = NULL;
DECLARE @CustomerOrderID   INT = NULL;
DECLARE @ProductID         INT = NULL;

SELECT cus.CustomerID,
       cus.FirstName,
       cus.LastName,
       ord.CustomerOrderID,
       ord.OrderNumber,
       prd.ProductName,
       dtl.QuantitySold,
       dtl.ProductPrice
FROM dbo.Customer cus
       INNER JOIN dbo.CustomerOrder ord
       ON cus.CustomerID = ord.CustomerID
       INNER JOIN dbo.OrderDetail dtl
       ON ord.CustomerOrderID = dtl.CustomerOrderID
       INNER JOIN dbo.Product prd
       ON dtl.ProductID = prd.ProductID
WHERE (cus.CustomerID = @CustomerID OR @CustomerID IS NULL)
       AND (ord.CustomerOrderID = @CustomerOrderID OR @CustomerOrderID
       IS NULL)
       AND (dtl.ProductID = @ProductID OR @ProductID IS NULL)
       AND prd.IsActive = 1
       AND EXISTS
```

```
        (
            SELECT *
            FROM dbo.ProductPriceHistory hist
            WHERE prd.ProductID = hist.ProductID
            GROUP BY hist.ProductID
            HAVING COUNT(*) > 3
        )
ORDER BY
        cus.CustomerID,
        CASE WHEN
        (
            cus.CustomerID = @CustomerID
            AND ord.CustomerOrderID = @CustomerOrderID
        )
            THEN 0
            ELSE 1
        END,
        ord.CustomerOrderID DESC,
        cus.LastName ASC;
```

This T-SQL statement has all the code required to generate the same output as the one from Listing 8-5. Depending on the indexes that exist on your tables and the join criteria, sometimes you will see better performance when selecting all your data in one query. Other times you may optimize your queries by getting subsets of data and combining them into one query. A portion of the execution plan for Listing 8-6 can be seen in Figure 8-4.

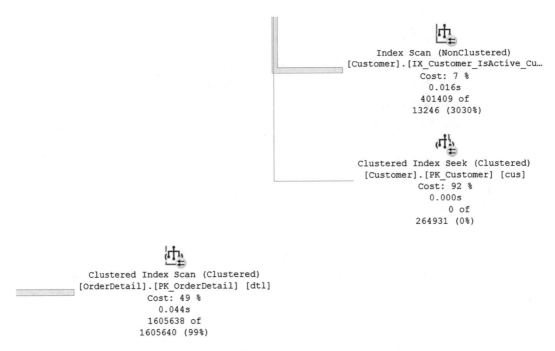

Figure 8-4. *Partial execution plan for Listing 8-6*

As shown in Figure 8-4, the step taking up the largest percentage of the execution plan has changed. Based on the actual execution plan, the largest percentage is spent performing a clustered index seek on the primary key of the Customer table. As this is a seek relating to the primary key of the table, it seems unlikely that there is a better alternative for performance tuning this query.

Optimizing Indexes

There are other factors that can contribute to slowness of running queries. In many scenarios, the best way to optimize these queries involves using indexes. You want to check execution plans for key lookups. These key lookups indicate that SQL Server is having to go from the non-clustered index to the clustered index to find additional fields that are needed as part of the query. In some cases, you may be able to change the values returned or the join conditions of your query to resolve the key lookups. Otherwise, you will need to see if the indexes can be changed in order to improve performance.

Creating and maintaining indexes is a topic that could take up a book by itself, but there are some things you can do when working with indexes. If you are at a point where you think you may need to consider adding indexes, you first want to be aware of what indexes currently exist on the tables in question. While it is outside the scope of this book, you want to determine if there are indexes that are no longer in use and can be dropped. Of the indexes that are remaining, you want to evaluate these carefully. One of these indexes may be able to be modified to allow it to continue to be effective for other T-SQL code but also to optimize the current query. You can create or modify an index so that additional columns are stored with the index. However, the index is not sorted by these columns. These columns can be referred to as a covering column. If a column is needed for a join or a WHERE clause, I would consider adding it to the index. Before deciding to add the column to the index, make sure you are familiar with how SQL Server uses indexes to search for data. The approach with some indexes involves adding a column as an included column on the index. This will allow SQL Server to return the column results without a key lookup, but it will not affect how SQL Server uses the index to retrieve data records.

Optimizing the duration of your T-SQL code can yield many benefits. One is improved performance of your applications. In some cases, you may be able to improve the duration of your queries by rewriting the code in a way that is more efficient. In other situations, you may want to consider if there are ways the code can be written differently to make better use of the existing indexes. Another option is to modify existing indexes or create new ones. If you choose to modify indexes, use caution as sometimes indexes can exist that cause more harm than they help. Regularly review the duration of your T-SQL code to see if you can find any queries that need performance tuning.

Automatic Database Tuning

In the previous sections, I discussed what you can do to optimize your T-SQL code regarding logical reads and duration. Over the past several releases of SQL Server, there have been many changes that can either help you optimize SQL Server or optimize your queries automatically. In some cases, this involves recording information about the performance of your queries. At other times this can be either SQL Server managing your execution plans or your indexes. While the topics covered in this section are related to optimization that SQL Server can perform for you, it is helpful to understand these concepts so that you have a better idea as to how SQL Server will handle your T-SQL code.

Automatic Plan Correction

Building on top of the functionality introduced in SQL Server 2016 with Query Store is a new feature introduced in SQL Server 2017. The next step was to see if SQL Server could use the access to historical information about execution plans, execution statistics, and wait statistics for those query executions to its benefit. Built into Query Store, this functionality can be configured so that no human intervention is required. In order to make that happen, this new functionality also has to include a way to verify the results.

Now that SQL Server can look at the query store, it can determine systematically if a new execution plan performs better or worse than the prior execution plan. This new functionality is referred to as Automatic Plan Correction. This feature is not enabled by default. Before it can be enabled, Query Store needs to be enabled, as shown in Listing 8-6. Once Query Store has been enabled, you can run the code shown in Listing 8-7 to enable Automatic Plan Correction.

Listing 8-7. Query to Enable Automatic Plan Correction

```
ALTER DATABASE Menu
SET AUTOMATIC_TUNING (FORCE_LAST_GOOD_PLAN = ON);
```

Once Automatic Plan Correction has been enabled, SQL Server can compare the new and previous execution plans to determine if the comparison meets the criteria where SQL Server can force the prior execution plan. In order to make sure that SQL Server does not spend extra effort microtuning performance, the threshold is set at a benefit of decreasing the CPU cost by 10 seconds or more. The other option is if the number of errors in the execution is less than the previous version. If the new execution plan cost more than 10 extra seconds on the CPU, SQL Server can force the previous plan automatically. Similarly, if the new execution plan has more errors than the previous plan, SQL Server can force the previous execution plan.

After SQL Server forces an execution plan automatically, it continues to monitor performance to confirm that the newly forced execution plan is working as expected. If SQL Server determines that the forced execution plan is no longer providing the performance benefit expected, it can undo forcing the execution plan. Automatic Plan Correction does not alter your T-SQL code; this feature only helps manage which execution plan is currently being used for your T-SQL code.

If you prefer to manually manage your execution plans, you can do so. Make sure that you do not run the T-SQL code shown in Listing 7-8. If you choose to manually plan choice correction, you need to regularly monitor which queries need to have plans forced. You also need to manually undo forcing query execution plans over time as the shape of your data and the associated statistics may change over time. Query Store can be used to monitor execution plans over time starting in SQL Server 2016. With SQL Server 2017, there is also the option of using the DMV `sys.dm_tuning_recommendations` to find queries that can benefit from forcing an execution plan.

While automatic or manual plan correction is outside the scope of T-SQL, it is helpful to know what SQL Server can do with your T-SQL queries. I still suggest that you design your T-SQL to run efficiently for a variety of scenarios, but it is nice to know that when issues like parameter sniffing are unavoidable, there are other options within SQL Server to help your overall query performance.

Automatic Index Management

In addition to allowing SQL Server to manage your execution plans and choose the best available plan, you also have the option of allowing SQL Server to systematically monitor and manage your indexes. This feature is currently only available in Azure SQL Database. Enabling Automatic Index Management allows SQL Server to create new indexes that it deems necessary and to also identify indexes that are unused or that seem to be like other indexes that have been created.

Like Automatic Plan Correction, SQL Server will monitor the performance of new indexes. If they are deemed to be less efficient, SQL Server will remove those indexes. The same process will be used if SQL Server modifies or drops indexes. It will still be possible to manually manage your indexes while using Azure SQL Database. However, allowing Azure SQL Database to promptly find and resolve indexing issues may save you money as less resources may be required to perform the same tasks.

Intelligent Query Processing

Along with the ability for SQL Server to automatically manage execution plans and indexes, there are other new features that can help automatically optimize T-SQL code performance. As discussed in Chapter 6, memory is a key resource used by SQL Server. When using memory with SQL Server, you want to be sure that memory is being used as efficiently as possible. Working with data sets is also critical to working with SQL Server. If SQL Server can convert a collection of rows into a batch and then perform any necessary actions, this will help optimize the query. The shape of the data is not always consistent in a data table. In those scenarios, it may be helpful to have an execution plan that is flexible depending on the types of data pulled back. These features can help improve the efficiency of the T-SQL code that is being executed.

Memory Grant Feedback

When executing a query, SQL Server will try to estimate the amount of memory required for that transaction. The amount of memory allocated to a query based on the estimate is referred to as a memory grant. While it is ideal that SQL Server estimate the memory correctly, there are times when the amount of memory estimated does not match the amount of memory used. Memory Grant Feedback first became available in SQL Server 2017. The addition of Memory Grant Feedback allows SQL Server to review previous memory usage for the previous execution of query and adjust the memory estimates if they are significantly under or over estimated. This allows SQL Server to minimize potential performance issues due to incorrectly estimated memory.

In order to make sure that memory grants are managed correctly, thresholds are defined for the variance between the memory grant and the actual memory usage. If the memory used is less than 1 MB, no additional analysis is required. If the memory grant is twice the amount of memory used, then the memory grant for the specific query can be recalculated. Similarly, the memory grant can be recalculated if the memory needed to execute the query is more than the memory grant.

Batch Mode on Rowstore

Having memory grants for batch mode operations is a necessary foundation for the next stage in the development of batch mode operations. Batch mode operations are where SQL Server can perform an action on a group of records all at once instead of one record at a time. When batch mode was originally introduced in SQL Server 2012, it was only available for columnstore indexes. Starting with SQL Server 2019, batch mode operations were also allowed to be used for a collection of rows. In this case, a collection of rows is also called a rowstore. Memory grants for batch mode operations allowing batch mode operations for heaps and indexes are the foundation for an additional type of query optimization.

Adaptive Joins

SQL Server uses statistics to help estimate the best plan. However, data is not always evenly distributed in a table. The plan it picks is often the best plan for some column values. The problem comes when it is poor for other column values. The chance of this happening has decreased in SQL Server 2019 due to new functionality that allows SQL Server to choose between the physical join operator of a nested loop and a hash match depending on the current execution of the query. This new functionality is called an adaptive join.

Adaptive joins were originally introduced in SQL Server 2017. However, adaptive joins can only be used as part of a batch mode operation. In SQL Server 2017, batch mode operations were only supported for columnstore indexes. Now that batch mode operations are also supported for heaps and B-tree indexes, adaptive joins can also be used on these database objects. Executing the query from Listing 8-6 generates an execution plan that contains an adaptive join. When you see the execution plan, you will see a physical operator for an adaptive join. On the graphical execution plan, you cannot tell what type of operator is used behind the scenes. However, if you mouse over the adaptive join in the execution plan, you will see a list of properties like the one shown in Figure 8-5.

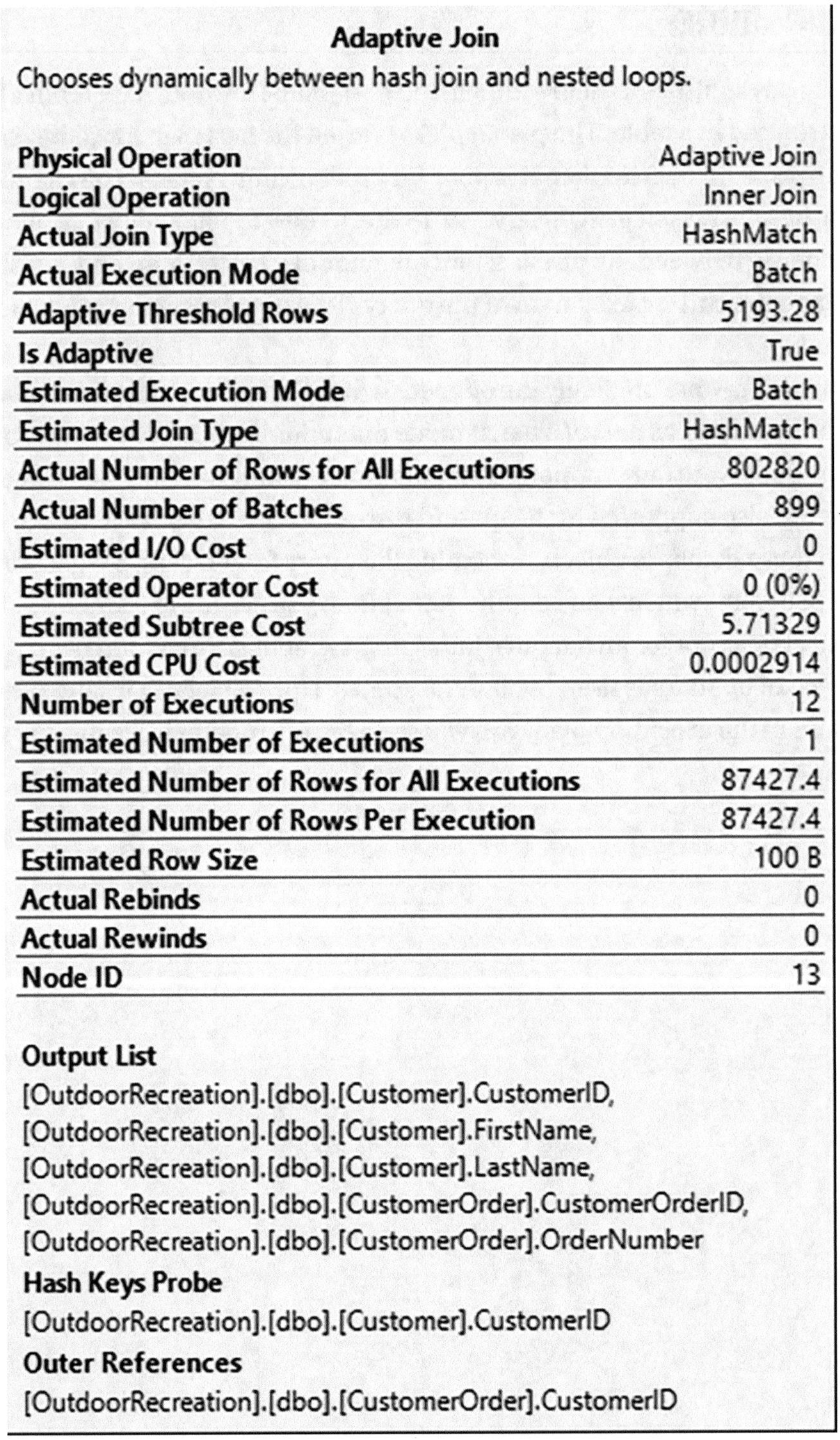

Adaptive Join

Chooses dynamically between hash join and nested loops.

Physical Operation	Adaptive Join
Logical Operation	Inner Join
Actual Join Type	HashMatch
Actual Execution Mode	Batch
Adaptive Threshold Rows	5193.28
Is Adaptive	True
Estimated Execution Mode	Batch
Estimated Join Type	HashMatch
Actual Number of Rows for All Executions	802820
Actual Number of Batches	899
Estimated I/O Cost	0
Estimated Operator Cost	0 (0%)
Estimated Subtree Cost	5.71329
Estimated CPU Cost	0.0002914
Number of Executions	12
Estimated Number of Executions	1
Estimated Number of Rows for All Executions	87427.4
Estimated Number of Rows Per Execution	87427.4
Estimated Row Size	100 B
Actual Rebinds	0
Actual Rewinds	0
Node ID	13

Output List
[OutdoorRecreation].[dbo].[Customer].CustomerID,
[OutdoorRecreation].[dbo].[Customer].FirstName,
[OutdoorRecreation].[dbo].[Customer].LastName,
[OutdoorRecreation].[dbo].[CustomerOrder].CustomerOrderID,
[OutdoorRecreation].[dbo].[CustomerOrder].OrderNumber
Hash Keys Probe
[OutdoorRecreation].[dbo].[Customer].CustomerID
Outer References
[OutdoorRecreation].[dbo].[CustomerOrder].CustomerID

Figure 8-5. *Adaptive join properties from Listing 8-6*

The original query from Listing 8-6 was to return information about customers, orders, and products based on parameters for all three. In Figure 8-5, you can see that the adaptive join type listed under the properties is the hash match. Figure 8-6 shows a partial screenshot from the live query statistics for the execution of Listing 8-6.

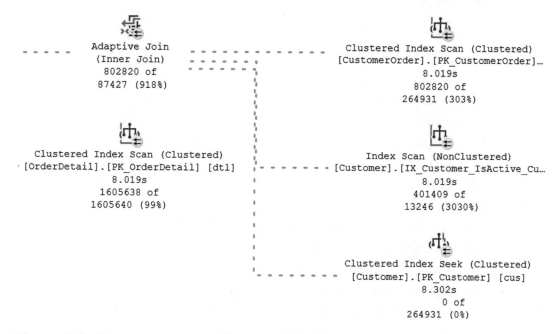

Figure 8-6. Live query statistics from Listing 8-6

You can see the total number of records processed by each step as the time spent on some of the steps. Looking at the live query statistics, you can see the percentage of records returned vs. the estimate. Figure 8-6 shows the live query statistics in progress. In this case, some records like the clustered index scan on the table `CustomerOrder` or the index scan on the table `OrderDetail` appear to be estimated correctly. It is also possible that other operators may not be estimated correctly. While these variances may cause performance issues, the reason I am pointing these values out is to compare them to the query execution after you change the value passed to the `@CustomerID`, `@CustomerOrderID`, and `@ProductID` variables.

If you limit the same query to one customer, order, and product, you may write T-SQL like what is shown in Listing 8-8.

Listing 8-8. Query for Recipe Information for a Specific Recipe

```
DECLARE @CustomerID        INT = 1;
DECLARE @CustomerOrderID   INT = 401508;
DECLARE @ProductID         INT = 1;

SELECT cus.CustomerID,
      cus.FirstName,
      cus.LastName,
      ord.CustomerOrderID,
      ord.OrderNumber,
      prd.ProductName,
      dtl.QuantitySold,
      dtl.ProductPrice
FROM dbo.Customer cus
      INNER JOIN dbo.CustomerOrder ord
      ON cus.CustomerID = ord.CustomerID
      INNER JOIN dbo.OrderDetail dtl
      ON ord.CustomerOrderID = dtl.CustomerOrderID
      INNER JOIN dbo.Product prd
      ON dtl.ProductID = prd.ProductID
WHERE (cus.CustomerID = @CustomerID OR @CustomerID IS NULL)
      AND (ord.CustomerOrderID = @CustomerOrderID OR @CustomerOrderID
      IS NULL)
      AND (dtl.ProductID = @ProductID OR @ProductID IS NULL)
        AND prd.IsActive = 1
        AND EXISTS
        (
            SELECT *
            FROM dbo.ProductPriceHistory hist
            WHERE prd.ProductID = hist.ProductID
            GROUP BY hist.ProductID
            HAVING COUNT(*) > 3
        )
```

```
ORDER BY
    cus.CustomerID,
    CASE WHEN
    (
        cus.CustomerID = @CustomerID
        AND ord.CustomerOrderID = @CustomerOrderID
    )
        THEN 0
        ELSE 1
    END,
    ord.CustomerOrderID DESC,
    cus.LastName ASC;
```

The differences between Listing 8-6 and Listing 8-8 are the first three lines. In Listing 8-6, the @CustomerID, @CustomerOrderID, and @ProductID is set to -1 so that all recipes are returned. In Listing 8-8, the @CustomerID, @CustomerOrderID, and @ ProductID are each set to a specific value. You can execute this query and look at the execution plan to see if SQL Server will handle this query execution differently now that there may be only one recipe affected. In Figure 8-7, you can see the properties for the adaptive join when executing Listing 8-8.

Adaptive Join

Chooses dynamically between hash join and nested loops.

Physical Operation	Adaptive Join
Logical Operation	Inner Join
Actual Join Type	NestedLoops
Actual Execution Mode	Row
Adaptive Threshold Rows	5193.28
Is Adaptive	True
Estimated Execution Mode	Batch
Estimated Join Type	HashMatch
Actual Number of Rows for All Executions	1
Actual Number of Batches	1
Estimated I/O Cost	0
Estimated Operator Cost	0 (0%)
Estimated Subtree Cost	5.71329
Estimated CPU Cost	0.0002914
Number of Executions	12
Estimated Number of Executions	1
Estimated Number of Rows for All Executions	87427.4
Estimated Number of Rows Per Execution	87427.4
Estimated Row Size	100 B
Actual Rebinds	0
Actual Rewinds	0
Node ID	13

Output List

[OutdoorRecreation].[dbo].[Customer].CustomerID,
[OutdoorRecreation].[dbo].[Customer].FirstName,
[OutdoorRecreation].[dbo].[Customer].LastName,
[OutdoorRecreation].[dbo].[CustomerOrder].CustomerOrderID,
[OutdoorRecreation].[dbo].[CustomerOrder].OrderNumber

Hash Keys Probe

[OutdoorRecreation].[dbo].[Customer].CustomerID

Outer References

[OutdoorRecreation].[dbo].[CustomerOrder].CustomerID

Figure 8-7. *Adaptive join properties from Listing 8-8*

The actual join type shown in Figure 8-7 is a nested loop. The difference between the adaptive join types in Figures 8-5 and 8-7 shows how the adaptive join can help optimize queries that previously were affected by parameter sniffing. The details of the live query statistics from Listing 8-8 are shown in Figure 8-8.

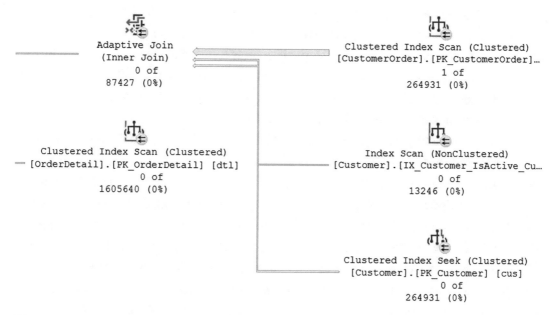

Figure 8-8. *Live query statistics from Listing 8-8*

In Figure 8-8, the same physical operators are present as in Figure 8-6. However, the actual number of rows processed vs. the estimated number of rows is significantly different. In the case of Figure 8-8, almost all the steps are severely overestimated. However, the query from Listing 8-8 will still benefit from the performance due to the use of the adaptive join. While Adaptive Joins can be beneficial when a query could benefit from using either a Hash Join or Nested Loop Join depending on the parameters provided, there are other queries where unequal data distribution within the table may affect query performance. SQL Server 2022 has a new feature for these types of scenarios called Parameter Sensitive Plan (PSP) optimization. When SQL Server attempts to create an execution plan, it will evaluate the tables associated with parameters to determine if there are uneven distributions. If SQL Server finds any, PSP allows SQL Server to create up to three execution plans to accommodate the different data distributions. For instance, if you executed the stored procedure dbo.GetCustomerAndOrderNumberByProductID for ProductID 1, the data distribution is different than if the stores procedure is executed for ProductID 4. With PSP, SQL Server can save an execution plan in the plan cache which is different for ProductID 1 than ProductID 4. One way to investigate these different execution plans is to use Query Store as discussed earlier in this chapter.

There are many ways that you can work toward optimizing for T-SQL code. Unless you are testing a new query, often the first step is to identify what T-SQL code needs to be optimized. After determining what query needs optimization, you may want to analyze execution plans to help determine if there is a step that stands out as needing optimization. You may also want to analyze information associated with the query such as average logical reads or average execution time. Combining this information may help you identify what can be tuned to improve performance.

In addition, there are features in SQL Server that can help automatically make your T-SQL code perform better. This includes allowing SQL Server to analyze your new execution plans and confirm that they are performing better than the previous execution plan. If the previous execution plan is expected to perform better, SQL Server can make sure that plan is automatically selected. If you are using Azure SQL Database, you have a similar option available when it comes to managing indexes. The use of adaptive joins allows SQL Server to make your execution plans more flexible. When an adaptive join is part of an execution plan, SQL Server can decide the correct physical operator to use depending on the values passed for that specific query execution. Whether you are manually optimizing your T-SQL code or letting SQL Server determine how to improve query execution, you have several tools available that should make your T-SQL code perform better.

CHAPTER 9

Coding Standards

One of the advantages of standardizing a codebase is that it will increase our ability to read and understand that code no matter the author. You can also think of standardization to get everyone to follow the rules not only in terms of formatting but also in what elements of the code are expected or are not allowed for your organization. Another benefit of standardization when naming database objects is that it can help increase the speed with which you and your team can quickly find a specific part of T-SQL code that you are trying to debug.

In this chapter, I will discuss various advantages to implementing coding standards. I will also go over what types of factors you should consider when defining standards. When developing them, you also want to determine how to implement those coding standards. I will cover the basic process needed to institute these standards.

Why Use Coding Standards

There are many different things you can do to improve your code quality. When improving your code quality, you want to think about your end goal. I want my T-SQL code to run efficiently, be able to be debugged quickly, and be easy to understand. This is often the result of creating consistency in how you design and write your T-SQL code. One option is to implement coding standards.

Oftentimes, there are specific T-SQL practices that you know you want people to follow. Some of these behaviors are easily agreed upon and most people use them by default. However, there can be other T-SQL best practices that you know are not common in general or in your organization. You want to create a set of guidelines that allows everyone to easily know what they should be doing.

There are also certain things that you know you do not want to see in T-SQL code no matter the reason. Once again, some of these topics are not common, but others may also be pervasive. Either way, you want to clearly define this all as part of your coding

E. Noble, *Pro T-SQL 2022*, https://doi.org/10.1007/978-1-4842-9256-3_9

standards. Using coding standards can minimize the back and forth regarding what types of T-SQL code are allowed or preferable vs. other code.

You can use coding standards to set boundaries for what is and is not allowed. I have come across times where software engineers or database developers want to use specific T-SQL because it is easier to read and write. However, there are times where the T-SQL code that makes sense easily to a human does not perform as well with SQL Server. While I want those same individuals to be able to come to me to ask questions about the current process, there are times where I have too many higher priority requests, and I do not have time to address their concerns.

It's nice to have these guidelines agreed on before their absence leads to conflict. This also should provide some reassurance that each topic has been discussed and multiple parties have come to the same conclusion that certain T-SQL code is either performing well for many scenarios or could be at a high risk to cause performance issues.

I know when I come into work my day is already full. Not only from the things I know I need to do but from the last-minute requests and one-off questions. The real goal of implementing coding standards is to make your life easier. This includes being able to rest easy knowing that quality T-SQL code is in your database. Ideally, you should be able to spend that time working on future database design enhancements or getting rid of technical debt.

Another factor affecting our lives is decision fatigue. This is the concept where a person gets worn down having to make decision after decision throughout the day. With the advent of technology, we experience that kind of fatigue every day. When it comes to making decisions regarding T-SQL coding, this type of decision fatigue can be even more overwhelming. There are many ways to accomplish the same thing in SQL Server. One of the other advantages to implementing T-SQL coding standards is that it can minimize the decisions a database developer needs to make when writing new code.

When you first implement coding standards, make sure to get buy-in from all parties. In many cases, you will not be able to have a unanimous decision. If you can, get a majority vote for any change you would like included in the coding standards. Another method is to make sure every individual agrees on the final standard before those standards are approved and implemented.

One of the main challenges with T-SQL in the workplace is that many of the people who are responsible for writing T-SQL are not database experts. This can cause frustration, and it can also contribute to poorly performing queries. One of the nicest and hardest aspects about T-SQL is how easy it is to write your first query. SQL is an abbreviation for Structured Query Language, and that is how simple queries are written. You can read them almost like a sentence.

However, this can give the false impression that what is happening with SQL Server behind the scenes is also simple. Most of us work in a high-stress, fast-paced environment. This often means we do not have time to stop and explain every decision we make. This can include why certain T-SQL code should not be used. This is where the strength of T-SQL coding standards really shines. It allows you to have the conversation once to set up the ground rules. After those rules or standards are in place, T-SQL developers and engineers can write their code in any way they want if it meets the predefined standards.

I have heard software developers say that having defined coding standards when writing applications can be very helpful. It allows them to easily jump into any code, whether they wrote it or not, and immediately feel comfortable. This is because while they may know they have never looked at this set of code, their brain already sees similarities with other code they have written. It gets rid of the instantaneous response that the code they are looking at is not theirs. The benefit is that they can immediately jump into reviewing the code or making the necessary changes.

Now that you have determined that you want to define coding standards, the next step is to implement these coding standards. This is where things can get tricky. It will be tempting to want every stored procedure that goes through script review to adhere to these standards. However, some of the code you will see is already out in Production. I have found there are times, especially when others are under strict deadlines, that it is especially frustrating when a stored procedure is rejected merely because it does not follow coding standards.

A possible compromise is to give a conditional approval and request that a new user story be created so that the T-SQL code can be updated to fit the new coding standards. This gives the developer reassurance that they can meet the deadlines of their current sprint, and it also lets you know that this T-SQL code should be corrected in a future release to meet coding standards.

An easy way to handle these new user stories is to add them to the following sprint. This allows them to get cleaned up while you still remember what needs to be changed. This also makes sure that the others performing script reviews know that the effort to get all T-SQL code compliant with the coding standards is important to all parties.

What to Include in Coding Standards

Ideally, coming up with coding standards will provide you with a framework that minimizes your overall challenges with reviewing and deploying T-SQL code. You want coding standards to cover how T-SQL code should look, how T-SQL code should function, how T-SQL code should perform, and how T-SQL code should be understood.

Some of the basics of coding standards have already been discussed in Chapter 4. This includes formatting T-SQL code by creating standards as to how the T-SQL is written. You will also want standards indicating how to name T-SQL database objects. It is also useful to have standards indicating how T-SQL code should be commented.

T-SQL Design

You can also define database design through coding standards. This can include how database objects should be organized including schemas. Coding standards can also indicate how data should be stored in the database. You can indicate what types of columns should be included in primary keys. It is also possible to indicate how tables should be clustered or when it is best to use clustered or non-clustered indexes.

ANSI STANDARD

One consideration is whether to keep your T-SQL code in compliance with ANSI standards. While SQL Server has some functionality that can be used, not all of this functionality is compliant with ANSI standards. In many cases, the SQL Server-specific commands and functions can be rewritten using ANSI standard code. Making sure you write your T-SQL code as ANSI standard allows you to easily move to another relational database management system that is also ANSI standard-compliant.

Normal Form

While covering T-SQL coding standards, you may also want to define design elements. This includes what and how data should be grouped together in tables and what information should be in those tables. There are various levels of normal forms, and you can use your T-SQL coding standards to indicate what those are. There are various types of database normalization that are commonly discussed. These include first normal form (1NF), second normal form (2NF), third normal form (3NF), and fourth normal form (4NF).

Each type of normal form builds on the one before it. The lowest-level normal form is the first normal form. This includes requiring that each table has a primary key and that each field or column only holds a single value.

Table Size

When creating tables, it is tempting to want to put all columns related to a specific item into the same table. This can cause tables to have many, many columns. One of the challenges of having a table with a significant number of columns is how the data is stored. This can ultimately lead to performance issues. It is possible to design your tables to prevent this kind of issue by analyzing the types of information you are storing and creating tables made up of subgroups of information. For instance, I may want to record everything about a product in the same table including all information about the manufacturer, product details, and sales price. However, it would be better to create one table for vendor information and one table for product information. This is in line with following best practices for database normalization. In addition, properly designed tables make the overall database design more adaptable as applications change over time.

Name Value Pair

When working with SQL Server, the goal is to think about set-based actions. Keeping this is mind, you want to be careful designing tables. You want to make sure that you minimize the number of columns to keep the table width small. You want to consider what kinds of columns are valuable. If you are using one column to define the value type and another column to define the actual value, you have designed a name-value pair relationship.

This type of design may be easier to understand and create simpler tables, but this design does not embrace the benefits of using SQL Server. When using name-value pairs, it becomes increasingly difficult to use indexes. Therefore, SQL Server need to look through more data to pull back the necessary values.

Primary Key

When creating and designing tables, think about what type of data will be stored. This not only has to do with how the data is ordered but also the table's relationship to other tables. In many cases, it is ideal to require primary keys as part of your coding standards. While a primary key is not required in all scenarios, it should help clarify what fields are used to define relationships to other tables.

Foreign Key

SQL Server is a relational database management system, and one of the main benefits of SQL Server is the relationships between tables. However, you need to specify the relationships between tables so that SQL Server can ensure that valid data is saved across the tables. When this happens, SQL Server checks the relationship between the table storing the values and the referencing table. SQL Server does this using a foreign key. Because SQL Server knows that it can trust the relationship, it can often filter out data more efficiently and find data faster. Therefore, it may be a good idea to specify that foreign key relationships are part of your T-SQL coding standards.

Non-Clustered Index

I have found that non-clustered indexes are a more highly debated topic than I would have ever expected. One of the challenges of using non-clustered indexes is that there is a cost associated with recording the data as part of the index or updating the index as the values change. However, SQL Server uses indexes to quickly find the data referenced by various queries. Make sure that the benefit of using non-clustered indexes outweighs the cost.

One of the ways that you can do this is to make sure that you properly define your indexes. Due to the cost associated with maintaining indexes, you want to make certain that any index you create is regularly being used by the available queries. You may also want to define how to determine which columns should be part of the index and which columns should be pulled back as part of the index.

Constraint Definition

Your tables can have one or more columns. Each of these columns holds some type of information. When it comes to that information, you may know that only certain values can be stored in that column. Using foreign keys can keep the data integrity in some situations, but there are other times when it may not make sense to use a foreign key. In these cases, you can specify a constraint on the record. The constraint can limit what type of information can be stored in those columns.

However, forcing SQL Server to manage those constraints puts an extra load on SQL Server. So, you may want to consider minimizing the use of constraints to limit what type of data can be stored in the database and rely on the application code to provide good data. Another use of constraints is to specify default values for certain fields. This can happen for columns where you know the most likely value that will exist when a record is created. For instance, you may want to specify a default value of True for an `IsActive` column as most records created will be active at the time they are created. Once again, this can be handled by the application, but you may also decide to enforce this as part of your T-SQL coding standards.

It is important to consider T-SQL coding standards that encourage good design practices. This includes determining how closely you will adhere to ANSI standards. There are other topics to include such as choosing the minimum normal form allowed as part of your database design. This decision may affect other aspects of your T-SQL design including primary keys, foreign keys, and non-clustered indexes. You may also consider how you want to handle constraints. Once you have determined the T-SQL coding standards you want to enforce for good T-SQL design practices, you may want to decide what coding standards are needed with regard to the overall performance of T-SQL.

T-SQL Performance

After determining the T-SQL coding standards related to database design and implementation, you want to determine what standards you need to help minimize and address any performance issues that may come up. This includes creating T-SQL coding standards that help make sure SQL Server does not get bogged down with unnecessary information. You also want to consider how T-SQL code needs to be written to minimize performance overhead.

Selecting Necessary Data

SQL Server can store quite a bit of data, and SQL Server can also retrieve large quantities of data. There are many scenarios where applications are retrieving data. When first learning about a database and the associated tables, it is often tempting to select all the columns in a table. While this is the easiest method to return data, it is not usually ideal.

First is the syntax used to select all rows by using the asterisks. The issue with this method is if the columns in the underlying object change, the code may not work as expected. Even worse, the code may not provide an error and users will not know they are getting bad data.

The second issue that can happen is more common. When you pull back all columns, there is considerably more work put on SQL Server. Not only must SQL Server return everything for all rows of data returned, but it is likely that SQL Server will not be able to use any indexes to return this data. This is the equivalent to reading this entire book each time you want to study one specific section. You would learn what you needed, but you would also spend a considerable amount of time reading topics that you were mostly likely going to disregard since they were not relevant for your needs at that time.

Sargeable

You want SQL Server to be able to easily search the database to find the information you are trying to access. There are some ways that you can write T-SQL that can let SQL Server take advantage of indexes and quickly find the necessary data. However, there are other methods of writing T-SQL that can give the same results but may take longer and require SQL Server to look through more data. The difference between these two scenarios is that the first scenario refers to making sure your T-SQL is sargeable, whereas the second option is when the T-SQL is not sargeable. This usually happens in the WHERE clause of the T-SQL statement. Listing 9-1 shows a query to find all customers that were created in October 2022.

Listing 9-1. Query Using Non-Sargeable Criteria

```
SELECT FirstName, LastName, Country
FROM dbo.Customer
WHERE DATEPART(MM, DateCreated) = 10
    AND DATEPART(YY, DateCreated) = 2022;
```

You can see the use of the DATEPART function on the date created to determine both the month and the year each record was created. In order for SQL Server to determine which records are in October 2022, it will need to check every record in the table. You can see this is true in the execution plan in Figure 9-1 with the index scan.

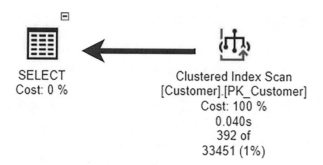

SELECT
Cost: 0 %

Clustered Index Scan
[Customer].[PK_Customer]
Cost: 100 %
0.040s
392 of
33451 (1%)

Figure 9-1. *Execution plan from non-sargeable criteria*

When execution plans are this simple, it can sometimes be difficult to get an idea of how performant these queries really are. One way you can get a better idea is to look at the properties associated with this execution plan. There is a lot of information in Figure 9-2, but let's focus on the Number of Rows Read.

Properties

Clustered Index Scan (Clustered)[Customer].[PK_Customer]

Name	Value
Physical Operation	Clustered Index Scan
Logical Operation	Clustered Index Scan
Estimated Execution Mode	Row
Actual Execution Mode	Row
Storage	RowStore
Actual Number of Rows for All Executions	392
Number of Rows Read	401408
Actual Number of Batches	0
Predicate	datepart(month,[OutdoorRecreation].[dbo...
Estimated I/O Cost	3.5009
Estimated CPU Cost	0.441706
Number of Executions	1
Estimated Number of Executions	1
> Object	[OutdoorRecreation].[dbo].[Customer]....

Figure 9-2. *Properties for the index scan from non-sargeable criteria*

The number of rows read for the index scan from Listing 9-1 is 401,408. To get a better idea of whether this query is performing well, let's write a query with sargeable values. In Listing 9-2, the code is still querying the dbo.Customer table for records created in October 2022, but no wit uses greater than or equal to and less than to specify an exact date range.

Listing 9-2. Query Using Sargeable Criteria

```
DECLARE @StartDate DATETIME2(2) = '2022-09-01';
DECLARE @EndDate DATETIME2(6) = DATEADD(mm, 1, @StartDate)

SELECT FirstName, LastName, Country, DateCreated
FROM dbo.Customer
WHERE DateCreated >= @StartDate
      AND DateCreated < @EndDate;
```

While this may look less clean or harder to read, the importance is in writing a query where SQL Server can quickly determine what records meet the criteria requested in the query. Figure 9-3 shows the execution plan for the query from Listing 9-2.

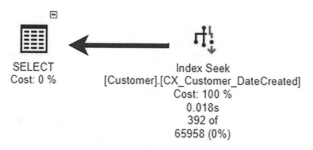

Figure 9-3. *Execution plan from sargeable criteria*

At a glance, the execution plan in Figure 9-3 looks very similar to the execution plan in Figure 9-1. When comparing execution plans that look similar, they can be said to have the same shape. While these execution plans have a similar shape, the items that make up the execution plan are different. In Figure 9-1, there was an index scan. In Figure 9-3, you can see that this execution plan is using an index seek. There is also a thinner line between the index seek from the SELECT in Figure 9-3 than there is in the index scan from the SELECT in Figure 9-1. All of this is a graphical representation of the overall performance of each query. However, you can also get some facts and figures to compare the performance to the queries in Listings 9-1 and 9-2. In Figure 9-2, the actual number of rows read was 32,242. Let's compare this value to the actual number of rows read from Figure 9-4.

Properties	

Index Seek (NonClustered)[Customer].[CX_Customer_DateCreated]

Name	Value
Physical Operation	Index Seek
Logical Operation	Index Seek
Estimated Execution Mode	Row
Actual Execution Mode	Row
Storage	RowStore
Actual Number of Rows for All Executions	392
Number of Rows Read	401408
Actual Number of Batches	0
Predicate	[OutdoorRecreation].[dbo].[Customer].[Da...
Estimated I/O Cost	0.439421
Estimated CPU Cost	0.132622
Number of Executions	1
Estimated Number of Executions	1
> Object	[OutdoorRecreation].[dbo].[Customer]....

Figure 9-4. *Properties for the index seek from sargeable criteria*

The actual number of rows read for Listing 9-2 is 1, as shown in Figure 9-4. Comparing 392 rows read for Listing 9-2 to 401,408 rows read for Listing 9-1, it becomes very clear which query is more efficient.

You can also look at the total CPU usage for both queries to see how each query performs. If you run both queries in Listings 9-1 and 9-2 at the same time, 98% of the total execution plan of both queries is spent on the query in Listing 9-1. You can also use SET STATISTICS TIME ON to find the CPU time and elapsed time. The CPU time is the total amount of time the query execution spent on the CPU or CPUs. The elapsed time is the total time for the query to execute. I ran both queries several times and found that the average CPU time for Listing 9-1 was 15 milliseconds and the average elapsed time for Listing 9-1 was 17 milliseconds. Each time the CPU time and elapsed time for Listing 9-2 was 0 millisecond. Comparing both the CPU time and the elapsed time, you can clearly see that Listing 9-2 performs better than Listing 9-1. Listing 9-1 read the data using an index scan and Listing 9-2 accessed the data using an index seek. This index seek allowed SQL Server to decrease the estimate I/O cost significantly as well as the estimate CPU cost. It is also important to note that the total elapsed time could be less than the total CPU time if there are multiple CPUs.

Implicit Conversion

The data in SQL Server has a data type. These data types were discussed in Chapter 2. When using these data types, it is important to make sure you keep the data types consistent. Otherwise, SQL Server must undergo an implicit conversion. This is where SQL Server converts one data type to another behind the scenes. This can cause additional load on SQL Server. In addition, there is a risk that the implicit conversion will fail. I see this most when an identification type column saves mostly integer values but occasionally strings.

SET NOCOUNT ON

There are many small tweaks that you can make to your T-SQL that will allow for some minor performance improvements. When you run T-SQL code by default, it will count the number of rows affected and can report them back. The cost of counting these records can be a few extra milliseconds. Therefore, a possible enhancement to the coding standards is to turn this functionality off, particularly when it involves stored procedures. The way to accomplish this is to make sure that SET NOCOUNT ON is included inside of a stored procedure. You can see this in Listing 9-3.

Listing 9-3. Stored Procedure Using SET NOCOUNT ON

```
/*-----------------------------------------------------------------*\
Name:            dbo.GetCustomer
Author:          Elizabeth Noble
Created Date:    2022-10-30
Description:     Get a list of all customers in the databases
```

```
Sample Usage:
      EXECUTE dbo.GetCustomer;
\*----------------------------------------------------------------*/
CREATE PROCEDURE dbo.GetCustomer
AS

SET NOCOUNT ON;

  SELECT
          CustomerID,
          FirstName,
          LastName,
          Address,
          City,
          PostalCode,
          Country,
          IsActive,
          DateCreated,
          DateModified,
          DateDisabled
    FROM dbo.Customer;
```

When SET NOCOUNT ON is included before the query code is executed, the stored procedure can execute in a couple fewer milliseconds.

NULL Values

Most of the T-SQL coding standards exist to help improve overall performance for SQL Server. However, some T-SQL coding standards exist to help improve query results or make it easier for people to write code that works as expected. One of the issues with NULL is that it does not work intuitively. NULL is treated as an unknown value in SQL Server. That means that NULL is neither true nor false. Therefore, where there are fields that can contain NULL values, the way these fields must be treated is different.

In addition, NULL values may indicate that tables were not designed efficiently. Before ending up in these scenarios, it may be beneficial to consider how the table should be designed. You want to make sure that the table really needs to include nullable columns. This is also due to how data is stored and how indexes are created. You want to consider how this data will be used.

NOLOCK

Best practices should also be a part of your coding standards. Some of the very common best practices include highly debated topics like if or when to use the NOLOCK hint in queries. One of the reasons I mention this specifically is that there are at least two very distinct groups involving NOLOCK. On the one hand, many database administrators view not using NOLOCK is a best practice. On the other hand, many developers see the use of NOLOCK is a best practice. This difference in perspective is based on a trade-off between data accuracy and performance.

The idea behind NOLOCK is to improve query performance by reducing the number of locks. In the case of NOLOCK, the reduction in lock activity is on the SELECT statement. Actions such as INSERT, UPDATE, and DELETE are not affected by NOLOCK. However, using NOLOCK on a SELECT statement can return results more quickly when a data modification action is holding a lock on that same table that the SELECT statement is trying to access.

You can get an idea of how these viewpoints are correct by looking at an example. Listing 9-4 shows a query to insert a record into the dbo.Customer table inside of an explicit transaction.

Listing 9-4. Inserting a Record into dbo.Customer

```
BEGIN TRAN
INSERT INTO dbo.Customer
(
    FirstName,
    LastName,
    Address,
    City,
    PostalCode,
    Country
)
VALUES
(
    'Stacy',
    'Parks',
    '123 Rua de Santa Catarina',
```

```
    'Porto',
    '1234-567',
    'Portugal'
);
```

In Listing 9-4, an explicit transaction has been started using BEGIN TRAN, but it has not specified a COMMIT or ROLLBACK. This will leave the transaction open with a lock on dbo.Customer. To simulate application performance, let's open a separate query window and run a query to find all records created in this table after October 1, 2022. You can see a sample of this query in Listing 9-5.

Listing 9-5. Query to Find Recent Customers

```
SELECT FirstName, LastName, Country
FROM dbo.Customer
WHERE DateCreated > '2022-10-01';
```

Due to the lock on dbo.Customer from the query in Listing 9-4, it seems like the query is continuing to run. The query in Listing 9-5 is waiting for the locks to be released before any data can be returned. In order to get results more quickly, you can change how SQL Server treats the locks on the table. In Listing 9-6, you modify the query from Listing 9-5 and included a query hint of WITH (NOLOCK).

Listing 9-6. Query to Find Recent Customers Using NOLOCK Hint

```
SELECT FirstName, LastName, Country
FROM dbo.Customer WITH (NOLOCK)
WHERE DateCreated > '2022-10-01';
```

When you run the query in Listing 9-5 in a separate query window, you get nearly instantaneous results. You can see an example of these results in Table 9-1.

Table 9-1. *Customers Created After October 1, 2022*

FirstName	LastName	County
Myra	Acharya	India
Stacy	Parks	Portugal

Looking at the preceding results, you can see that the record inserted in Listing 9-4 is included in the results. However, this record has not been committed to SQL Server. You could roll back the transaction from Listing 9-4 and undo the insert. This would cause the results from Table 9-1 to be inaccurate. This discrepancy where queries return results that are not fully committed to the database is known as a *dirty read*. This is the largest risk when using NOLOCK in your queries. Before deciding that you should use NOLOCK in your T-SQL code, make sure that the business, including your end users, understands the potential risks of using this hint.

RECOMPILE

Besides NOLOCK, another possible query hint that is often considered is RECOMPILE. You may find yourself dealing with a query that is affected by parameter sniffing, as discussed in Chapter 5. This means that the query creates an execution plan that may perform well for some values, but when other parameter values are used, the performance can degrade significantly. One of the workarounds that can be easily and quickly implemented is the query hint RECOMPILE. In Listing 9-7, you can see the additional line needed when creating a stored procedure to allow the stored procedure to recompile on execution.

Listing 9-7. Adding WITH RECOMPILE to a Stored Procedure

```
/*-------------------------------------------------------------*\
Name:              dbo.GetCustomerAndOrderNumberByProductID
Author:            Elizabeth Noble
Created Date:      2022-10-30
Description:       Get customer and products ordered for an order number
Sample Usage:
     EXECUTE dbo.GetRecipeAndIngredientByMealTypeID 1;
\*-------------------------------------------------------------*/
CREATE PROCEDURE dbo.GetCustomerAndOrderNumberByProductID
     @ProductID    INT
WITH RECOMPILE
AS
     SELECT
          cus.FirstName,
          cus.LastName,
```

```
        ord.OrderNumber,
        ord.OrderDate,
        prd.ProductName,
        SUM(dtl.QuantitySold),
        dtl.ProductPrice
    FROM dbo.Customer cus
        INNER JOIN dbo.CustomerOrder ord
        ON cus.CustomerID = ord.CustomerID
        INNER JOIN dbo.OrderDetail dtl
        ON ord.CustomerOrderID = dtl.CustomerOrderID
        INNER JOIN dbo.Product prd
        ON prd.ProductID = dtl.ProductID
    WHERE prd.ProductID = @ProductID
    ORDER BY cus.FirstName, cus.LastName;
```

While this is a quick fix, it can increase the CPU load on the server. I suggest trying to redesign the query if possible. If not, you may need to change the stored procedure to only recompile for the values that fall outside of the majority. This is to minimize the resources needed to create a new execution plan every time the stored procedure is run. If the recompile is limited to a smaller set of data, then the store procedure will not need to generate an execution plan as frequently.

For your T-SQL coding standards, it is important to include guidelines related to writing T-SQL that performs well. You also want to include some rules for what actions are or are not allowable in order to try and fix poorly performing T-SQL. The last part of your T-SQL coding standards is a catch-all generally related to security, futureproofing, and maintainability.

T-SQL Usability

Having T-SQL coding standards that encourage good database design and address performance issues is a good start. However, you are also going to want some coding standards to help with other aspects of T-SQL. Some of this includes having T-SQL coding standards for potential security issues. There are other coding standards that you can put in place that are best practices but may not affect performance. They may be in place either to help keep your T-SQL functioning even if the underlying data structure changes or to encourage T-SQL commands that help make your T-SQL code easier to read or understand.

Linked Server

Linked servers are one of those things that may be overlooked as part of the coding standards. It seems unlikely that you will need to use linked servers, but linked servers have a way of seeming necessary when you least expect it. This is why it is a good idea to include specifications about how to handle linked servers as part of your T-SQL coding standards. Due to the general security risks associated with using linked servers, it is recommended that you do not use linked servers unless necessary. I suggest clearly defining exactly what is considered necessary. This will help reduce any contention should you find yourself wanting to implement linked servers.

Column Definition

One of the key factors of writing T-SQL is specifying what columns you are using or affecting. While this is related to making sure you only interact with the data you need, there are other benefits to requiring your T-SQL code to explicitly state column names. When inserting data into SQL Server, it is possible to not state the column names or order you are using for the insert. If you are inserting data into every column in the table and you are inserting the data in the same order as the columns in the table, you will not have any issues. However, this can cause stored procedures or other T-SQL code to stop functioning if columns are added or removed from the table or if the column order is changed in the future. Therefore, a good habit is to explicitly state your column names on all T-SQL. For these examples, this specifically includes selects and inserts.

BETWEEN

There are also situations when you have multiple choices on how to write T-SQL code, and all those options seem to perform about the same. This can happen when you are trying to get a subset of data that covers a continuous range. Defining a T-SQL coding standard in this situation does not necessarily correlate to improving the performance of SQL Server. This is more closely related to improving the consistency of the T-SQL code. An example of how to write T-SQL using BETWEEN is shown in Listing 9-8.

Listing 9-8. Query with BETWEEN

```
SELECT FirstName, LastName, Country
FROM dbo.Customer
WHERE CustomerID BETWEEN 100 AND 20000;
```

In terms of readability, you may decide that all ranges that cover inclusive values should be written using BETWEEN. This may be preferable to using greater than or equal to and less than or equal to get the same range.

Stored Procedure Parameters

While improving code readability is important, there are times that improving readability of T-SQL may make debugging the code harder when it comes to performance issues. This type of situation can happen depending on how you configured your stored procedure parameters. You can either define each parameter individually or you can create a user-defined table that you can use to pass in a multitude of variables. If you choose to use a user-defined table, your T-SQL code may be cleaner, but it may take more time to debug performance issues going forward. In addition, your stored procedure will work differently because you are working with a table variable instead of handling each data field individually.

UNION

You will have times where you want to combine data from two different queries. This type of combination involves appending one data set to another. When these two data sets share the same number of columns with the same data types, there is the possibility to use a UNION statement to combine this data. The advantage of using a UNION is that the queries are readable and you can easily tell by reading the T-SQL code what is happening. The challenge with using UNION is that the performance of a UNION may be worse than the performance of each query independently. In addition to UNION, there is also the UNION ALL functionality. The main difference between a UNION and a UNION ALL is how the data is returned. In a UNION statement, a distinct set of records is returned, whereas in a UNION ALL statement, the actual number of records from each separate query is included in the result set. When designing your coding standards, you want to decide if UNION and UNION ALL statements are allowed. You may also want to decide if there are specific scenarios where they would or would not be allowed.

CAST or CONVERT

When writing code, you may find yourself in a situation where you want to change the data type from one value to another. Changing data types can be important with performing mathematical functions on integer values. Due to how SQL Server performs mathematical operations, if you divided one integer by another integer, you get an integer as the answer. If you want SQL Server to provide a decimal as a result, you need to change the data type from an integer to a decimal. Similarly, you may want to display a string of text as part of a SQL Server query. Alternatively, if you include an integer when concatenating with a string, you get an error when SQL Server tries to execute the query. However, if you change the integer to a varchar data type, you can parse the string correctly.

For instance, you may specify that all code should use ANSI SQL standards when possible. If you implemented this policy, the developers would have to use CAST for all code unless they need to format a date. Then the developer would be able to use CONVERT. Or you may indicate that all date formatting must be handled in the application. Therefore, CONVERT would never be allowed as part of the coding standard.

Cursors

Cursors are a source of controversy when it comes to databases. In Chapter 6, I went over set-based operations, which is where SQL Server performs best. The issue with cursors is that they do not take advantage of these set-based operations. This can cause considerable overhead when it comes to handling data. To compound the challenges with cursors, they are written in a way that is more akin to how application code is written than T-SQL. This can make it very tempting to use cursors as it may be easier to understand how to write the code to get the desired results. Like other factors when developing your T-SQL coding standards, you may not be able to rule out cursors entirely. If so, try to create some criteria where you believe cursors would be beneficial and limit cursor usage to only those situations.

ORDER BY

It is often tempting to want SQL Server to get all of the data exactly how your application needs the data. While SQL Server can do this, you want to consider if it is worth the cost to SQL Server to do all the work you are requesting. Such can be the situation when you want data to be sorted for your application. SQL Server can sort the data using the ORDER BY statement, but it may be a better use of resources to have the application sort this data. If you decide this is how you want to handle sorting data, it may be a good idea to include in your T-SQL coding standards that data should not be sorted in SQL Server.

If you know there are specific situations where this will be unavoidable, you can state in your coding standards the exact scenarios where using an ORDER BY is allowed in your T-SQL code.

Case Statements

T-SQL code can be versatile. While you may choose to keep your T-SQL code limited to application functionality, database code is also used for other purposes such as reporting. In many applications, you may be both processing transactions and allowing your users to search and filter data. This type of activity can be a reporting activity. Oftentimes, users do not want to see data in the same manner the data is stored. For instance, you may have a table that includes a status type. A given record may have several statuses over time. However, a user may want to see one line with all of the statuses for that specific record. This is where you would want to use a case statement so that you could convert multiple rows into various columns. Performing this type of activity is not a purely transactional use of T-SQL, and you may want to limit this type of behavior as part of your coding standards.

TRY... CATCH

Including error handling in T-SQL code can be helpful and may be considered best practice in your workplace. You want your application to gracefully handle procedures that fail. One of the situations you may find yourself in is in the unfortunate event that a stored procedure is a deadlock victim. The TRY... CATCH block can allow the deadlock stored procedure to either rerun or exit gracefully. See Listing 9-9.

Listing 9-9. Query Using TRY... CATCH

```
DECLARE @FirstName    VARCHAR(40) = 'Stacy';
DECLARE @LastName     VARCHAR(100) = 'Parks';
DECLARE @Address      VARCHAR(100) = '123 Rua de Santa Catarina';
DECLARE @City         VARCHAR(100) = 'Porto';
DECLARE @PostalCode   VARCHAR(20) = '1234-567';
DECLARE @County       VARCHAR(75) = 'Portugal';

BEGIN TRY
    BEGIN TRAN
    INSERT INTO dbo.Customer
```

```
    (
        FirstName,
        LastName,
        Address,
        City,
        PostalCode,
        Country
    )
    VALUES
    (
        @FirstName,
        @LastName,
        @Address,
        @City,
        @PostalCode,
        @County
    );
    COMMIT TRANSACTION
END TRY
BEGIN CATCH
    PRINT 'Insert Failed';
    ROLLBACK TRANSACTION
END CATCH
```

Once you have determined what you want to include in your T-SQL coding standards, the next step is to get buy-in from your coworkers or other departments that will also be writing T-SQL. Getting everyone to agree to a set standard can solve many issues. First, it helps those that are onboarding to the company. When they review code, they will see a consistent code style. This will allow them to focus on what the T-SQL is doing instead of trying to interpret how the T-SQL code is written.

If you create a thorough and well-defined coding standard, there should be less back and forth during script reviews when there is T-SQL that is not believed to be best practice. With the T-SQL coding standard in place, all parties know what is allowed and what is deemed as undesirable or bad practice. New hires will also know what T-SQL is acceptable. Everyone can be held to the same standard, and it allows others to see that the rules for writing T-SQL are fair.

Source Control

Writing T-SQL code that is manageable is a worthwhile goal to build upon a solid foundation of understandable and maintainable code. Chapter 4 discussed how to standardize your T-SQL code. This continued in Chapter 10 with implementing SQL coding standards. The purpose of this foundation is to create a consistent code base for your database. While developing a consistent code base can help improve code quality, this effect is diminished if you are unable to maintain your T-SQL code.

Developing manageable T-SQL code covers many different aspects of writing database code. The previous chapter focused on coding standards as a way to help guide you and others to writing T-SQL code that performs well. Having database code that performs well and is easy to read can help your applications and your development process. The next step on that path is to consider how you are storing your code.

One option is to use source control to save T-SQL code associated with creating various database objects. Why is source control important and what can it do to help make T-SQL code development better? Knowing that you want to implement source control is different from defining a process for managing source control. Setting up guidelines on how to handle source control puts you in a good place to begin creating your first database project in source control.

Reasons to Use Source Control

Without having a way to manage code, you can end up spending hours reviewing scripts and preparing for software releases. This kind of manual work involves locating files for script review, manually comparing code between production and a manual script, figuring out which scripts to include in a deployment, or manually running each script as part of the deployment. This is where you can benefit from having maintainable code. This includes making sure you can find the T-SQL code for any database object. You also want to know that you are modifying the correct version of the code. Serious issues can

E. Noble, *Pro T-SQL 2022*, https://doi.org/10.1007/978-1-4842-9256-3_10

occur when the wrong version of T-SQL code is modified and deployed. It will also help you to know what version of code needs to be deployed at any point in time. For these reasons, database code can benefit from incorporating source control.

Keeping T-SQL code together to be easily accessed can be a challenge. Source control can help keep all T-SQL code together and organized. Source control is no longer something that only exists for application development. Source control allows you to organize code, and it can be used to help create structure around database development. Standardizing your T-SQL and implementing coding standards can be more easily managed with source control by using third-party tools as part of your commit, build, and deployment processes. When you make changes to database code, you have the option to make those changes locally. If you choose to use SQL Server Data Tools (SSDT) and keep all your database code in the same project, you can build all the databases together to confirm any database dependencies are working as expected. SSDT allows you to manage your database code with or without source control. This is an advantage over deploying code manually to SQL Server. As part of the build process, the database project will verify that the fields in your views, functions, stored procedures, or other T-SQL code exist within the database.

There are other issues that can happen when writing T-SQL code. You may have times when multiple people or teams need to change the same database objects. Depending on how your company handles deploying code, you may end up with some database objects that have multiple layers of changes. Source control can help manage these changes and make sure they are implemented correctly. In addition, defining processes for managing code can help everyone use the correct version of database code for their needs.

If you keep all your databases in the same solution, you can add references between databases if there are dependencies. If you remove a column from a table in one database, a stored procedure that depends on this column in another database will fail to build. The build failure identifies the affected stored procedure as well as the missing column reference. This can be especially useful when you are adding columns or changing column names. There may come a time when you want to refactor a table or some other database object. If your applications and databases are saved in the same solution, you will have the option to automatically refactor the code.

Some changes to T-SQL code can be complex and involved. Other times you may be working with database objects or code that is critical to running your company. To start working on changing code, you want to make sure you are working with the most up-to-date version of the code. Prior to source control, I had a very manual process for reviewing code that was time consuming. As a result of implementing source control, the speed with which you can review database code can be greatly improved. Using source control allows you to ensure you are implementing your changes consistently.

You may want a place where you can change code, test code, and repeat this process until you get to the desired output. Source control can pull the most recently saved T-SQL code down to your local machine. You can then work on making your modifications to the T-SQL code on your local desktop. When you are ready to save that work, you can save those changes locally. This allows you to work independently of other developers. When you are sure of your changes, you can save your T-SQL code to the centralized location. This centralized repository becomes your source for all database changes.

Another benefit of using source control is that it speeds up the process to identify what T-SQL code has changed. Prior to using source control, I had to manually review an entire database object to confirm what changed. The best process I found was to visually compare the current Production stored procedure to the new version of the stored procedure. While this was somewhat effective, it was also possible for me to easily miss something.

After getting the database added into source control, I could easily see all code that changed as part of the script review. This allowed me to quickly see all T-SQL code that changed. I could also use source control to easily compare T-SQL code to previous versions. As part of the comparison, sections of the code that had been modified were highlighted. Even more helpful was that the code that was added vs. modified or removed was highlighted in two different colors.

Having access to your T-SQL code can make it easier and faster to get scripts together for software releases. Source control also helps protect unapproved T-SQL code from being deployed in error. Without source control for T-SQL, getting ready for a deployment can be a hassle.

You need to be able to access scripts for different databases and software releases but also keep track of changes over time. The business may decide to revert back to a previous version of code. When that code is saved in source control, it is easier to search through the versions of the specific database object and find the change history. With source control I can save time by finding when a change was implemented. If you implement automated deployments, as discussed in Chapter 13, you may have even faster methods to revert to a previous version of code.

You can combine source control with testing strategies, discussed in Chapter 12, and automated software releases. This will allow you to minimize the manual effort needed for code reviews, which may help business relationships between IT departments. Using similar processes to manage database code as application development can help increase source control adoption. When T-SQL code is stored in source control, this opens up the possibility of pointing third-party tools at it. These tools can analyze an entire T-SQL codebase and help automate tasks such as automatically rejecting or correcting formatting issues.

Tip   One method of automating code formatting is through the use of precommit hooks with Git

---

Another advantage of source control is it allows you to have one more tool to help in the case of disaster recovery. If you lose all your hardware and backups, how long will it take you to get your business up and running again? While you may know that your backups need to be tested on a regular basis, you may not have had the opportunity to test them lately. Depending on how your company developed its disaster recovery plan and what happens when disaster strikes could mean you lose access to your current Production servers and all the associated data. If this unlikely situation happens, you may find yourself wondering how you will get your applications running again. As a plan of last resort, if your databases are in source control along with the necessary data in your base tables, you have a chance of getting your company's systems up and running.

How to Use Source Control

One of the things I found out when first implementing source control was the discussions that needed to happen internally prior to implementing source control. I found that the database team, the development teams, and the QA teams needed to come to an agreement as to how code would be managed going forward. It is ideal to learn each team's goals and needs so that you can design an effective process to manage database code. There may be differences in how each team wants to manage their respective codebases. Some things to cover are

- Guidelines for when to use local vs. centralized repositories

- How to save your changes to source control

- How to resolve bugs that have been deployed

- What should be included with your database code

Source control allows you to work with code locally on your machine. You can create database objects or change database objects, and when you build the code locally, you have an additional check that the database project can build successfully. A successful build indicates that several checks have been run against the database to confirm that objects can be created successfully. Once you have tested and confirmed your database code, you can check it into a centralized location. The location can either be a server you have set up on-premises or in the cloud, such as the case with GitHub. This central repository can receive code changes from you and any other members of your team that are authorized to make changes to this database project. In addition, a repository can allow developers or development teams to work on code independently of one another.

Saving changes to T-SQL code locally is often referred to as a *commit*. When committing code, you can add comments to your commit. You can also implement standards as to how your commit messages should be written. One example is to precede the commit message with a ticket or user story number. Once a central repository is set up, individual users can make a copy of the centralized code. This copy is usually stored locally on the developer's machine and is called a *branch*. This name stems from the centralized code, which is referred to as a *trunk*. In modern terminology, this is called the *main branch*. Adding a reference to the issue worked can be helpful when preparing branches for software releases. Git and GitHub allow you to save changes before they are committed permanently to the repository. *Staging changes* is the term for when you save changes that are not immediately committed to the repository. Staging changes for your commit can be done through Azure Data Studio or the command line.

With the desire for more companies to allow any combination of Agile, Kanban, Scrum, Continuous Integration, or Continuous Delivery, it has become increasingly important to have a source control solution that is more flexible. This solution needs to allow for multiple teams to simultaneously work on the same code base without negatively affecting software releases. That is where the popularity of Git originates.

If you are using SQL Server Data Tools and Visual Studio, each code repository will contain at least one database solution. Within the database solution, each database will have a single database project. You have the option of choosing if each database project will have its own solution or if all projects will share the same solution. Azure Data Studio or Visual Studio Code has an extension for database projects. These database projects live within a workspace and are similar to a solution. The workspace provides a way to access the database projects within a given folder. It is possible to have all applications and databases in the same solution, but that is outside the scope of this book. These decisions are not only based on preference and desired functionality. As you will see in Chapter 13, how you organize your repository will also determine how your code is deployed.

Inside of the repository, there is the concept of one or more branches. One branch is the main branch. Think of it similarly to the set of code you regularly go to if you need to deploy these changes. This branch is called the main. Any time you want to make changes to the main branch, it is generally best to create a new branch to write your T-SQL code. This allows the main branch to remain unaffected by code that is in development and is not ready to be deployed. In this way, the main branch can match the code that is currently deployed to Production.

As these commits happen per branch, you may find yourself in a situation where you need to deploy two different branches during the same deployment. This is when you will want to try to combine this code. In order to combine this code, take the changes in the branch and add them back to the main or release branch. Combining a feature branch to the main branch is called a *merge*. One aspect that can happen as part of this merge is called a *conflict*. This can happen when many people have been working on the same database object over the same period of time or there has been a delay in merging a previous feature branch with the main branch. Make sure to work with your development teams to get a better understanding of how to avoid merge conflicts and how they can be resolved.

Rollback Changes

One thing that happens more often than some of us would like to admit is when code is deployed and then does not work as intended. I have been in situations where those bugs were found during deployment. Other times those bugs are not found until days, weeks, or months after deployment. In either scenario, the key is to figure out how to quickly restore the database to a more functional state. One of the discussions I had with developers and QA was how to handle this on deployment night. A bug can be manually fixed by a T-SQL script. Depending on how you manage your database code software releases, it is possible that this bug fix can be undone in a future deployment. If you put the bug fix into source control, you can make sure this bug fix will not be undone going forward.

As a result, we adopted what we called a rollforward strategy. If we could quickly find and resolve the issue, we would check those changes into source control and deploy them up through the environments. A rollforward follows the same process as manually deploying a hotfix. However, adding the changes to source control ensures that this fix will not be rolled back in a future software release. This rollforward strategy was only permitted on the night of the deployment. When we adopted the strategy, the concept was that we were going to deploy all code that had been merged to a main branch. If you choose to deploy a different version of the database project than the most recent version, you will not be able to use this method.

We also adopted a method to use a hotfix. These were changes that were needed as soon as possible due to a critical loss in functionality of an application. As there may be various items in development, we could not go ahead and just deploy the most recent database code. In these cases, I would still check the modified T-SQL code into source control. That code may have been deployed to development and tested in our QA environment, but the code would be manually deployed to production. The concept was that the next time the database code was deployed, this database object would already exist.

Designing how to save database code also involves conversations with the development, QA, and release management teams. There are pros and cons to the various methods that exist. You can save all of your database projects in the same solution with all of your application code. While this may take longer for your projects to build, if you create the right relationships, you can be certain that changes in your database will not affect the functionality of your applications. Depending on the number of applications that exist in your company, this may be a difficult task. There is also the option of having all your database projects saved in the same solution. Saving all database projects in the same solution will also cause them to be saved in the same repository. If you have cross-database dependencies, this method will help protect your databases. This is particularly helpful when you make changes to one database object and you are not certain if these changes will break functionality in a different database. The final option is to create one solution per database. The advantage of this method is that you can develop each database independently. The downside is that you may make changes to a database that breaks functionality for another database.

Prior to setting up your first database in source control, I recommend discussing the topics in this section with the other teams at your company. Make sure everyone is in agreement when it comes to writing, testing, and saving changes to your database code.

Get others on board when it comes to fixing database code once it has been deployed. Also consider how you want your database projects to interact with one another and your applications. Once you take all of this under consideration, you are ready to create your first database project.

Setting Up Source Control

Now that you have decided you would like to implement source control for your database, and you have figured out some general guidelines on how you want to set up your database projects, let's set it up. This section assumes that someone else is responsible for procuring, installing, and configuring source control. There are many factors involved in the initial setup for source control and they are outside the scope of this book. One of the first things to do is get whatever IDE you are using to connect to source control. Once you are connected to source control, create a way to store the source control for your databases. You want to figure out how to make and save changes to your database code after you have a place for your database source control.

In this section, I will be using Azure Data Studio, the Database Projects extension, Git, and GitHub to get a database into source control. In order to manage database projects in Azure Data Studio, you need to install the Database Projects extension. Figure 10-1 shows how to add the Database Project extension in Azure Data Studio.

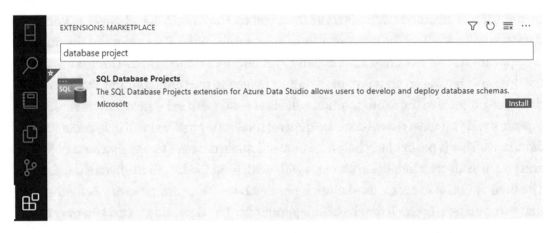

Figure 10-1. *Installing the Database Projects extension in Azure Data Studio*

Once you have installed the Database Projects extension in Azure Data Studio, there will be a new icon on the far left had side of Azure Data Studio that has the shape of two application windows on top of one another. Now you can create a workspace to work on a database project.

Note   When working with database projects in Azure Data Studio or VS Code, a workspace file is created to manage the database project. In Visual Studio, a solution file is created to manage database projects.

Azure Data Studio has several options you can use to start working with database projects:

- From the Database Projects window

  - Create new

  - Open existing

- From the menu on the Database Projects window

  - Create project from database

  - Update project from database

  - Generate SQL Project from OpenAPI/Swagger spec

These options cover all sorts of scenarios that you may consider when creating your database project. If you choose Create new from the Database Projects window, Azure Data Studio will create a new, empty database project. If you already have a database project saved locally, you want to use the Open existing option in Azure Data Studio. This option can be used if you are already using a database project that was created in Azure Data Studio, VS Code, or Visual Studio. However, neither of these options are the best option if you want to create new database project based on an existing database or database structure.

One of the easiest ways to start using source control is to add an existing database to source control. Azure Data Studio makes this easy by allow you to create a database project from an existing database. The best part is that this will also sort all of your database objects into folders so that you can easily manage your code. When creating a database object from an existing database, you can choose how the database objects are organized in your new database project.

When creating the database project, you can choose to organize the folder structure as file, flat, object type, schema, or schema/object type. If you choose file, all the database objects will be saved in a single file. If you are planning on adding new T-SQL for database objects to this file, they need to be appended to the single file. The next option available is flat. The flat option creates a single .SQL file for each database object. Primary keys, foreign keys, constraints, and indexes are all included in the .SQL file for the specified table. This option lets you more easily manage individual objects than the file option, but to modify any existing object, you will have to search the entire list of files to find the specific object.

The other three options of object type, schema, and schema/object type are similar. The object type folder option creates folders for each object type. All tables are saved in one folder and another folder contains all stored procedures. If you prefer to save the .SQL files by schema, this is also an option. This can be helpful if you create database objects in more schemas than dbo. The schema/object type creates folders for each schema and subfolders within each schema for the database object type. While choosing how you would like to organize the files is a matter of personal preference, the file organization will be the same for all developers. Therefore, you may want to discuss which organization method to choose prior to implementation.

Now that you know more information about creating data projects and the available options, you can create a database project. To add a new, empty database in source control, select the Database Projects extension, and select either Create new or Open existing. For this example, choose Create new so you can build an entirely new database. Once you select Create new, you get a slide-out window named *Create new database project*, as shown in Figure 10-2.

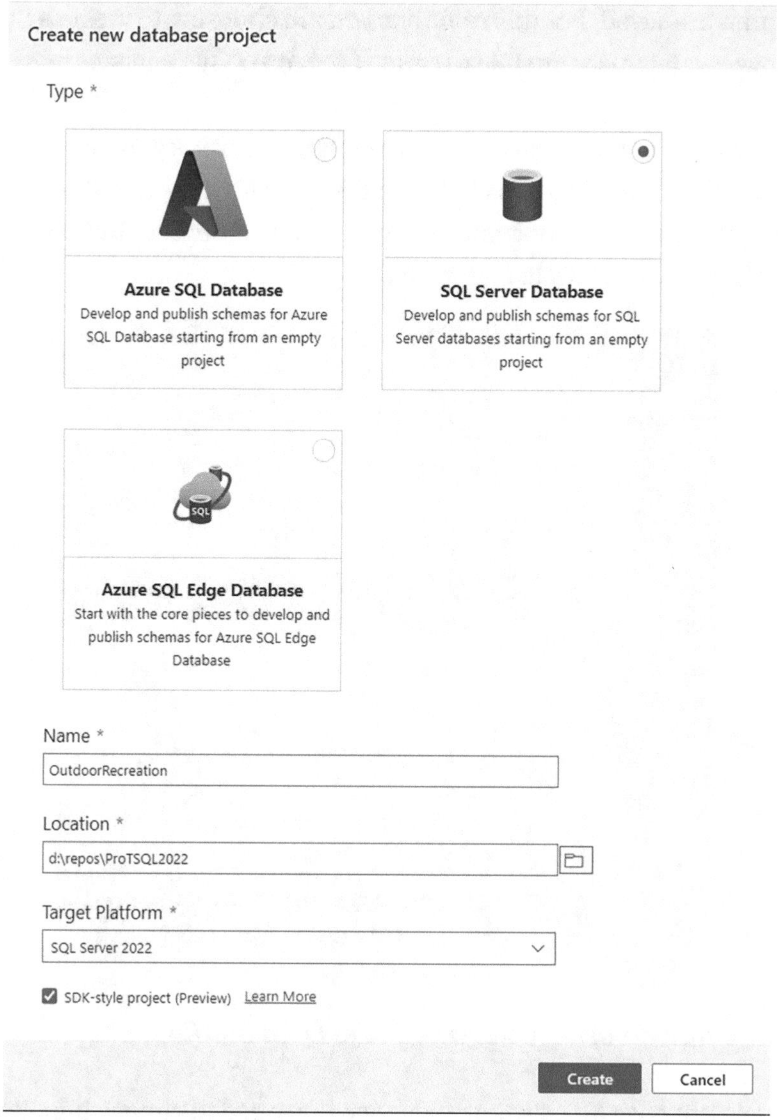

Figure 10-2. *Creating a new database project*

In this step, you are creating a new workspace with a new database project. Save the OutdoorRecreation database project to D:\repos\. In the current state of source control, such as with Git, there is a concept of having a centralized repository. This is the location where all code is saved and accessible for users. The expectation is that users will create a copy of the code on their local machines and make changes on their local machine. This is sometimes called a *local repository*. This is the same location where your other local repositories are saved. For this example, you are choosing to create a SQL Server Database. However, it is also possible to create an Azure SQL Database or Azure SQL Edge Database.

The next step is to add the workspace to a GitHub repository. When you select the Source Control icon, which has two circles on the top with lines connecting them to one circle on the bottom, the slide-out window gives you the option to Initialize Repository or Publish to GitHub, as shown in Figure 10-3.

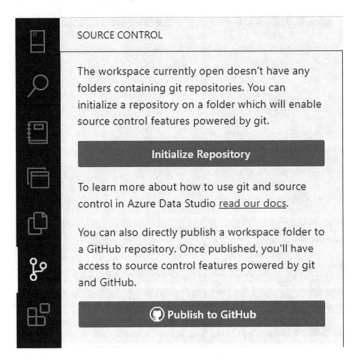

Figure 10-3. *Initial repository setup in Azure Data Studio*

Since you do not have an existing repository, you need to choose Initialize Repository. This will launch a pop-up window asking for permission to let the GitHub extension sign in using GitHub. This will allow you to initialize and create the repository at the same time.

Note   Git and GitHub are two separate things. Git is the software used to manage changes for distributed version control. GitHub is a hosting service used to host web-based Git repositories.

Name the repository OutdoorRecreation. Give the repository the description of Database project for Menu. Select a license for the repository. However, it is beyond the scope of this book to go into detail regarding Git ignore or the available licensing options. The last part to specify is a private repository. The main difference between a public and private repository is whether you would like others to be able to access, download, and make suggestions regarding your code.

Figure 10-4 shows a new repository that is linked to my GitHub account.

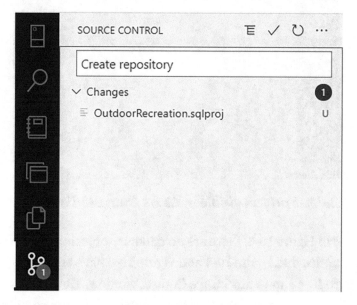

Figure 10-4. *Local repository visible in Azure Data Studio*

You can see in the Source Control window that the Outdoor Recreation workspace is now set up as a local repository. If you go back to the Database Projects window, you will be able to see the all objects currently associated with the database project. The dialog window is shown in Figure 10-5.

Figure 10-5. *Database project visible in Azure Data Studio*

As you can see in Figure 10-5, there are no database objects associated with this project. You may notice that Figure 10-4 and Figure 10-5 have almost exactly the same layout. Figure 10-4 shows the Source Control window. The options in the upper right corner are the options to how to view the proposed changes, commit the changes, refresh the changes displayed, or a menu of additional source control options. The options in Figure 10-5 are the ability to create a new database project, open an existing project, refresh the database project, or a menu of specific actions related to managing database projects.

If you want to update the database project with the objects in an existing database, you can do that easily by selecting the menu, which can be opened by selecting the ... in the upper right corners of the Database Project window. You can then choose Update Project From Database. This will open the *Update project from database* window where you can specify the source database, target projects, and update actions, as shown in Figure 10-6.

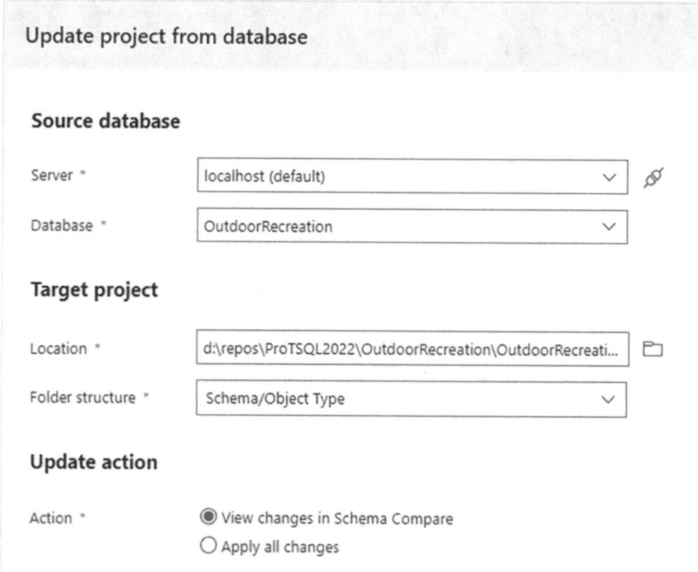

Figure 10-6. *Update project from database window*

One of the useful features of the *Update project from database* window is the option to either view changes in Schema Compare or apply all changes. For this example, let's view the changes before you update the database project. Also, specify that the folder structure should have all objects stored by schema and then by object type. Once you select the Update button, you will get a new window, as shown in Figure 10-7, comparing the database OutdoorRecreation to the objects currently in source control. Since you just created this workspace, there are no objects in source control.

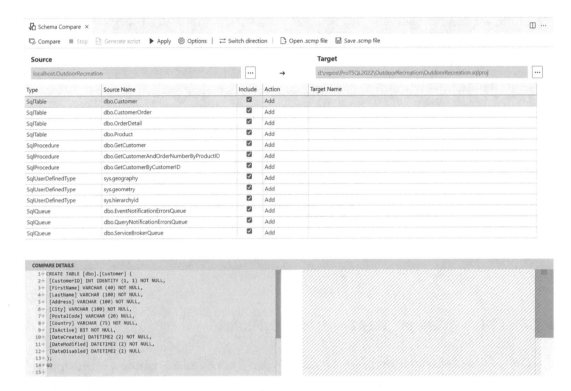

Figure 10-7. *Schema Compare window*

The top menu bar in Figure 10-7 shows the many options available in Schema Compare. Use this to add code to source control in the local repository that is missing. The two most useful options are Apply and Options. Apply takes all of the items listed under source and performs the action in the center (in this case, Add) to the target. For example, the SQL table dbo.Customer that exists in the OutdoorRecreation database will be added to the OutdoorRecreation local repository. While source control is the tool used to manage changes, a repository is the location where the changes are stored. Options gives you control over what items will be compared, and thus modified, as part of this schema compare. Figure 10-7 includes adding some user defined types and queues. If you want to exclude them, you can select options and navigate to the Include Object Types tab. Deselecting the check boxes for Queues and User-Defined Types (CLR) removes these objects from the comparison, and if you apply the changes after the removing them, they will not be added into the local repository. If you exclude the queues and user-defined types from the comparison, these objects will not be added to your repository. If you later decide you want to add them to your repository, you will need to compare the source and target again. Once you select Apply, you get the option to confirm that you want to make these changes.

Now that the changes have been applied, you can see them in the *Database Projects* window as shown in Figure 10-8.

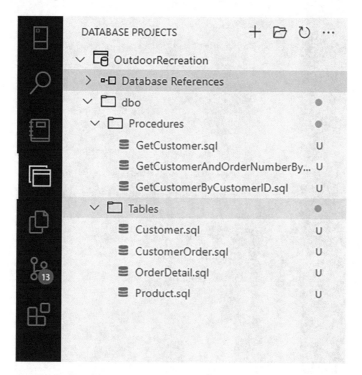

Figure 10-8. *Database Projects window with new objects*

Figure 10-8 shows a folder named dbo for the dbo schema. Under the dbo folder are two subfolders, one for Procedures and one for Tables. Within each of these folders are the individual scripts for each database object that exists in the respective schema/object type group.

On the left-hand bar, the source control icon also shows that there are 13 changes pending. In Figure 10-9, you can see the changes viewed as a tree.

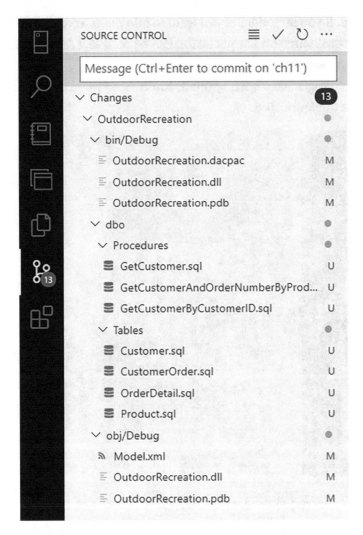

Figure 10-9. *Changes to source control as a tree*

In order to commit the changes, type a message in the text box where you see the text *Message (Ctrl+Enter to commit on 'ch11')*. To commit the message, either select the check box in the upper right-hand corner or use Ctrl+Enter. A pop-up window will ask, *would you like to stage all your changes and commit them directly?* Once you select yes, the changes are committed locally.

The source control window will update. All of the objects previously displayed will no longer be listed. Instead, you'll see a blue button right below the text box to add a message to the commit. In Figure 10-10, the button shows one commit that can be synced to the GitHub repository.

Figure 10-10. *Syncing changes*

Before selecting this button, the changes are only stored on your local machine. To allow these changes to be saved in the central repository, you need to sync these changes. This will also allow anyone else with access to this repository to see the changes associated with the *ch11* branch.

If you have additional tasks you need to perform on this branch, you can create additional objects. By right-clicking the Procedures folder, you can select *Add Stored Procedure*. This will open a window with a template for how to create stored procedures. The new file named GetProduct.sql will also be added to the Database Projects window to the left, as shown in Figure 10-11.

Figure 10-11. *Adding stored procedures*

Figure 10-11 shows the T-SQL code to create the stored procedure dbo.GetProduct on the right-hand side. In order to save this change, you should commit the change locally. This should be about as quick as saving a file with the added step of including a description of what changed. Once you are done with your work within a branch of a repository, you should sync the change to GitHub so that other developers can pull down any changes you have made if they are working on the same branch.

Note   When using sync with GitHub, any changes to the current branch on GitHub are updated locally. This is called *pull first*. Then changes, like the creation of the stored procedure, are updated at GitHub. This is called a *push*. Sync is a pull followed by a push.

If you are finished with all necessary changes for the *ch11* branch, you can merge the changes to the *main* branch with a pull request. Pull requests are useful, especially when working in teams, because they allow others to easily see what changes were made in the branch. It is also possible to add various approvals and validations as part of resolving a pull request, but that is outside the scope of this book.

Creating a pull request can be done through the terminal on Azure Data Studio or accessing the repository on github.com. When I go to the ProTSQL2022 repository on GitHub, I can see the new changes that have been pushed for the *ch11* branch, as shown in Figure 10-12.

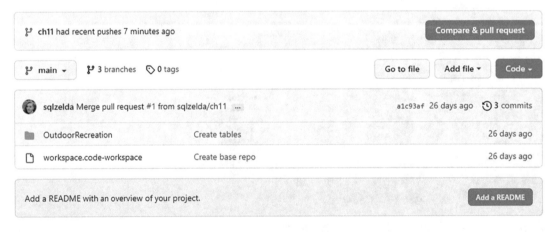

Figure 10-12. *Repository in GitHub.com showing changes*

To create a pull request, select the Compare & pull request button. This will open a pull request. You have the option to merge the branch *ch11* into any branch that exists at github.com. For any branch you select to merge into, GitHub will run a quick check to see if the branch can be merged.

For this example, I am going to merge *ch11* into the *main* branch. This will take all of the changes in *ch11* and add them to the *main* branch. Before creating the pull request, I can review the files changed if I scroll down. Once I am ready to create the pull request, I can select the Create pull request button.

Tip   In many organizations, the pull request is used as part of the code review process.

Once a pull request is created, GitHub will run additional validations to confirm there are no merge conflicts. This pull request will stay open until it is merged. In my example, once the code is merged, all of the changes will be added to the main branch. After the code is merged, anyone pulling down a copy of the *main* branch will also have the updated changes from the *ch11* branch.

Implementing source control is a big step in getting your database projects to be more manageable. Champion a source control initiative at your company. Reach out to other departments and put procedures in place that make sure everyone feels comfortable implementing source control. You also walked through the beginning steps of getting your database added to source control. This is the beginning of a journey that will have some hiccups but can save you time in the long run. Now that you have implemented source control, you are ready for the next steps in managing your T-SQL code. The next chapter will focus on the various methods you can use to test your T-SQL code and confirm that you are complying with various coding standards.

CHAPTER 11

Testing

When you need to write or modify some T-SQL code, you may be tempted to just start writing the code. In many cases, the necessary database code is simple enough that no additional analysis is needed. Eventually, the data being queried or the T-SQL code is complex enough that you want to make certain your code is working as expected. During these times, you may want to test your T-SQL changes. While you can start testing T-SQL code at any time, you may find it helpful to start certain habits early on before dealing with complex scenarios.

You may be ready to start testing your code, but you do not know where to start. The type of testing you will do will depend on what you are trying to accomplish. You can implement testing to confirm that a single piece of functionality is working as expected. It is also possible to test interactions between two or more pieces of code. This type of testing can also be useful when trying to confirm the downstream effects of implementing changes to your T-SQL code. You can also test to ensure that the code you write matches your coding standards. While any type of testing is valuable, the most significant benefits come when using all three in conjunction.

Unit Testing

You have your next task, and you are ready to start writing some T-SQL. You also want to implement functionally testing your code. When you test a single piece of code, this is called *unit testing*. Understanding what unit tests are and why you should use them can help improve your T-SQL code quality. Unit tests are beneficial because they allow you to quickly and easily verify the accuracy of your T-SQL code. Let's get started writing your first unit tests for SQL Server. This section will go over the process of creating your first unit test. This will include designing a test case, writing a unit test, confirming that the unit test is working, and updating your code to produce the correct results for your unit test.

© Elizabeth Noble 2023
E. Noble, *Pro T-SQL 2022*, https://doi.org/10.1007/978-1-4842-9256-3_11

The concept of unit testing is basic. You have a single change that you want to make to your T-SQL code. Unit testing allows you to test and confirm the functionality for a single piece of code. One of the common methods of using unit tests is to create a test case that fails, such as expecting the count of customers that are inactive to be zero when executing `dbo.GetCustomer`. This will fail because the current code for the stored procedure selects all customers. Then you write the T-SQL code, run the unit test, and repeat until the unit test passes. This is *test-driven design*. Whether you are implementing new functionality or resolving a bug in T-SQL, unit tests can help verify your code.

When creating unit tests, you need to think differently than you normally do when you set out to write T-SQL code. You are creating unit tests to confirm that the code you are writing works as expected. In order to verify that your T-SQL code is working as expected, you want your unit test to indicate a pass. When creating your unit test, your first execution of the unit test should fail. Starting with a failing unit test indicates that the desired functionality does not exist.

There are many different implementations of running unit tests. Unit tests can be written inside of Visual Studio. You can also use a free third-party unit testing framework that creates database objects in T-SQL. Another option is to use a paid third-party tool to create and run your unit tests. There are benefits and drawbacks to each of these options.

Another factor in determining how you will implement unit testing is in how you want to run your unit tests. If you have not had a chance to develop an automated way to manage code and deployments, you may decide that you prefer to manually run your unit tests. However, if you have an automated build and deployment pipeline, you may find it easier to automate your unit tests. The easiest method that has the least amount of overhead is manually running your unit tests. This can be running these tests with a stored procedure or through a GUI.

You can use unit tests to verify just about anything with your database schema. Most of those unit tests are for testing functionality for your database objects like stored procedures, views, and functions. I may be biased, but I hope you have far more stored procedures than views or queries. Do not be concerned if you do not have any unit tests in place now. You can create unit tests as you need them. This may mean that you do not have complete code coverage for your unit tests, but it prevents you from spending time implementing unit tests for code that is not modified frequently.

Before you write your first unit test, you need to know what functionality you will be developing. Let's change the stored procedure `dbo.GetCustomer` to only display customers that are active. When I first started unit testing my T-SQL code, I would run my unit tests manually. In this case, let's look for customers that are currently not active. You can create a unit test to check for inactive records. If your unit test finds any inactive records, it will fail. If your unit test does not find any inactive records, it will succeed or pass. Let's run the query shown in Listing 11-1 to find any customers that are not active.

Listing 11-1. Finding Inactive Customers

```
SELECT CustomerID,
       FirstName,
       LastName,
       IsActive
FROM dbo.Customer
WHERE IsActive = 0;
```

When running this query, you may get the results displayed in Table 11-1.

Table 11-1. *Inactive Customers*

CustomerID	FirstName	LastName	IsActive
12	Selena	Tiesto	False
27	Ian	West	False

Once you get the results in Table 11-1, you know what records will be affected by dbo.GetCustomer changing to pull back active customers instead of all customers. The unmodified stored procedure is shown in Listing 11-2.

Listing 11-2. Original Stored Procedure

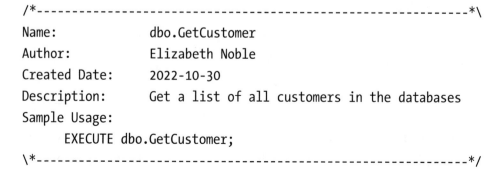

```
/*----------------------------------------------------------------*\
Name:           dbo.GetCustomer
Author:         Elizabeth Noble
Created Date:   2022-10-30
Description:    Get a list of all customers in the databases
Sample Usage:
       EXECUTE dbo.GetCustomer;
\*----------------------------------------------------------------*/
```

```
CREATE OR ALTER PROCEDURE dbo.GetCustomer
AS
  SELECT
        CustomerID,
        FirstName,
        LastName,
        Address,
        City,
        PostalCode,
        Country,
        IsActive,
        DateCreated,
        DateModified,
        DateDisabled
  FROM dbo.Customer;
```

When executing this stored procedure, you expect to see all customers in the table being returned. After executing this stored procedure, you get the records shown in Table 11-2.

Table 11-2. *Sample of All Customers*

CustomerID	FirstName	LastName	IsActive
1	Myra	Acharya	True
2	Jose	Gomez	True
12	Selena	Tiesto	False
27	Ian	West	False
401409	Stacy	Alexander	True
401407	Karim	Khalil	True
401405	Marty`	Bethel	True

You can see in Table 11-2 that both active and inactive customers are returned when executing the stored procedure. In this way, you have created a basic unit test, the query in Listing 11-1, and confirmed that this test failed when running the stored procedure in Listing 11-2 since the inactive records were also returned with the result set.

The next step is to figure out how to get the unit test to pass. For this example, the change is simple. Let's add a line at the end of the stored procedure where only active customers are returned, as shown in Listing 11-3.

Listing 11-3. Stored Procedure After Modification

```
/*----------------------------------------------------------*\
Name:              dbo.GetCustomer
Author:            Elizabeth Noble
Created Date:      2022-10-30
Description:       Get a list of all active customers in the databases
Sample Usage:
        EXECUTE dbo.GetCustomer;
\*----------------------------------------------------------*/
CREATE OR ALTER PROCEDURE dbo.GetCustomer
AS
  SELECT
        CustomerID,
        FirstName,
        LastName,
        Address,
        City,
        PostalCode,
        Country,
        IsActive,
        DateCreated,
        DateModified,
        DateDisabled
  FROM dbo.Customer
    WHERE IsActive = 1;
```

Once this stored procedure has been created, you can execute it to confirm that the new functionality is working as expected. In this case, you want to verify that CustomerIDs 2 and 5 are no longer being returned. Based on the preceding code, you expect the result set from Listing 11-3 to match what is shown in Table 11-3.

Table 11-3. *Sample Active Customers*

CustomerID	FirstName	LastName	IsActive
1	Myra	Acharya	True
2	Jose	Gomez	True
401409	Stacy	Alexander	True
401407	Karim	Khalil	True
401405	Marty`	Bethel	True

You have confirmed that the changes you made to Listing 11-3 have correctly removed the inactive customers from the result set. This is how T-SQL code is commonly tested. Executing and comparing results before and after a change is a valid way to test code changes, but it comes at the cost of repeatability. Building a collection of unit tests allows you to retest changes in each deployment to ensure that functionality is not lost from one software release to the next.

This method of testing your code is a good place to start, but it can be difficult to follow consistently. You may have some tables that can store data in various states. For instance, if you want to find the information about the frequency of orders for an on-sale product, the logic to test the results gets more complex. This is where using third-party tools can be helpful.

Finding individual sample sets for your data can be time consuming and error prone. In addition, you may spend more time trying to find the right test case rather than writing or testing the T-SQL code. Another challenge is that you may skip over important test cases due to the time and energy spent manually finding test data that already exists in the database. However, using T-SQL to find specific test cases in your data is not your only option. You can manually insert test data and perform your tests on the records that have been inserted. This method allows you to determine the best scenarios for the code you are testing. In most cases, this sample data will not remain in a centralized location. You may still need to rewrite specific examples each time you test a new piece of functionality.

There are different types of unit testing tools available to you. Unit testing can be handled by adding additional T-SQL objects to your database. Another option is to pay for third-party tools that can help manage your unit tests. Another option is to use Visual Studio to create and manage unit tests. While all these options are valid and have their own benefits, I want to focus on what you can accomplish by creating unit tests natively in Visual Studio. Figure 11-1 shows the first step to create a unit test in Visual Studio.

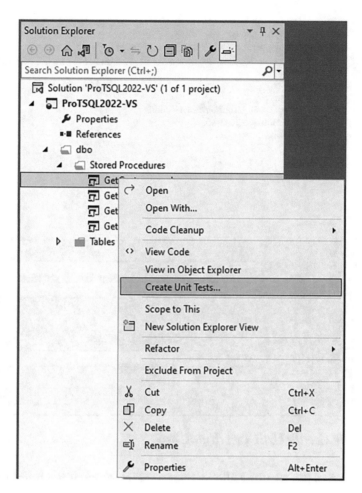

Figure 11-1. *Creating a unit test*

Once you select the option to create a unit test, Visual Studio will walk you through the process of creating your first unit test. The dialog box in Figure 11-2 will open.

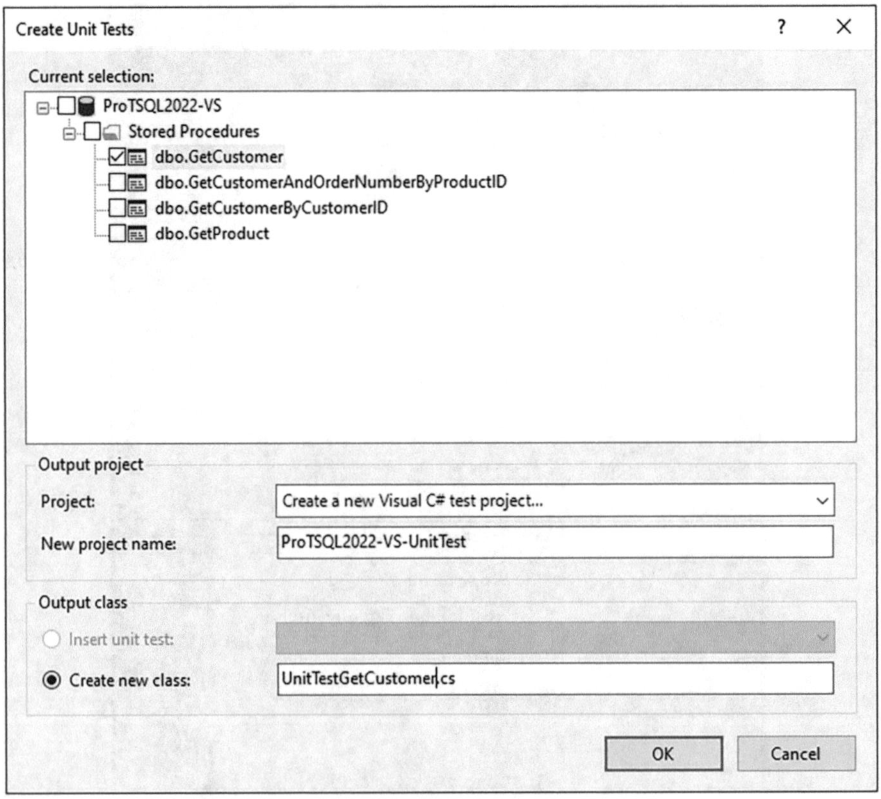

Figure 11-2. The Create Unit Test dialog box

The top portion of the window allows you to select which objects should be used to create unit tests. For this example, let's work on creating a new unit test for the dbo. GetCustomer stored procedure. You are also creating your first unit test associated with this database project. You can select that you want to create a new Visual C# test project. However, you do not need to know C# to start creating your own unit tests in Visual Studio. Give this new project a name and create a new class. You can reuse this class for other unit tests going forward.

Once you select OK on the dialog window, you will get another pop-up, as shown in Figure 11-3.

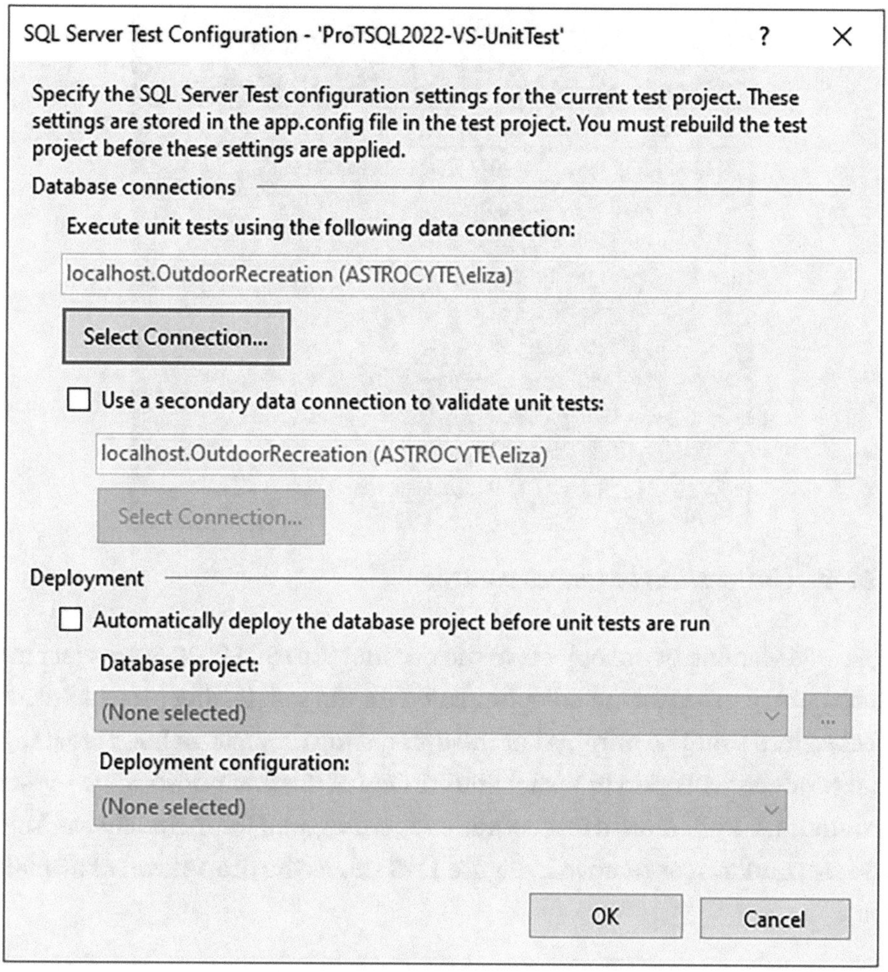

Figure 11-3. *Setting the connection string*

There are a couple of options that can be set here. Most of this has to do with selecting the data source you are using where you can perform the unit tests. Select the pre-existing Menu database to run the unit tests. You have the option to automatically deploy the database before running the unit tests. However, let's only deploy the database if the unit tests passes.

Once you have set the connection string and configured the additional settings, Visual Studio will add a new project to the existing solution. You can see in Figure 11-4 how your database project will look along with the unit testing project.

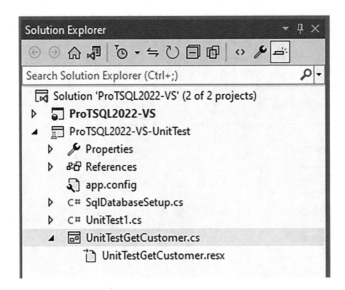

Figure 11-4. *Unit testing in source control*

In Figure 11-4, none of the objects in the original ProTSQL2022-VS project have
been altered. You can see all the objects created for the unit testing project are available
to be checked into source control. After the unit testing project has been created, some
additional windows will open in Visual Studio. One of these windows allows you to
set test conditions. By default, a test condition is configured for Inconclusive. You can
leave this test condition or remove it. Figure 11-5 shows the drop-down of available test
conditions.

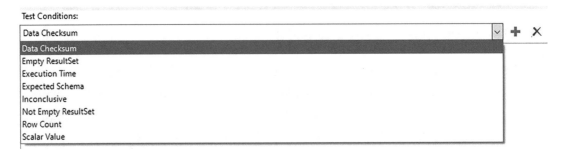

Figure 11-5. *Available unit test options*

Before you begin creating your unit test, let's define the purpose of each of these
conditions in Table 11-4.

Table 11-4. *Unit Test Conditions*

Test Condition	Description
Data Checksum	Finds the CheckSum of the unit test. Test passes if the CheckSum matches the original unit test.
	This should only be used if the data returned in the result set will remain the same.
Empty ResultSet	Checks to see if any data is returned. Test passes if no data is returned.
Execution Time	Checks the overall execution time of the query. Test passes if the query completes in the specified amount of time.
Expected Schema	Checks the schema of the object returned. Test passes if the columns and data types match the expected schema.
Inconclusive	This is created by the system as a placeholder and should be removed once the first unit test is created.
Not Empty ResultSet	Checks to see if any data is returned. Test passes if data is returned.
Row Count	Checks the number of rows returned. Test passes if the row count returns matches the expected count.
Scalar Value	Checks the value returned. Test passes if the value returned matches the expected value.

You want to create a unit test to verify that inactive customers are not being returned by the dbo.GetCustomer stored procedure. Similar to the manual unit test you wrote previously, you want to confirm that there are no inactive customers returned by the stored procedure dbo.GetCustomer. You can do this by selecting the condition of Empty ResultSet. You can see this test condition in Figure 11-6.

Test Conditions:

Empty ResultSet				∨ ✚ ✕
Name	Type	Value	Enabled	
emptyResultSetCondition1	Empty ResultSet	ResultSet 1 must have zero rows.	True	

Figure 11-6. *Unit test to check for Empty ResultSet*

Now that you've created a test condition, you need to write some T-SQL code for this unit test. Select Empty ResultSet as the test condition. For this unit test to pass when it is run, the T-SQL code inside the unit test must not return any results.

After you change the stored procedure, you do not want any inactive customers to be returned. In this case, a passing test case is to have no inactive customers returned. This also matches the test conditions that were created in Figure 11-6. Listing 11-4 shows the code for the unit test.

Listing 11-4. Code to Run the Unit Test

```
-- database unit test for dbo.GetCustomer

-- Create table variable to hold results
DECLARE @CustomerList TABLE
(
    CustomerID      INT,
    FirstName       VARCHAR(40),
    LastName        VARCHAR(100),
    [Address]       VARCHAR(100),
    City            VARCHAR(100),
    PostalCode      VARCHAR(20),
    Country         VARCHAR(75),
    IsActive        BIT,
    DateCreated     DATETIME2(2),
    DateModified    DATETIME2(2),
    DateDisabled    DATETIME2(2)
);

-- Insert results from dbo.GetCustomer into table variable
INSERT INTO @CustomerList
(
    CustomerID,
    FirstName,
    LastName,
    [Address],
    City,
    PostalCode,
```

```
    Country,
    IsActive,
    DateCreated,
    DateModified,
    DateDisabled
)
EXECUTE [dbo].[GetCustomer];

-- Get count of customers that are inactive
---- The unit test will pass if there are no inactive customers
---- The unit test will fail if there are inactive customers
SELECT CustomerID
FROM @CustomerList
WHERE IsActive = 0;
```

You first create a table variable. The next section of the unit test inserts the results from the stored procedure dbo.GetCustomer into the table variable. The final step is to select only the inactive records from the table variable. Once you add the preceding code to UnitTestGetCustomer.cs and save the file, you are ready to run your first unit test. You can go to the Test menu to run the unit tests as shown in Figure 11-7.

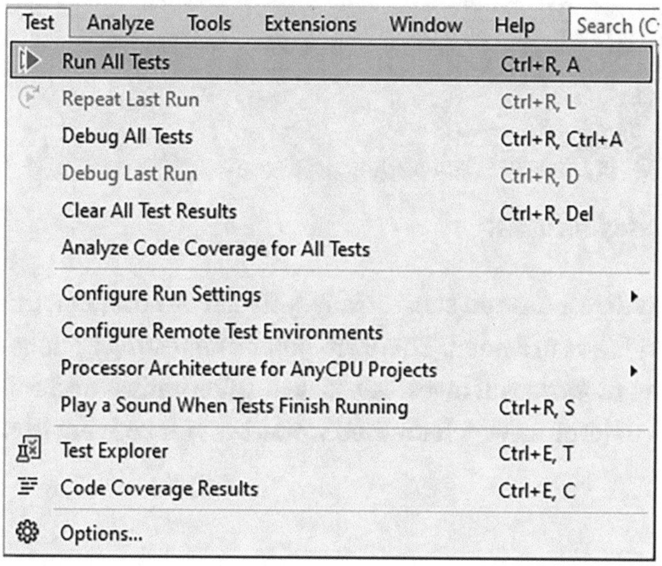

Figure 11-7. *Manually running a unit test*

You are using test-driven design for the unit tests, and you are testing this unit test before changing the original stored procedure. For this scenario, you are expecting the unit test to fail. You can see the results of running this unit test in Figure 11-8.

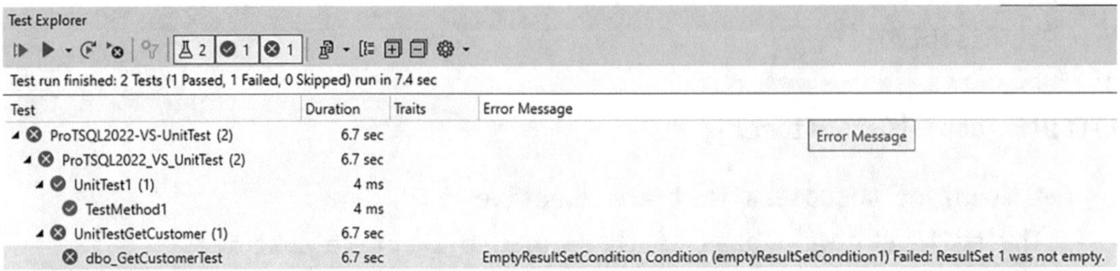

Figure 11-8. *Failed unit test*

The original stored procedure still returns inactive customers. This causes the unit test to fail. Once you update the stored procedure `dbo.GetCustomer` with the T-SQL code from Listing 11-3 and repeat the unit test, you will get the results in Figure 11-9.

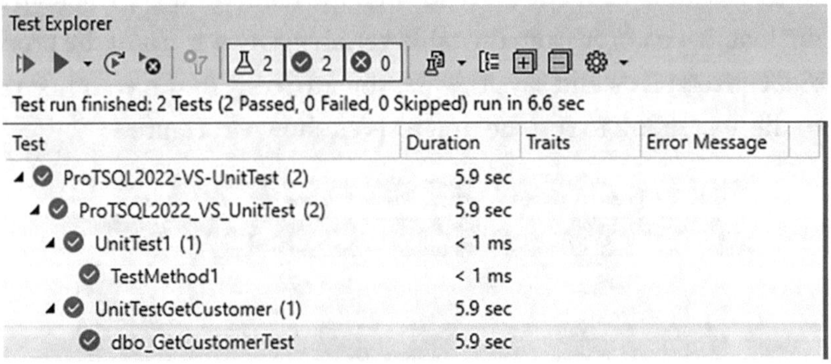

Figure 11-9. *Passed unit test*

Now that the unit test has run successfully, you can be confident that your new T-SQL code is working as intended. There are other unit testing options available for database projects. I propose you investigate several alternatives and collaborate with your coworkers to determine which method works best for your environment.

Integration Testing

While it is good to know that a single piece of database code is working as expected, most T-SQL code does not exist in isolation. The very nature of relational design infers that items in the database are related to one another. We normally think of the relationships between tables. However, stored procedures access data that exists in tables. If you want to verify an insert of data, you may run a unit test. This will confirm that the data you expected to be inserted has been inserted.

Issues can arise when there is more than one way to access the same data in the database. Oftentimes, these queries were written at different periods in time. This can cause the logic in the queries to be slightly different. I have also seen instances where different business units in a company have different calculations for the same data. If a calculation for one business unit is reused for another business unit, it can cause what appears to be inaccurate results.

This brings up a question as to how to keep your T-SQL code and query results consistent across multiple different database objects. This is where integration testing can be useful. *Integration testing* is the term used to indicate testing that is designed to work with more than a single piece of code. If you are using an application to insert data and you want to verify that the data is inserted correctly, this can be considered integration testing. You are testing both the application's ability to connect to SQL Server and the T-SQL code to insert the data into the database.

This is only one scenario where integration testing can be used. A common situation I find myself in is working with two stored procedures that are intended to pull back generally the same information. There are times that changes to one of the underlying tables or code in one of the stored procedures may cause these two stored procedures to return different results. Unfortunately, these differences in results are not usually found until well after the T-SQL code is deployed. This causes an overall loss of confidence in the applications.

While it is preferred that these intertwined stored procedures are documented or, better yet, refactored down to a single stored procedure, this is not always an option. There are costs associated with having multiple versions of similar code, but there are also costs with having multiple processes relying on the same code. For the rest of this chapter, we will assume that the T-SQL code cannot be rewritten to get rid of the dependency.

Just like unit testing database code, you can begin your integration testing manually by using T-SQL queries. The biggest factor in your integration is understanding how your environment works together. Sometimes this is found by accident, like when something breaks. Other times you may be a subject matter expert and already know the interactions. Either way, in order to begin integration testing, you first need to have at least two things to test.

You can begin by testing a data insert along with a data select of the same table(s). You can also use integration testing to compare the results of two queries. This can happen if you have one query where you return all values and another query where you search for a specific value. While these two stored procedures will not match for every record, they may have matching results for a specific record. This type of integration testing will confirm that the values returned in the columns are consistent between one another.

If you start making changes to a stored procedure that selects data, you may want to test the insert of the data along with the select for that same data. You may be updating the stored procedure `dbo.GetCustomer` to only return active customers. You can unit test this stored procedure by creating a unit test for inactive customers and a unit test for active customers. You can also use integration testing to confirm that this stored procedure will still return expected results after creating a new customer. This type of testing may be considered trivial now, but as the application grows and matures, they may become increasingly useful. Often a business needs answers faster than they can be provided. This sometimes causes database objects to be used in ways they were not originally intended.

This integration test consists of inserting a new customer into the `dbo.Customer` table. After inserting the record, you execute the `dbo.GetCustomerAndOrderNumberByProductID` stored procedure to verify that the new customer is returned. The stored procedure used to insert the record into `dbo.Customer` is shown in Listing 11-5.

Listing 11-5. Inserting a Record into the dbo.Customer Table

```
/*--------------------------------------------------------------*\
Name:           dbo.InsertCustomer
Author:         Elizabeth Noble
Created Date:   2022-10-30
Description:    Used to create a customer
```

```
Sample Usage:
    EXECUTE dbo.InsertCustomer
      'Elizabeth',
      'Noble',
      '123 Main Steet',
      'Some City',
      '00000',
      'United States',
      1,
      GETDATE(),
      GETDATE(),
      GETDATE();
\*------------------------------------------------------------*/
CREATE OR ALTER PROCEDURE dbo.InsertCustomer
    @FirstName      VARCHAR(40),
    @LastName       VARCHAR(100),
    @Address        VARCHAR(100),
    @City           VARCHAR(100),
    @PostalCode     VARCHAR(20),
    @Country        VARCHAR(75),
    @IsActive       BIT,
    @DateCreated    DATETIME2(2),
    @DateModified   DATETIME2(2),
    @DateDisabled   DATETIME2(2)
AS

INSERT INTO dbo.Customer
(

    FirstName,
    LastName,
    [Address],
    City,
    PostalCode,
    Country,
    IsActive,
```

```
    DateCreated,
    DateModified,
    DateDisabled
)
VALUES
(
    @FirstName,
    @LastName,
    @Address,
    @City,
    @PostalCode,
    @Country,
    @IsActive,
    @DateCreated,
    @DateModified,
    @DateDisabled
);
```

Now that you know how you will be adding the customers to the database, you should identify the other stored procedures needed for your integration test. Listing 11-6 shows the T-SQL code for the stored procedure to create the customer order.

Listing 11-6. Inserting a Record into the dbo.CustomerOrder Table

```
/*-------------------------------------------------------------*\
Name:           dbo.InsertCustomerOrder
Author:         Elizabeth Noble
Created Date:   2022-10-30
Description:    Used to create the header for a customer order
Sample Usage:
    EXECUTE dbo.InsertCustomerOrder
        3,
        99999,
        '2022-10-31',
        NULL;
\*-------------------------------------------------------------*/
```

```
CREATE OR ALTER PROCEDURE dbo.InsertCustomerOrder
    @CustomerID     INT,
    @OrderNumber    VARCHAR(15),
    @OrderDate      DATETIME2(2),
    @ShipDate       DATETIME2(2)
AS

INSERT INTO dbo.CustomerOrder
(
    CustomerID,
    OrderNumber,
    OrderDate,
    ShipDate,
    IsActive,
    DateCreated,
    DateModified,
    DateDisabled
)
SELECT
    @CustomerID,
    @OrderNumber,
    @OrderDate,
    @ShipDate,
    1,
    SYSDATETIME() AS DateCreated,
    SYSDATETIME() AS DateModified,
    NULL AS DateDisabled;
```

This code creates a record in the dbo.CustomerOrder table. Once the record has been
created in the dbo.CustomerOrder table, you can insert data into the dbo.OrderDetail
table. The stored procedure to create the order detail information is in Listing 11-7.

Listing 11-7. Inserting a Record into the dbo.OrderDetail Table

```
/*------------------------------------------------------------------*\
Name:               dbo.InsertOrderDetail
Author:             Elizabeth Noble
```

```
Created Date:      2022-10-30
Description:       Used to create line items for the order detail
Sample Usage:
     EXECUTE dbo.InsertOrderDetail
          111111,
          1,
          599.00,
          1;
\*----------------------------------------------------------------*/
CREATE OR ALTER PROCEDURE dbo.InsertOrderDetail
    @CustomerOrderID       INT,
    @ProductID             INT,
    @ProductPrice          DECIMAL(6,2),
    @QuantitySold          INT
AS

INSERT INTO dbo.OrderDetail
(
    CustomerOrderID,
    ProductID,
    ProductPrice,
    QuantitySold,
    IsActive,
    DateCreated,
    DateModified,
    DateDisabled
)
SELECT
    @CustomerOrderID,
    @ProductID,
    @ProductPrice,
    @QuantitySold,
    1,
    SYSDATETIME() AS DateCreated,
    SYSDATETIME() AS DateModified,
    NULL AS DateDisabled;
```

You use the above stored procedures to create a customer and populate order information for this customer.

The next step is to review what stored procedure you will be using for the integration test. In Listing 11-8, you can see the stored procedure dbo. GetCustomerAndOrderNumberByProductID.

Listing 11-8. Selecting a Customer and Order by Product

```
/*----------------------------------------------------------------*\
Name:              dbo.GetCustomerAndOrderNumberByProductID
Author:            Elizabeth Noble
Created Date:      2022-10-30
Description:       Get customer and products ordered for an order number
Sample Usage:
    EXECUTE dbo.GetCustomerAndOrderNumberByProductID 1;
\*----------------------------------------------------------------*/
CREATE OR ALTER PROCEDURE dbo.GetCustomerAndOrderNumberByProductID
    @ProductID    INT
AS
    SELECT
        cus.CustomerID,
        cus.FirstName,
        cus.LastName,
        ord.OrderNumber,
        ord.OrderDate,
        prd.ProductName,
        SUM(dtl.QuantitySold) AS QuantitySold,
        dtl.ProductPrice
    FROM dbo.Customer cus
        INNER JOIN dbo.CustomerOrder ord
        ON cus.CustomerID = ord.CustomerID
        INNER JOIN dbo.OrderDetail dtl
        ON ord.CustomerOrderID = dtl.CustomerOrderID
        INNER JOIN dbo.Product prd
        ON prd.ProductID = dtl.ProductID
    WHERE prd.ProductID = @ProductID
```

```
    GROUP BY cus.FirstName,
        cus.LastName,
        ord.OrderNumber,
        ord.OrderDate,
        prd.ProductName,
        dtl.ProductPrice
    ORDER BY cus.FirstName, cus.LastName;
```

In order to perform integration testing, you need to write some code so that you can insert into the customer. Afterward, you run the second stored procedure. You can insert these results into a temporary table and then verify that the customer created in dbo.InsertCustomer exists in the results from the stored procedure dbo.GetCustomerAndOrderNumberByProductID. In the example in Listing 11-9, you also need to add some products to the order so that the dbo.GetCustomerAndOrderNumberByProductID stored procedure can to pull some results.

Listing 11-9. Manual Integration Testing

```
-- Declare variables to be used later
DECLARE @Customer       INT;
DECLARE @Product        INT = 1;
DECLARE @CustomerOrder  INT;

-- Create CustomerID 1
EXECUTE dbo.InsertCustomer          @FirstName = 'Elizabeth',
        @LastName = 'Noble',
        @Address = '123 Main Steet',
        @City = 'Some City',
        @PostalCode = '00000',
        @County = 'United States',
        @IsActive = 1,
        @DateCreated = GETDATE(),
        @DateModified = GETDATE(),
        @DateDisabled = NULL;

-- Create order for CustomerID 1
EXECUTE dbo.InsertCustomerOrder
    @CustomerID = @Customer,
```

```
    @OrderNumber = 99999,
    @OrderDate = '2022-10-31',
    @ShipDate = NULL;

-- Get most recent insert
SELECT @CustomerOrder = SCOPE_IDENTITY();

-- SELECT TOP 1 * FROM dbo.CustomerOrder ORDER BY 1 DESC;
-- DELETE FROM dbo.CustomerOrder WHERE CustomerOrderID = 802820
-- DBCC CHECKIDENT(CustomerOrder, NORESEED)
-- DBCC CHECKIDENT(CustomerOrder, RESEED, 802819)
-- Add order detail for OrderNumber 10050 for CustomerID 1
EXECUTE dbo.InsertOrderDetail
    @CustomerOrderID = @CustomerOrder,
    @ProductID = 1,
    @ProductPrice = 599.00,
    @QuantitySold = 1;

-- Create table variable to store results below
DECLARE @OrderInfo TABLE
(
    CustomerID      INT,
    FirstName       VARCHAR(50),
    LastName        VARCHAR(100),
    OrderNumber     VARCHAR(15),
    OrderDate       DATETIME2(2),
    ProductName     VARCHAR(25),
    QuantitySold    INT,
    ProductPrice    DECIMAL(6,2)
);

-- Lookup customers and orders that have ordered ProductID 1
INSERT INTO @OrderInfo (CustomerID, FirstName, LastName, OrderNumber,
OrderDate, ProductName, QuantitySold, ProductPrice)
EXECUTE dbo.GetCustomerAndOrderNumberByProductID @Product;

-- Verify integration of stored procedures by confirming results are
returned for CustomerID 1
```

```
SELECT FirstName, LastName, OrderNumber
FROM @OrderInfo
WHERE CustomerID = @Customer;
```

When determining what you should be integration testing, think about any dependencies related to the T-SQL code that you are writing.

Some T-SQL code has a more obvious need for integration testing than others. One of the scenarios that needs the most integration testing involves different database objects that return the same data. This can be two different stored procedures. It is also possible that the integration testing can compare the results between functions and stored procedures or views and functions. While these database objects may return different columns in the result set or in a different order, the columns that are the same can be compared.

Other times you may have T-SQL code where one database object depends on the data handled in a previous step. You may have a stored procedure that updates a value in the table. A view or stored procedure may only return a specific subset of values. Using integration testing can allow you to execute the first stored procedure where you will update a lookup value in the table. Depending on the testing required, you can execute the stored procedure and confirm that the record appears. Unless the record should no longer appear, you can use integration testing to confirm that the record no longer appears.

A common situation when this can occur is when you want to soft delete or disable a data record from your application. You can use one set of T-SQL to disable the record. There may be one or more database objects that should then be tested to confirm that the disabled records no longer appear. Creating a way to keep all your integration testing scenarios together and making sure that they are repeatable is what will protect your applications in the future. Integration testing your code now confirms that your current version of T-SQL code will pass. However, automating and repeating your integration testing going forward will allow you to continue to verify that new bugs have not been introduced into your T-SQL code.

Depending on the design and complexity of your system, you may have data that is entered in one application and is sent to or used by another application. Throughout the business activities, this data may end up in different databases or different tables. This can involve different stages of data throughout your business. This can also include using integration testing between the transactional databases and a data warehouse. Using integration testing in this manner can ensure that the data entered in your applications remains consistent when it is migrated into a data warehouse.

There are more graceful methods that can help with integration testing. However, I have found that most of them reference unit testing. The only difference for using these tools with integration testing is how the tests are written. This means you can use the unit testing functionality within Visual Studio as shown in the preceding section. There are other tools you can use for your unit and integration testing, but they will not be covered in this book.

Load Testing

Another aspect of working with SQL Server is handling large data sets quickly. It's easy to hope that T-SQL code that is functionally correct will also perform well. However, this is not always what happens. While you can use execution plans to get a good idea of the relative performance of a query, this does not guarantee that the code will perform well under a heavy load. If you want to get an idea of how the T-SQL code will perform under stress, you need to perform *load testing.*

Load testing presents some very special issues. One challenge is that the hardware is often different between the load testing environment and Production. In addition to hardware differences, there is usually a difference in the data that exists in the lower environments. This can be anything from having less data in lower environments to the data in the lower environments being cleansed and having different statistics. Additional differences can include data that has been entered in the lower environments that does not match Production. In many cases, these differences cannot be resolved.

Unless you have the exact hardware and the exact Production databases, your load testing will not match Production with complete certainty. It is still beneficial to load test your T-SQL code. Even if you are unable to create the perfect load testing environment, you can still compare the relative performance of T-SQL code in your load testing environment. The next step is to figure out how to implement load testing. A simple but not very reliable method is to create T-SQL scripts to generate dummy load testing data. This method will give you a general idea of performance, but without significant analysis of existing Production data, it will not accurately reflect Production performance.

There are several third-party tools available for load testing and many of them are free. These tools should make it simpler to begin load testing. However, you are faced with the same issue of the tests not accurately reflecting Production activity. While implementing load testing is an important aspect when developing your T-SQL code, the steps needed to load test are outside the scope of this book.

Static Code Analysis

Creating standards for formatting and developing T-SQL coding standards is only a start when it comes to writing T-SQL code. In Chapter 3, I wrote about standardizing your T-SQL code. T-SQL coding standards were covered in Chapter 9. These standards are only useful if they are followed. Many times, the standards are lengthy and can be difficult to remember. There are better ways to ensure these standards are followed than trying to remember all the rules. *Static code analysis* can be used to confirm that your standards are being followed.

As discussed, there are benefits to standardizing how you and your coworkers write T-SQL. This can make the code easier to read and save time debugging issues in the T-SQL code. Unfortunately, the benefits of standardization cannot be realized if the T-SQL code getting checked into source control does not match the formatting standards. This is one situation where static code analysis can help.

Static code analysis allows you to prevent code that does not meet your T-SQL coding standards from ending up in Production. Once your code is saved and checked into source control, you can verify that the code complies with your standards prior to deploying the database code. There are options to enforce T-SQL formatting, but the main option is a third-party tool.

In addition to using static code analysis for standardization of formatting for database code, you can use static code analysis for your database coding standards. There is built-in functionality in Visual Studio 2017. You can find the window in Figure 11-10 by selecting the Code Analysis option from the Properties menu.

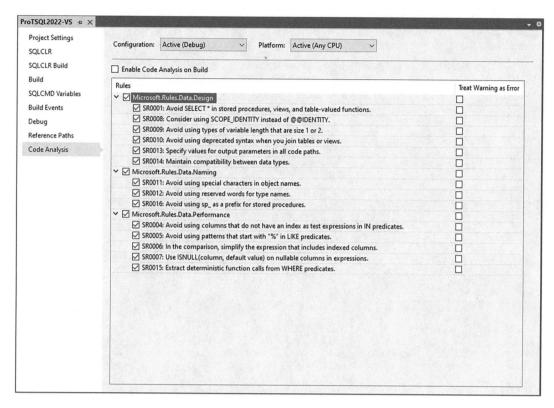

Figure 11-10. *Code analysis in database projects*

You can select code analysis to be run every time you build the database project. You also have the option of selecting which items should be included as part of your code analysis. These options include best practices and items that can affect the performance of the T-SQL code. In addition, there is the option to escalate some of these rules to error and fail instead of sending a warning message.

The benefit of static code analysis is that it automates the process of ensuring that the T-SQL code meets your business' coding standards. This can help code rejections feel less personal; the code is being reviewed and rejected as part of the overall build process. The build process will also communicate the warning or error message in a consistent method.

Getting your database code into source control is only half of the issue. The real challenge can come when trying to deploy database changes that are only saved in source control. Determining how you want to deploy your code will help you determine what method to use to save your T-SQL code. Deploying T-SQL code from source control will be discussed further in Chapter 13.

CHAPTER 12

Deployment

Throughout the course of developing software, there will come a time when you need to implement new functionality. One of the prevailing issues with new functionality is implementing that functionality in a manner that does not affect current performance. For many businesses today, the need to have applications up and running 24 hours per day is critical. This creates a scenario where any form of downtime or loss in current functionality can be incredibly expensive. While the deployment method used can help minimize the overall risk associated with new functionality, there are other options that can be used when writing new code.

A frequent issue that comes up is related to how software is developed in correlation with how code is deployed. In many projects, the amount of time needed to implement new functionality is greater than the frequency at which T-SQL code is deployed. Determining how source control is managed can mitigate some of these risks. There are different ways T-SQL code can be deployed. Understanding these methods and the best times to use them will help improve your database deployments. There are also options when it comes to how your users interact with the database code.

Methodology

Each development environment is different. Before deciding how to deploy T-SQL code, it helps to get a better understanding of how development is handled at your company. You want to know how many database developers are at your company and how many different development teams use SQL Server. Another factor you want to know is how these development teams write and deploy code. Collecting all this information enables you to determine the best method to deploy T-SQL code for your environment.

When working with SQL Server, the risks associated with code issues can often be larger than with application code. These risks are compounded when there are multiple individuals accessing the same T-SQL code. If you are in an environment where you are

© Elizabeth Noble 2023
E. Noble, *Pro T-SQL 2022*, https://doi.org/10.1007/978-1-4842-9256-3_12

the only database developer, there may be less of a chance of having issues with merge conflicts. If there are multiple database developers or teams writing T-SQL code, there is more of a chance of having more than one person working on the same database code. While some of this can be managed through source control, it is also important to be mindful of how database code is deployed.

Types of Deployment

Part of determining your deployment method includes understanding the current process you use to deploy your database code. Right now, your business may have scripts that are manually deployed. Depending on your organizational structure, you may have an environment where those scripts can be deployed at any point in time to a specific environment or you may have conditions about what days of the week those T-SQL scripts can be deployed. Knowing who is developing database code, how changes are coded and managed, and the frequency of your deployments can help you determine whether a migration or state-based approach is best for you.

If there are certain days you can deploy to various environments, this is known as a *gated deployment*. You may be using database projects in a version control system. In Chapter 11, the topic of branching and merging was covered. Your company may only use one branch for your database project. All development work by all individuals is done in the same place. On the other hand, your company may utilize *branching*. This is where your developers use a copy of the main code base and make changes to that copy. Some companies may deploy directly from a branch. This can be particularly helpful if you are not writing your database code to be able to be deployed at any point in time. Other companies, particularly ones that write code to be deployed at any point in time, may choose to have all branches merged back to master or the main branch once the work is complete. In this case, all deployments are from the main branch.

Sometimes how teams manage their workflows is determined by the frequency of their deployments. For many companies, the goal is to be able to deploy frequently. However, this does not mean that every company is ready for that frequency of deployments. For the development teams that write code in a more Kanban style, there may be no pattern for when code is deployed to Production. Other teams may have a set cadence or sprint cycle for when they deploy their code. These sprint cycles can range from weeks to months. If your company is still in the process of determining how often to release code, I caution against longer sprint cycles as it often means more changes are being deployed at once. This increases the risk of having issues in your deployment.

You also want to understand the volume of database changes happening on an average deployment. You may find that on average there are not that many database changes getting deployed every sprint. If this is the case, make sure you do not end up having a deployment with a significant number of database changes. When there are multiple changes happening to the database during a single deployment, there is not only a greater risk of having a bug, but there is also the possibility depending on your deployment method that one change to T-SQL code may overwrite another.

Before getting into two of the main methods of deploying database code, there is one additional factor you should consider. While we all want every database deployment to go out and work as expected, there may come a time where you need to undo or roll back one or more database changes from a deployment. If you do not have a rollback strategy in place, now is a good time to start considering a solid rollback strategy. When a rollback is needed, it's a bad time to start figuring out how to quickly and effectively roll back your T-SQL code. Having a method to do this repeatedly can significantly help increase the confidence you have in your deployments. Your company may use rollback scripts to streamline when you need to revert to the previous version of database code. If you are using version control, you have the option to revert to a different version of your database code. To build upon this, if you are using continuous integration, you may have a prepackaged version of the previous database code that can be deployed against your Production database in a manner of minutes.

Migration- Based Deployments

This ultimately leads us to consider the deployment methods commonly used for database deployments. One method consists of bundling all the scripts that will be deployed together. This is considered a *migration-based approach*; another option is to take everything that exists in source control and treat it as the source of truth for your database. When using this type of method, whatever database you are deploying to will be overwritten to match the database objects that exist in source control. This is commonly called a *state-based deployment*.

Now that you know what the migration-based deployment method is, you can start determining if it is the best method for your deployments. One of the main benefits of using the migration-based approach is that you can control exactly what is deployed to your database. This method of deployment often involves having all the scripts that will be deployed saved in a single location, and these scripts are usually named in a way that allows them to be deployed in a specific order. This can make your deployments easy to manage. You can quickly find at the folder where the scripts are saved and know exactly what is getting deployed.

If you use this deployment method, I recommend that you have a separate folder that keeps track of the rollback scripts that need to be deployed and the order in which these rollback scripts should be deployed. This will help if you have to roll back on deployment night and it should help you quickly find the code that needs to be rolled back if you need to roll back several deployments at once. There are some limitations with the migration-based deployment method. One of the main challenges is if you need to roll back a specific piece of code. Depending on how your source control is managed, it may not be as simple as viewing the history of that database object and restoring a previous version from source control.

A migration-based deployment method can be set up manually. You and the rest of your team can write your T-SQL code files and save them in numerical order. This really consists of creating a script in SQL Server Management Studio and saving the file with a specific naming convention. This naming convention includes specifying the deployment order such as prefixing the filename with the step number to indicate the deployment order.

You may create a file named 001_20230620_DB232_ActiveProduct.sql. However, you may then receive a request to make additional modifications to the same stored procedure. In this case, you need to remove the date columns from the stored procedure dbo.GetProduct. In Listing 12-1, you can find the T-SQL code.

Listing 12-1. Sample Script for Migration-Based Deployment

```
PRINT N'Altering [dbo].[GetProduct]...';
GO
/*-------------------------------------------------------------*\
Name:           dbo.GetProduct
Author:         Elizabeth Noble
Created Date:   2022-10-30
Description:    Get a list of all products in the databases
Updated Date:   2023-05-23
Description:    Add feature flag. If feature flag is enabled, only
                Show active products. Otherwise, show all products.
Updated Date:   2023-06-20
```

Description: Remove the feature flag. Leave only the new logic.
                         The stored procedure now only returns active products.
Updated Date: 2023-06-21
Description: Remove dates.
                         The stored procedure now only returns active products.

Sample Usage:
        EXECUTE dbo.GetProduct;
--/
CREATE OR ALTER PROCEDURE dbo.GetProduct
AS
  SELECT
        ProductID,
        ProductName,
        ProductPrice,
        IsActive
  FROM dbo.Product
  WHERE IsActive = 1;

Once you have completed your changes to the database code, you can save this code as a SQL script. Save this code with the filename 002_20230620_DB232_RemoveDates. sql. In order to make sure that your deployment runs smoothly, you can put both files in the same folder. Figure 12-1 shows the two files as they would be displayed in a file folder.

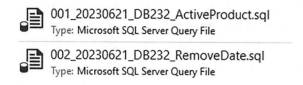

001_20230621_DB232_ActiveProduct.sql
Type: Microsoft SQL Server Query File

002_20230621_DB232_RemoveDate.sql
Type: Microsoft SQL Server Query File

Figure 12-1. *Migration-based file list*

The first script you created begins with 001. This is the first script in order by filename. This is also the first script that should be run during the next deployment. The second script you created begins with 002. These files are named specifically so that they will be run in ascending order by filename during the next software release. Writing T-SQL scripts and saving them manually is not the only method that can be used as part of a migration-based deployment. Third-party tools can help manage this process for you.

There are many proponents of migration-based deployments. One of the main challenges in developing any database code is managing how the code is maintained when multiple developers are working off the same code base. In Chapter 11, I covered branching and merging. This is the main method used to make sure that everyone developing T-SQL code for the database project can work in a manner that limits inconsistencies when multiple developers are working on the same database object. If you are working with a team that is not accustomed to source control, using a migration-based approach may be more logical. A migration-based deployment process is better suited to handle multiple changes to the data in your database. This can be part of a data cleanup or related to refactoring database objects. Another advantage of using a migration-based deployment method is that it can be easier to pick and choose exactly what database objects will be deployed. If you make frequent changes to your databases, you may end up with many scripts, which may increase the amount of time required for deployment.

Due to these factors, there are some scenarios where you may find a migration-based deployment is more effective than a state-based deployment. Smaller development teams may find a migration-based approach easier to use. If you are using source control for your database, you still need to make sure that your team synchronizes the database code for their development. The same may also be true for environments that have fewer development teams. If your team is not doing frequent deployments during the same day or has a larger maintenance window available for deployments, then the migration-based deployment method may also work well for you.

The one risk you need to keep in mind when using a migration-based approach involves database changes that happen outside of source control. You may find yourself in a situation where you need to deploy a change immediately to production. Often these changes are deployed to production without having them deployed to the lower environments or checked into source control. If you need to deploy a hotfix or a patch and this code does not end up in your source control, your environments may become out of sync. While future deployments will not overwrite your changes, you may find inconsistent behavior between your environments. In order to resolve this, any hotfix that is made manually should be added back to source control so that your development environments remain in sync with production.

State-Based Migrations

State-based rollouts involve copying the entire database schema from one environment to another environment. Migration-based deployments are not the only option available when deploying your T-SQL code. Another popular option for database deployments involves using a source for your database schema and updating your target environment to have that same database schema. This is known as a *state-based approach*. Typically, this is used with source control, but this is all not always necessary. The concept is that the target database will end up similar to the source database or source control once the deployment is complete. This method does not require source control, but it is easier to manage through source control.

Whereas each change is saved individually in its own script file when using the migration-based approach, this is not the case for a state-based deployment. In a state-based deployment, you can have many changes to the same database object, but there is only one set of T-SQL code that is deployed to your target database instance. This single T-SQL script combines all the changes into one net change. If the database object is in source control or the source database is different from the target, the change script is run on the target instance. I also like the fact that I know exactly what state the database will be in once a deployment is complete. The database in the target instance should have the same database objects that exist in the source location after the deployment is complete.

Using the same example as the one for the migration-based approach, I will walk through how this is handled as part of the state-based deployment. The first step involves going into source control and making sure that you have the latest version. Once you have the latest version, you can open the stored procedure dbo.GetProduct. After you have made these changes, you can check these changes into source control.

Suppose someone else is making changes to match the T-SQL code in Listing 12-1. If another developer wants to change this procedure, they need to be sure they are working with the latest copy. They do this by checking source control for any check-ins by another developer. In this example, they will find the change you made. If they skip this step, your code change could be lost or there could be a merge conflict.. They can then make changes to the dbo.GetProduct stored procedure. These changes can then be merged back into the master branch. When it is time to deploy this code, the source location will have both changes. These changes will be to only show active products and to remove the date columns. Instead of deploying these changes one at a time, the stored procedure dbo.GetProduct will be deployed to the target instance once. This single update to the stored procedure will include both changes.

When working with many developers or many different development teams, there may be a benefit to using a state-based deployment method. This is due to the frequency of changes that may be happening in the overall database project. While the state-based migration can work for database projects that have a few or many changes, this deployment method is better at managing frequent changes. This is because those many developers making many changes means many steps to the rollout process when using migration, but fewer files are changed in a state-based approach. When using a state-based approach, your rollout will be faster and less prone to someone making a tiny typo of the wrong file name and causing an issue deploying the code. When using the state-based approach, you can be confident that any changes in your source location will exist in your target location after the deployment is complete. This also means that if there are many changes made to Production that were not put into source control, these changes will be overwritten during the next deployment. If your team is performing frequent updates especially throughout the day, you may find the state-based approach takes less time for a deployment. At the very least, this is since there are usually less changes being deployed through the state-based approach when there are frequent deployments.

One of the largest challenges in using the state-based approach has to do with deploying data manipulation changes. These data changes can involve managing configuration tables, managing feature flags, adding default values, or correcting data that was affected by a prior bug. The state-based approach is excellent for comparing the overall database schema. However, there are limitations when it comes to changing the data within the database. In most cases, this is done through manual files that may be executed after deployment. If you are using source control, this can be managed through the pre-deployment and post-deployment scripts. There is only one predeployment and one postdeployment script if you are using source control. This can make the process of changing data somewhat more complicated as you will either need to write your T-SQL code to be able to run once and then be ignored or go into source control and frequently change either your predeployment or postdeployment script.

Styles of Development

There are several different ways that database development teams can manage their workflows. The methodology used can contribute to what type of deployment method should be used.

Kanban

My first job that involved consistently writing database code did not have any strict timelines. The goal was to make changes and deploy them as quickly as possible. This was often because I was creating SQL Server Reporting Service (SSRS) reports. Typically, this type of development can be referred to as Kanban. Kanban refers to a methodology for managing change requests. The high-level concept is that there is a continuous queue of work. Requests go into a backlog and are worked, usually one at a time, until they are complete.

Scrum

The Scrum method of code development involves more structure that Kanban. Scrum involves several steps such as ensuring work items are well defined, estimating how long it will take to complete a specific work item, and determining when the item will be completed. To determine when code is expected to be complete and deployable, organizations identify how often they intend to deploy code. This length of time is called a *sprint or sprint cycle*. Each sprint is expected to have a fixed quantity of work that can be completed. Using the estimates, work items are added to a sprint based on priority until the estimated work matches the expected quantity of work in a sprint. This is a high-level definition and not intended to be an in-depth resource on how to implement Scrum or Kanban for your database teams. For these deployments, all user stories in the sprint are expected to be deployed as part of the sprint. While there are some ways to deploy everything in a sprint without changing functionality, our code was often not written that way.

If your business is trying to move toward being able to deploy changes at any point in time, consider changing how you develop your database code. This change can be a shift in how you think about your solutions and how you write your code. Concepts like using feature flags will help you. Essentially you want to write your T-SQL code in a way that it can be deployed at any point in time and your applications will not break. However, getting to this point requires several fundamental steps. The first is knowing how your company develops its T-SQL code. You may want to handle deployments differently if you have many developers working on T-SQL code for a single application than if you have each developer working on a separate application. This will help you determine what method of deployment will work best for you.

Feature Flags

You may be asked to make some changes to an application that will require many different user stories. To put it differently, you may be refactoring an application where that process is expected to take months. At the same time, you know your business may deploy database code every two weeks. The issue becomes how to develop T-SQL code where you can confirm the code works in the existing database structure but also make sure that these database changes do not end up in Production before they are ready.

This is a question not only many database developers but also software developers have asked themselves. At the heart of the issue is how to write database code that can be turned on and off. One method that attempts to handle this is the use of feature flags. Feature flags are a programmatic way to enable or disable functionality. They are not a SQL Server feature but rather a method of implementing T-SQL code. Ideally, feature flags are used to allow code to be deployed as soon as possible while allowing fine-tuned control over when the functionality will be enabled. The intention with feature flags is to leave them in place for a limited amount of time as they are only intended to allow code to be deployed before enabling the features. The high-level process is the following:

1. Add a feature flag to the database as disabled.

2. Update the stored procedure to use IF ((SELECT IsActive FROM dbo.FeatureFlag WHERE FeatureFlagID = <FeatureFlagID>) = 1)... EXISTS...

3. Enable the feature from the database table.

4. Update the stored procedure to remove the IF... EXISTS and only use the new logic.

5. Disable or delete the feature from the database table.

There are many ways to implement feature flags. The goal remains the same, to create database code and database objects that can be configured to work in one scenario or another.

When using feature flags, you have the option to enable or disable new functionality at will. This method of managing your database code can allow you to write code, deploy the code to production, and enable the new functionality at a later time chosen by the business. In addition to being able to determine exactly when to enable new functionality, you get the added benefit of being able to roll back changes almost instantaneously by updating a single value in a database. There are some foundations you want to have in place before fully embracing feature flags. For instance, you want to be in the habit of unit testing your database code. When it comes to feature flags, you need to unit test when the feature flag is enabled, and you also need to unit test when the feature flag is disabled to confirm that your applications are using the pre-existing database logic.

I suggest you wait until you have fully implemented source control for your databases before embracing feature flags. One of the reasons for this recommendation is that there is additional effort in managing your feature flags. When you create feature flags for your database objects, you need to create some additional logic to allow your applications to use the pre-existing T-SQL code or the new database code. This requires both discipline and defined processes to determine when to remove the feature flags from the code. While feature flags will work great for database objects like stored procedures, functions, or views, feature flags are not the solution for everything you develop. Some changes, such as changes to database columns, cannot be toggled on and off. To manage these types of changes to database objects, I will discuss some solutions at the end of this section.

When using feature flags for your T-SQL code, you have a couple options to determine what feature flags are enabled at any given time. There are two main solutions I've heard proposed when it comes to feature flags and databases. The first one may be more application code-based. It consists of supplying the feature flag values in a configuration file. The second option is more of a T-SQL-based solution. This solution involves creating a table to store the feature flags in their current status such as enabled or disabled. There are benefits and downsides to each option. Using application code to manage feature flags may be easier to implement and manage. However, it may be more difficult for the database administrators to support these feature flags. If you keep the feature flag values in the database, you need to be disciplined in managing those feature flags and removing them. It can become very easy to end up with a table that is cluttered with deprecated feature flags. The downside is that only users with access to the database table can confirm the value associated with each feature flag.

When you deploy your database code, you can deploy the feature flag as disabled. Once you are ready to enable the new functionality, you can set the feature flag to enabled. You want to define a process for determining when it is time to switch entirely to the new functionality. When you are ready to operate entirely on the new functionality, remove the previous T-SQL code. Also remove any reference to feature flags as part of this process. The challenge with this method is it can become easy to skip over the process of removing the prior database code. If your T-SQL code is not cleaned up on a regular basis, this can greatly diminish the manageability of your code going forward.

If you need to update a stored procedure to use new logic, you can use feature flags in order to deploy this change whenever you want. Refer to Listing 12-2, you can find the original stored procedure that has not been modified.

Listing 12-2. Original Stored Procedure

```
/*---------------------------------------------------------------*\
Name:               dbo.GetProduct
Author:             Elizabeth Noble
Created Date:       2022-10-30
Description:        Get a list of all products in the databases
Sample Usage:
        EXECUTE dbo.GetProduct;
\*---------------------------------------------------------------*/
CREATE OR ALTER PROCEDURE dbo.GetProduct
AS
  SELECT
        ProductID,
        ProductName,
        ProductPrice,
        IsActive,
        DateCreated,
        DateModified,
        DateDisabled
  FROM dbo.Product;
GO
```

This stored procedure pulls various information about all products. In this T-SQL code, the stored procedure does not differentiate between active and inactive products. Information about all products is returned. You may find that this stored procedure was only supposed to return active products. You need to update this stored procedure to only return active products and exclude the IsActive column. Removing this column prevents this code change from being enabled as soon as it is deployed.

In this case, you need to use something like feature flags to allow you the flexibility to create these changes in the stored procedure and control when these changes are available to the application. When working with feature flags, you need a way to determine whether a feature flag is enabled or not. This is how you and the database code will know which T-SQL code should be executed at a given time. One option is to create a table to store the information about the feature flags. You can create a table like the one shown in Listing 12-3.

Listing 12-3. Creating a Feature Flag Table

```
CREATE TABLE dbo.FeatureFlag
(
        FeatureFlagID      SMALLINT,
        IsActive           BIT,
        DateCreated        DATETIME2,
        DateModified       DATETIME2
);
```

This table is simple. There is an integer value for the feature flag, a value that indicates if the feature flag is enabled, a date when the feature flag was created, and a date when the feature flag values were last updated. This table allows you to store information about what feature flags are enabled. In order to use this feature flag table, you need to enter information about this feature flag into the table created in Listing 12-3. The INSERT statement in Listing 12-4 shows an insert into the dbo. FeatureFlag table.

Listing 12-4. Inserting a Feature Flag Record

```
INSERT INTO dbo.FeatureFlag
(
        FeatureFlagID,
        IsActive,
        DateCreated,
        DateModified
)
VALUES (947,0,SYSDATETIME(),SYSDATETIME());
```

You have inserted a record for Feature Flag 947. At the time of the insert, the feature flag is disabled. The goal is that the existing stored procedure will continue to return the same results as it did before the feature flag was added. In the stored procedure in Listing 12-5, you add logic to allow the stored procedure to return different results depending on whether Feature Flag 947 is disabled or enabled.

Listing 12-5. Stored Procedure with Feature Flag

```
/*----------------------------------------------------------------*\
Name:            dbo.GetProduct
Author:          Elizabeth Noble
Created Date:    2022-10-30
Description:     Get a list of all products in the databases
Updated Date:    2023-05-20
Description:     Add feature flag. If feature flag is enabled, only
                 Show active products. Otherwise, show all products.

Sample Usage:
     EXECUTE dbo.GetProduct;
\*----------------------------------------------------------------*/
CREATE OR ALTER PROCEDURE dbo.GetProduct
AS

    IF ((SELECT IsActive FROM dbo.FeatureFlag WHERE FeatureFlagID =
    947) = 1)
         BEGIN
             SELECT
                 ProductID,
                 ProductName,
                 ProductPrice,

                 DateCreated,
                 DateModified,
                 DateDisabled
             FROM dbo.Product
             WHERE IsActive = 1;
         END
    ELSE
```

```
BEGIN
        SELECT
                ProductID,
                ProductName,
                ProductPrice,
                IsActive,
                DateCreated,
                DateModified,
                DateDisabled
        FROM dbo.Product;
    END;
```

The first portion of this query now only return results if Feature Flag 947 is enabled. For any other scenario, the stored procedure returns the results from the second query. The original state for the feature flag is to be disabled. When the feature flag is disabled, all products will be returned. Once this code has been deployed to Production, there will come a time where you are ready to enable the new functionality. When this happens, running the T-SQL code in Listing 12-6 will enable the feature flag.

Listing 12-6. Enabling the Feature Flag

```
UPDATE dbo.FeatureFlag
SET    IsActive = 1,
       DateModified = GETDATE()
WHERE FeatureFlagID = 947;
```

Enabling this feature flag will cause the stored procedure dbo.GetProduct to now only return active products.

Once you are confident that the new code is working as intended and there is no business need to roll back, update the stored procedure to only return results for the new database code. Removing the feature flag will also protect this stored procedure from returning inaccurate results if the feature flag gets updated in error. The T-SQL code in Listing 12-7 shows the final state of the dbo.GetProduct stored procedure.

Listing 12-7. Final Stored Procedure

```
/*------------------------------------------------------------*\
Name:              dbo.GetProduct
Author:            Elizabeth Noble
Created Date:      2022-10-30
Description:       Get a list of all products in the databases
Updated Date:      2023-05-20
Description:       Add feature flag. If feature flag is enabled, only
                   Show active products. Otherwise, show all products.
Updated Date:      2023-06-20
Description:       Remove the feature flag. Leave only the new logic.
                   The stored procedure now only returns active products.

Sample Usage:
      EXECUTE dbo.GetProduct;
\*------------------------------------------------------------*/
CREATE OR ALTER PROCEDURE dbo.GetProduct
AS
  SELECT
        ProductID,
        ProductName,
        ProductPrice,

        DateCreated,
        DateModified,
        DateDisabled
  FROM dbo.Product
  WHERE IsActive = 1;
```

The database code in the stored procedure dbo.GetProduct has been updated. Before any code changes, this stored procedure returned all products. After creating the feature flag, the stored procedure is updated to include logic to either return all products or only active products depending on the feature flag status. When the changes have been confirmed, you can remove the logic for the feature flag. This leaves the stored procedure in place with only the updated T-SQL code. You can either clean up the dbo. FeatureFlag table by setting IsActive to FALSE or delete the row for FeatureFlagID 947.

How you manage your branching and merging in source control may determine how frequently you need to deploy database code that is incomplete. You may find yourself in a situation where you are working on developing database code but it is not complete before your next deployment. It is often easiest to write code in a way that it can be deployed when it is completed. However, with the move toward Agile software development, it has become increasingly important to write T-SQL code in a manner where it can be deployed at any moment in time. This is where the true benefit of feature flags can be realized.

Automated Deployment

There are many ways to handle your database deployments. There are different tools you can use to automate your database deployments and there are different deployment strategies you can use. Determining what method to use for your database deployments depends on what types of issues you are trying to prevent or resolve. These issues can include failing to update code during a deployment, overwriting code during a deployment, preventing unwanted code from being deployed, or improving the speed of your deployments. These deployment strategies depend on what type of T-SQL code is being deployed. Other methods of deploying database code involve deploying your database in a way that can help you catch issues in development before the changes are deployed to all other environments including production.

There are ways to streamline and automate deploying T-SQL code using SQL Server Management Studio, Visual Studio, or PowerShell. If you want to automate your database deployments without having your database in source control, you want to take some additional steps to protect your database. SSDT allows all objects to begin with CREATE. When deploying code, SSDT determines if an object should use CREATE or ALTER. If you want to change data in the database using DML, you need to use predeployment or postdeployment scripts. When doing so, your T-SQL code should be written in a way to allow the code to be run more than once. This may not be the method you are using now, but you should consider what would happen if someone accidentally tried to deploy the same scripts again. Write your scripts so that they will run successfully no matter how many times they are executed. If you are using source control already, your source control should manage this functionality for you.

When deploying T-SQL code as part of a migration-based deployment, the process may function differently if you are not using source control. For migration-based deployments, you usually have a set of scripts that needs to be run for your deployment. When not using source control, the most complicated step can sometimes be determining exactly what should be deployed. When you are ready to deploy your T-SQL code, ideally the scripts will be saved in the same folder. At this point, you can either manually run all these migration scripts or determine what can be done to automate running the scripts. If you choose to run the scripts manually, you must open each script and make sure that you are connected to the correct instance of SQL Server. There are other options you can use to improve the consistency and speed of deploying these migration scripts. You can use batch files or PowerShell can help you automate these deployments. Listing 12-8 includes the PowerShell needed to run all SQL script files saved in the folder `C:\Deploy`.

Listing 12-8. PowerShell to Run SQL Scripts

```
Invoke-DbaQuery -SQLInstance localhost -Database OutdoorRecreation -File
"C:\Deploy\*.sql"
```

This code indicates that all files with the extension of `.sql` in the `C:\Deploy` folder should be executed on the localhost SQL Server on the `OutdoorRecreation` database.

Tip   This code is executed using the PowerShell module dbatools. This module is a SQL Server community-built open source project. For more details, you can visit `https://dbatools.io/`.

If you are using a state-based migration approach and you are not using source control, it can also be automated using PowerShell. These DACPACs can be generated from a database that already exists and an instance of SQL Server. Depending on how you choose to work with DACPACs, you can either have the target database updated to match the code from the DACPAC or you can create a script file based off the differences between the DACPAC and the target database. Once you locate the DACPAC file that is generated from your solution or workspace, you can run the PowerShell code shown in Listing 12-9.

Listing 12-9. PowerShell to Compare DACPAC

```
Publish-DbaDacPackage -SQLInstance localhost -Database OutdoorRecreation -Path
C:\temp\OutdoorRecreation.dacpac
```

This PowerShell is also from the dbatools module. Instead of executing all SQL Server files in the `C:\temp` folder, this PowerShell compares the schema from the DACPAC file to the schema of the `OutdoorRecreation` database on the localhost server. This PowerShell command includes some additional toggles such as `-GenerateDeploymentReport` or `-ScriptOnly`. The `-GenerateDeploymentReport` creates an XML file showing the changes that are made to the database. The `-ScriptOnly` option outputs a SQL Script file that can be executed manually. Depending on how you choose to work with DACPACs, you can either have the target database updated to match the code from the DACPAC or you can create a script file based off the differences between the DACPAC and the target database.

The easiest way to move towards a fully automated deployment is to use third-party tools. However, this is not the only option available to you. If you are interested in migration-based deployments, there is at least one free third-party tool available: DbUp. While this tool may be helpful for managing migration-based deployments, I will not be covering DbUp as part of this book. Be aware that if you are going to use migration-based deployments and source control, you will need an extension or another tool like DbUp.

If your database is in source control and you are using state-based migrations, you have several alternatives to deploy your database changes. You have the option of deploying the changes directly from Visual Studio to your target database instance. While you are still manually deploying your code, there can be a significant time savings so that you don't have to open up multiple files and execute each one individually. However, without using third-party tools to further automate your deployments, you will need to create PowerShell scripts to create the DACPAC or SQL script file and deploying those files to the target instance.

In the previous section of deployment methods, I went over migration-based and state-based deployments. When deploying changes to that modify data, such as with data manipulation language (DML) queries, you want to make certain that you cannot accidentally modify the data more than once. While we may want to make sure that every script can be written in a way where they could not update the data more than once, there may be times where it is not possible to write a script to prevent this from happening. If this happens, you can use a similar concept to feature flags. This is where you create a table to record when a data modification script has been run. The first time this script completes, the table can be updated with a value indicating that all records were updated. For instance, if you want to increase the product price by 10%, your T-SQL code should be written in a way that does not update the product prices each time the database project is deployed. The script can also check to make sure that this value does not exist in the table prior to running the script. This table can also be checked and populated either as pass or fail for the entire T-SQL script or each individual record can be recorded when the update is complete.

You may also find that there are times where database code is ready to be deployed but the business is not ready to enable the new functionality. Earlier in this chapter, I covered how feature flags can help you control whether applications use the current state or a future state of database code. There is a deployment method that can help in these situations. The largest advantage here is that you can deploy database code without having your applications use this new T-SQL code. Depending on the database objects that are changing, this can be relatively easy or difficult to manage.

When you want to deploy T-SQL code changes, but you are not ready for those changes to be released to the Production environment, you can use a deployment method to help you. This deployment method is referred to as *dark deployment*. This method uses a feature flag or a similar concept. You deploy T-SQL code so that the database code continues to function as it always has. When you are ready to enable the new functionality, you can enable the feature flags. This switches how the database code works so that it uses the new functionality instead of the original database code.

The beginning state of the application and the database is shown in Figure 12-2.

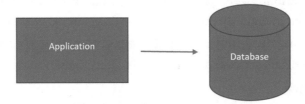

Figure 12-2. *Unmodified application and database*

The next step in a dark deployment is to update the database by deploying the SQL scripts. If you are using feature flags, the feature flags should be disabled. The database in Figure 12-3 has been updated with the new database code.

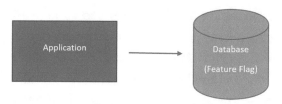

Figure 12-3. *Deploying database changes*

After the T-SQL code with feature flags has been deployed, you are now ready to deploy the application. Once you deploy the application and enable the feature flag, your application and database will be in the same state, as in Figure 12-4.

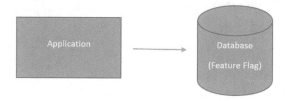

Figure 12-4. *Deploying the application and enabling feature flags*

These steps can allow you to deploy your database changes dark.

There are many risks involved with database deployments. These risks can involve T-SQL code or application code that no longer work as expected. There are also risks that the same code may appear to work but does not work as expected. In some cases, this issue may be cosmetic. Other times, a bug in the database code may negatively affect the quality of the data that is saved in the database. This can include altering the data in a way that the data is no longer usable. In order to avoid these types of scenarios, different deployment methods can be used to protect the database and the applications.

One potential deployment method is where one set of hardware is swapped out for a set of hardware with the updated software. This type of deployment method is known as *blue-green*. This can work well for applications, but this can be more difficult when databases are involved. If your application is only using a database to read data, you can use the blue-green method as is. However, since the concept is to replace the code entirely, this does not work well for databases that need to allow for write activity.

There is a modified version of the blue-green method that can be used for databases. In this method, you still have two sets of applications: the original application and the new application. When users are connecting to the original application, you deploy any scripts that can be updated and still allow the original application to work as intended.

If you use feature flags, you deploy the database objects that use feature flags. Once you are ready to start using the new application code, you can update the stored procedures to start using the feature flags for the new application code. After you are confident that the updates to the applications and the database code are working as intended, you can remove the feature flags. At this point, you will have transitioned entirely over to the new application code and all feature flags will be removed from the T-SQL code.

The initial state for your blue-green deployment is shown in Figure 12-5.

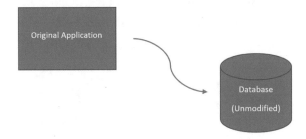

Figure 12-5. *Unmodified application and database*

The application and the database are both unmodified before the deployment. The next step in a blue-green database deployment is to deploy the database changes that will work for either the original or new application. Figure 12-6 shows the database having some changes applied.

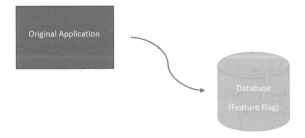

Figure 12-6. *Deploying database changes*

The original application will continue to connect to the modified database. The blue-green deployment method is based on the concept of replacing code, not overwriting code. In order to follow this deployment method, you want to stand up the hardware and software needed for the new application. Figure 12-7 shows the state of the database and the updated application.

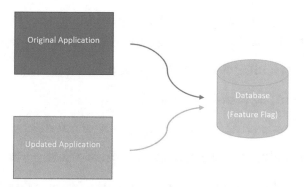

Figure 12-7. *Deploying a new application*

With the feature flags in place, both applications continue to function in the same manner as the original application. Now that the application code is ready, the feature flags can be enabled in the database. Figure 12-8 shows the updated application connecting to the updated database.

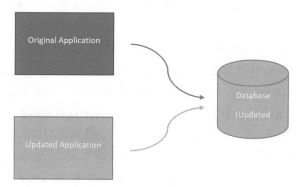

Figure 12-8. *Removing feature flags*

The updated application and database are up and running, and the original application has been decommissioned. The new state would be like Figure 12-9.

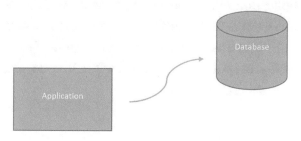

Figure 12-9. *Removing the original application*

Removing the original application information completes the blue-green deployment process. To reiterate, the process for a blue-green deployment is as follows:

1. Start with an unmodified application and database.

2. Add a feature flag to the database.

3. Deploy an updated application using the new feature flag.

    a. The unmodified application can continue to work as before.

    b. The modified application will use the new features due to the feature flag.

4. Remove the unmodified application.

5. Update the remaining application code to have the same functionality without the feature flag.

6. Remove the feature flag.

This deployment method lets you manage how you deploy and enable your new database code.

While impacting the quality of the data is one issue, there are also concerns related to the performance of changes that are made to the database code. In some cases, database objects may be added or modified in a way that causes a severe degradation of performance. Depending on how the applications are configured, this can cause the applications to fail. There are some deployment strategies that can be implemented to help identify potential performance issues before they are visible to the end users.

You may also want to test your new code before letting everyone use the new T-SQL code. It is possible to get a general idea of the performance of your T-SQL code by using a separate database where the changes to the T-SQL code have been applied. Due to the nature of SQL Server at this time, you can only test read transactions on this secondary database. When you use this method, you are using a *canary deployment method*. The concept is that the application will connect to both databases. The second database will only perform read transactions. With additional hardware, you can have most of the transactions sent to the original database and a small portion of the activity sent to the second database. As you gain confidence in the new T-SQL code, you can increase the volume of activity sent to second database.

When designing code that is deployable, you want to start at the very beginning. You must understand how your teams are structured, your development cycle, and when your code is deployed across your environments. The goal is to write maintainable and manageable T-SQL code. You can choose to deploy your T-SQL code using a migration-based approach where you can control exactly what is getting deployed to your environments. You can instead choose to use a state-based deployment method where you control what your database will be after the deployment. You can also determine how to handle developing code that is not ready to be deployed. Using branching and merging strategies, you can keep the code that is in development separate from the code that will be deployed. There is also the option of using feature flags so that you can deploy code at any point in time and control when the new functionality is enabled. Regardless of the methods you chose, you want to determine a deployment strategy that can be defined and is repeatable.

CHAPTER 13

Functionality

Over the course of this book, we have covered many different topics. Most of these chapters involve best practices. These best practices involve naming conventions, formatting T-SQL code, or designing database objects. Despite your best efforts, you may find yourself in a situation that is outside the scope of best practices. These times can correlate to periods of high stress or tight deadlines. The goal of this chapter is to help you prepare for the situations when you must make quick decisions about complex topics.

Designing database code for applications that are created to let users insert or update data can be challenging. You may find yourself dealing with applications where you need to disable permissions or functionality. When dealing with legacy application code, there may be additional challenges particularly if those applications are using ORM (Object-Relational Mapping) software. As organizations grow, there may be a need for additional reporting, but there may not be the time required to develop a data warehouse. Within SQL Server, there is the ability to make your T-SQL code more flexible, but you must ensure that you do not sacrifice functionality at the cost of flexibility.

In this chapter, you will review common programing requirements and T-SQL coding methods that can be used to meet those requirements. For each method, you will review pros and cons to help you make a quick decision.

Inserting and Updating Data

One common situation that T-SQL code needs to handle is how to insert or update data. This section starts by discussing the easiest, but most troublesome, solution using MERGE statements. Another method of using an IF statement is discussed; it allows SQL to determine if a record exists. If it does, the record will be updated. Otherwise, the record will be inserted.

© Elizabeth Noble 2023
E. Noble, *Pro T-SQL 2022*, https://doi.org/10.1007/978-1-4842-9256-3_13

There are many scenarios where you want the ability to pass in a set of values. If the records do not exist, you may want to insert the information, but if the record does exist, you may want to update that record. Often, when we are under pressure, we want to use the fastest, easiest way to do things. Other times, we may be focused more on T-SQL code readability than what is best for the database engine. While it is important to ensure that your database code can be understood by others, it is equally as important to consider the performance of your database code when writing T-SQL.

This can be equally true when using T-SQL to insert or update database records. It may be easier and more straightforward for an application to execute the same stored procedure regardless of whether the user is inserting a new record or updating an existing record. This type of action can also be referred to as an upsert. It does not matter how you find yourself in the situation; the important thing is to design T-SQL code that works reliably and effectively.

There is T-SQL database code that seems like it will make the process of performing an insert or an update in a single query. This functionality is called a MERGE statement. The benefit of using a MERGE statement is that the logic is straightforward. However, there are many known issues with the MERGE statement. The most significant issue with the MERGE statement is in relation to deleting data from tables that use indexed views. When data is deleted from the table, the associated indexed view updates intermittently. It has also been reported that using MERGE statements with temporal tables does not always work as expected. Other issues include partitioned tables not updating full-text indexes when the MERGE statement modifies a string column that is part of the full-text index. Unique key violation errors can occur when using MERGE to DELETE or INSERT data into a table using nonfiltered unique indexes.

I suggest not using a MERGE statement unless you are willing to accept these potential issues. Listing 13-1 shows an example of a MERGE statement.

Listing 13-1. Stored Procedure with a Merge Statement

```
CREATE PROCEDURE dbo.CustomerOrderMerge
    @CustomerOrderID INT,
    @CustomerID INT,
    @OrderNumber VARCHAR(15),
    @OrderDate DATETIME2(2),
    @ShipDate DATETIME2(2),
    @IsActive BIT,
```

```
        @DateCreated DATETIME2(2),
        @DateModified DATETIME2(2),
        @DateDisabled DATETIME2(2)
AS
MERGE dbo.CustomerOrder AS [Target]
USING
(VALUES
        (
                @CustomerOrderID,
                @CustomerID,
                @OrderNumber,
                @OrderDate,
                @ShipDate,
                @IsActive,
                @DateCreated,
                @DateModified,
                @DateDisabled
        )
) AS [Source]
        (
                CustomerOrderID,
                CustomerID,
                OrderNumber,
                OrderDate,
                ShipDate,
                IsActive,
                DateCreated,
                DateModified,
                DateDisabled
        )
ON ([Target].CustomerOrderID = [Source].CustomerOrderID)
WHEN MATCHED THEN
        UPDATE SET
                [Target].CustomerID = [Source].CustomerID,
                [Target].OrderNumber = [Source].OrderNumber,
```

```
            [Target].OrderDate = [Source].OrderDate,
            [Target].ShipDate = [Source].ShipDate,
            [Target].IsActive = [Source].IsActive,
            [Target].DateCreated = [Source].DateCreated,
            [Target].DateModified = [Source].DateModified,
            [Target].DateDisabled = [Source].DateDisabled
WHEN NOT MATCHED BY TARGET THEN
        INSERT (
            CustomerOrderID,
            CustomerID,
            OrderNumber,
            OrderDate,
            ShipDate,
            IsActive,
            DateCreated,
            DateModified,
            DateDisabled
            )
        VALUES (
            [Source].CustomerOrderID,
            [Source].CustomerID,
            [Source].OrderNumber,
            [Source].OrderDate,
            [Source].ShipDate,
            [Source].IsActive,
            [Source].DateCreated,
            [Source].DateModified,
            [Source].DateDisabled
            );
```

This MERGE statement updates a customer order if the order already exists in the dbo.CustomerOrder table. The logic for this MERGE statement is easy to follow, and the format can be easy to write. You want to be aware of these issues before implementing MERGE statements in your environment.

I once implemented MERGE statements before fully understanding the issues these statements presented. When I tried to replace the MERGE statements, there were concerns that the logic would be too difficult. To replace the logic from Listing 13-1, you can write a query like the one in Listing 13-2.

Listing 13-2. Stored Procedure to Insert or Update

```
CREATE PROCEDURE dbo.CustomerOrderUpsert
      @CustomerOrderID INT,
      @CustomerID INT,
      @OrderNumber VARCHAR(15),
      @OrderDate DATETIME2(2),
      @ShipDate DATETIME2(2),
      @IsActive BIT,
      @DateCreated DATETIME2(2),
      @DateModified DATETIME2(2),
      @DateDisabled DATETIME2(2)
AS
IF EXISTS (SELECT CustomerOrderID FROM dbo.CustomerOrder WHERE
CustomerOrderID = @CustomerOrderID)
      BEGIN
            UPDATE dbo.CustomerOrder
            SET   CustomerID = @CustomerID,
                  OrderNumber = @OrderNumber,
                  OrderDate = @OrderDate,
                  ShipDate = @ShipDate,
                  IsActive = @IsActive,
                  DateModified = @DateModified,
                  DateDisabled = @DateDisabled
            WHERE CustomerOrderID = @CustomerOrderID;
      END;
ELSE
      BEGIN
            INSERT dbo.CustomerOrder
```

```
            (
                        CustomerOrderID,
                        CustomerID,
                        OrderNumber,
                        OrderDate,
                        ShipDate,
                        IsActive,
                        DateCreated,
                        DateModified,
                        DateDisabled
            )
            VALUES
            (
                        @CustomerOrderID,
                        @CustomerID,
                        @OrderNumber,
                        @OrderDate,
                        @ShipDate,
                        @IsActive,
                        @DateCreated,
                        @DateModified,
                        @DateDisabled
            )
    END;
```

Replacing the logic from the MERGE statement, you can use an IF... ELSE statement to control the flow of actions inside the SQL Server query. In Listing 13-2, if the order exists in the dbo.CustomerOrder table, the record will update all fields except DateCreated. Otherwise, a new record in dbo.CustomerOrder will be inserted.

MERGE statements are not limited to inserting or updating data in a target table. MERGE statements can be expanded to handle other scenarios such as inserting or deleting data. MERGE statements can also be created so that missing records are inserted, changed records are updated, and orphaned records are deleted as part of a single statement. While the data modifications can be combined as part of single statement, you should use caution when using MERGE statements because they can be prone to performance issues and data inconsistencies as discussed. Due to the ease of writing MERGE statements, it is possible to compare data between two tables in a way that is not efficient for SQL Server. While the tables are only being compared once, if the comparison is not efficient, this can have a significant impact on the performance tables being compared. There have also been instances where unique key violations can occur when using filtered indexes. MERGE statements can also create foreign key constraint violations in specific circumstances. This includes using two tables with foreign key constraints where the foreign key is set to NOCHECK and then rolled back. I suggest researching known issues with MERGE statements and performing adequate testing to confirm the T-SQL code will work as expected. The code in Listing 13-2 shows that it is not overly complex to write code that can handle either an insert or an update. Prior to SQL Server 2019, either the code in Listing 13-1 or Listing 13-2 may have been subject to parameter sniffing. Now that SQL Server 2019 has adaptive joins, this should be less of an issue.

Disable Functionality

One challenge when working with applications is how to make changes to backend table design without affecting business continuity. This section discusses how you can update data so that records can be deleted from the database when the current application does not support soft deletes, where the records are marked as inactive instead of removed from the database. These methods can include disabling a foreign key constraint or creating a dummy record. Afterwards, the record should be able to be deleted. This section will also cover how to use soft deletes and some methods to decide when to toggle allowing users to find all records or only those that have not been soft deleted. You may also be able to use the concept of application rules to allow the ability to toggle functionality. This can also be used with feature flags, as discussed in Chapter 13.

When designing applications, often the first goal is to focus on meeting the specified requirements. In many cases, the product owners or business units are asking for functionality that they need right now. However, the same individuals do not have your knowledge of application and database development. Therefore, the same people may not request the ability to enable or disable specified functionality upon their request. In this case, functionality can either be considered the ability for a user or a role to perform an action or for an application to behave in a certain way. It may be that they are counting on you to know how they may want to use the same applications in the future.

One of the most frequent things that can be forgotten when designing a new application is the ability to enable or disable certain functionality for a user role. You can tell you are in this situation if the existence of a record in a table means that it is available to the application. For this example, table dbo.CustomerOrder is created using the T-SQL statement in Listing 13-3.

Listing 13-3. Creating the dbo.Customer Table

```
CREATE TABLE [dbo].[Customer] (
    [CustomerID]      INT              IDENTITY (1, 1) NOT NULL,
    [FirstName]       VARCHAR (40)                     NOT NULL,
    [LastName]        VARCHAR (100)                    NOT NULL,
    [Address]         VARCHAR (100)                    NOT NULL,
    [City]            VARCHAR (100)                    NOT NULL,
    [PostalCode]      VARCHAR (20)                         NULL,
    [Country]         VARCHAR (75)                     NOT NULL,
    [DateCreated]     DATETIME2 (2)                    NOT NULL
            CONSTRAINT [DF_Customer_DateCreated] DEFAULT (SYSDATETIME()),
    [DateModified]    DATETIME2 (2)     NOT NULL
            CONSTRAINT [DF_Customer_DateModified] DEFAULT (SYSDATETIME()),
    CONSTRAINT PK_Customer PRIMARY KEY CLUSTERED (CustomerID)
);
```

In Table 13-1, you can examine the records from the dbo.Customer table.

Table 13-1. *Customer Table Sample Data*

CustomerID	FirstName	LastName	DateCreated
1	Myra	Acharya	2022-08-30
2	José	Gomez	2022-08-30
12	Selena	Tiësto	2022-08-30
27	Ian	West	2022-08-30
401405	Marty`	Bethel	2022-10-02

For instance, if an order is displayed in an application because it is in the dbo. Customer table, this is a case where you can't control how an application interacts with customer orders. The only option you have to keep a customer order from being used by an application is to delete the customer order record. This action is referred to as a *hard delete*.

The tables you need to delete a record from depend on whether this deletion may be prevented by foreign key relationships. In these scenarios, you only have a couple options available. One option is to drop the foreign keys and then delete the specified record. For this table design, if you want to remove the customer Ian from the database, you need to drop any foreign keys referencing the dbo.CustomerOrdertable and then delete the record. The query in Listing 13-4 drops the foreign key.

Listing 13-4. Dropping the Foreign Key

```
ALTER TABLE [dbo].[CustomerOrder]
    DROP CONSTRAINT [FK_CustomerOrder_Customer];
```

Once any foreign keys that referenced the dbo.CustomerOrder table have been dropped, you need to remove the customer record to make sure that it is no longer available. Listing 13-5 shows the statement to remove the specific customer.

Listing 13-5. Deleting a Customer Record

```
DELETE FROM dbo.Customer
WHERE FirstName = 'Ian';
```

The resulting table has the records shown in Table 13-2.

Table 13-2. *Customer Table After Deleting Ian*

CustomerID	FirstName	LastName	DateCreated
1	Myra	Acharya	2022-08-30
2	José	Gomez	2022-08-30
12	Selena	Tiësto	2022-08-30
401405	Marty`	Bethel	2022-10-02

There is a significant issue with this method. You should take caution when you are faced with the decision to drop foreign key relationships between tables. This can not only negatively affect query performance but can also affect your data quality. Foreign keys are one of the final pieces that can help ensure that data between your tables remains consistent.

Another possibility is to insert a dummy record into the table with the foreign key relationship. You can add a customer to the dbo.Customer table with the name Inactive Deactivated. This can be inserted using the query in Listing 13-6.

Listing 13-6. Inserting a Dummy Customer Record

```
SET IDENTITY_INSERT dbo.Customer ON;
INSERT INTO dbo.Customer
(
        CustomerID,
        FirstName,
        LastName,
        [Address],
        City,
        PostalCode,
        Country,
        DateCreated,
        DateModified,
        DateDisabled
)
VALUES
(
        0,
        'Inactive',
        'Deactivated',
        '',
        '',
        '',
        '',
        GETDATE(),
```

```
        GETDATE(),
        NULL
);
SET IDENTITY_INSERT dbo.Customer OFF;
```

Inserting this dummy record into the dbo.Customer table is only the first step. You need to update the records in the dbo.CustomerOrder table for Ian to use the CustomerID for Inactive Deactivated. The update is shown in Listing 13-7.

Listing 13-7. Updating Inactive Customers in the Customer Order Table

```
UPDATE dbo.CustomerOrder
SET CustomerID = 0,
      DateModified = GETDATE()
WHERE CustomerID = 27;
```

This may not prevent your application from showing the specific value unless your application has been configured in such a way to always ignore that value. If neither of these options can be used, there is another option available. With this table design involved, another option is to remove the orders associated with the customer Ian.

Due to these limitations, the concept of a hard delete may not be ideal for your environment. There are other options available to you. It is possible to design your tables so that you can toggle whether the customers are active. This allows you to enable or disable functionality without deleting the data record. To use this option, you need the dbo.Customer table to include a column such as IsActive. To change the table created in Listing 13-3, execute the query in Listing 13-8.

Listing 13-8. Adding the IsActive Column to the dbo.Customer Table

```
ALTER TABLE dbo.Customer
ADD IsActive BIT
CONSTRAINT DF_Customer_IsActive DEFAULT ((1)) NOT NULL;
```

This will usually be a value that indicates a true or false. For SQL Server, this is often represented with a one for true and a zero for false. If you set the IsActive to true and run a query that filtered results where the IsActive value is true, you will only have a listing of active customers. Once you have added the IsActive column to the dbo.Customer table, you can modify your T-SQL code to display either orders for active or inactive customers based on how they are written.

You have the option to only show results based on the value assigned to `IsActive`. When the `IsActive` value is set to 1, the value is true. If you want to only show active customers, you modify your T-SQL code to use `IsActive = 1` in the WHERE clause. This also gives you the ability to have some screens that only show active customers and other screens that only show inactive or disabled customers.

In addition to disabling or enabling functionalities for users or roles, there are occasions when you want to be able to control how an application works. Companies often want to change how their business operates over time. This can usually be done by adding, changing, or removing functionality in the applications that the business uses.

For instance, if a business wants to expand outside its current market, it may choose to add new functionality to its existing applications. The easiest way to add this new functionality is to add new application code. However, the business may find that this new market or new line of business is not working the way it intended and the company decides to roll back this new functionality. Depending on how the code was written, this may be a complex change requiring another code rewrite or a simple change allowing the application to use a different part of the code.

Depending on your business environment, you may find that it is easier to manage the changes in functionality through the database instead of the application code. This is even more likely when you want functionality to change based on seasonality or by region. This allows you to exert finely tuned control that can be changed rapidly. You want to carefully consider the best place to manage this functionality. The best advice I can offer is to keep business logic in the application when higher-level management needs to sign off on any changes. For business logic that can change rapidly and with little oversight, it may be best to leave the business logic in the database.

If you want to manage some of your application business logic from within the database, you want to create a table to manage whether certain features are enabled. This table is similar in concept to the table created for feature flags in Chapter 12. If you want to manage the functionality in the database, you may want to create a table like the one in Listing 13-9.

Listing 13-9. Creating an Application Rule Table

```
CREATE TABLE dbo.ApplicationRule
(
    ApplicationRuleID              IDENTITY(1,1) INT    NOT NULL,
    ApplicationRuleDescription     VARCHAR(50)          NOT NULL,
```

```
IsActive                          BIT                       NOT NULL,
DateCreated                       DATETIME                  NOT NULL,
DateModified                      DATETIME                      NULL,
CONSTRAINT PK_ApplicationRule_ApplicationRuleID
        PRIMARY KEY CLUSTERED (ApplicationRuleID)
);
```

If you are creating rules for a single, centralized application, this table design will work for your needs. If you are managing multiple applications, consider how these rules are used by applications. If most or all rules are unique per application, you may want to add a column to this table to indicate the application affected.

There could be a business reason why you may want to toggle your application to show only active customers or show all customers. This scenario could happen if there are justifiable business reasons why the application may need to show all customers or only the active customers. The value for this rule can be stored in Table 13-3.

Table 13-3. *Application Rule Table*

Application RuleID	ApplicationRule Description	IsActive	DateCreated	DateModifed
1	Show only active customers	1	2023-04-12	2023-04-12

The entry in this table indicates that only active customers will be shown when this application rule is enabled. If you want the same application to show all customers, you need to update the IsActive value to false. While you could update all your database code and stored procedures to use IF... THEN statements depending on when this application rule is enabled, I suggest handling this functionality within the application.

This is where it becomes important to develop your code to be flexible. While the topic of this book is not application code development, you will need a database that works with your application code to handle these scenarios. Conceptually this can work similarly to feature flags, as discussed in Chapter 12. This is where you can make a table to store a reference to the specified functionality. In some environments, this may be referred to as application rules.

Supporting Legacy Code

Applications are developed over time, and how the applications are developed will determine how easy they can be to maintain them over time. When you are trying to change the table schema by adding or removing columns, you may be able to use views so that the applications continue to work as expected while the backend changes are made. Similarly, you may find that there are many denormalized tables in your database. This section also discusses how you can use views to help move towards a more normalized database schema.

One of the key issues in software development involves dealing with technical debt. For many organizations, applications are initially developed with a timeline in order to meet the current business needs. This can cause applications to be developed rapidly without having the time to plan for how this application will be supported in the future. This often becomes the single source of tension between development and the database administrators.

The concern with modifying a table is how to change it without breaking the entire application. There are strategies that can be used to allow you to add new columns to an existing table without breaking existing code. You want a way to both allow existing code to reference the table as is and store this new information in a manner that works with your existing standards. The options discussed in this section are intended to support new functionality on a short-term basis. It is recommended that you update your application code and database objects to remain compliant with best practices.

The real challenge is that when an application is developed, it usually is not well documented. If the application is not well documented, this can make supporting legacy code even more difficult if the T-SQL queries are saved directly in the application code. If the database code is in the application, it will require more effort not only to locate the specific database code but also to get the database code updated. This is because it is not merely as simple as altering a table or stored procedure to increase the flexibility and maintainability of the T-SQL code.

As businesses grow and change, the same application may need to be modified to handle new functionality. This new functionality may require storing new information. To store this information, you may want to add a column to a table or create a new table entirely. The challenge becomes trying to understand all the items that depend on this table. While you can verify dependencies between database objects, the issue is that you do not know how the application is currently accessing this table. Your applications may be accessing the data table through prepared statements and ad hoc queries. If your application is using prepared statements or ad hoc queries, you may have to change your application code when adding a new column to a table especially if your coding standards do not specify that column names must always be specified with your T-SQL queries.

The simplest option that you can use to allow for additional columns in a table is to create another table with the same primary key as the table you want to modify. In this scenario, you also need to rename the existing table so that a view can be created with the same name as the original table. All queries that would access the original unmodified table will now access this view. When you are ready to update all the application code, the view can be dropped and the table can be renamed back to its original name.

These new columns can be added to this second table. You may find that due to how legacy application code was written, you cannot implement the change from Listing 13-8. You may want to add the IsActive column to the dbo.Customer table, but your application may have embedded T-SQL queries within the application. Therefore, you may not be certain what will break if you add that new column. Creating a new table named dbo.CustomerIsActive in Listing 13-10 is one option.

Listing 13-10. Creating a Copy of the dbo.Customer Table with the IsActive Column

```
CREATE TABLE dbo.CustomerIsActive(
        CustomerID      INT             IDENTITY(1,1)   NOT NULL,
        FirstName       VARCHAR(40)                     NOT NULL,
        LastName        VARCHAR(100)                    NOT NULL,
        Address         VARCHAR(100)                    NOT NULL,
        City            VARCHAR(100)                    NOT NULL,
        PostalCode      VARCHAR(20)                         NULL,
        Country         VARCHAR(75)                     NOT NULL,
        IsActive        BIT                             NOT NULL,
            CONSTRAINT DF_CustomerIsActive_IsActive DEFAULT ((1)),
        DateCreated     DATETIME2(2)                    NOT NULL
            CONSTRAINT DF_CustomerIsActive_DateCreated DEFAULT (SYSDATETIME()),
        DateModified    DATETIME2(2)                    NOT NULL
            CONSTRAINT DF_CustomerIsActive_DateModified DEFAULT (SYSDATETIME ()),
```

```
DateDisabled    DATETIME2(2)                              NULL
      CONSTRAINT DF_CustomerIsActive_DateDisabled DEFAULT (NULL),
   CONSTRAINT PK_CustomerIsActive PRIMARY KEY CLUSTERED (CustomerID ASC)
);
```

You can move all the data from the dbo.Customer table to the dbo.CustomerIsActive table. Then you can allow the applications to continue to insert or update the data records. You will need to drop the dbo.Customer table and create a view with the same name. However, if the date is quite large or has a significant amount of data, you may want to try another method. One method is to rename the dbo.Customer table to dbo.CustomerXYZ. You then create a view named dbo.Customer that mimics the schema of the old dbo.Customer table. After this is complete, you can start added columns to the dbo.CustomerXYZ table. An example of the view is in Listing 13-11.

Listing 13-11. Creating a View to Match the Original Schema of dbo.Customer

```
CREATE VIEW dbo.Customer
AS
      SELECT CustomerID,
             FirstName,
             LastName,
             [Address],
             City,
             PostalCode,
             Country,
             DateCreated,
             DateModified
      FROM dbo.CustomerIsActive;
```

Existing application code can reference the view to select or modify data. This is not an ideal long-term solution and is intended to allow you to move toward the goal of refactoring your applications to use the new table over time. If you have database code written directly in the application, the transition period needed to drop the view and rename the table back to dbo.Customer may require additional effort to manage. When determining how to modify your database objects while allowing existing code to function, you want to focus on implementing a solution that will allow you to easily continue to develop T-SQL code going forward.

Besides views, you also have the option to make a new object with the desired specifications. This would be making the same table as in Listing 13-10. You can then add a trigger to allow any data modifications for the original table to be passed into this new database object. You need to create one DML trigger each for the insert, update, and delete actions. Listing 13-12 shows how to create an insert trigger; you still need to create a trigger for an update and a trigger for a delete.

Listing 13-12. Creating a Trigger when Records Are Inserted into dbo. CustomerOrder

```
CREATE TRIGGER CustomerOrder_InsertCustomerOrderIsActive
ON dbo.CustomerOrder
FOR INSERT
AS
INSERT INTO dbo.CustomerOrderIsActive
(
        CustomerID,
        FirstName,
        LastName,
        [Address],
        City,
        PostalCode,
        Country,
        IsActive,
        DateCreated,
        DateModified,
        DateDisabled
)
SELECT
        CustomerID,
        FirstName,
        LastName,
        [Address],
        City,
        PostalCode,
        Country,
```

```
        IsActive,
        DateCreated,
        DateModified,
        DateDisabled
FROM inserted;
```

This will allow you to continue using the original database object for all your application code. You can leave this additional table and trigger in place until you are ready to start using the new table in your database code.

In addition to adding new columns, you may want to use some other strategies to refactor tables. This can include increasing the normalization of your databases. It is quite common to come across legacy tables with many more columns than would be expected for a database with a high level of normalization. By creating a space where you can modify the table design and create an abstraction layer, you can modify your database objects without affecting application performance.

Sometimes it is easier to start with your end goal in mind. In this case, you are trying to redesign one legacy table into two or more normalized tables. The idea is to accomplish this while allowing your applications to function as normal. For this example, you have a table like the one from Listing 13-13.

Listing 13-13. Original Denormalized Table

```
CREATE TABLE dbo.OrderDetail(
        OrderDetailID       INT             IDENTITY(1,1)   NOT NULL,
        CustomerOrderID     INT                             NOT NULL,
        ProductName         VARCHAR(25)                     NOT NULL,
        ProductPrice        DECIMAL(6,2)                    NOT NULL,
        QuantitySold        SMALLINT                        NOT NULL,
        IsActive            BIT                             NOT NULL,
        DateCreated         DATETIME2(2)                    NOT NULL,
        DateModified        DATETIME2(2)                    NOT NULL,
        DateDisabled        DATETIME2(2)                        NULL,
    CONSTRAINT PK_OrderDetail PRIMARY KEY CLUSTERED (CustomerOrderID ASC,
    OrderDetailID ASC)
);
```

Once you know which table you would like to normalize, you want to design the tables you will use to replace this original table. Listing 13-14 shows an example of the tables that can be created so that you can transition to more normalized data tables.

Listing 13-14. Normalized Table

```
CREATE TABLE dbo.Product(
        ProductID       INT             IDENTITY(1,1)   NOT NULL,
        ProductName     VARCHAR(25)                     NOT NULL,
        ProductPrice    DECIMAL(6,2)                    NOT NULL,
        IsActive        BIT                             NOT NULL,
        DateCreated     DATETIME2(2)                    NOT NULL,
        DateModified    DATETIME2(2)                    NOT NULL,
        DateDisabled    DATETIME2(2)                        NULL,
 CONSTRAINT PK_Product PRIMARY KEY CLUSTERED (ProductID ASC)
);

CREATE TABLE dbo.OrderDetail_Normal(
        OrderDetailID   INT             IDENTITY(1,1)   NOT NULL,
        CustomerOrderID INT                             NOT NULL,
        ProductID       INT                             NOT NULL,
        ProductPrice    DECIMAL(6,2)                    NOT NULL,
        QuantitySold    SMALLINT                        NOT NULL,
        IsActive        BIT                             NOT NULL,
        DateCreated     DATETIME2(2)                    NOT NULL,
        DateModified    DATETIME2(2)                    NOT NULL,
        DateDisabled    DATETIME2(2)                        NULL,
 CONSTRAINT PK_OrderDetail PRIMARY KEY CLUSTERED (CustomerOrderID ASC,
   OrderDetailID ASC)
);
```

In the preceding example, if you know that there will be no data modifications to the dbo.Product table, you can also use a view to interact with the dbo.OrderDetail table. Listing 13-15 shows a view to use these new tables.

Listing 13-15. View Using the Normalized Table

```
CREATE VIEW dbo.OrderDetail
AS
    SELECT dtl.OrderDetailID,
           dtl.CustomerOrderID,
           prd.ProductName,
           dtl.ProductPrice,
           dtl.QuantitySold,
           dtl.IsActive,
           dtl.DateCreated,
           dtl.DateModified,
           dtl.DateDisabled
    FROM dbo.OrderDetail_Normal dtl
        INNER JOIN dbo.Product prd
        ON dtl.ProductID = prd.ProductID;
```

Like the logic in Listing 13-11, you can create a view with the name dbo.OrderDetail so that the applications can interact with the new table going forward. Depending on the purpose of the original and new tables, you may not be able to update all code to use these new tables. If so, you may have to rely on triggers to update these tables.

Reporting on Transactional Data

Oftentimes, we find that one of the main requests for a database is to provide reporting. This section covers how you can use parameters to improve the code reusability when you are trying to get the same information based on different criteria. There is also an example of how to use views to create a standardized data set that can be reused across multiple applications. This view can be reused in other code. A view that includes another view is called a *nested view*. However, it is important to note that using views, especially nested views, should be used with caution, as will be discussed later in the section.

Most databases used by applications are designed to handle a large volume of transactions. The overall design of these databases is referred to as online transaction processing or OLTP. These databases are usually designed to store and retrieve data quickly. This type of behavior involves many writes to the database. However, your business may ultimately decide that it needs summary or reporting information from this same database that is running one of your applications. Ideally, you only have your OLTP applications, as opposed to reporting applications, accessing databases on your transactional servers. You want to have a good understanding of your business and the impact the impact any reporting queries could have on application performance. You may be able to run very simple SELECT statements that are only accessing a small set of data without negatively impacting your applications. You should do everything in your power to limit the additional load put on SQL Server for data requests outside of your applications. When large quantities of data are accessed for reporting purposes, this can cause performance degradation of the primary applications or OLTP applications. This includes additional CPU resources to generate execution plans that have been flushed from the cache to make way for running queries for reporting workloads. You may also have issues with application data that exists in memory getting cleared from the buffer pool after large quantities of data have been moved to memory for reporting. These issues can cascade into a scenario where your application performance is affected by reporting workloads. If you find yourself in the situation where you need to report directly from a transactional database, communicate with your management team what kind of impact reporting may have on your applications.

When you need to access data for reporting, you need to have a high number of reads from this same database. Transactional data is not designed for handling the large quantities of data one might need for reporting. It is generally tuned for queries that read smaller amounts of data like reading one order or one customer for an application screen. There are other challenges.

In some cases, gathering this reporting data can be simple. There may be a small number of joins or the underlying logic may not be very complex. You can end up writing a single report, and due to the quality of the report, you may be asked to create additional reports. These additional reports may involve many tables or the overall logic for these queries may be more complex. This can often be because these tables were not designed with reporting in mind. In some cases, you may find that you are being asked to report on data that does not exist.

To develop reports quickly, it is often easiest to write specific logic for each individual report. Over time this can cause you to end up with a significant number of reports that should return the same or similar results. The best-case scenario is that the results are similar but that the underlying code is different. This can get even more complex as the business may change the functionality of some applications. It may be easy to identify some reports that need to be updated while other reports are missed and start returning inaccurate results.

At some point in time, you may receive a request to generate a report from your transactional data. Often these requests can start out as a simple one-time request for data. Say a user wants to access order information for customers with the first name Stacy. While this may start as a request to run a query and get some data, you may find that eventually your users want this report available to be run any time or by a select group of people. At that point in time, you may write a query like the one in Listing 13-16.

Listing 13-16. Stacy Customer Orders

```
SELECT cus.FirstName,
       cus.LastName,
       ord.CustomerOrderID,
       ord.OrderNumber,
       prd.ProductName,
       dtl.QuantitySold,
       dtl.ProductPrice
FROM dbo.Customer cus
       INNER JOIN dbo.CustomerOrder ord
       ON cus.CustomerId = ord.CustomerID
       INNER JOIN dbo.OrderDetail dtl
       ON ord.CustomerOrderID = dtl.CustomerOrderID
       INNER JOIN dbo.Product prd
       ON dtl.ProductID = prd.ProductID
WHERE cus.FirstName = 'Stacy';
```

While the specifics of report development are outside of the scope of this book, I have seldom worked in an environment where some type of reporting data was not regularly requested off the transactional databases. The preceding query does not show a stored procedure, but you can just as easily use a stored procedure to select this data. The issue with the query in Listing 13-16 is that it is hard-coded to only return results for the customer with a first name of Stacy.

Over time, businesses often need different or additional information when it comes to analyzing data. This can come in the format of needing a new report showing information about another customers. Now your users want a report with information about Myra's orders. This may also be a request to replace the report for Stacy with a report for Myra. In either scenario, you need to create a query like the one in Listing 13-17.

Listing 13-17. Myra Customer Orders

```
SELECT cus.FirstName,
       cus.LastName,
       ord.CustomerOrderID,
       ord.OrderNumber,
       prd.ProductName,
       dtl.QuantitySold,
       dtl.ProductPrice
FROM dbo.Customer cus
       INNER JOIN dbo.CustomerOrder ord
       ON cus.CustomerId = ord.CustomerID
       INNER JOIN dbo.OrderDetail dtl
       ON ord.CustomerOrderID = dtl.CustomerOrderID
       INNER JOIN dbo.Product prd
       ON dtl.ProductID = prd.ProductID
WHERE cus.FirstName = 'Myra';
```

While you have met the requirements for creating one report for Stacy and a new report for Myra, you have also added overhead to maintaining your reports. The queries from Listings 13-16 and 13-17 are maintained separately. If there are changes to how data is pulled from one report, you need to remember that the other report may also need to be changed.

If you find yourself in this situation, the next step is to figure out how to start collapsing the data sets in your reports. You first want to identify which reports return similar results. These can be reports that deal with the same business application or the same functionality. You want to create a query that returns all relevant information for that application or functionality. This will be the base data source that you can use to update your existing reports. The query in Listing 13-18 shows one way to write a query that can be used for both reports.

Listing 13-18. Order Informaiton from Several Joins

```
DECLARE @FirstName VARCHAR(40);
SELECT cus.FirstName,
       cus.LastName,
       ord.CustomerOrderID,
```

```
        ord.OrderNumber,
        prd.ProductName,
        dtl.QuantitySold,
        dtl.ProductPrice
FROM dbo.Customer cus
        INNER JOIN dbo.CustomerOrder ord
        ON cus.CustomerId = ord.CustomerID
        INNER JOIN dbo.OrderDetail dtl
        ON ord.CustomerOrderID = dtl.CustomerOrderID
        INNER JOIN dbo.Product prd
        ON dtl.ProductID = prd.ProductID
WHERE cus.FirstName = @FirstName;
```

In this query, you are using a parameter named @FirstName. This parameter allows you to set a value for the @FirstName variable. This value can be changed depending on which report is being run. When it comes to using Report Server, the value for @FirstName can be set for each report. This type of query allows you to use a single set of code for multiple types of report. This allows you to use the same query for Stacy and Myra or a report request for a specific customer.

Creating the query in Listing 13-18 allows your overall code to be reusable. This can solve one of the issues related to generating reports off transactional data. Another issue that can occur when reporting off transactional data is the intricacy of the logic between the tables. In Listing 13-19, the information about customers and orders has been flattened to more closely align with how a data warehouse is designed.

Listing 13-19. Customer Order Information

```
CREATE VIEW dbo.CustomerOrderInformation
AS
SELECT
        cus.FirstName,
        cus.LastName,
        cus.FirstName + ' ' + cus.LastName AS FullName,
        cus.[Address],
        cus.City,
        cus.Country,
```

```
        cus.PostalCode,
        cus.IsActive AS CustomerIsActive,
        ord.CustomerOrderID,
        ord.OrderNumber,
        prd.ProductName,
        dtl.QuantitySold,
        dtl.ProductPrice,
        prd.IsActive AS ProductIsActive
FROM dbo.Customer cus
        INNER JOIN dbo.CustomerOrder ord
        ON cus.CustomerID = ord.CustomerID
        INNER JOIN dbo.OrderDetail dtl
        ON ord.CustomerOrderID = dtl.CustomerOrderID
        INNER JOIN dbo.Product prd
        ON dtl.ProductID = prd.ProductID;
```

Like the query in Listing 13-18, the query in Listing 13-19 is designed to allow your T-SQL code to be reusable for a variety of scenarios. The design decreases the complexity of the logic required for your queries or reports. The query in Listing 13-20 has the same functionality as the query in Listing 13-18.

Listing 13-20. Recipe Ingredients from a View

```
CREATE PROCEDURE dbo.CustomerOrderByFirstName
        @FirstName VARCHAR(40)
AS
SELECT
        co.FirstName,
        co.LastName,
        co.CustomerOrderID,
        co.OrderNumber,
        co.ProductName,
        co.QuantitySold,
        co.ProductPrice
FROM dbo.CustomerOrderInformation co
WHERE co.FirstName = @FirstName;
```

The main difference between these two queries is that the overall logic required for Listing 13-20 is much simpler and more straightforward. This can allow less technical users the ability to create reports off this same data set. While this can help keep data consistent and easy to access, this method may not have the best performance. When using this method to access your data for reporting, be sure to monitor performance and confirm that the reports are returning data without timing out. SQL Server 2022 can also help you create reports off of a near real-time copy of your transactional databases by using Azure Synapse Link for SQL Server. Azure Synapse Link will send data to Azure Synapse Analytics with minimal overhead on your current production systems. In order to setup Azure Synapse Link for SQL Server, you will need to create an Azure Data Lake Storage Gen2 account in your tenant on the Azure portal as well as ensuring your database has a master key. Then you can connect your SQL Server 2022 instance to Azure Synapse Analytics with Azure Synapse Link through Synpase Studio at `https://ms.web.azuresynapse.net/en/`. You will need to create a SQL pool in Synapse Studio and then create a master key for that pool. Once that is complete, you can create a linked service to SQL Server. In order to connect to your SQL Server 2022 instance, you will need a self-hosted integration runtime. Once this is complete, you should add a linked service to the Azure Data Lake Storage Gen2 account. Now that Synapse Studio has linked services to SQL Server 2022 and Azure Data Lake Storage Gen2, you can integrate a linked connection between both linked services. You are able to select which tables you wanted synced when you setup this connection. After you successfully publish these changes, you can then start Azure Synapse Link. You will need to wait a few minutes before confirming your data has been copied to Azure Synapse Analytics.

This base data set can then be used throughout all your reports. Once you have updated the reports to use this base data set, confirm that this data set will be able to handle your reporting needs going forward. This gives you an idea of the structure of the data that you will need if you would like to move toward a data warehouse.

As stated in the beginning of this section, the concept of using one view to get data from another view is referred to as nesting views. The idea of nesting views is very enticing because views can make T-SQL easier to read and understand. However, that readability often comes at the cost of performance. When a view is accessed, SQL Server executes the SELECT statement at run time. This essentially makes a view a shortcut for executing a query that you run frequently. The view still needs to determine if there is an execution plan and find the data to return. This is true even if the results of the view are going to be used in another view. Depending on the design of the views, this can even cause SQL Server to access the same table multiple times. In the case of a view that is nested into another view where both views access the dbo.Customer table, SQL Server would need to go to the dbo.Customer table two times, once for the nested view and once for the other view.

Dynamic SQL

Sometimes it is ideal to write T-SQL that can be reused in numerous and possibly different scenarios. In this section, you'll learn how dynamic SQL can be used to allow for code reuse. This section should be reviewed with caution as there are many issues with dynamic SQL including the risk of allowing your database to be exploited or corrupted. This can happen by including a ;DELETE FROM dbo.Customer as part of the input on a form. When this happens, it is referred to as a SQL injection because SQL code is being injected into the database.

Depending on what T-SQL code you are trying to write, you may find it difficult to write your database code to use set-based design. In these situations, it may be tempting to write your code in a way that is more iterative. You may want to write T-SQL code that is highly variable and can be modified depending on the parameters and values passed into it. Dynamic SQL makes it so you can use a mixture of variables and T-SQL code to generate a SQL statement when the code is executed. Using dynamic SQL may seem like the solution you have been wanting. In most cases, the drawbacks of dynamic SQL can far outweigh the benefits, but there are times where dynamic SQL can be one of the right solutions.

In Chapter 7, I covered how to read execution plans. When using dynamic SQL, a new execution plan needs to be calculated each time the query is executed. This causes additional strain on the database engine.

Most of the cases where you would want to use dynamic SQL involve times when you need additional flexibility. Many of the times where dynamic SQL is desirable relate to database administration activities. Most of these activities involve performing the same actions on more than one database on the SQL Server instance. There is some additional functionality available with dynamic SQL that can make using it especially appealing.

When executing T-SQL, you cannot use a database name or a table name as a variable in standard T-SQL. Using dynamic SQL gives you the option to write queries that can be executed on more than database object. The query in Listing 13-21 shows an example of dynamic SQL.

Listing 13-21. Dynamically Retrieving Data from Tables

```
CREATE PROCEDURE dbo.TableByDynamicValues
      @TableName SYSNAME,
      @ColumnName SYSNAME,
      @ColumnValue NVARCHAR(25)
AS
DECLARE @ObjectID INT;
DECLARE @ColumnList NVARCHAR(MAX);
DECLARE @Query NVARCHAR(MAX);

SET @ObjectID = OBJECT_ID(@TableName);

SELECT @ColumnList = STRING_AGG (cast([name] as nvarchar(max)), ',')
FROM sys.columns
WHERE [object_id] = @ObjectID
      AND [name] NOT IN (N'IsActive',N'DateCreated',N'DateModified',
      N'DateDisabled') ;

SET @Query =
      N'SELECT ' + @ColumnList +
      N' FROM ' + @TableName +
      N' WHERE ' + @ColumnName + N' = @ColumnValue';
EXECUTE sp_executesql @Query,
      N'@ColumnName SYSNAME, @ColumnValue NVARCHAR(25)',
      @ColumnName = @ColumnName,
      @ColumnValue = @ColumnValue;
```

This query allows a user or application to pass in a table name. This is the table name that will be queried for values. The other two parameters allow a column name and a column value to be passed in as part of the query. This column name will be used to filter the data out. Listing 12-22 shows how this code functions.

Listing 13-22. Executing a Store Procedure with Different Values

```
EXECUTE dbo.TableByDynamicValues N'Product', N'ProductID', N'1';
EXECUTE dbo.TableByDynamicValues N'Customer', N'FirstName', N'Marty`';
```

There are two occurrences of the same stored procedure in Listing 13-22. The first execution returns results from the Product table. The second execution returns results from the Customer table. Executing the queries in Listing 13-22, you get the results in Table 13-4.

Table 13-4. *Dynamic SQL Results*

DateDisabled	ProductID	ProductName	ProductPrice
NULL	1	Telescope	599.00

Address	City	Country	Customer ID	Date Disabled	First Name	Last Name	Postal Code
750 Cherry Rd	Memphis	United States	410405	2022-08-30	Marty`	Bethel	38117

The first set of data returned is the columns from the Product table for the ProductID of 1. The stored procedure in Listing 13-21 excludes the columns IsActive, DateCreated, DateModified, and DateDisabled. All other columns in the table are returned. The values in the second data set are the records from the Customer table for the FirstName of Marty`. From a software development perspective, this may seem like the ideal method to use when writing database code.

However, this method of using T-SQL does not take how the database engine executes a query into consideration. This will cause SQL Server to generate a new execution plan each time the stored procedure is executed as the data being requested can change dramatically between each execution. While it may seem like dynamic SQL can help make your application code more flexible, there is a cost to this method of writing T-SQL. I have used dynamic SQL when trying to create an ETL process and I wanted to programmatically determine which tables had primary keys and which ones didn't. Then I could easily generate a script that dropped primary keys only for those tables that had them. In general, I avoid using dynamic SQL for most scenarios when I need to write T-SQL code. Trying to write your code without dynamic SQL will encourage you to practice writing database code in a manner that uses the strengths of the SQL Server database engine.

Using dynamic SQL can also increase the risk that additional T-SQL code is executed beyond the purpose you originally intended. This type of behavior is referred to as SQL injection. The concept of SQL injection is that additional T-SQL code is inserted, or injected, into the original statement. The additional T-SQL code that has been inserted allows for functionality that was not originally intended for the query execution. This can include viewing data that should not be accessible to this user. This same user may also be able to modify data or database objects through SQL injection. If you want to use dynamic SQL, you can minimize the risk of SQL injection by using parameters to pass values to the dynamic SQL. The method of parameterizing the dynamic SQL will make it more difficult for users to view or modified data in ways that you did not intend.

When writing T-SQL code, you want to write code that is functional and effective. This means writing code that is readable and maintainable. Writing code that can grow with your business is also a critical skill. If you are writing code to handle inserts and updates or variety of data modifications, you want to make sure you are writing code that is easily understood and supported going forward. During application development, consider how you want to handle disabling permissions or application functionality. If not, you want to consider strategies that allow you to deactivate data values in a way that does not break relationships between the tables in your database. You may also have to support legacy code. One of the challenges with supporting legacy code is making changes without breaking existing functionality. There are times you may need to pull data for reporting from your transactional database. Try to design your queries to allow for flexibility and reusability. While flexibility is good, also use caution as to how much flexibility you implement in your T-SQL code. After improving the functionality of your database code, you may find that you want to determine how to track changes to your data. You can learn about logging in Chapter 14.

CHAPTER 14

Logging

During your time working with SQL Server, you will get a wide variety of requests from your company. Some of these requests may involve changing business logic or adding new functionality. There are other times that your company may want to track what happened in the past. There are a variety of third-party tools that can help track performance and other functionality related to database maintenance. However, your business may be interested in tracking data changes or understanding where something went wrong.

This type of logging related to data modifications or error handling can be implemented using T-SQL. When logging these types of changes, you have several options available to you. These options include minimally logging activity all the way to logging the most granular of activities. You also want to consider how this information will be accessed and used going forward. This will help you log information in a way that can be beneficial to your organization in the future. This will also prevent you from logging data that ends up never being used.

Data Modification

This section gives examples of how you can track changes to the data within your databases. This section covers setting up change tracking and what types of information you can expect to gather when using change tracking. There is also a portion on enabling change tracking as well as accessing the data generated from change tracking.

Choosing a method to track data modifications requires understanding what types of information your organization needs to track. You may want to only log information when something has changed. Depending on your business case, you may need to know not only when something changed but also what changed. There are also a couple options on how you can track these changes. You have the option to either use SQL Server to track these changes for you or you can create database objects that will log this information for you.

© Elizabeth Noble 2023
E. Noble, *Pro T-SQL 2022*, https://doi.org/10.1007/978-1-4842-9256-3_14

One of the things to consider when implementing any sort of logging is the performance overhead. This can be even more critical when tracking data modifications. You want to make sure that you choose a logging method that allows you to both track the necessary changes and have the expected performance impact. As you may expect, the more detailed logging you implement, the greater the performance overhead.

Out of all the options discussed in this chapter, Change Tracking has the least amount of overhead. If you want to record more detailed information and you are willing to increase resource utilization, you may want to consider Change Data Capture. Another possible implementation of tracking change involves using database triggers. While the use of database triggers allows you to finely tune what is logged and how it is logged, it can come at the cost of even higher resource utilization.

An intermediate option may be using SQL Server Audit depending on the type of data you want to log. SQL Server Audit can be used to track server or database-level activity. In the context of logging changes related to applications, you want to focus on database audits. The database audit actions within SQL Server Audit can track changes related to all types of data activity including accessing or modifying data. SQL Server uses extended events to monitor the audit activity. The data that can be retrieved includes the time the action happened, information about the user that triggered the audit, and the object affected. It may also be possible to record the statement issued when the audit action took place.

Another minimal logging activity available with regard to data modifications involves logging the most recent time a record was changed and incrementing the number of changes that have occurred for that data record. This type of tracking is handled by Change Tracking within SQL Server, a built-in feature that will automatically record changes to data within tables and report those changes in custom table objects. To use Change Tracking, you will first need to enable it on the database. Throughout this book, we have been using the Menu database. You need to run the T-SQL code shown in Listing 14-1 to enable Change Tracking on the Menu database.

Listing 14-1. Enabling Change Tracking on the OutdoorRecreation Database

```
ALTER DATABASE OutdoorRecreation
SET CHANGE_TRACKING = ON
(CHANGE_RETENTION = 2 DAYS, AUTO_CLEANUP = ON);
```

To enable Change Tracking on the Menu database, you need to specify the database name and indicate that you want to turn Change Tracking on. The last line in the preceding T-SQL code is optional. These values indicate how long you want to retain changes and if the retention history should be cleaned up automatically.

Once you have enabled Change Tracking in the Menu data, you can configure tables to use Change Tracking. The table where you will implement Change Tracking must have a primary key. If this table does not have a primary key, you must add one before you can enable Change Tracking on this table. In this case, you will be enabling Change Tracking on the dbo.CustomerOrder table; refer to Listing 14-2.

Listing 14-2. Enabling Change Tracking on the dbo.CustomerOrder Table

```
ALTER TABLE dbo.CustomerOrder
ENABLE CHANGE_TRACKING
WITH (TRACK_COLUMNS_UPDATED = ON);
```

Change Tracking is now enabled on the dbo.CustomerOrder table. Change Tracking can either record that an entire data row has changed or specify that specific columns have changed. When you track column changes, SQL Server will record that a change happened and the specific column or columns that have changed. If you do not specify a value for TRACK_COLUMNS_UPDATED, SQL Server will use the default value of off and will only tell you that a row has been added to, removed from, or modified within the table without further detail.

After setting up Change Tracking, you may want to determine what kind of information is available or has changed. While the changes in the table dbo.CustomerOrder are tracked by SQL Server, this information is not available from a table that you can find in Object Explorer. Instead, you need to access the CHANGETABLE associated with the table dbo.CustomerOrder. Once Change Tracking has been enabled, records are initialized and can be found in the CHANGETABLE. The query in Listing 14-3 shows how you would find these initialized records.

Listing 14-3. Querying Initialized Records

```
SELECT ord.CustomerOrderID,
       ord.OrderNumber,
       ord.OrderDate,
       chng.CustomerOrderID,
```

```
        chng.SYS_CHANGE_VERSION,
        chng.SYS_CHANGE_CONTEXT
FROM dbo.CustomerOrder AS ord
        CROSS APPLY CHANGETABLE
        (VERSION CustomerOrder,
                (CustomerOrderID), (ord.CustomerOrderID)) AS chng;
```

This query returns information from the dbo.CustomerOrder table and information from the CHANGETABLE. Table 14-1 shows an example of the initialized records.

Table 14-1. *Initialized Records*

Customer OrderID	SYS_CHANGE_VERSION	SYS_CHANGE_CONTEXT
1	NULL	NULL
2	NULL	NULL
3	NULL	NULL
4	NULL	NULL

The records in Table 14-1 are from the CHANGETABLE. There is a column for the CustomerOrderID, the primary key on the table, and columns to track information about the changes. Since none of the data records have been modified, the values are all NULL.

You can modify the records in the table dbo.CustomerOrder. In Listing 14-4, you update the DateModified.

Listing 14-4. Updating DateModified

```
UPDATE dbo.CustomerOrder
SET ShipDate = SYSDATETIME()
WHERE CustomerOrderID = 3;
```

Now that a record has been modified, you can get a better idea of how information is being stored when it comes to Change Tracking. If you run the query from Listing 14-3 again, you will get the results shown in Table 14-2.

Table 14-2. *Records After Changing ShipDate*

Customer OrderID	SYS_CHANGE_VERSION	SYS_CHANGE_CONTEXT
1	NULL	NULL
2	NULL	NULL
3	1	NULL
4	NULL	NULL

The table shows that the SYS_CHANGE_VERSION has changed from the initialized value of NULL to 1. This shows that CustomerOrderID 3 has been modified since the change tracking was originally initialized.

If you want to find more information about what columns were changed. Listing 14-5 shows the query needed to find information about changes to dbo.CustomerOrder that occurred since the last automatic cleanup.

Listing 14-5. Finding Changed Records

```
SELECT CustomerOrderID,
     SYS_CHANGE_OPERATION AS ChangeOperation,
     CHANGE_TRACKING_IS_COLUMN_IN_MASK
     (COLUMNPROPERTY
          (OBJECT_ID('CustomerOrder'), 'OrderNumer', 'ColumnId'),
     SYS_CHANGE_COLUMNS) AS OrderNumberChange,
     CHANGE_TRACKING_IS_COLUMN_IN_MASK
     (COLUMNPROPERTY
          (OBJECT_ID('CustomerOrder'), 'OrderDate', 'ColumnId'),
     SYS_CHANGE_COLUMNS) AS OrderDateChange,
     CHANGE_TRACKING_IS_COLUMN_IN_MASK
     (COLUMNPROPERTY
          (OBJECT_ID('CustomerOrder'), 'ShipDate', 'ColumnId'),
     SYS_CHANGE_COLUMNS) AS ShipDateChange,
     CHANGE_TRACKING_IS_COLUMN_IN_MASK
     (COLUMNPROPERTY
          (OBJECT_ID('CustomerOrder'), 'DateCreated', 'ColumnId'),
```

```
    SYS_CHANGE_COLUMNS) AS CreatedChange,
    CHANGE_TRACKING_IS_COLUMN_IN_MASK
    (COLUMNPROPERTY
        (OBJECT_ID('CustomerOrder'), 'DateModified', 'ColumnId'),
    SYS_CHANGE_COLUMNS) AS ModifiedChange,
    CHANGE_TRACKING_IS_COLUMN_IN_MASK
    (COLUMNPROPERTY
        (OBJECT_ID('CustomerOrder'), 'DateDisabled', 'ColumnId'),
    SYS_CHANGE_COLUMNS) AS DisabledChange,
    SYS_CHANGE_CONTEXT
FROM CHANGETABLE
(CHANGES dbo.CustomerOrder,0) as ChngTbl
ORDER BY SYS_CHANGE_VERSION;
```

This version information is needed to find the state of the changes on this table. The query in Listing 14-5 shows you one way that you can use to access this information. Table 14-3 shows the results for the query in Listing 14-5.

Table 14-3. *Change Tracking Result Set*

Customer OrderID	Change Operation	Order Number Changed	Order Date Changed	Ship Date Changed	Created Changed	Modified Changed
3	U	False	False	True	False	False

These results are recorded from the update issued in Listing 14-4.

The CustomerOrderID affected is listed in the first column of Table 14-3. This matches the same CustomerOrderID updated in Listing 14-4. The ChangeOperation is listed as a U for update. This also matches the DML action in Listing 14-4. The final five columns in Table 14-3 are populated using specific functions to unmask the columns indicated in the Change Tracking tables. The function involved returns a true value if the column was modified and a false value if the data was not modified. In the case of Listing 14-4, the only column updated was the DateModified. This matches the result in Table 14-3. The columns NameChange, DescChanged, IsActiveChanged, and CreatedChanged are all false. These values were not changed. However, the column ModifiedChanged is true. This indicates that the column referenced, DateModified, was changed.

There are some potential issues regarding consistency when using Change Tracking. Storing the data does not affect the consistency of the data. The consistency of the data is affected as part of the data retrieval. You can do everything possible to make sure you are accessing the most recent data in the Change Tracking table. This includes checking for the last synchronized version in Change Tracking and confirming that this version is still available. However, if the version in Change Tracking is older than the retention period, this data may be cleaned up before the data can be retrieved. With Change Tracking, you may also have occasions where a data modification occurs after the last synchronization. This can cause additional versions or modified records to be returned. Any of these scenarios can affect the consistency of the data returned with Change Tracking. The best practice to minimize issues with consistency is to use the snapshot isolation level.

If you need to know more than the row or column that was changed and the number of changes that occurred for that record since implementing Change Tracking, you may want to consider Change Data Capture. Like Change Tracking, there are benefits and drawbacks of using Change Data Capture. The single largest benefit is that Change Data Capture will capture the details related to the data record that was changed.

For inserted data, you will be able to identify exactly what was added to the table. Similarly, you will be able to determine all the columns for a data record that was deleted. When updating data, you will be able to access both the data before and after the update. A downside is that each change to the table requires that at least one record is written to a tracking table. Another downside is that two SQL Server Agent jobs are created for each table that is tracked. As you increase the number of tables under Change Data Capture, the amount of resources used will increase as well. This can cause the performance hit associated with Change Data Capture to be severe enough to prevent you from implementing Change Data Capture.

If you decide to move forward with Change Data Capture, you can update a table in a database to use Change Data Capture. Before doing this, you need to allow Change Data Capture to occur on your database. You can enable Change Data Capture per database by running the T-SQL code in Listing 14-6.

Listing 14-6. Enabling Database Tracking on the Menu Database

```
USE OutdoorRecreation;
GO
EXECUTE sys.sp_cdc_enable_db;
GO
```

Now that you have enabled Change Data Capture, you want to choose a table where you are only concerned with knowing when a record has changed. Let's implement Change Data Capture on the table dbo.CustomerOrder. Before enabling Change Data Capture on this table, you need to make sure that SQL Server Agent is running on this instance. In Listing 14-7, you can find the database code needed to implement Change Data Capture on this table.

Listing 14-7. Enabling Database Tracking on the dbo.CustomerOrder Table

```
USE OutdoorRecreation;
GO
EXECUTE sys.sp_cdc_enable_table
      @source_schema = 'dbo',
      @source_name = 'CustomerOrder',
      @role_name = NULL;
GO
```

At a minimum you need to specify the table schema, table name, and the database roles that can access this data. If you specify NULL for the role name, the information recorded by Change Data Capture will be accessible to everyone. Once this table has been enabled for Change Data Capture, you will be able to find the new jobs created in SQL Server Agent. You will receive a message once the T-SQL code in Listing 14-7 completes. You can examine an example of this message in Figure 14-1.

```
Job 'cdc.OutdoorRecreation_capture' started successfully.
Job 'cdc.OutdoorRecreation_cleanup' started successfully.
```

Figure 14-1. *Message showing SQL Server Agent jobs created*

The process of enabling Change Data Capture also creates several system tables in the cdc schema. In Figure 14-2, you can find the system tables that were created to manage Change Data Capture.

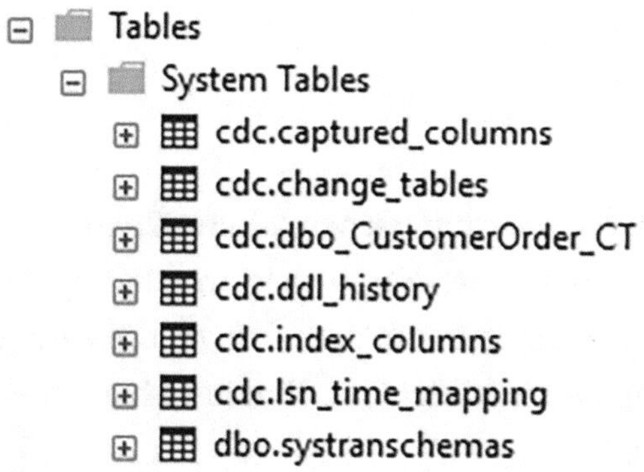

☐ 🖿 Tables
    ☐ 🖿 System Tables
        ⊞ ▦ cdc.captured_columns
        ⊞ ▦ cdc.change_tables
        ⊞ ▦ cdc.dbo_CustomerOrder_CT
        ⊞ ▦ cdc.ddl_history
        ⊞ ▦ cdc.index_columns
        ⊞ ▦ cdc.lsn_time_mapping
        ⊞ ▦ dbo.systranschemas

Figure 14-2. *System tables created for Change Data Capture*

The table that you will use to track changes on dbo.CustomerOrder is the cdc.dbo_
CustomerOrder_CT table.

If you implement Change Data Capture on an empty table, you will be able to track
when your data records have changed but you will also be able to track the number of
changes that have happened since the table was created. Listing 14-8 contains a script to
insert records into dbo.CustomerOrder.

Listing 14-8. Inserting Customer Order into dbo.CustomerOrder

```
INSERT INTO dbo.CustomerOrder
(
    CustomerID,
    OrderNumber,
    OrderDate,
    IsActive,
    DateCreated,
    DateModified
)
VALUES
(
    3,
    'T15493',
    SYSDATETIME(),
    1,
```

```
        SYSDATETIME(),
        SYSDATETIME()
);
```

This can work somewhat differently when adding Change Data Capture to an existing table. If you add Change Data Capture to an existing table, you will still be able to track when changes have happened to your data records, but you will only be able to determine the number of data modifications that have happened since Change Data Capture was implemented.

Previously in Listing 14-8, you enabled Change Data Capture on the dbo. CustomerOrder table. If you assume that the table was empty and you insert some records into the table, you will be able to determine when these records were added. Executing the query in Listing 14-9 shows the records in the Change Data Capture table.

Listing 14-9. Querying the Change Data Capture Table for dbo.CustomerOrder

```
SELECT __$start_lsn,
       __$end_lSN,
       __$seqval,
       __$operation,
       __$update_mask,
       CustomerOrderID,
       CustomerID,
       OrderNumber,
       OrderDate,
       ShipDate,
       IsActive,
       DateCreated,
       DateModified,
       DateDisabled,
       __$command_id
FROM cdc.dbo_CustomerOrder_CT;
```

You can examine a subset of the information that has been tracked about the data records in Table 14-4.

Table 14-4. *Change Tracking Output for dbo.CustomerOrder*

__$start_lsn	__$operation	Customer OrderID	Customer Order
0x000000AF0001FA500005	2	802821	T15493

It may not seem like there is much information being recorded, but the information saved in this table can be quite helpful. The column __$operation indicates the action that occurred on this table. The __$operation tells you which type of activity was performed. In this case, the value of 2 in the column __$operation signifies that a record was inserted into the table. The columns CustomerOrderID, CustomerID, and DateCreated in cdc.dbo_CustomerOrder_CT are some of the values that were inserted.

Executing the code in Listing 14-10 updates a record in the table allowing you to review the differences in the change tracking table.

Listing 14-10. Updating a Customer Order into dbo.CustomerOrder

```
UPDATE dbo.CustomerOrder
SET OrderNumber = 'T-15493',
    DateModified = GETDATE()
WHERE CustomerOrderID = 802821;
```

In this query, you are changing the order number from T15493 to T-15493. To find the result of this update, you can rerun the T-SQL from Listing 14-9. Table 14-5 has the results of that query.

Table 14-5. *Change Tracking Output for dbo.CustomerOrder*

__$start_lsn	__$operation	Customer OrderID	Customer Order
0x000000AF0001FA500005	2	802821	T15493
0x000000AF0001FC300003	3	802821	T15493
0x000000AF0001FC300003	4	802821	T-15493

There will be two entries in the table cdc.dbo_CustomerOrder_CT table with the same starting LSN of 0x000000AF0001FC300003. Both of these lines are associated with the update executed from Listing 14-10. The first row in the table with a __$start_lsn of 0x000000AF0001FC300003 has an $__operation of 3. This operation type is

used for the values in the table before the update. The second row for __$start_lsn
0x000000AF0001FC300003 has an $__operation of 4. This operation value indicates
the values in this row are the values after the update completed. In order case,
CustomerOrderID remained the same. However, CustomerOrder changed. The
__$operation 3 with a CustomerOrder of T15493 is the old value for the CustomerOrder;
the __$operation 4 with the CustomerOrder of T-15493 is the new value.

I covered inserting and updating data in a table with change data capture enabled.
The last action to review is deleting a record from the table. The code in Listing 14-11
deletes the record added from Listing 14-8.

Listing 14-11. Deleting Customer Order into dbo.CustomerOrder

```
DELETE FROM dbo.CustomerOrder
WHERE CustomerOrderID = 802821;
```

Once this record is deleted, you can execute the T-SQL from Listing 14-10 to
determine if there are any new records added to the tracking table. The results of this
query are in Table 14-6.

Table 14-6. *Change Tracking Output for dbo.CustomerOrder*

__$start_lsn	__$operation	Customer OrderID	Customer Order
0x000000AF0001FA500005	2	802821	T15493
0x000000AF0001FC300003	3	802821	T15493
0x000000AF0001FC300003	4	802821	T-15493
0x000000B0000003A00008	1	802821	T-15493

The last record in this table was added to track the delete from Listing 14-11. The
__$operation of 1 is used to indicate the record is tracking a delete performed on the table.

If the table already existed and you enabled Change Data Capture, you would not
find entries for the original data records until they had been updated. Once these records
are modified, they will show up in the cdc.dbo_CustomerOrder_CT table. While Change
Data Capture can be easy for setup and implementation, you should use caution when
adding tables to Change Data Capture. Each table added to Change Data Capture causes
two SQL Server Agent jobs to be created. There is also a significant amount of logging
that occurs as a result of tracking changes on these tables. Both can cause SQL Server to
use additional resources.

You can use Change Tracking, Change Data Capture, or database triggers to track data modifications. All of these options have their own strengths and limitations. When choosing the right option for your organization, you want to consider what type of data you need to record and the performance overhead you are willing to incur tracking these changes. If you need better performance, you generally have to choose less functionality. The more information you want to collect or the more you want to customize logging data modifications will come at a cost of increased hardware utilization and potential performance overhead.

Error Handling

This section discusses how you can write T-SQL code that function expectedly, if not gracefully, when an error is encountered. One solution is to use a TRY... CATCH block. This is a popular method in terms of writing T-SQL code. However, it does require some potential modifications to applications that are not designed to handle SQL Server errors gracefully. Another less robust option is to create database tables to record historical information as well as logging activities. This may not help as much in preventing an application from crashing, but it may help show when an issue started happening.

In addition to logging data modifications, you may also benefit from logging certain types of errors that occur within the database. While there are SQL Server-specific errors that can occur, this is not the focus of this section. There are also errors that occur as a result of the application interacting with the database. Many of these errors can be logged outside of SQL Server as part of your application development. However, you may find that some issues need to be accessible from within SQL Server.

When considering error handling, you want to consider how that information is logged and how the application handles errors. One of the more common options from within SQL Server is to use a TRY... CATCH block. This code wraps the ability to try the T-SQL code and perform a specific action if that attempt failed. If the code succeeds, then the T-SQL code will execute as expected. Listing 14-12 shows a TRY... CATCH block.

Listing 14-12. Try... Catch Block to Insert Customer Order

```
CREATE PROCEDURE dbo.CustomerOrderInsert
    @CustomerID INT,
    @OrderNumber VARCHAR(15),
    @OrderDate DATETIME2(2),
```

```
        @ShipDate DATETIME2(2),
        @IsActive BIT,
        @DateCreated DATETIME2(2),
        @DateModified DATETIME2(2),
        @DateDisabled DATETIME2(2)
AS
BEGIN TRY
    BEGIN TRANSACTION;
            INSERT INTO dbo.CustomerOrder
            (
                    CustomerID,
                    OrderNumber,
                    OrderDate,
                    ShipDate,
                    IsActive,
                    DateCreated,
                    DateModified,
                    DateDisabled
            )
            VALUES
            (
                    @CustomerID,
                    @OrderNumber,
                    @OrderDate,
                    @ShipDate,
                    @IsActive,
                    @DateCreated,
                    @DateModified,
                    @DateDisabled
            );
    COMMIT TRANSACTION;
END TRY
BEGIN CATCH
    ROLLBACK TRANSACTION;
END CATCH;
```

This block of code inserts a record if there are no errors. However, if an error is encountered, the transaction will be rolled back. There are some ways to integrate this with your application code so that the user is aware there was an error with the transaction. The goal of using this method is to prevent the application from crashing or prevent the end user from expecting the transaction to save correctly.

You can also add error handing in the CATCH block that can provide more information about the reason for failure. You can update the stored procedure in Listing 14-12 to include an error output as displayed in Listing 14-13.

Listing 14-13. Try... Catch Block to Insert Customer Order with Error Information

```
CREATE OR ALTER PROCEDURE dbo.CustomerOrderInsert
      @CustomerID INT,
      @OrderNumber VARCHAR(15),
      @OrderDate DATETIME2(2),
      @ShipDate DATETIME2(2),
      @IsActive BIT,
      @DateCreated DATETIME2(2),
      @DateModified DATETIME2(2),
      @DateDisabled DATETIME2(2)
AS
BEGIN TRY
      BEGIN TRANSACTION;
            INSERT INTO dbo.CustomerOrder
            (
                  CustomerID,
                  OrderNumber,
                  OrderDate,
                  ShipDate,
                  IsActive,
                  DateCreated,
                  DateModified,
                  DateDisabled
            )
            VALUES
```

```
            (
                    @CustomerID,
                    @OrderNumber,
                    @OrderDate,
                    @ShipDate,
                    @IsActive,
                    @DateCreated,
                    @DateModified,
                    @DateDisabled
            );
        COMMIT TRANSACTION;
END TRY
BEGIN CATCH
    SELECT ERROR_NUMBER() AS ErrorNumber,
            ERROR_SEVERITY() AS ErrorSeverity,
            ERROR_STATE() AS ErrorState,
            ERROR_PROCEDURE() AS ErrorProcedure,
            ERROR_MESSAGE() AS ErrorMessage;

    ROLLBACK TRANSACTION;
END CATCH;
```

Now if the there is a reason the insert fails, the user will receive a message with information about the failure. This gives the user the option to correct the issue and retry the action.

For instance, if you execute the T-SQL code in Listing 14-14, you will create a situation where the insert will fail.

Listing 14-14. Executing a Stored Procedure with TRY... CATCH with an Error Message

```
ALTER TABLE [dbo].[CustomerOrder] WITH CHECK
ADD CONSTRAINT [FK_CustomerOrder_Customer]
      FOREIGN KEY([CustomerID])
      REFERENCES [dbo].[Customer] ([CustomerID]);

DECLARE @Date DATETIME2(2) = CAST(SYSDATETIME() AS DATETIME2(2))
```

```
EXEC dbo.CustomerOrderInsert
      @CustomerID = 50000000,
      @OrderNumber = 12345,
      @OrderDate = @Date,
      @ShipDate = NULL,
      @IsActive = 1,
      @DateCreated = @Date,
      @DateModified = @Date,
      @DateDisabled = NULL;
```

This code with fail because CustomerID 50000000 does not exist in the table
dbo.Customer. This failure is to the foreign key constraint. The output of the query in
Listing 14-14 is in Table 14-7.

Table 14-7. *Error Output from TRY... CATCH*

ErrorNumber	ErrorSeverity	ErrorState	ErrorProcedure	ErrorMessage
547	16	0	dbo. CustomerOrderInsert	The INSERT statement conflicted with the FOREIGN KEY constraint "FK_CustomerOrder_Customer". The conflict occurred in database "OutdoorRecreation", table "dbo. Customer", column 'CustomerID'.

The table confirms that the insert did not happen due to a foreign key constraint. The
user can then fix the values to provide a valid CustomerID, or the user may decide this
change is not needed.

You may find that your application is able to write or update data in the database
without any issues. However, you may have a process that sends data from one system
to another. There may be infrastructure issues or inconsistencies with data types that
can cause failures when sending data from one database object to another. You need to
determine how these errors should be handled. You still want a method to handle these
failures, but you may also need more instantaneous reporting that these records failed
to be sent or received. Business today requires a constant state of uptime and successful
interactions. You can control your effectiveness in responding to these issues by how you
record failures when trying to process data.

Database tables that store information that needs to be moved through a system often store a status type column in the data table. Whatever process updates the status of the record may either have issues updating the record status or updating the record status to a failed state. When there is not a large amount of data in the table, finding these failed records can be easy. It usually require a search of records where the status has not changed in a specified period or where the records are in a failed or error status.

Depending on how you use the information about customer orders, you may want to log when each customer order is prepared. You may have an application that allows you to indicate when a customer order was started and completed. This information can be recorded with a customer order status. You need to create a table to indicate the customer order history status. An example of the information can be found in Table 14-8.

Table 14-8. *Data Within the dbo.CustomerOrderHistoryStatus Table*

CustomerOrder History StatusID	CustomerOrderHistory StatusName	IsActive	DateCreated	DateModified
1	Started	True	2023-02-12	2023-02-13
2	Completed	True	2023-02-13	2023-02-13
3	Cancelled	True	2023-02-13	2023-02-13
4	Error	True	2023-02-13	2023-02-13

This table includes the status available when recording occurrences where someone has started preparing a customer order. To log each instance of a customer order being prepared, you need to create a table to store information about when each customer order is prepared. There are several ways this can be recorded. For the sake of this chapter, let's create a single record each time a customer order is started. Once the customer order is started, the customer order can end up in a completed, cancelled, or error status. The query for storing the customer order history can be found in Listing 14-15.

Listing 14-15. Creating the dbo.CustomerOrderHistory Table

```
CREATE TABLE dbo.CustomerOrderHistory
(
        CustomerOrderHistoryID        INT           NOT NULL,
        CustomerOrderID               INT           NOT NULL,
```

```
CustomerOrderHistoryStatusID  TINYINT      NOT NULL,
DateCreated                   DATETIME2(2)  NOT NULL,
DateModified                  DATETIME2(2)      NULL,
CONSTRAINT PK_CustomerOrderHistory_CustomerOrderHistoryID
      PRIMARY KEY CLUSTERED (CustomerOrderHistoryID),
CONSTRAINT FK_CustomerOrderHistory_CustomerOrder
      FOREIGN KEY (CustomerOrderID)
      REFERENCES dbo.CustomerOrder(CustomerOrderID),
CONSTRAINT FK_CustomerOrderHistory_CustomerOrderHistoryStatus
      FOREIGN KEY (CustomerOrderHistoryStatusID)
      REFERENCES dbo.CustomerOrderHistoryStatus(Customer
              OrderHistoryStatusID)
);
```

This table can store each unique time a customer order is started. An example of the data stored in this table can be found in Table 14-9.

Table 14-9. *Data Within the dbo.CustomerOrderHistory Table*

CustomerOrder HistoryID	Customer OrderID	CustomerOrder History StatusID	DateCreated	DateModified
1	1	2	2023-02-13	2023-02-13
2	1	3	2023-02-13	2023-02-13
3	3	4	2023-02-13	2023-02-13
4	4	1	2023-02-13	2023-02-13

The records in Table 14-9 indicate customer orders that have been started and their various statuses. The first record is for CustomerOrderID of 1 with a status of completed. The second record is for CustomerOrderID of 1 with a status of cancelled. The third record is for CustomerOrderID of 3 with a status of error. The last record displayed is for CustomerOrderID of 4 with a status of started.

When there is an error for any of the records, those records will have a
`CustomerOrderHistoryStatusID` of 4 in the `dbo.CustomerOrderHistory` table. Initially
the amount of data in this table will not be very large, and it will be easy to find the recent
error records within this table. However, over time this table will grow to a considerable
size. This can cause SQL Server to search through many records in order to find any
recent error records. If you plan for the table `dbo.CustomerOrderHistory` to grow to
a size where it will be difficult to search, you may implement error logging differently.
There may be other scenarios where you want to keep all records that have errored in an
error status, but you also want to know what to be able to resolve any issues with recently
errored records.

In either of these scenarios, it may be beneficial to create a table specifically for
logging recent error records. Before creating this table, you may also want to consider
how this table must be managed over time. Unlike the `dbo.CustomerOrderHistory`
table, you want to make sure that this new table does not get too large. You also want to
only keep recent error records in this table. Keeping a small number of records in the
table allows the table to be easily searched. The goal of this new table is only be to alert
users of any recent error records. Considering the purpose of this table, you also want to
design a process to purge data from this table regularly.

If you choose to create an additional logging table for error records, you may end up
creating a table like the one in Listing 14-16.

Listing 14-16. Creating the dbo.CustomerOrderHistoryLog Table

```
CREATE TABLE dbo.CustomerOrderHistoryLog
(
        CustomerOrderHistoryLogID INT              NOT NULL,
        CustomerOrderHistoryID    INT              NOT NULL,
        DateCreated               DATETIME2(2)     NOT NULL,
        DateModified              DATETIME2(2)     NULL,
        CONSTRAINT PK_CustomerOrderHistoryLog_CustomerOrderHistoryLogID
                PRIMARY KEY CLUSTERED (CustomerOrderHistoryLogID),
        CONSTRAINT FK_CustomerOrderHistoryLog_CustomerOrderHistoryID
                FOREIGN KEY (CustomerOrderHistoryID)
                REFERENCES dbo.CustomerOrderHistory(CustomerOrderHistoryID)
);
```

Any errors on the dbo.CustomerOrderHistory table can have a corresponding record entered to the table in Listing 14-16. In Table 14-9, there was an error record for CustomerOrderHistoryID 2. If you had created the table in Listing 14-16 before that error record was created, you might find an entry like the one in Table 14-10.

Table 14-10. *Data Within the dbo.CustomerOrderHistoryLog Table*

CustomerOrder HistoryLogID	CustomerOrder HistoryID	DateCreated	DateModified
1	2	2023-02-13	2023-02-13

Once you have a record in the dbo.CustomerOrderHistoryLog table, you can generate an alert based on the existence of a record in this table. One option is to have a stored procedure that is executed every 15 minutes. The purpose of this stored procedure may be to generate an email if there are any records found in the dbo.CustomerOrderHistoryLog table. If you choose this method to create your alerts, make certain that you remove data from this table regularly. In this case, you also need a stored procedure to regularly remove data from this table.

Regardless of which method you choose to implement logging errors between your applications and SQL Server, you should make sure that these errors are tracked somewhere that can be accessible to multiple parties. One of the more difficult issues to troubleshoot is when there is no logging available. The goal of logging errors related to SQL Server is to allow individuals within your organization to quickly find where issues are occurring so that they can resolve them efficiently. You may choose to implement most of your error handling from the application. However, it may be possible to generate automated reports from within SQL Server for errors that need to be corrected promptly.

As part of your application development, you want to consider what type of logging is necessary for your organization. In industries where there is the possibility for greater theft, it may be more important to track when a data modification occurs and who modified the data. The information needed will determine what type of logging you implement for data modifications. You also want to consider how to manage errors associated with the database. These are not errors that are specific to SQL Server but are errors that occur as a result of the T-SQL code that has been written for use by your applications. After determining how to manage logging for your application, you may want to consider how to design your T-SQL code to be reusable.

CHAPTER 15

Enhancement

This chapter continues the focus on building maintainable T-SQL. There are many times when you need to update a database schema to add new application functionality. The first section gives several examples you can use to implement changes to existing database objects. The second section highlights some challenges you may experience while trying to phase out poor database design or deprecated functionality.

Adding New Functionality

Ideally, adding functionality to existing applications is a regular part of software development. This section discusses options for how you can add functionality to existing applications while keeping existing functionality. For the purposes of this book, I will use application rules to reference the ability to enable functionality by updating values stored in a database table. This method will not require any application or code changes. However, feature flags will be used to refer to when functionality is enabled through how data is passed to SQL Server, including the use of parameters. If you are adding functionality by adding data to tables, row-level security may allow you to control when the new functionality goes live. You can also use triggers if you need to add new functionality for recording log or historical information about your data. Other options to implement logging are covered in Chapter 14.

Application Rules

Using application rules consists of creating a place to store all of the available application rules and their statuses. In Chapter 14, the T-SQL to create a table for application rules was shown in Listing 14-9. For reference, this code is shown here in Listing 15-1.

E. Noble, *Pro T-SQL 2022*, https://doi.org/10.1007/978-1-4842-9256-3_15

Listing 15-1. Creating an Application Rule Table

```
CREATE TABLE dbo.ApplicationRule
(
        ApplicationRuleID              INT           IDENTITY(1,1)  NOT NULL,
        ApplicationRuleDescription     VARCHAR(50)                  NOT NULL,
        IsActive                       BIT
            CONSTRAINT DF_ApplicationRule_IsActive     DEFAULT 1       NOT NULL,
        DateCreated                    DATETIME2(2)
            CONSTRAINT DF_ApplicationRule_DateCreated DEFAULT SYSDATETIME()
                                                                      NOT NULL,
        DateModified                   DATETIME2(2)
            CONSTRAINT DF_ApplicationRule_DateModified DEFAULT SYSDATETIME()
                                                                      NULL,
        CONSTRAINT PK_ApplicationRule_ApplicationRuleID
            PRIMARY KEY CLUSTERED (ApplicationRuleID)
);
```

You will notice the code above varies slightly as there are now default constraints for the IsActive, DateCreated, and DataModified columns. Now that you have a place to store application rules, you can insert your first rule. Listing 15-2 shows the code to create the application rule.

Listing 15-2. Populating an Application Rule Table

```
INSERT INTO dbo.ApplicationRule (ApplicationRuleDescription)
VALUES ('Show only active customers');
```

Once you've inserted the record, this application rule will exist in the dbo. ApplicationRule table. Table 15-1 shows what you should expect to find in the database.

Table 15-1. *Application Rule Table*

Application RuleID	ApplicationRule Description	IsActive	DateCreated	DateModifed
1	Show only active customers	1	2023-04-12	2023-04-12

These concepts were discussed in Chapter 14, and this section will continue to walk through the entire process. In Chapter 12, there were two examples of a stored procedure named dbo.GetCustomer in Listing 12-2 and Listing 12-3. The difference between these two was the addition of a WHERE clause of where IsActive = 1. Listing 15-3 shows the original T-SQL code for the stored procedure.

Listing 15-3. Original Stored Procedure

```
/*-----------------------------------------------------------------*\
Name:               dbo.GetCustomer
Author:             Elizabeth Noble
Created Date:       2022-10-30
Description:        Get a list of all customers in the databases
Sample Usage:
        EXECUTE dbo.GetCustomer;
\*-----------------------------------------------------------------*/
CREATE OR ALTER PROCEDURE dbo.GetCustomer
AS
    SELECT
            CustomerID,
            FirstName,
            LastName,
            Address,
            City,
            PostalCode,
            Country,
            IsActive,
            DateCreated,
            DateModified,
            DateDisabled
    FROM dbo.Customer;
```

When we discussed modifying the stored procedure in Listing 15-3 in Chapter 12, we only included adding a line item at the end of the query to hardcode changing the store procedure to only allow active customers. However, you may want to deploy this change prior to when the application is ready for this change. Fortunately, there is a way to toggle this functionality within the stored procedure. Listing 15-4 shows the updated stored procedure so that the application rule table determines if all customers or only active customers are shown.

Listing 15-4. Stored Procedure Using an Application Rule

```
/*----------------------------------------------------------------*\
Name:               dbo.GetCustomer
Author:             Elizabeth Noble
Created Date:       2022-10-30
Description:        Get a list of all customers in the databases

Updated Date        2023-04-12
Description:        Updated to use IsActive application rule

Sample Usage:
      EXECUTE dbo.GetCustomer;
\*----------------------------------------------------------------*/
CREATE OR ALTER PROCEDURE dbo.GetCustomer
AS
  DECLARE @OnlyActive BIT;

  SELECT @OnlyActive = IsActive
      FROM dbo.ApplicationRule
      -- This is the hardcoded value for 'Show only active customers'
      ---- If ApplicationRuleID 1 is enabled, @OnlyActive = 1
      ---- If ApplicationRuleID 1 is disabled, @OnlyActive = 0
      WHERE ApplicationRuleID = 1;

  SELECT
        CustomerID,
        FirstName,
        LastName,
        Address,
        City,
        PostalCode,
        Country,
        IsActive,
```

```
        DateCreated,
        DateModified,
        DateDisabled
    FROM dbo.Customer
    -- Stored procedure will always show Active customers
    WHERE IsActive = 1
                -- This will use 1 if ApplicationRule 1 is enabled
                ---- This will return only active customers
                -- This will use 0 if ApplicationRule 1 is disabled
                ---- This will return inactive customers
                AND IsActive = @OnlyActive;
```

At some point in the future, you may decide that the application rule is no longer needed. When this happens, you can update the stored procedure to remove the dependency on the application rule. In this scenario, let's update the stored procedure to only show active customers, as indicated in Listing 15-5.

Listing 15-5. Stored Procedure Using an Application Rule

```
/*--------------------------------------------------------------*\
Name:              dbo.GetCustomer
Author:            Elizabeth Noble
Created Date:      2022-10-30
Description:       Get a list of all customers in the databases

Updated Date       2023-04-12
Description:        Updated to use IsActive application rule

Updated Date       2023-06-13
Description:        Updated only show IsActive customers

Sample Usage:
      EXECUTE dbo.GetCustomer;
\*--------------------------------------------------------------*/
CREATE OR ALTER PROCEDURE dbo.GetCustomer
AS
  SELECT
        CustomerID,
```

```
        FirstName,
        LastName,
        Address,
        City,
        PostalCode,
        Country,
        IsActive,
        DateCreated,
        DateModified,
        DateDisabled
   FROM dbo.Customer
   -- Stored procedure will always show Active customers
   WHERE IsActive = 1;
```

Application rules can be applied to other T-SQL database objects where input parameters are not supported, such as views. Listing 15-6 shows how you can control the functionality of a view with an application rule.

Listing 15-6. View Using an Application Rule

```
CREATE OR ALTER VIEW dbo.vwCustomer
AS
  SELECT
        CustomerID,
        FirstName,
        LastName,
        Address,
        City,
        PostalCode,
        Country,
        IsActive,
        DateCreated,
        DateModified,
        DateDisabled
  FROM dbo.Customer
  -- This view will always show Active customers
  WHERE
```

```
      -- This is the hardcoded value for
      -- 'Show only active customers'
   IsActive = 1
            -- This will use 1 if ApplicationRule 1 is enabled
            ---- This will return only active customers
            -- This will use 0 if ApplicationRule 1 is disabled
            ---- This will return inactive customers
         AND IsActive =
               (
                  SELECT IsActive
                  FROM dbo.ApplicationRule
                  WHERE ApplicationRuleID = 1
               );
```

This is one way to toggle functionality. Another option is the use of feature flags, as discussed in Chapter 12. They are conceptually similar to application rules. However, in many cases there may be an external piece of code that determines if the new functionality should be toggled on or off.

Feature Flags

When using a feature flag, you can add an input parameter to your stored procedure that can control the behavior of the T-SQL code. Listing 15-7 shows the stored procedure dbo.Customer from Listing 15-3 updated to use feature flags.

Listing 15-7. Stored Procedure Using Feature Flags

```
/*----------------------------------------------------------------*\
Name:             dbo.GetCustomer
Author:           Elizabeth Noble
Created Date:     2022-10-30
Description:      Get a list of all customers in the databases

Updated Date      2023-04-12
Description:      Updated to use IsActive feature flag
```

Sample Usage:

```
      EXECUTE dbo.GetCustomer
\*------------------------------------------------------------*/
CREATE OR ALTER PROCEDURE dbo.GetCustomer
      @OnlyActive BIT = 0 -- Defaults to show all customers
AS
  SELECT
        CustomerID,
        FirstName,
        LastName,
        Address,
        City,
        PostalCode,
        Country,
        IsActive,
        DateCreated,
        DateModified,
        DateDisabled
  FROM dbo.Customer
  -- Stored procedure will always show Active customers
  WHERE IsActive = 1
            -- This will use 1 if ApplicationRule 1 is enabled
            ---- This will return only active customers
            -- This will use 0 if ApplicationRule 1 is disabled
            ---- This will return inactive customers
            AND IsActive = @OnlyActive;
```

In the stored procedure above, the @OnlyActive value is passed into the stored procedure. A benefit of using a parameter to toggle functionality in a stored procedure is that you can default the value to maintain existing functionality.

There may also be instances where you want to add data to the database, but you may not want the applications to be able to use the data until a future date. This can happen when you are migrating or integrating a new business or application into an existing database. If you find yourself needing to populate data in a table, but you don't want the data to be accessed, then you may be able to try using row-level security. For an additional information on row-level security, you can refer to Chapter 21.

You may find yourself in a situation where you would like to log behavior on a table. While it may be ideal to have the application log the information directly, this may not be possible. In this case, you may want a trigger to record this information. As an example, you can log when a product is added, changed, or deleted using triggers. You may want to record when a new product is added as well as the login that added the product. Listing 15-8 shows a table to log the behavior on the dbo.Product table.

Listing 15-8. Creating the ProductLog Table

```
CREATE TABLE dbo.ProductLog(
      ProductLogID     INT                            IDENTITY(1,1)   NOT NULL,
      ProductID        INT                                            NOT NULL,
      ProductName      VARCHAR(25)                                    NOT NULL,
      ProductPrice     DECIMAL(6,2)                                   NOT NULL,
      IsActive         BIT
            CONSTRAINT DF_ProductLog_IsActive       DEFAULT (1)      NOT NULL,
      DateCreated      DATETIME2(2)
            CONSTRAINT DF_ProductLog_DateCreated  DEFAULT (SYSDATETIME())
                                                                     NOT NULL,
      DateModified     DATETIME2(2)
            CONSTRAINT DF_ProductLog_DateModified DEFAULT (SYSDATETIME())
                                                                     NOT NULL,
      DateDisabled     DATETIME2(2)                                       NULL,
 CONSTRAINT PK_ProductLog PRIMARY KEY CLUSTERED (PK_ProductLogID ASC)
);
```

Now that you have created the table, you can get add a trigger to the table so that when a record is inserted or updated in the dbo.Product table, a record of the new data will be saved in the dbo.ProductHistory. Since there will already be a trigger on the table, you can also add logic to update the DateModified in the dbo.Product table. Listing 15-9 shows how to create a trigger that logs product changes if a product is inserted or updated.

Listing 15-9. Creating the ProductLog Table

```
CREATE TRIGGER dbo.LogProductHistory
ON dbo.Product
```

```
AFTER INSERT, UPDATE
AS
      INSERT INTO dbo.ProductHistory
        (
            ProductID,
            ProductPrice,
            ProductName
        )
      SELECT
            ProductID,
            ProductPrice,
            ProductName
      FROM inserted;

      UPDATE prd
      SET DateModified = SYSDATETIME()
      FROM dbo.Product prd
            INNER JOIN deleted del
            ON prd.ProductID = del.ProductID;
```

In addition to inserting a record into the dbo.ProductHistory table after a record has been added or changed, this trigger also updates the DateModified on the dbo. Product table so that there is a record of the when the record was most recently changed.

Like writing any other code, you should test this and confirm the trigger is working as expected. To test this trigger, execute the T-SQL from Listing 15-10.

Listing 15-10. Testing the Insert and Updating the Trigger

```
UPDATE dbo.Product
SET IsActive = 1
WHERE ProductID = 5;

INSERT INTO dbo.Product (ProductName, ProductPrice)
VALUES ('Kayak',1299.00);
```

In Listing 15-10, you update ProductID of 5 to be active. You also run a separate query to insert a new product kayak into the table dbo.Product. Since the trigger dbo. LogProductHistory has been added to the dbo.Product table, you expect to find two new entries in the dbo.ProductHistory table.

408

The first query should not only add a record to the dbo.ProductHistory table but should also update the DateModified in the dbo.Product table. The second query should add a record to the dbo.ProductHistory table because a new product has been created. Refer to Listing 15-11.

Listing 15-11. Checking Results from the Trigger

```
SELECT ProductLogID,
       ProductID,
       ProductName,
       ProductPrice,
       DateCreated
FROM dbo.ProductHistory;

SELECT ProductID,
       ProductName,
       DateCreated,
       DateModified,
       DateDisbled
FROM dbo.Product
WHERE ProductID = 5;
```

After running these queries, you can check the results. As stated, you should find two new records in the dbo.ProductHistory table. In addition, the DateModified should be updated in dbo.Product for ProductID 5. Table 15-2 shows the results from the first query.

Table 15-2. *Product History Results*

Product Log ID	Product ID	Product Name	Product Price	Date Created
1	5	Disk Golf Disk - Large	12.99	202304-12 11:58 AM
2	7	Kayak	1299.00	2023-04-12 11:58 AM

Once you have confirmed that the logging portion of the trigger is working as expected, you can check to confirm that DateModified has been updated in dbo.Product. The results from the second query above are shown in Table 15-3.

Table 15-3. *Product Table Update*

Product ID	Product Name	Date Created	Date Modified	Date Disabled
5	Disk Golf Disk - Large	2023-02-12 8:27 AM	2023-04-12 11:58 AM	NULL

This allows you to confirm that the `DateModified` in the `dbo.Product` table has been updated as expected.

Using application rules, feature flags, row-level security, or triggers can be useful when trying to implement new functionality for your database. This can include changing how stored procedures or other database code functions, limiting access to information for certain users, or adding logging to your data tables. However, there are also times where you may want to remove existing functionality from your database. Continue to the next section for more ideas on how you can use T-SQL to manage application enhancements.

Phasing Out Old Technology

You can also find yourself in situations where you want to refactor or rework existing tables or database code. Like adding new functionality, this section will cover some techniques that can be used to allow you to change the database schema in ways that will not affect the current functionality of applications. When trying to improve database normalization, you may be able to temporarily use views to allow applications to behave like they are still using the previous table schemas. If you need to create more dynamic functionality with stored procedures, you can use input parameters to allow the application to use previous functionality. This can be accomplished using either application rules or feature flags. When you are ready to migrate away from current tables for your application, you may not be ready to discontinue the use of those tables for other purposes. You can use triggers to ensure that the data is saved to the legacy data tables as well.

The main challenge with phasing out old technology is ensuring your applications continue to work as expected until the applications can be updated to use the new T-SQL code. However, many of the same techniques referenced in the section "Add New Functionality" can be used to phase out existing functionality.

CHAPTER 16

Managing Data Growth

When a database is first created, for a given amount of time, the tables in the database will remain small. Depending on the nature of the data stored in the table or the amount of time that has passed, you may find yourself in a situation where one or more of your tables have experienced a significant amount of growth since the table was first created. There can be many motivations for managing the relative age of the data stored in a table or how data is stored overall. This chapter will focus on organizing your data in a way that can be managed long term. While many companies also have the goal of improving performance when it comes to managing data, that will not be the focus of this chapter.

SQL Server provides the functionality to separate or sort your data into various groups or categories. When it comes to managing data growth, this data is normally sorted by date. You are not limited to organizing your data by a given date, but for the purposes of this chapter, which will be our focus. You first want to figure out how to organize your data, not only how the data will be grouped but also how the data will be stored. Setting up the functionality for sorting and storing your data allows you to start moving your data into those various groups that you have created. There are options for grouping data, and you can use different ways to store your data. This allows you to design a solution that can support a highly transactional throughput for recent data and allow older data to be designed in a way to support reporting.

Partitioning

When reviewing one of your database tables, you may find that this table has grown to a size that makes it difficult to manage. A big table is hard to manage. Your indexes are big. Too big to defrag. Your stats don't get enough steps to build solid plans. Deleting the older rows from that table can create locks that include brand new rows. Yikes!

© Elizabeth Noble 2023
E. Noble, *Pro T-SQL 2022*, https://doi.org/10.1007/978-1-4842-9256-3_16

The process of organizing this data by some value is partitioning. Partitioning allows us to make that one big table into many smaller tables, each of which is easier to manage. These smaller tables can even be stored on different disks so you don't waste prime SSD space on year-year-old rows that no one ever reads but Legal won't let you delete. The remainder of this section will go through the steps you need to do in order to partition your tables.

First, you want to identify tables that should be partitioned before they grow to that size. However, you can still partition a table after it has grown extremely large. In either scenario, you have identified a table where you would like to better manage archiving data or maintaining indexes. Conceptually you want to think about how you access this data. Ideally, a clustered index includes values that don't change often so that the table doesn't get rearranged frequently. In addition, when implementing partitioning, you want to choose a column that will always be used when accessing this data.

Partition Foundation

In order to implement partitioning through a partitioned table, you need to create several other database objects to partition the table. The first step in partitioning is figuring out how you want to consistently access your data. You will be working with the dbo.CustomerOrderHistory table. For the purposes of this chapter, this table represents information about when CustomerOrders have been used over the past two years. You may decide for legal, user experience, or other reasons that you want to start the process of archiving some of this historical information. Since this is a historical table, you will be choosing to partition (that is, organize or sort) this data based upon the DateCreated. Choosing how this data will be partitioned leads to the next decision that must be made.

Once you have decided how the data will be sorted, you also need to decide specifically what data will be sorted together in groups. Groups of data that are sorted together are called *ranges*. One thing to consider when choosing ranges to be partitioned is to think about how frequently data will be accessed within each range. For most applications, this mean that recent data is accessed frequently and data that is much older is accessed less frequently. If you have five years of CustomerOrder history data, there may be a business reason why you have data for this long of a period, but for day-to-day operations you may normally only access information on a daily, weekly, monthly, or annual basis.

Knowing how the data is accessed in general allows you to determine the ranges you need to partition the data. Once you figure out the ranges, you need to decide how to store your data. Within any installation of SQL Server, there is a single primary data file per database. This file contains the objects and data stored within the database, and the file extension is .mdf. This data file exists within a primary filegroup. It is also possible to add other files and filegroups to your database. Files can be added to the primary filegroup or another filegroup, and each filegroup can exist on a different drive. Using filegroups can benefit you by allowing you to choose how you store your data.

You can keep more frequently used data in filegroups on faster storage. You can also keep less frequently used data in filegroups on slower storage. This can allow you to change how your data is stored in a way that allows you to save money. The filegroups operate like a logical structure as to how the data will be sorted. When you use a database that does not have any additional filegroups, you will have a single filegroup named primary. The T-SQL code to create these filegroups is shown in Listing 16-1.

Listing 16-1. Creating Filegroups

```
ALTER DATABASE OutdoorRecreation
ADD FILEGROUP CustomerOrderHistory2021;

ALTER DATABASE OutdoorRecreation
ADD FILEGROUP CustomerOrderHistory2022Q1;

ALTER DATABASE OutdoorRecreation
ADD FILEGROUP CustomerOrderHistory2022Q2;

ALTER DATABASE OutdoorRecreation
ADD FILEGROUP CustomerOrderHistory2022Q3;
```

In this example, there are four different filegroups. The first filegroup will hold the CustomerOrder history prior to 2022. The next two filegroups are each for the first two quarters of the calendar year in 2022. The third filegroup is designed for the third quarter of 2022. Once you create the filegroups, you need to create any files that will be used by the filegroups. For the example in this chapter, you will be creating one file per filegroup. You can create these files using T-SQL in Listing 16-2.

Listing 16-2. Adding Filegroups to the OutdoorRecreation Database

```
ALTER DATABASE OutdoorRecreation
ADD FILE
(
     NAME = CustomerOrderHistoryFG2021,
     FILENAME = 'D:\SQLData\CustomerOrderHistoryFG2021.ndf',
     SIZE = 50MB
)
TO FILEGROUP CustomerOrderHistory2021;

ALTER DATABASE OutdoorRecreation
ADD FILE
(
     NAME = CustomerOrderHistoryFG2022Q1,
     FILENAME = 'D:\SQLData\CustomerOrderHistoryFG2022Q1.ndf',
     SIZE = 50MB
)
TO FILEGROUP CustomerOrderHistory2022Q1;

ALTER DATABASE OutdoorRecreation
ADD FILE
(
     NAME = CustomerOrderHistoryFG2022Q2,
     FILENAME = 'D:\SQLData\CustomerOrderHistoryFG2022Q2.ndf',
     SIZE = 50MB
)
TO FILEGROUP CustomerOrderHistory2022Q2;

ALTER DATABASE OutdoorRecreation
ADD FILE
(
     NAME = CustomerOrderHistoryFG2022Q3,
     FILENAME = 'D:\SQLData\CustomerOrderHistoryFG2022Q3.ndf',
     SIZE = 50MB
)
TO FILEGROUP CustomerOrderHistory2022Q3;
```

Reviewing at this T-SQL code, you are altering the `OutdoorRecreation` database and adding a file to the database. When you create the file, you specify the logical name, the filename and file path, the file size, and the filegroup associated with that file.

The filegroups and the files determine where your data will be saved. You must configure how to save that data to those files and filegroups. There are couple different database objects that need to be created in T-SQL before data can be stored in the filegroups. You have already determined how you want the data sorted, and now all you need is to issue T-SQL commands so that SQL Server also knows how to sort this data. This first step is to create a function that tells SQL Server how to sort data for a partition. This type of function is known as a *partition function*. In Listing 16-3, you can find the T-SQL code to create the partition function.

Listing 16-3. Creating a Partition Function

```
CREATE PARTITION FUNCTION CustomerOrderHistoryFunc(DATETIME2(2))
AS RANGE RIGHT FOR VALUES
(
        '2022-01-01',
        '2022-04-01',
        '2022-07-01'
);
```

In Listing 16-3, you specify the range of the function as `RIGHT`. The range is directly related to the values provided as part of the partition function. In the case of a right range, this signifies that the value is on the right-hand side of the boundary when separating your partitions. When using the T-SQL code from Listing 16-3, any value up to January 1, 2022 will end up in the first partition. The second partition will contain all values beginning exactly with January 1, 2022 up to April 1, 2022. However, any data from April 1, 2022 until right before July 1, 2022 will exist in the third partition. As the partition function is currently designed, all data that is created on or after July 1, 2022 will end up in the fourth partition. An example of how data is stored when using a right partitions is displayed in Figure 16-1.

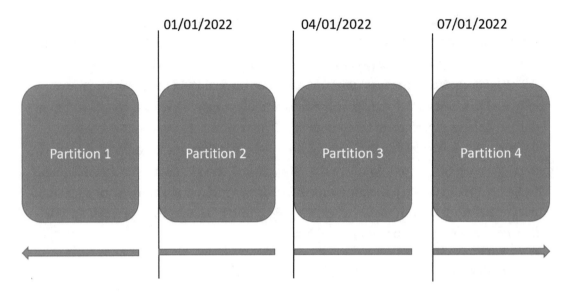

Figure 16-1. *Partitions using a right range*

The other option when creating a partition function is specifying the range as LEFT. If you specified a left range or did not specify left or right, the first partition would include any values up to and *including* January 1, 2022. In Figure 16-2, you can find how the data is stored in the partitions if you use a left range.

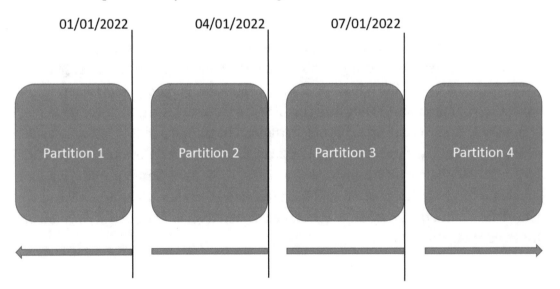

Figure 16-2. *Partitions using a left range*

With the data you are using, the data type is DATETIME2(7). If you use the left range, any data happening 1/10th of a microsecond after midnight on January 1, 2022 will end up in the second partition. You can now understand how important it is to understand your data and your data types when creating partition functions.

Creating a partition function is helpful. A partition function lets SQL Server know how to separate the data into different segments. However, you also need to indicate how SQL Server should use that partition function. This is where you want to create a partition scheme. A partition scheme maps a specific partition function to filegroups. You can find the T-SQL code to create a partition scheme in Listing 16-4.

Listing 16-4. Creating a Partition Scheme

```
CREATE PARTITION SCHEME CustomerOrderHistoryRange
AS PARTITION CustomerOrderHistoryFunc TO
(
    CustomerOrderHistory2021,
    CustomerOrderHistory2022Q1,
    CustomerOrderHistory2022Q2,
    CustomerOrderHistory2022Q3
);
```

The partition scheme has a specific name and references a partition function to use. One difference you can identify between the partition function and the partition scheme is that the partition function specified three values. However, the partition scheme has four values. Since you specified that the range on the partition function was right, all values before the first date in the partition function specified will end up in the first filegroup. Reviewing the T-SQL code in Listing 16-3 and Listing 16-4, you can determine that the first value specified in the partition function correlates with the begin date for the first quarter of 2022.

The reason you want to use your partitioning column in all your T-SQL code is due to how SQL Server uses partitions. Once you have partitioned your data, SQL Server will search through partitioned data differently than non-partitioned tables. Once a partition has been implemented, SQL Server will use the partition to figure out which section of the table has the data that a query is requesting. If you search for a record by date, SQL Server will very quickly know exactly which partition to access to find the data. However, if you do not specify a date and you are wanting information about a specific CustomerOrder, SQL Server will search through every partition to find the information you have requested. Selecting a well partitioned column is important when implementing partitioning in your database. If you do not choose a column that is frequently or almost always used as part of your queries, you may incur additional performance overhead associated with having a partition.

It is generally advised that you should not implement partitioning primarily to improve performance. While the overall goal is to simplify managing your data over time, you can implement some functionality in order to increase the possibility of improving performance. One such method involves how you index your partitioned table. You want to create indexes that are segmented like the partition on your table. These indexes are known as *aligned partitioned indexes*. Aligned partitioned indexes can be clustered or non-clustered.

As an example, the partition function in Listing 16-3 creates a range based on DATETIME2. The partition scheme in Listing 16-4 uses the function in Listing 16-3 to allocate the data in the ranges to the filegroups specified. When the table is created or modified to use the partition scheme, the data will be saved in the filegroups specified. What data ends up in what partition will be determined by the partition function. As I will discuss in Listing 16-6 below, the partition scheme will use the column `DateCreated` to determine what data ends up in the partitions. The `DateCreated` column is then the partition column. Since you want to use the `DateCreated` column as the partition column, you need to make sure the data is ordered by the `DateCreated` column. This is done by creating a clustered index that uses the `DateCreated` column. This new index can be referred to as a partitioned aligned index or aligned index.

There are different requirements depending on if the aligned partitioned index is unique. However, the general outcome is the same. Both types of aligned partitioned indexes include a reference to the partitioned column. In the case of a unique aligned clustered or non-clustered index, the partitioned column must be part of the index. On the other hand, when creating a non-unique aligned index, you do not have to specify the partitioned column. If the partitioned column is not part of the aligned index, SQL Server will add a reference back to the partitioned column as part of the index.

There is also the possibility of creating indexes that use a different partition than its table. These are considered *non-aligned partitioned indexes*. Creating non-aligned partitioned indexes is something you only want to do in limited circumstances. These scenarios include wanting a partitioned index on a non-partitioned table, to check for uniqueness on a column other than the partition column, or you want to join one partitioned table to another partitioned table using a different column than the partition column.

Note   If you create an index and do not specify the partition, the index will default to an aligned index.

Ultimately, the goal when using partitioning is to reduce the number of records SQL Server is accessing when trying to read or update data. You can write your queries in such a way that SQL Server can quickly determine exactly which partitions have the data requested and ignore all the other partitions. When SQL Server generates an execution plan ignoring specific partitions, this is known as *partition elimination*. SQL Server can treat a very large table like many smaller tables. In so doing, SQL Server only needs to interact with a subset of the partitioned table. This is your best chance to improve performance as a result of partitioning. However, in order to have your queries take advantage of partition elimination, you will need to reference the partitioning column in your query. Otherwise, SQL Server will not know which partition to access.

Previously, you created new filegroups and added them to the current database. You also created a new partition function and scheme. In Listing 16-5, you can refer to the T-SQL to add a new partition.

Listing 16-5. Adding a New Partition to an Existing Partition

```
ALTER DATABASE OutdoorRecreation
ADD FILEGROUP CustomerOrderHistory2022Q4;

ALTER DATABASE OutdoorRecreation
ADD FILE
(
    NAME = CustomerOrderHistoryFG2022Q4,
    FILENAME = 'D:\SQLData\CustomerOrderHistoryFG2022Q4.ndf',
    SIZE = 50MB
)
TO FILEGROUP CustomerOrderHistory2022Q4;

ALTER PARTITION SCHEME CustomerOrderHistoryRange
NEXT USED CustomerOrderHistory2022Q4;

ALTER PARTITION FUNCTION CustomerOrderHistoryFunc()
SPLIT RANGE ('2022-10-01');
```

In order to create a new partition, you need to take the existing partition function and break the existing partition at a specified point. Before running the T-SQL code in Listing 16-5, the last range in the partition function included all data on and after July 1, 2022. The SPLIT RANGE code on the last partition takes the last partition beginning on July 1, 2022 and breaks it into two partitions. The partition is separated on the date October 1, 2022, provided in Listing 16-5. The previous partition is then split into two partitions. The first of these two partitions includes all dates beginning on July 1, 2022, up to but not including October 1, 2022. The second partition covers all dates on October 1, 2022 and later.

Most of the preceding database code follows the same logic as shown previously in this chapter. You create a new filegroup and add the file to the database. You also need to change the partition scheme to let SQL Server know the next filegroup that should be used as part of the partition scheme. Once that is complete, you can update the partition function. This will allow SQL Server to save data in the correct filegroup based upon the new specifications. If you forget and need to partition the data later, update the partition scheme and function. SQL Server will move the data to the correct partition.

Almost any time someone talks about partitions, they also specify that partitions are not necessarily something that is used to improve performance. There are many reasons that partitions may not improve performance, and some of those reasons are because partitions may not always be properly implemented. When considering partitioning, you want to focus on what data column you will be using to partition your data. This is known as the *partitioning column*. The reason you will want to be aware of your partitioning column is because this partitioning column will determine how you write your T-SQL code going forward.

Partitioned Tables

While you have created filegroups, files, partition functions, and partition schemes, none of this partitioning logic has been applied to any data within the databases. You have the option of creating a new table or partitioning an existing table. For this example, let's start with creating a new table that is partitioned as part of the table creation. You can refer to the T-SQL to create the partitioned table in Listing 16-6.

Listing 16-6. Creating a Partitioned Table

```
CREATE TABLE dbo.CustomerOrderHistory
(
    CustomerOrderHistoryID        BIGINT    IDENTITY(1,1)   NOT NULL,
    CustomerOrderID               INT                       NOT NULL,
    CustomerOrderHistoryStatusID  TINYINT                   NOT NULL,
    DateCreated                   DATETIME2(2)              NOT NULL,
    DateModified                  DATETIME2(2)                  NULL,
    CONSTRAINT PK_CustomerOrderHistory_CustomerOrderHistoryID
    PRIMARY KEY NONCLUSTERED
        (CustomerOrderHistoryID, DateCreated),
    CONSTRAINT FK_CustomerOrderHistory_CustomerOrder
        FOREIGN KEY (CustomerOrderID)
        REFERENCES dbo.CustomerOrder(CustomerOrderID),
    CONSTRAINT FK_CustomerOrderHistory_CustomerOrderHistoryStatus
        FOREIGN KEY (CustomerOrderHistoryStatusID)
        REFERENCES dbo.CustomerOrderHistoryStatus
        (CustomerOrderHistoryStatusID)
) ON CustomerOrderHistoryRange (DateCreated);
```

In this code, the last line indicates that the table should be created on the partition scheme from Listing 16-4. This is how the table is partitioned. The partition scheme on the table sorts the data into partitions using the partition function.

Once the partitioned table is created in Listing 16-6, the structure of the table will be conceptually similar to Figure 16-3.

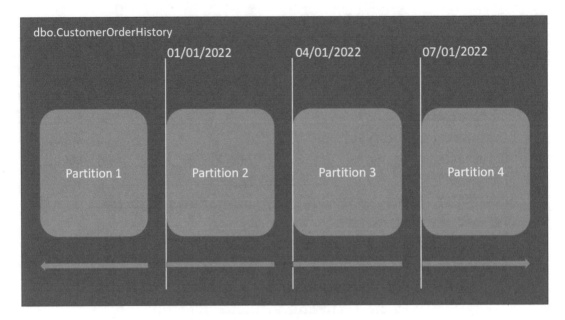

Figure 16-3. *Partitioned table data structure*

Inside of the partitioned table, you can identify each partition clearly. Within the partitioned table, you can also determine how the right range on the partition function has broken out the data into each partition. You can confirm how the table is partitioned by running the query in Listing 16-7.

Listing 16-7. Viewing Partitions for Partitioned Table

```
SELECT tbl.[name] AS TableName,
       sch.[name] AS PartitionScheme,
       fnc.[name] AS PartitionFunction,
       prt.partition_number,
       fnc.[type_desc],
       rng.boundary_id,
       rng.[value] AS BoundaryValue,
       prt.[rows]
FROM sys.tables tbl
       INNER JOIN sys.indexes idx
       ON tbl.[object_id] = idx.[object_id]
       INNER JOIN sys.partitions prt
```

```
        ON idx.[object_id] = prt.[object_id]
                AND idx.index_id = prt.index_id
        INNER JOIN sys.partition_schemes AS sch
        ON idx.data_space_id = sch.data_space_id
        INNER JOIN sys.partition_functions AS fnc
        ON sch.function_id = fnc.function_id
        LEFT JOIN sys.partition_range_values AS rng
        ON fnc.function_id = rng.function_id
                AND rng.boundary_id = prt.partition_number
WHERE tbl.[name] = 'CustomerOrderHistory'
        AND idx.[type] <= 1
ORDER BY prt.partition_number;
```

This query shows the table name, the partition scheme used on the table, the partition function used on the table, the partition number, the value to partition the data, and the number of rows in each partition. Figure 16-4 shows the results from the query in Listing 16-7.

	TableName	PartitionScheme	PartitionFunction	partition_number	type_desc	boundary_id	BoundaryValue	rows
1	CustomerOrderHistory	CustomerOrderHistoryRange	CustomerOrderHistoryFunc	1	RANGE	1	2022-01-01 00:00:00.000	0
2	CustomerOrderHistory	CustomerOrderHistoryRange	CustomerOrderHistoryFunc	2	RANGE	2	2022-04-01 00:00:00.000	0
3	CustomerOrderHistory	CustomerOrderHistoryRange	CustomerOrderHistoryFunc	3	RANGE	3	2022-07-01 00:00:00.000	0
4	CustomerOrderHistory	CustomerOrderHistoryRange	CustomerOrderHistoryFunc	4	RANGE	4	2022-10-01 00:00:00.000	0
5	CustomerOrderHistory	CustomerOrderHistoryRange	CustomerOrderHistoryFunc	5	RANGE	NULL	NULL	0

Figure 16-4. *Data for a partitioned table*

The preceding results were taken immediately after the partitioned table was created. You can confirm that the partition scheme used is CustomerOrderHistoryRange and the partition function is CustomerOrderHistoryFunc. The preceding boundary values match the ranges specified in Listing 16-3 when the partition function was created. Reviewing the value in the rows column from Figure 16-4 you can confirm all the values are 0. This is because there are no rows in the table.

You inserted data from a pre-existing table into the partitioned table. Executing the same query from Listing 16-7, you can determine how the data has been stored in the partitions. In Figure 16-5, you can find the number of rows per partition.

	TableName	PartitionScheme	PartitionFunction	partition_number	type_desc	boundary_id	BoundaryValue	rows
1	CustomerOrderHistory	CustomerOrderHistoryRange	CustomerOrderHistoryFunc	1	RANGE	1	2022-01-01 00:00:00.000	0
2	CustomerOrderHistory	CustomerOrderHistoryRange	CustomerOrderHistoryFunc	2	RANGE	2	2022-04-01 00:00:00.000	0
3	CustomerOrderHistory	CustomerOrderHistoryRange	CustomerOrderHistoryFunc	3	RANGE	3	2022-07-01 00:00:00.000	0
4	CustomerOrderHistory	CustomerOrderHistoryRange	CustomerOrderHistoryFunc	4	RANGE	4	2022-10-01 00:00:00.000	802818
5	CustomerOrderHistory	CustomerOrderHistoryRange	CustomerOrderHistoryFunc	5	RANGE	NULL	NULL	3

Figure 16-5. *Data added to the partitioned table*

In Figure 16-4, you can verify the row counts per partition before any data was added to the dbo.CustomerOrderHistory table. Figure 16-5 shows the number of rows per partition after the table is fully populated. The fourth partition has 802,818 rows. You know the actual number of rows in the partition, but you may still want to confirm that the table is partitioning data as we would expect. Listing 16-8 shows a query to count the number of records by date ranges.

Listing 16-8. Query to Confirm Row Counts

```
SELECT
     SUM(
          CASE WHEN DateCreated < '2022-01-01'
               THEN 1
               ELSE 0
          END
     ) AS Partition1,
     SUM(
          CASE WHEN DateCreated >= '2022-01-01'
                    AND DateCreated < '2022-04-01'
               THEN 1
               ELSE 0
          END
     ) AS Partition2,
     SUM(
          CASE WHEN DateCreated >= '2022-04-01'
                    AND DateCreated < '2022-07-01'
               THEN 1
               ELSE 0
          END
     ) AS Partition3,
```

```
    SUM(
        CASE WHEN DateCreated >= '2022-07-01'
                    AND DateCreated < '2022-10-01'
            THEN 1
            ELSE 0
        END
    ) AS Partition4,
    SUM(
        CASE WHEN DateCreated >= '2022-10-01'
            THEN 1
            ELSE 0
        END
    ) AS Partition5
FROM dbo.CustomerOrderHistory;
```

The first column in the query returns a count of records that have a created date before January 1, 2022. Assuming the partition function is partitioning data as you expect, the number of rows shown for the first partition from Figure 16-5 should match the value returned for column one from Listing 16-8. The query results from Listing 16-8 are shown in Figure 16-6.

	Partition1	Partition2	Partition3	Partition4	Partition5
1	0	0	0	802818	3

Figure 16-6. *Query results showing row count*

Each column in Figure 16-6 shows the number of records that exist in each date range. The first column represents the number of records with a date created before January 1, 2022. The second column is the number of records with a created date starting on January 1, 2022 up to but not including April 1, 2022. The third column follows a similar pattern for records with a date created of April 1, 2022 all the way until July 1, 2022. The last column is for all records created on or after October 1, 2022. Comparing the values in these five columns to the rows column from Figure 16-5 can help you confirm that your partition function is working as expected. In your case, the value from the rows column from Figure 16-5 does correspond to the column values from Figure 16-6. This confirms that your data is being partitioned as expected.

You have verified that the data is getting sorted into the correct partition. However, you have not confirmed that you have any data that has a value that matches the exact date for your range partitions. One way you can verify this is to run a query, like the one in Listing 16-9, that shows the number of records with the exact date and time as the one specified for your partition function.

Listing 16-9. Query to Confirm Range Function

```
SELECT COUNT(*)
FROM dbo.CustomerOrderHistory
WHERE DateCreated = '2022-08-01';
```

When you run the preceding query, you end up getting 14,720 results returned. This lets you know that your partition function is working as expected. If you had zero results returned, you might not be certain on which partition any records with the exact date and time of August 1, 2022, 12:00:00:00.000 would end up. However, since your partitions show the correct counts by date and time grouping, you know it is working as expected.

Previously, you created an empty partitioned table. Once you partition the table, you are ready to manage the growth of this table over time. This process of managing data growth is not a one-time occurrence but something that will need to be maintained going forward. In the case of the table, you need to add partitions going forward. This process will be like the one shown in Listing 16-5. Adding partitions to an existing partitioned table is not the only time that you may need to partition tables. You may also find yourself in a situation where you did not originally intend to partition a table, but for any number of circumstances, you now need to partition the table. In Listing 16-10, you can refer to the T-SQL code required to change a non-partitioned table to a partitioned table.

Listing 16-10. Adding a Partition to an Existing Table

```
ALTER TABLE dbo.CustomerOrderHistory
DROP CONSTRAINT PK_CustomerOrderHistory_CustomerOrderHistoryID
   WITH (MOVE TO CustomerOrderHistoryRange(DateCreated));

ALTER TABLE dbo.CustomerOrderHistory
ADD CONSTRAINT PK_CustomerOrderHistory_CustomerOrderHistoryID
   PRIMARY KEY NONCLUSTERED (CustomerOrderHistoryID, DateCreated);
```

```
CREATE CLUSTERED INDEX IX_CustomerOrderHistory_DateCreated
ON dbo.CustomerOrderHistory (DateCreated)
ON CustomerOrderHistoryRange (DateCreated);
```

Prior to implementing the partition, all the data in the table is ordered by the primary key. In this case, the primary key is the `CustomerOrderHistoryID`. However, once you partition the table, you want the table segmented by the created date. This requires changing how the data in the table is stored. To get SQL Server to update how the data is stored, you need to drop the original clustered key. If the primary key is clustered, then you also need to drop the primary key. At that time, you can create a new non-clustered primary key along with the date created. Including the date created as part of the partitioning column on the clustered key is necessary for the partitioned table. Once this is done, you can create a clustered index on the date created. This index will be created on the partition scheme. When an index is created on a partition scheme, it is called an *aligned index*.

Caution   Be aware that adding a non-aligned primary key to a partitioned table will prevent you from easily moving partitions into and out of the table. This concept is called *partition switching* and is discussed in detail in Chapter 17.

If all the data in your existing non-partitioned table exists within one of the partitions on your new table, you have the option to easily move the data from the non-partitioned table to the partitioned table. Listing 16-11 shows the T-SQL code necessary to accomplish this task.

Listing 16-11. Switching All Data Out of a Partitioned Table to a Non-Partitioned Table

```
ALTER TABLE dbo.CustomerOrderHistory
WITH CHECK ADD CONSTRAINT CK_CustomerOrderHistory_MinDateCreated
CHECK
(
    DateCreated IS NOT NULL
    AND DateCreated >= '2021-08-01'
);
```

```
ALTER TABLE dbo.CustomerOrderHistory
WITH CHECK ADD CONSTRAINT CK_CustomerOrderHistor_MaxDateCreated
CHECK
(
    DateCreated IS NOT NULL
    AND DateCreated < '2023-01-01'
);

ALTER TABLE dbo.CustomerOrderHistory SWITCH PARTITION 1
TO dbo.CustomerOrderHistoryArchive;
```

To switch the data from the non-partitioned table, the tables need to use the same filegroup as well as verify that the data in the non-partitioned table can exist within the partition that you will be using on the partitioned table. You first need to create constraints on the partitioning column that match the range for the partition. Once the constraints have been created, you can switch all the data from the non-partitioned table into the partition specified on the partitioned table.

If you have two partitioned tables, you may want to move a partition from one table to another. This process can be referred to as partition switching. The T-SQL code required to do this is less complex than the code from Listing 16-11. Listing 16-12 shows database code that will switch the partition from the current table to a new archive table.

Listing 16-12. Switchig Out of Partitioned Table to Another Partitioned Table

```
ALTER TABLE dbo.CustomerOrderHistory SWITCH
    PARTITION 1
TO dbo.CustomerOrderHistoryArchive
    PARTITION 1;
```

For this example, you move the records from the fourth quarter of 2021 from the dbo.CustomerOrderHistory table to the dbo.CustomerOrderHistoryArchive table. In order to switch a partition from one table to partition in a different partitioned table, you must specify the partitions for each table. The partition in the target table must also be empty in order for this T-SQL code to execute. This method is a particularly straightforward and easy method of managing your data growth over time. If you create a specific data management plan and move data from your main OLTP tables to an archive table, you can keep all your data but also allow your highly transactional tables to maintain only the most relevant data for your business.

Now that we have covered how to partition new and existing tables, let's determine what partitioning can mean for query execution. Data is usually recorded in the order that each transaction occurred. This can correlate to a specific time period, but that may not always be the case. In addition, even though data is recorded in a specific order, there are often reasons why the business may want to analyze data based on a specific date range. You may want to find the CustomerOrders that were started for a specific date range. By issuing the query in Listing 16-13, you can search the dbo.CustomerOrderHistory table to find this information.

Listing 16-13. Accessing Data Before Partitioning Table

```
SELECT CustomerOrderHistoryID,
    CustomerOrderID,
    CustomerOrderHistoryStatusID,
    DateCreated
FROM dbo.CustomerOrderHistory
WHERE DateCreated BETWEEN '2022-10-07' AND '2022-10-09';
```

After querying the dbo.CustomerOrderHistory table for a specific date range, you can also review how SQL Server executed that T-SQL code to find the data I requested. The execution plan in Figure 16-7 shows how the data was retrieved.

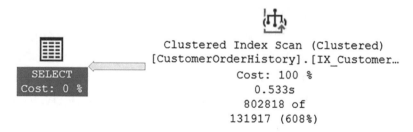

```
                            Clustered Index Scan (Clustered)
                            [CustomerOrderHistory].[IX_Customer...
  SELECT                           Cost: 100 %
  Cost: 0 %                           0.533s
                                    802818 of
                                  131917 (608%)
```

Figure 16-7. *Execution plan for unpartitioned table*

The dbo.CustomerOrderHistory table was not partitioned when this query was executed, and the table was ordered by the clustered primary key. In this case, that is the CustomerOrderHistoryID. While the data may have been stored in the order the records were created, SQL Server has no way to know that is true based on how the table is configured. To make sure that SQL Server retrieves all data based on the date created, SQL Server will need to review each record in the table. This is represented earlier with the Clustered Index Scan operator on the execution plan. Figure 16-8 shows some of the properties associated with the query from Listing 16-3.

Properties	▼ ⊣ ✕
Clustered Index Scan (Clustered)	▼

⊟ **Misc**

Actual Execution Mode	Row
⊟ **Actual I/O Statistics**	
⊞ Actual Lob Logical Reads	0
⊞ Actual Lob Physical Reads	0
⊞ Actual Lob Read Aheads	0
⊞ Actual Logical Reads	3392
⊞ Actual Physical Reads	2
⊞ Actual Read Aheads	3458
⊞ Actual Scans	1
⊞ Actual Number of Batches	0
⊞ Actual Number of Rows for All Executions	802818

Figure 16-8. *Reads associated with a clustered index scan*

The number of total records returned for this query is 802,818. The total number of local reads is 3,392. This represents the total number of pages that were accessed to determine the number of records that met the criteria for this query.

The preceding values represent how SQL Server would execute a query on a non-partitioned table. You can compare the performance of the query in Listing 16-13 between a non-partitioned and partitioned table. You can add a partition to the dbo.CustomerOrderHistory table and compare the results to the preceding non-partitioned table. You first need to drop the existing primary key and add a new non-clustered primary key like the one from Listing 16-10. Since this table no longer has a clustered index, you will get an execution plan like the one in Figure 16-9 if you try to rerun the query from Listing 16-13.

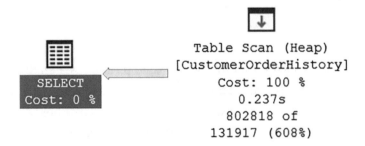

Figure 16-9. *Partitioned table without a clustered index on a partitioning key*

If you forget to add a new clustered index on the partitioning column including the partition range, you will end up with a heap. In this case, the result is a full scan of the table to find any records that matches the date criteria specified. While you might expect the number of logical reads to be the same for this example and the previous example, Figure 16-10 shows a different result.

Properties	▾ ⇥ ✕
Table Scan (Heap)	▾
▣ Misc	⌃
Actual Execution Mode	Row
⊟ Actual I/O Statistics	
⊞ Actual Lob Logical Reads	0
⊞ Actual Lob Physical Reads	0
⊞ Actual Lob Read Aheads	0
⊞ Actual Logical Reads	3375
⊞ Actual Physical Reads	0
⊞ Actual Read Aheads	0
⊞ Actual Scans	2
⊞ Actual Number of Batches	0
⊞ Actual Number of Rows for All Executions	802818

Figure 16-10. *Reads for a query partitioned table without a clustered index on a partitioning key*

In the first example, Figure 16-8 shows 3,392 logical reads to find all records in dbo. CustomerOrderHistory that match the date range specified. Partitioning the table and replacing the original primary key with both the CustomerOrderHistoryID and DateCreated has caused the number of logical reads to drop from 3,392 to 3,375, as shown in Figure 16-10. While the number of logical reads has dropped significantly, it is not ideal to perform queries where full table scans are required on the partitioning column of the partitioned table. The point is to make sure you have a clustered index on your partitioned table that can take advantage of the partitioning column.

To take better advantage of your partitioned table, you want to include a clustered index on your partitioned table. This included having a clustered index that is aligned on the partition scheme by the partition column. Once you have done this, you can run the T-SQL code from Listing 16-13. You will get an execution plan like the one in Figure 16-11.

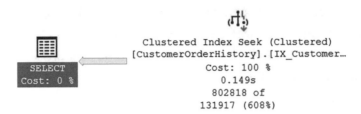

Figure 16-11. *Partitioned table with a clustered index on a partitioning key*

You can verify that SQL Server now uses a clustered index seek to find the correct data. You can also examine the properties for this operator to identify what kind of impact having a clustered index that includes the partitioning key really has. You can see the I/O statistics and rows return in Figure 16-12.

Properties	▾ ⊣□ ✕
Clustered Index Seek (Clustered)	▾
⊟ **Misc**	⌃
Actual Execution Mode	Row
⊟ Actual I/O Statistics	
⊞ Actual Lob Logical Reads	0
⊞ Actual Lob Physical Reads	0
⊞ Actual Lob Read Aheads	0
⊞ Actual Logical Reads	4199
⊞ Actual Physical Reads	2
⊞ Actual Read Aheads	4190
⊞ Actual Scans	2
⊞ Actual Number of Batches	0
⊟ Actual Number of Rows for All Executions	802818

Figure 16-12. *Reads for a query partitioned table with a clustered index on a partitioning key*

When you originally ran this query on a non-partitioned table, there were 3,392 logical reads. After partitioning table without a clustered index, the number of logical reads dropped to 3,375. While the lower number of logical reads does not indicate with certainty that the performance will be better, you can confirm that SQL Server will read less data querying a partitioned table with a clustered index on the partitioning column. Now that there is a clustered index on the partition table, the total logic reads has dropped from 3,375 to 4,190 logical reads, as shown in Figure 16-12 above.

Creating a partitioned table correctly is only part of the challenge if you want to improve performance. The main way this can be done is by writing T-SQL code that includes criteria that allows for partition elimination. The data code in Listing 16-14 is an example of T-SQL code that does not specify the partitioning column as part of the criteria.

Listing 16-14. Accessing Data Without Using a Partitioned Column

```
SELECT CustomerOrderHistoryID,
    CustomerOrderID,
    CustomerOrderHistoryStatusID,
    DateCreated
FROM dbo.CustomerOrderHistory
WHERE CustomerOrderID = 401408
    AND CustomerOrderHistoryStatusID = 1;
```

As a result, this query will be executed on all partitions in the table. Even if there is an index for the columns specified, the query will still need to search the data in each partition separately to confirm that all data requested is returned. Once you decide on a partitioning column, you should include the partitioning column in all your queries so that you can take advantage of the partitioned table. To do that for the query from Listing 16-15, you need to include the `DataCreated` in the WHERE clause. In order to keep from accessing all partitions, you also want to specify an actual date range for this value, such as `DateCreated BETWEEN '2022-10-07' AND '2022-10-09'`.

Partitioned Views

You can break a single table up into multiple segments by creating a partitioned table. Conversely, you have the option of combining several smaller tables together in a way that will allow them to act like one large table. The tables that are joined in this manner can be partitioned or not. Similar to creating a partitioned table, you also have the option of creating a partitioned view.

Like partitioned tables, you should not expect the use of partitioned views to necessarily mean that you will get better performance from the queries that will use this database object going forward. However, there are some design principles that may allow you to achieve improved performance. When using partitioned tables, there is the concept of *partition elimination*. The same sort of concept can be found with partitioned views. Listing 16-15 shows two tables with the same schema as one another.

Listing 16-15. Creating Tables for a Partitioned View

```
CREATE TABLE dbo.CustomerOrderHistory2021
(
      CustomerOrderHistoryID        BIGINT     IDENTITY(1,1)    NOT NULL,
      CustomerOrderID               INT                         NOT NULL,
      CustomerOrderHistoryStatusID TINYINT                      NOT NULL,
      DateCreated                   DATETIME2(2)                NOT NULL,
      DateModified                  DATETIME2(2)                    NULL,
      CONSTRAINT PK_CustomerOrderHistory2021_CustomerOrderHistoryID
            PRIMARY KEY NONCLUSTERED (CustomerOrderHistoryID, DateCreated),
      CONSTRAINT FK_CustomerOrderHistory2021_CustomerOrder
            FOREIGN KEY (CustomerOrderID)
            REFERENCES dbo.CustomerOrder(CustomerOrderID),
      CONSTRAINT FK_CustomerOrderHistory2021_CustomerOrderHistoryStatus
            FOREIGN KEY (CustomerOrderHistoryStatusID)
            REFERENCES dbo.CustomerOrderHistoryStatus
            (CustomerOrderHistoryStatusID)
);

CREATE CLUSTERED INDEX IX_CustomerOrderHistory2021_DateCreated
ON dbo.CustomerOrderHistory2021 (DateCreated)
ON CustomerOrderHistoryRange (DateCreated);

CREATE TABLE dbo.CustomerOrderHistory2022
(
      CustomerOrderHistoryID        BIGINT     IDENTITY(1,1)    NOT NULL,
      CustomerOrderID               INT                         NOT NULL,
      CustomerOrderHistoryStatusID TINYINT                      NOT NULL,
      DateCreated                   DATETIME2(2)                NOT NULL,
      DateModified                  DATETIME2(2)                    NULL,
      CONSTRAINT PK_CustomerOrderHistory2022_CustomerOrderHistoryID
            PRIMARY KEY NONCLUSTERED (CustomerOrderHistoryID, DateCreated),
      CONSTRAINT FK_CustomerOrderHistory2022_CustomerOrder
            FOREIGN KEY (CustomerOrderID)
            REFERENCES dbo.CustomerOrder(CustomerOrderID),
```

```
    CONSTRAINT FK_CustomerOrderHistory2022_CustomerOrderHistoryStatus
        FOREIGN KEY (CustomerOrderHistoryStatusID)
        REFERENCES dbo.CustomerOrderHistoryStatus
        (CustomerOrderHistoryStatusID)
);

CREATE CLUSTERED INDEX IX_CustomerOrderHistory2022_DateCreated
ON dbo.CustomerOrderHistory2022 (DateCreated)
ON CustomerOrderHistoryRange (DateCreated);
```

While each of these tables is on the same partitioning scheme, there is nothing to limit the type of data that will be stored in these tables. The first table is intended to store data for 2022, and the second table is for data from 2021. However, you need to add constraints to these tables to ensure that the correct records exist in each table. In Listing 16-16, you can find the constraints that will be added to both tables.

Listing 16-16. Adding Constraints to Tables

```
ALTER TABLE dbo.CustomerOrderHistory2022
WITH CHECK ADD CONSTRAINT CK_CustomerOrderHistory2022_MinDateCreated
CHECK
(
    DateCreated IS NOT NULL
    AND DateCreated >= '2022-01-01'
);

ALTER TABLE dbo.CustomerOrderHistory2022
WITH CHECK ADD CONSTRAINT CK_CustomerOrderHistory2022_MaxDateCreated
CHECK
(
    DateCreated IS NOT NULL
    AND DateCreated < '2023-01-01'
);

ALTER TABLE dbo.CustomerOrderHistory2021
WITH CHECK ADD CONSTRAINT CK_CustomerOrderHistory2021_MinDateCreated
CHECK
```

```
(
      DateCreated IS NOT NULL
      AND DateCreated >= '2021-01-01'
);

ALTER TABLE dbo.CustomerOrderHistory2021
WITH CHECK ADD CONSTRAINT CK_CustomerOrderHistory2021_MaxDateCreated
CHECK
(
      DateCreated IS NOT NULL
      AND DateCreated < '2022-01-01'
);
```

The table for 2022 now has a constraint that only allows records with a DateCreated from January 1, 2022, up to but not including January 1, 2023. There is also a constraint on the table for 2021 with similar logic so that only records that were created in 2021 can be stored in this table.

You now have tables for two different date ranges, and you have applied constraints to these tables. The next step is to create a partitioned view. The process of creating a partitioned view is relatively simple and consists of adding a UNION ALL between each select statement on the underlying tables. An example of creating a partitioned view can be found in Listing 16-17.

Listing 16-17. Creating a Partitioned View

```
CREATE VIEW dbo.vwCustomerOrderHistory
WITH SCHEMABINDING
AS
-- Select data from current read/write table
SELECT CustomerOrderHistoryID,
      CustomerOrderID,
      CustomerOrderHistoryStatusID,
      DateCreated,
      DateModified
FROM dbo.CustomerOrderHistory2022
UNION ALL
-- Select data from partitioned table
```

```
SELECT CustomerOrderHistoryID,
    CustomerOrderID,
    CustomerOrderHistoryStatusID,
    DateCreated,
    DateModified
FROM dbo.CustomerOrderHistory2021;
```

Notice that the column lists are in the same order for both SELECT statements used within the partitioned view. This is a requirement of creating a partitioned view. You must also specify the full column list of the table when creating a partitioned view. Once the partitioned view has been created, you may want to check how querying a partitioned view works.

Back in Listing 16-13 you queried the dbo.CustomerOrderHistory table on the date range between October 7, 2022 and October 9, 2022. You can query the partitioned view for the same date range, as shown in Listing 16-18.

Listing 16-18. Accessing Data Using a Partitioned Column

```
DECLARE @StartDate  DATETIME2(2) = '2022-10-07';
DECLARE @EndDate    DATETIME2(2) = '2022-10-09';

SELECT CustomerOrderHistoryID,
    CustomerOrderID,
    CustomerOrderHistoryStatusID,
    DateCreated,
    DateModified
FROM dbo.vwCustomerOrderHistory
WHERE DateCreated > @StartDate
    AND DateCreated <= @EndDate;
```

The T-SQL code is very similar between Listing 16-13 and Listing 16-18. This shows how easy it can be to shift to using a partitioned view instead of the current table names in your queries. However, what you are really interested in confirming is how the execution plan has changed with the use of a partitioned view. Figure 16-13 shows the execution plan that is generated as a result of running the query in Listing 16-18.

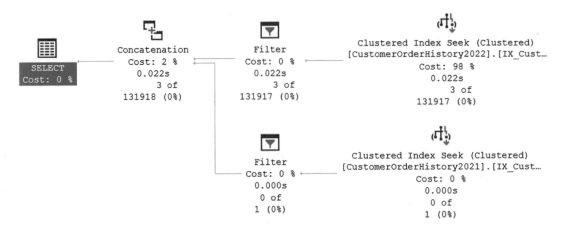

Figure 16-13. *Execution plan for a partitioned view*

Like the partitioned table referenced earlier in this chapter, the execution plan for the partitioned view also uses a clustered index seek. Even though the partitioned view includes both the 2022 and 2021 tables, you can determine from the execution plan that SQL Server only returns results from the dbo.CustomerOrderHistory2022 table when finding the results from the query in Listing 16-18. The percentage for dbo.CustomerOrderHistory is 0%. You can also examine the properties of the clustered index seek in Figure 16-14.

Properties	▼ ⊕ ✕
Clustered Index Seek (Clustered)	▼

⊟ **Misc**	
Actual Execution Mode	Row
⊟ Actual I/O Statistics	
⊞ Actual Lob Logical Reads	0
⊞ Actual Lob Physical Reads	0
⊞ Actual Lob Read Aheads	0
⊞ Actual Logical Reads	7
⊞ Actual Physical Reads	3
⊞ Actual Read Aheads	8
⊞ Actual Scans	2
⊞ Actual Number of Batches	0
⊞ Actual Number of Rows for All Executions	3

Figure 16-14. *Reads for a query partitioned view with a clustered index on a partitioning key*

You can determine based on the number of rows returned that the data in the 2021 table is different from the partitioned tables referenced previously in this chapter. You can also determine that the relative number of logical reads is low and trends similarly to the partitioned table earlier in this chapter.

The T-SQL code executed in Listing 16-18 accessed the partitioned view based on the partitioned column in each of the tables and on the constraint specified for each of the tables. You saw that SQL Server was able to quickly determine which table to access when querying the data. There may be times when you want to run a query that does not include the partitioning column, like the one in Listing 16-19.

Listing 16-19. Accessing Data Without Using a Partitioned Column

```
SELECT CustomerOrderHistoryID,
       CustomerOrderID,
       CustomerOrderHistoryStatusID,
       DateCreated
FROM dbo.vwCustomerOrderHistory
WHERE CustomerOrderID = 401408
       AND CustomerOrderHistoryStatusID = 1;
```

This query searches for a specific CustomerOrder that has a certain status. However, there is no indication that any of these records exist in a specific table within the indexed view. Since SQL Server does not have the ability to rule out certain date ranges as part of the query, you get the execution plan in Figure 16-15.

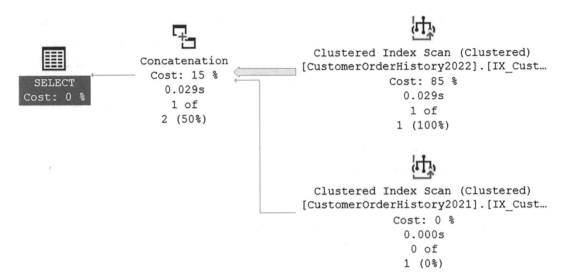

Figure 16-15. *Execution plan for a partitioned view*

You can determine that in this execution plan, SQL Server must access the table containing the 2021 data and the table containing the 2022 data. In this example, you can determine that there is no benefit on the number of tables accessed as part of this request.

Using partitioned views can help you take more than one table and combine them together into one database object. By accessing this single database object, you can simplify your T-SQL code across multiple ranges. You have also learned that using a partitioned view can be beneficial in limiting the number of tables accessed, but if you do not use the partitioning column as part of your queries, you will still need to access all tables included in the view. While partitioned tables break one table up into multiple segments and partitioned views combine tables together into one database object, you may find advantages to combining them both.

Hybrid Workloads

Companies have been using databases for many years and may have acquired a significant amount of data. Often, these same companies may be generating reports from this data. In many cases, these same companies may not have prioritized building a data warehouse. For these situations, one database is often trying to perform two tasks at the same time. The first role is to continue to store transactional data. However, the second role is to also act as a data warehouse for analytical processing. In many situations, the database design needed for transaction processing does not match the best design for analysis processing. While your company may be willing to move toward a data warehouse someday, you may find yourself in a situation where you need to implement designs that can function well with this hybrid workload.

In combining partitioned and non-partitioned tables with a partitioned view, you can give yourself additional flexibility. Using a partitioned view will allow you to use a single database object and name to access any data for a specific purpose. In this example, let's continue to work with the data recorded as a result of CustomerOrders being started. Since a partitioned view allows you to combine several tables together, you can investigate how those tables can be created. One advantage of using multiple tables is that each table can use different indexes. This difference in indexes can change both how data is stored and accessed. You can also have the option to make some tables as read only, which can signify that you do not intend to add data to these tables.

You will be creating a partitioned view to access all the CustomerOrder history data. The first table is only to hold all the older data that you want to archive. You can also partition this table to allow for partition elimination when searches are performed based on the partitioning key of the table. In Listing 16-20, you can refer to the T-SQL needed to create your partitioned table for archived data.

Listing 16-20. Creating Partitioned Tables for Archived Data

```
CREATE TABLE dbo.CustomerOrderHistoryPartition
(
        CustomerOrderHistoryID          BIGINT          NOT NULL,
        CustomerOrderID                 INT             NOT NULL,
        CustomerOrderHistoryStatusID    TINYINT         NOT NULL,
        DateCreated                     DATETIME2(2)    NOT NULL,
        DateModified                    DATETIME2(2)        NULL,
        CONSTRAINT PK_CustomerOrderHistoryPartition_CustomerOrderHistoryID
                PRIMARY KEY (CustomerOrderHistoryID, DateCreated),
        CONSTRAINT FK_CustomerOrderHistoryPartition_CustomerOrderID
                FOREIGN KEY (CustomerOrderID)
                REFERENCES dbo.CustomerOrder(CustomerOrderID),
        CONSTRAINT FK_CustomerOrderHistoryParition_
        CustomerOrderHistoryStatusID
                FOREIGN KEY (CustomerOrderHistoryStatusID)
```

```
        REFERENCES dbo.CustomerOrderHistoryStatus
            (CustomerOrderHistoryStatusID)
)
ON CustomerOrderHistoryRange (DateCreated);
```

This partitioned table is created like many of the partitioned tables already included in this chapter. Like the partitioned tables created earlier in this chapter, this table was also created on the partition scheme `CustomerOrderHistoryRange`. Now that you have a partitioned table, you want to create a non-partitioned table for data that is being actively used by the application right now. The table created in Listing 16-21 is an example of a non-partitioned table.

Listing 16-21. Creating a Table for Active Data

```
CREATE TABLE dbo.CustomerOrderActive
(
    CustomerOrderHistoryID          BIGINT          NOT NULL,
    CustomerOrderID                 INT             NOT NULL,
    CustomerOrderHistoryStatusID    TINYINT         NOT NULL,
    DateCreated                     DATETIME2(2)    NOT NULL,
    DateModified                    DATETIME2(2)        NULL,
    CONSTRAINT PK_CustomerOrderActive_CustomerOrderHistoryID
        PRIMARY KEY (CustomerOrderHistoryID),
    CONSTRAINT FK_CustomerOrderActive_CustomerOrderID
        FOREIGN KEY (CustomerOrderID)
        REFERENCES dbo.CustomerOrder(CustomerOrderID),
    CONSTRAINT FK_CustomerOrderActive_CustomerOrderHistoryStatusID
        FOREIGN KEY (CustomerOrderHistoryStatusID)
        REFERENCES
        dbo.CustomerOrderHistoryStatus(CustomerOrderHistoryStatusID)
);
```

The creation of this table does not specify that partition scheme of `CustomerOrderHistoryRange`. This table will be a standard table created on the PRIMARY filegroup in the database.

Once the underlying tables have been created, you can create a single database object that can allow you to access both tables. This will be the same as the partitioned view created in the previous section. Listing 16-22 has the T-SQL code needed to create a partitioned view.

Listing 16-22. Creating a Partitioned View

```
CREATE VIEW dbo.vwCustomerOrderHistory_PT
AS
-- Select data from current read/write table
SELECT CustomerOrderHistoryID,
      CustomerOrderID,
      CustomerOrderHistoryStatusID,
      DateCreated,
      DateModified
FROM dbo.CustomerOrderActive
UNION ALL
-- Select data from partitioned table
SELECT CustomerOrderHistoryID,
      CustomerOrderID,
      CustomerOrderHistoryStatusID,
      DateCreated,
      DateModified
FROM dbo.CustomerOrderHistoryPartition;
```

This partitioned view allows you to keep the most recent and highly active data in a table without partitions. This table can be specifically indexed to allow for the best write speeds. Any other tables included in the partitioned view can be indexed based on their usage. The partitioned table included in the preceding partitioned view may only include inactive data. As a result, you may expect this data to only be read going forward. Knowing this, you can use a different strategy to index this table.

Now let's determine the behavior of SQL Server when querying a non-partitioned table. The query in Listing 16-23 shows a query to find all records for a specific date range in the dbo.CustomerOrderHistory table.

Listing 16-23. Access Data Before Partitioning Table and View

```
DECLARE @StartDate  DATETIME2(2) = '2022-10-07';
DECLARE @EndDate    DATETIME2(2) = '2022-10-09';

SELECT CustomerOrderHistoryID,
       CustomerOrderID,
       CustomerOrderHistoryStatusID,
       DateCreated,
       DateModified
FROM dbo.CustomerOrderHistory
WHERE DateCreated > @StartDate
       AND DateCreated <= @EndDate;
```

This query will be run on a non-partitioned table. At the time of the query execution, this table is ordered by the original primary key, which is the CustomerOrderHistoryID. As a result, the execution plan from the query in Listing 16-23 is shown in Figure 16-16.

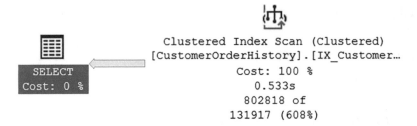

Figure 16-16. *Execution plan for an unpartitioned table*

Based on the execution plan in Listing 16-16, you can confirm that SQL Server uses a clustered index scan to find the relevant records. This is because there is no index that includes the DateCreated. With the table not being partitioned by date, SQL Server also needs to go through the entire table to find the data records that satisfy the query in Listing 16-23.

After running this query, you can review additional information about the operators in the execution plan. Specifically, you want to identify the number of logical reads and rows returned for this query execution. Using Figure 16-17, you can identify the logical reads and number of rows.

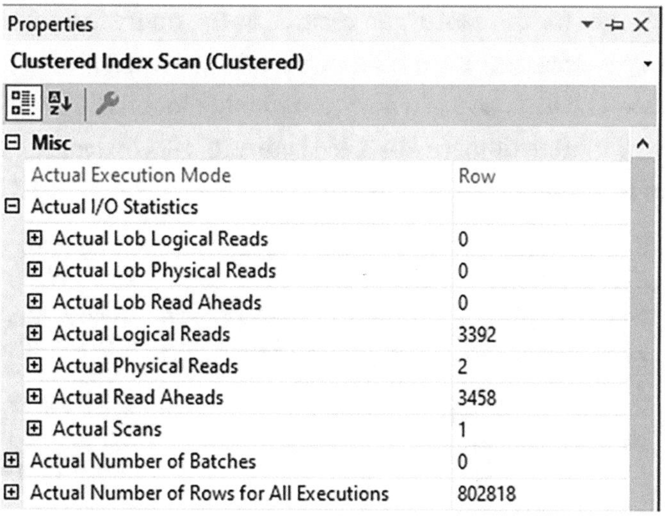

Figure 16-17. *Reads associated with the clustered index scan*

You can see that this query returned 802,818 rows with a total number of 3,392 pages read as logical reads. You will be comparing these values to the performance associated with a partitioned view that contains both a partitioned and non-partitioned table.

Previously, in Listing 16-22, you created a partitioned view that contained a partitioned table for all 2021 data records and non-partitioned table for all 2022 data records. To compare how a partitioned view performs differently than a non-partitioned table, you can run the query in Listing 16-24.

Listing 16-24. Accessing Data Using a Partitioned Column in a Partitioned Table

```
DECLARE @StartDate   DATETIME2(2) = '2022-10-07';
DECLARE @EndDate     DATETIME2(2) = '2022-10-09';

SELECT CustomerOrderHistoryID,
       CustomerOrderID,
       CustomerOrderHistoryStatusID,
       DateCreated,
       DateModified
FROM dbo.vwCustomerOrderHistory_PT
WHERE DateCreated > @StartDate
      AND DateCreated <= @EndDate;
```

This query searches for the same data records as the query from Listing 16-23. However, this query is accessing a partitioned view instead of a non-partitioned table. The partitioned view is composed of a partitioned table for all of 2021 and a non-partitioned table containing data for 2022. In Figure 16-18, you can see the execution plan generated for this query.

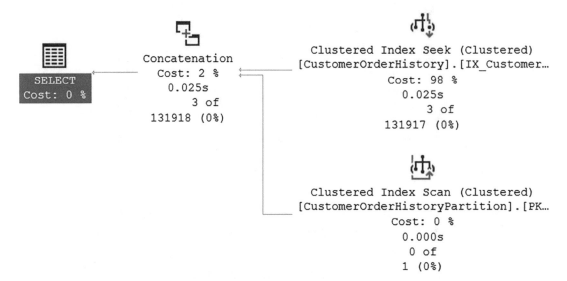

Figure 16-18. *Execution plan for a partitioned view*

One of the important things to note is that this execution plan uses a clustered index seek instead of a clustered index scan. This lets you know that SQL Server could determine where to find the relevant data records efficiently and without having to go through all or most of the records in the table. Another thing that stands out is that the clustered index seek is performed on the partitioned dbo.CustomerOrderHistory table. You can also find the properties associated with the clustered index seek to get additional information. In Figure 16-19, you can see the number of logical reads and the number of records returned.

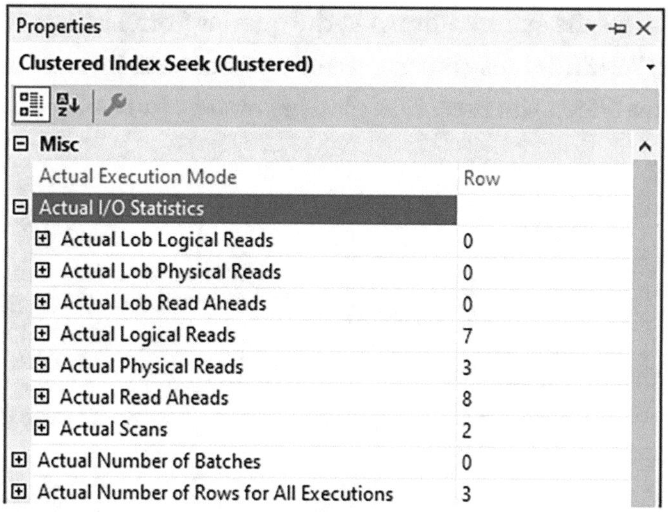

Figure 16-19. *Reads for a query partitioned view with a clustered index on a partitioning key*

The total number of rows returned is 3 with a total number of 7 data pages read from memory. The decrease in the number of total data pages read from memory indicates that this query is more efficient at finding the relevant data than the query in Listing 16-23.

You have seen how querying a partitioned view on a column that references a partitioned table performs. The next step is to see how querying a partitioned view works when accessing a non-partitioned table. Listing 16-25 shows a query to access data from the non-partitioned table of the partitioned view.

Listing 16-25. Accessing Data Using a Partitioned Column Not in a Partitioned Table

```
SELECT CustomerOrderHistoryID,
       CustomerOrderID,
       CustomerOrderHistoryStatusID,
       DateCreated
FROM dbo.vwCustomerOrderHistory
WHERE CustomerOrderID = 401408
       AND CustomerOrderHistoryStatusID = 1;
```

This query returns the same columns as the queries from Listings 16-23 and 16-24. The criteria in the WHERE clause is accessing data from 2022 instead of 2021. To see how this change in dates affects the execution plan generated, you can see the difference in Figure 16-20.

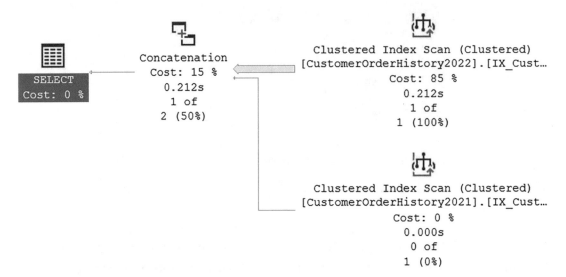

Figure 16-20. *Execution plan for a partitioned view not on a partitioned table*

In Figure 16-20, the preceding execution plan used a clustered index scan on the dbo.CustomerOrderHistory2022 table. While the execution plans between the partitioned and non-partitioned tables are similar, how much data is retrieved from SQL Server can vary between the two execution plans. Figure 16-21 can show you how much data is accessed for the query in Listing 16-25.

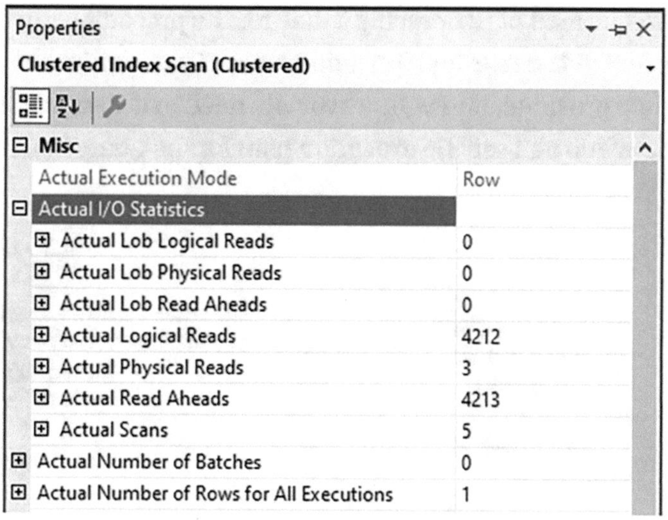

Figure 16-21. *Reads for a query partitioned view on a non-partitioned table*

In Figure 16-21, you can see there are 4,212 data pages read from memory and 1 records returned. This performance is still much better than the performance when all data existed in a single non-partitioned table.

You have confirmed that partitioned views work well for queries that access partitioned tables and non-partitioned tables within the partitioned view. Like partitioned tables, it is still best to query data using the columns that are part of the partition. In Listing 16-26, you query the partitioned view using columns that are not part of the partition.

Listing 16-26. Accessing Data Without Using a Partitioned Column

```
SELECT CustomerOrderHistoryID,
     CustomerOrderID,
     CustomerOrderHistoryStatusID,
     DateCreated
FROM dbo.vwCustomerOrderHistory_PT
WHERE CustomerOrderID = 401408
     AND CustomerOrderHistoryStatusID = 1;
```

You can see that instead of referencing a date for the preceding query, you want to return all records for CustomerOrderID of 4 that have a CustomerOrderHistoryStatusID of 2. There is no date provided, and SQL Server will need to access all tables within the partitioned view. You can see the execution plan for the query in Listing 16-26 in Figure 16-22.

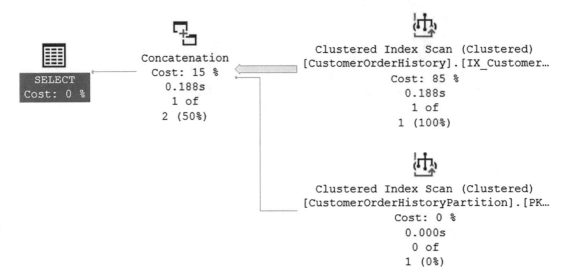

Figure 16-22. *Execution plan for a partitioned view not on a partitioning key*

As expected, the execution plan shows a clustered index scan on dbo. CustomerOrderHistory and dbo.CustomerOrderHistoryPartition. There is no date range provided in Listing 16-26, which causes SQL Server to access both tables in the partitioned view. The criteria for the query do not take advantage of any indexes on the tables which causes the need for a clustered index scan. The key point here is to use the partitioning column as much as possible. This gives you the best chance to take advantage of any performance gains associated with partitioning your data.

The longer your applications and databases are in use, the more new challenges you will face in managing the data generated. When working with hybrid workloads, you may find that you need too many different methods to manage and access your data. Combining tables and partitioned tables in a partitioned view can give you some of the flexibility you need. Breaking your data up into multiple non-partitioned and partitioned tables can allow you to create different indexes on the tables based on how you will be accessing the data within those tables. This sort of strategy can allow you to keep a table with only recent data separate from any data used for reporting purposes. The table containing recent and current data can then be configured to maximize application performance.

One of the options available within SQL Server is the use of partitioning. You have the option to partition information into various filegroups. You can also create partition functions and partition schemes that help SQL Server determine how to segment data. Once the partition scheme is applied to a column on a table, the table is now a partitioned table. The column used for the partition scheme is known as the partitioning key. When queries are designed to use the partitioning key, SQL Server can use partition elimination to find the records that meet the query criteria. In addition to using partitioned tables, you also have the option of using partitioned views. Partitioned views can allow you to combine multiple database objects into a single object that can be referenced by your application code. When running a query, SQL Server will determine which objects need to be accessed to meet the query criteria. You can also combine non-partitioned tables and partitioned tables into the same partitioned view. This method may be able to help you if you find yourself in a situation where your database needs to be able to handle both transactional and analytical queries.

CHAPTER 17

Managing Data Long-Term

In the previous chapter, I introduced the concepts of partitioned tables and partitioned views. This chapter continues the discussion on partitions by discussing how to use partition switching. The first section introduces the concept of partition switching. The second section guides you to use all the information you have learned about partition switching to manage data retention and archival.

Data Retention and Archival

Managing data long-term should allow you to store data effectively and remove data quickly. This section covers how to swap data to be expunged into a new table so that the data can be removed. The last two partitions in the table will be merged so that these oldest data remains in the last partition. Finally, the new partition will be split to that new data can be saved in the newest partition. This entire process is referred to as *a sliding window partition*. If you decide to implement one of these, it may be best to automate this process using a SQL Server Agent job.

Let's get familiar with the T-SQL for tables you will use for this process. The first table is dbo.CustomerOrderActive. This table is used to hold active orders as determined by the business rules. The table in Listing 17-1 is used to hold the current month of customer orders.

Listing 17-1. Customer Orders Last Month

```
CREATE TABLE dbo.CustomerOrderActive
(
        CustomerOrderHistoryID          BIGINT          NOT NULL,
        CustomerOrderID                 INT             NOT NULL,
        CustomerOrderHistoryStatusID    TINYINT         NOT NULL,
        DateCreated                     DATETIME2(2)    NOT NULL,
        DateModified                    DATETIME2(2)        NULL,
```

E. Noble, *Pro T-SQL 2022*, https://doi.org/10.1007/978-1-4842-9256-3_17

```
    CONSTRAINT PK_CustomerOrderActive_CustomerOrderHistoryID
        PRIMARY KEY (CustomerOrderHistoryID),
    CONSTRAINT FK_CustomerOrderActive_CustomerOrderID
        FOREIGN KEY (CustomerOrderID)
        REFERENCES dbo.CustomerOrder(CustomerOrderID),
    CONSTRAINT FK_CustomerOrderActive_CustomerOrderHistoryStatusID
        FOREIGN KEY (CustomerOrderHistoryStatusID)
        REFERENCES
    dbo.CustomerOrderHistoryStatus(CustomerOrderHistoryStatusID)
);
```

The expectation is that all orders will be fulfilled within in a three-month period. Therefore, the most activity is expected for the most recent three months.

The second table is used to keep customer history for the past 12 months. This data is used for reporting and analysis within the business. In Listing 17-2, the T-SQL shows that this table is partitioned.

Listing 17-2. Partitioned Table for Customer Orders in the Last 12 Months

```
CREATE TABLE dbo.CustomerOrderHistory
(
    CustomerOrderHistoryID       BIGINT     IDENTITY(1,1)    NOT NULL,
    CustomerOrderID              INT                         NOT NULL,
    CustomerOrderHistoryStatusID TINYINT                     NOT NULL,
    DateCreated                  DATETIME2(2)                NOT NULL,
    DateModified                 DATETIME2(2)                    NULL,
    CONSTRAINT PK_CustomerOrderHistory_CustomerOrderHistoryID
        PRIMARY KEY NONCLUSTERED
        (CustomerOrderHistoryID, DateCreated),
    CONSTRAINT FK_CustomerOrderHistory_CustomerOrder
        FOREIGN KEY (CustomerOrderID)
        REFERENCES dbo.CustomerOrder(CustomerOrderID),
    CONSTRAINT FK_CustomerOrderHistory_CustomerOrderHistoryStatus
        FOREIGN KEY (CustomerOrderHistoryStatusID)
        REFERENCES dbo.CustomerOrderHistoryStatus
        (CustomerOrderHistoryStatusID)
) ON CustomerOrderHistoryRange (DateCreated);
```

The third table is a table to hold archival data needed to regulatory purposes, which this case is customer order information older than a year old. After 15 months, the data will be removed from this table. This table is also partitioned, as shown in Listing 17-3 below.

Listing 17-3. Partitioned Table to Archive Customer Orders in the Last 15 Months

```
CREATE TABLE dbo.CustomerOrderHistoryArchive
(
        CustomerOrderHistoryID          BIGINT      IDENTITY(1,1)   NOT NULL,
        CustomerOrderID                 INT                         NOT NULL,
        CustomerOrderHistoryStatusID    TINYINT                     NOT NULL,
        DateCreated                     DATETIME2(2)                NOT NULL,
        DateModified                    DATETIME2(2)                    NULL,
        CONSTRAINT PK_CustomerOrderHistoryArchive_CustomerOrderHistoryID
                PRIMARY KEY NONCLUSTERED
                (CustomerOrderHistoryID, DateCreated),
        CONSTRAINT FK_CustomerOrderHistoryArchive_CustomerOrder
                FOREIGN KEY (CustomerOrderID)
                REFERENCES dbo.CustomerOrder(CustomerOrderID),
        CONSTRAINT FK_CustomerOrderHistoryArchive_CustomerOrderHistoryStatus
                FOREIGN KEY (CustomerOrderHistoryStatusID)
                REFERENCES dbo.CustomerOrderHistoryStatus
                (CustomerOrderHistoryStatusID)
) ON CustomerOrderHistoryArchiveRange (DateCreated);
```

The last table is the table to temporarily hold the data to be purged. This table must have the same format as the other tables, as shown in Listing 17-4.

Listing 17-4. Table to Purge Customer Orders Over 15 Months

```
CREATE TABLE dbo.CustomerOrderPurge
(
        CustomerOrderHistoryID          BIGINT      IDENTITY(1,1)   NOT NULL,
        CustomerOrderID                 INT                         NOT NULL,
        CustomerOrderHistoryStatusID    TINYINT                     NOT NULL,
```

```
    DateCreated                     DATETIME2(2)                 NOT NULL,
    DateModified                    DATETIME2(2)                     NULL,
    CONSTRAINT PK_CustomerOrderPurge_CustomerOrderHistoryID
    PRIMARY KEY NONCLUSTERED
        (CustomerOrderHistoryID, DateCreated),
    CONSTRAINT FK_CustomerOrderPurge_CustomerOrder
        FOREIGN KEY (CustomerOrderID)
        REFERENCES dbo.CustomerOrder(CustomerOrderID),
    CONSTRAINT FK_CustomerOrderPurge_CustomerOrderHistoryStatus
        FOREIGN KEY (CustomerOrderHistoryStatusID)
        REFERENCES dbo.CustomerOrderHistoryStatus
        (CustomerOrderHistoryStatusID)
);
```

Now that you have the tables created, the next part is go through the process of moving these partitions at month's end.

Switching Partitions

In Chapter 18, I introduced the idea of partitioning in SQL Server. This section will go through the process of managing partitions after you have created them. The first example will go through using partition switching between two tables that are not partitioned. The second example will show how to switch partitions from a non-partitioned table to a partition table. The last example will show how partitions can be switched between partitioned tables.

For the first example, you will create a non-partitioned table using the T-SQL code in Listing 17-5.

Listing 17-5. Creating a Non-Partitioned Table

```
CREATE TABLE dbo.CustomerOrderNonParitition(
    CustomerOrderHistoryID          BIGINT       NOT NULL,
    CustomerOrderID                 INT          NOT NULL,
    CustomerOrderHistoryStatusID    TINYINY      NOT NULL,
    DateCreated                     DATETIME2(2) NOT NULL,
```

```
    DateModified                        DATETIME2(2)    NULL,
  CONSTRAINT [PK_CustomerOrderNonPartition]
      PRIMARY KEY CLUSTERED ([CustomerOrderHistoryID], [DateCreated])
);
```

This is a new empty table with the same schema as the table dbo.
CustomerOrderActive. Both tables have not been partitioned. You should get a count of the number of records in each table before you switch the data from one table to the other table. This is because a non-partitioned table is treated as a table consisting of one partition. The query in Listing 17-6 gets the count of records for the dbo.
CustomerOrderActive and dbo.CustomerOrderNonPartition tables.

Listing 17-6. Getting Counts of Records in the Source and Destination Tables

```
SELECT COUNT(*)
FROM dbo.CustomerOrderActive;

SELECT COUNT(*)
FROM dbo.CustomerOrderNonParitition;
```

The output of the queries above has been formatted into Table 17-1 to show the record count for the number customers in each table.

Table 17-1. *Count of Records per Table*

Table Name	Record Count
dbo.CustomerOrderActive	802,821
dbo.CustomerOrderNonPartition	0

The dbo.CustomerOrder table has 802,821 records before the partition switch, and the table dbo.CustomerOrderNonPartition has 0 records. The T-SQL in Listing 17-7 shows how you can switch data to another non-partitioned table.

Listing 17-7. Moving Data Between Non-Partitioned Tables

```
ALTER TABLE dbo.CustomerOrderActive
SWITCH TO dbo.CustomerOrderNonParitition;
```

After the partition, which in this case is the entire table, is switched from dbo.CustomerOrderActive to dbo.CustomerOrderNonPartition, you can run a query to check the row counts of both tables as shown in Listing 17-8.

Listing 17-8. Number of Records in Non-Partitioned Tables

```
SELECT COUNT(*)
FROM dbo.CustomerOrderActive;

SELECT COUNT(*)
FROM dbo.CustomerOrderNonParitition;
```

After running this T-SQL, you get the record count for both tables as shown in Table 17-2.

Table 17-2. *Count of Records per Table*

Table Name	Record Count
dbo.CustomerOrderActive	0
dbo.CustomerOrderNonPartition	802,821

This table indicates that there are no rows in dbo.CustomerOrderActive and 802,821 rows in dbo.CustomerOrderNonPartition. This is what you would expect since the entire table of dbo.CustomerOrderActive was switched into dbo. CustomerOrderNonPartition. If you want to reset the tables back to how they were before the partition switch, you could execute the T-SQL in Listing 17-9 to switch back from dbo.CustomerOrderNonParitition to dbo.CustomerOrderActive.

Listing 17-9. Moving Data Back to the Original Table

```
ALTER TABLE dbo.CustomerOrderNonParitition
SWITCH TO dbo.CustomerOrderActive;
```

Now that the partition has been switched back, all of the records are once again in dbo.CustomerOrderActive. If data had been written to the dbo.CustomerOrderActive table, you would not be able to switch the data back to the original table. The target table must be empty. Listing 17-10 has a query you can execute to confirm that dbo. CustomerOrderNonPartition does not have any partitions.

Listing 17-10. Query to View Partition Information for CustomerOrderNonPartition Table

```
SELECT tbl.[name] AS TableName,
      sch.[name] AS PartitionScheme,
      fnc.[name] AS PartitionFunction,
      prt.partition_number,
      fnc.[type_desc],
      rng.boundary_id,
      rng.[value] AS BoundaryValue,
      prt.[rows]
FROM sys.tables tbl
      INNER JOIN sys.indexes idx
      ON tbl.[object_id] = idx.[object_id]
      INNER JOIN sys.partitions prt
      ON idx.[object_id] = prt.[object_id]
            AND idx.index_id = prt.index_id
      INNER JOIN sys.partition_schemes AS sch
      ON idx.data_space_id = sch.data_space_id
      INNER JOIN sys.partition_functions AS fnc
      ON sch.function_id = fnc.function_id
      LEFT JOIN sys.partition_range_values AS rng
      ON fnc.function_id = rng.function_id
            AND rng.boundary_id = prt.partition_number
WHERE tbl.[name] = 'CustomerOrderNonParitition'
      AND idx.[type] <= 1
ORDER BY prt.partition_number;
```

The examples above indicate how to partition switch between two non-partitioned tables. However, it is much more likely that you will want to use partition switching with at least one table that is partitioned.

Next, you will work through an example where you will partition switch from a non-partitioned table to a partitioned table. As a refresher, Listing 17-11 shows how to create a partition function and partition scheme.

Listing 17-11. Creating a Partition Function and Partition Scheme

```
CREATE PARTITION FUNCTION CustomerOrderHistoryFunc(DATETIME2(2))
AS RANGE RIGHT FOR VALUES
(
      '2022-01-01',
      '2022-02-01',
      '2022-03-01'
);

CREATE PARTITION SCHEME CustomerOrderHistoryRange
AS PARTITION CustomerOrderHistoryFunc TO
(
      [PRIMARY],
      [PRIMARY],
      CustomerOrderHistory202202,
      CustomerOrderHistory202203
);
```

One important note when switching partitions is that the both the source that is being switched out and the target being switched to must be in the same filegroup. For your example, dbo.CustomerOrderActive is in the PRIMARY filegroup. Therefore, if you are switching out to the first partition in dbo.CustomerOrderHistory, the first partition must also be in the filegroup PRIMARY. Otherwise, you would have to move dbo.CustomerOrderActive to the same filegroup as the first partition in dbo.CustomerOrderHistory.

Before switching the records from dbo.CustomerActive to dbo.CustomerOrderHistory, you can check the record counts using the query in Listing 17-12.

Listing 17-12. Number of Records in the Non-Partitioned and Partitioned Tables

```
SELECT COUNT(*)
FROM dbo.CustomerOrderActive;

SELECT COUNT(*)
FROM dbo.CustomerOrderHistory;
```

The results from these two queries are displayed in Table 17-3.

Table 17-3. *Count of Records per Table*

Table Name	Record Count
dbo.CustomerOrderActive	802,821
dbo.CustomerOrderNonPartition	0

The record counts indicated that 802,821 records are in the table dbo. CustomerOrderActive, and there are zero records in dbo.CustomerOrderNonPartition.

Before you can try to switch the partitions, you need to confirm that all records in dbo.CustomerOrderActive exist within the partition you will be using in dbo. CustomerOrderNonPartition. To do this, you need to add check constraints to dbo. CustomerOrderActive. Listing 17-13 shows the T-SQL used to add check constraints.

Listing 17-13. Adding Check Constraints to the Source Table

```
ALTER TABLE dbo.CustomerOrderActive
WITH CHECK ADD CONSTRAINT CK_MaxDateCreated
CHECK (DateCreated IS NOT NULL AND DateCreated < '2022-01-01');
```

When switching data from a non-partitioned table to a partition in a partitioned table, you must first verify that all of the data in the non-partitioned table can exist in the partition in the partitioned table. To do this, you need to add a check constraint to the non-partitioned table. The check constraint above confirms that all data in dbo. CustomerOrderActive was created before January 1, 2022. This is the same date range that exists for the first partition in dbo.CustomerOrderActive.

Note   If creating the check constraint fails because there is data outside of the date range for the partition, you will not be able to use partition switching to move the data from the non-partitioned to the partitioned table. Similarly, you will not be able to use partition switching if you only want to move some data from the non-partitioned table to the partitioned table or if you want to move all data from the non-partitioned table to the target table in a partition that is not empty.

Once the check constraint has been added, you can use the T-SQL in Listing 17-14 to switch all of the data from the non-partitioned table dbo.CustomerOrderActive to the first partition in the dbo.CustomerOrderHistory table.

Listing 17-14. Partition Switch from Non-Partitioned Table to Partitioned Table

```
ALTER TABLE dbo.CustomerOrderActive
SWITCH TO dbo.CustomerOrderHistory PARTITION 1;
```

As you have done before, once the partition is successfully switched, you can execute the T-SQL in Listing 17-15 to confirm the record counts in each table affected.

Listing 17-15. Number of Records in the Non-Partitioned and Partitioned Tables

```
SELECT COUNT(*)
FROM dbo.CustomerOrderActive;

SELECT COUNT(*)
FROM dbo.CustomerOrderHistory;
```

The results from these queries are as expected. There are 0 records remaining in dbo.CustomerOrderActive and 802,821 records are in dbo.CustomerOrderNonPartition, as shown in Table 17-4.

Table 17-4. *Count of Records per Table*

Table Name	Record Count
dbo.CustomerOrderActive	0
dbo.CustomerOrderNonPartition	802,821

This confirms that all records have been switched from dbo.CustomerOrderActive to dbo.CustomerOrderNonPartition.

You will switch the partition back to reset the demo. Before you switch the partitions back, you can run an additional query to verify the partition in dbo.CustomerOrderNonPartition that contains these records. Listing 17-16 has the query to execute to verify these results.

Listing 17-16. Query to View Partition Information for the
CustomerOrderHistory Table

```
SELECT tbl.[name] AS TableName,
      sch.[name] AS PartitionScheme,
      fnc.[name] AS PartitionFunction,
      prt.partition_number,
      fnc.[type_desc],
      rng.boundary_id,
      rng.[value] AS BoundaryValue,
      prt.[rows]
FROM sys.tables tbl
      INNER JOIN sys.indexes idx
      ON tbl.[object_id] = idx.[object_id]
      INNER JOIN sys.partitions prt
      ON idx.[object_id] = prt.[object_id]
            AND idx.index_id = prt.index_id
      INNER JOIN sys.partition_schemes AS sch
      ON idx.data_space_id = sch.data_space_id
      INNER JOIN sys.partition_functions AS fnc
      ON sch.function_id = fnc.function_id
      LEFT JOIN sys.partition_range_values AS rng
      ON fnc.function_id = rng.function_id
            AND rng.boundary_id = prt.partition_number
WHERE tbl.[name] = 'CustomerOrderHistory'
      AND idx.[type] <= 1
ORDER BY prt.partition_number;
```

Running this T-SQL code, you will find that all 802,821 records are in the first
partition as expected. This indicates you have successfully switched the data from a
non-partitioned to a partitioned table. If you want to switch the partition back, you need
to run the T-SQL shown in Listing 17-17.

Listing 17-17. Switching Back from the Current Partitioned Table to the Original Non-Partitioned Table

```
ALTER TABLE dbo.CustomerOrderActive
DROP CONSTRAINT CK_MaxDateCreated;

ALTER TABLE dbo.CustomerOrderHistory
SWITCH PARTITION 1 TO dbo.CustomerOrderActive;
```

Before switching the partitions back, you need to remove the check constraint on dbo.CustomerOrderActive so that the table schemas match dbo.CustomerOrderHistory. If the table schemas do not match, you will not be able to switch the partition. This requirement is one of the reasons partition switching can be so much faster than inserting the data into the target table.

Once you remove this constraint, you can successfully switch the data from dbo.CustomerOrderHistory back to dbo.CustomerOrderActive.

If you reran the T-SQL from Listing 17-9 and Listing 17-10, you would move data back into the dbo.CustomerOrderHistory table. After switching the data from dbo.CustomerOrderActive to dbo.CustomerOrderHistory, you will have 802,821 records in dbo.CustomerOrderHistory. When this is complete, you we are ready to implement partition switching between two partitioned tables. Before beginning the process of partition switching, you should execute Listing 17-18 to confirm how many records are in each table.

Listing 17-18. Number of Records in Partitioned Tables

```
SELECT COUNT(*)
FROM dbo.CustomerOrderHistory;

SELECT COUNT(*)
FROM dbo.CustomerOrderHistoryArchive;
```

The results from the queries above indicate the row count for the dbo.CustomerOrderHistory and dbo.CustomerOrderHistoryArchive tables. These row counts are shown in Table 17-5.

Table 17-5. *Count of Records per Table*

Table Name	Record Count
dbo.CustomerOrderHistory	802,821
dbo.CustomerOrderHistoryArchive	0

You are able to confirm that dbo.CustomerOrderHistory has 802,821 records and dbo.CustomerOrderHistoryArchive has 0 records. Now that you know the record counts before you switch partitions, you can switch the first partition from dbo.CustomerOrderHistory to the first partition in dbo.CustomerOrderHistoryArchive as indicated in Listing 17-19.

Listing 17-19. Partition Switch from Partitioned Table to Partitioned Table

```
ALTER TABLE dbo.CustomerOrderHistory SWITCH PARTITION 1
TO dbo.CustomerOrderHistoryArchive PARTITION 1;
```

Once this partition switch is complete, you can again verify the row counts in dbo.CustomerOrderHistory and dbo.CustomerOrderHistoryArchive. Listing 17-20 shows the T-SQL to verify these row counts.

Listing 17-20. Number of Records in Partitioned Tables

```
SELECT COUNT(*)
FROM dbo.CustomerOrderHistory;

SELECT COUNT(*)
FROM dbo.CustomerOrderHistoryArchive;
```

The results from these queries show that there are no records remaining in dbo.CustomerOrderHistory. Table 17-6 also shows that all 802,821 records are now in the dbo.CustomerOrderHistoryArchive table.

Table 17-6. *Count of Records per Table*

Table Name	Record Count
dbo.CustomerOrderHistory	0
dbo.CustomerOrderHistoryArchive	802,821

The table indicates that the partition has been successfully switched. If you would like to switch the partition back to the original partitioned table, you can execute the T-SQL in Listing 17-21.

Listing 17-21. Partition Switch Back from Partitioned Table to Partitioned Table

```
ALTER TABLE dbo.CustomerOrderHistoryArchive SWITCH PARTITION 1
TO dbo.CustomerOrderHistory PARTITION 1;
```

This T-SQL will move all of the data in the first partition of dbo. CustomerOrderHistoryArchive back to the first partition in dbo. CustomerOrderHistory. Listing 17-22 shows information about the partitions for dbo. CustomerOrderHistoryArchive.

Listing 17-22. Query to View Partition Information for CustomerOrderHistoryArchive Table

```
SELECT tbl.[name] AS TableName,
      sch.[name] AS PartitionScheme,
      fnc.[name] AS PartitionFunction,
      prt.partition_number,
      fnc.[type_desc],
      rng.boundary_id,
      rng.[value] AS BoundaryValue,
      prt.[rows]
FROM sys.tables tbl
      INNER JOIN sys.indexes idx
      ON tbl.[object_id] = idx.[object_id]
      INNER JOIN sys.partitions prt
      ON idx.[object_id] = prt.[object_id]
            AND idx.index_id = prt.index_id
      INNER JOIN sys.partition_schemes AS sch
      ON idx.data_space_id = sch.data_space_id
      INNER JOIN sys.partition_functions AS fnc
      ON sch.function_id = fnc.function_id
      LEFT JOIN sys.partition_range_values AS rng
      ON fnc.function_id = rng.function_id
            AND rng.boundary_id = prt.partition_number
```

```
WHERE tbl.[name] = 'CustomerOrderHistoryArchive'
    AND idx.[type] <= 1
ORDER BY prt.partition_number;
```

Once you have reviewed this information, you can confirm that you have successfully switched partitions between two partitioned tables.

This section covered how to switch partitions between two non-partitioned tables, a non-partitioned and partitioned table, and two partitioned tables. While each of these processes separately can be helpful, combining them to suit your business needs may be even better. In the next section, you will go through an example of how switching partitions across multiple tables can help with your data retention and archival processes. The demo in the next section will apply these concepts to allow you to have a table for active application activity, a table for reporting purposes, a table for storing data for compliance reasons, and a table to quickly remove data from the database.

Sliding Window Partition

The goal of this example is show how you can switch partitions between multiple tables, both partitioned and non-partitioned. For this example, you'll use a preloaded small set of sample data in several of the tables, as shown in Table 17-7.

Table 17-7. *Count of Records per Table for Managing Customer Orders*

Table Name	Record Count
dbo.CustomerOrderActive	1
dbo.CustomerOrderHistory	3
dbo.CustomerOrderHistoryArchive	12
dbo.CustomerOrderPurge	0

The single record in dbo.CustomerOrderActive is for the month of April 2023. The three records in dbo.CustomerOrderHistory are for January, February, and March 2023. In dbo.CustomerHistory there are 12 records, one for each month for the past 4 to 15 months.

This process assumes you are at the beginning of May 2023. This is the point in time when you would be ready to update dbo.CustomerOrderActive to be for May 2023. Following the pattern where dbo.CustomerOrderHistory is for the most recent three historical months, this table will be updated to hold data from February 2023 to April 2023, and dbo.CustomerOrderHistoryArchive will have data for to February 2022 through January 2023.

For this example, start by moving the oldest month of data out of dbo.CustomerOrderHistoryArchive into dbo.CustomerOrderPurge. Before you do this, you can verify the row counts for each partition for dbo.CustomerOrderHistoryArchive by executing the T-SQL in Listing 17-23.

Listing 17-23. Merge Partitions for Customer Orders Over 15 Months Old

```
SELECT SCHEMA_NAME(tbl.[schema_id]) AS SchemaName,
      tbl.[name] AS TableName,
      pt.partition_number AS PartitionNumber,
      pt.[rows] AS NumberRecords,
      rv.[value] AS BoundaryValue,
      CASE WHEN ISNULL(rv.[value], rv2.[value]) IS NULL
            THEN 'N/A'
            ELSE
                  CASE WHEN fnc.boundary_value_on_right = 0
                          AND rv2.[value] IS NULL THEN '>='
                       WHEN fnc.boundary_value_on_right = 0
                          THEN '>'
                       ELSE '>='
                  END + ' '
                       + ISNULL(CONVERT(varchar(64), rv2.value),
                       'Min Value') + ' ' +
                  CASE fnc.boundary_value_on_right
                       WHEN 1 THEN 'and <'
                       ELSE 'and <='
                  END
                  + ' ' + ISNULL(CONVERT(varchar(64), rv.value),
                       'Max Value')
            END AS TextComparison
```

```
FROM sys.tables AS tbl
     INNER JOIN sys.indexes AS idx
     ON tbl.[object_id] = idx.[object_id]
     INNER JOIN sys.partitions AS pt
     ON idx.[object_id] = pt.[object_id]
          AND idx.index_id = pt.index_id
     INNER JOIN sys.partition_schemes AS pch
     ON idx.data_space_id = pch.data_space_id
     INNER JOIN sys.partition_functions AS fnc
     ON pch.function_id = fnc.function_id
     LEFT JOIN sys.partition_range_values AS rng
     ON fnc.function_id = rng.function_id
          AND rng.boundary_id = pt.partition_number
     LEFT JOIN sys.partition_range_values AS rv
     ON fnc.function_id = rv.function_id
          AND pt.partition_number = rv.boundary_id
     LEFT JOIN sys.partition_range_values AS rv2
     ON fnc.function_id = rv2.function_id
          AND pt.partition_number - 1= rv2.boundary_id
WHERE tbl.[name] = 'CustomerOrderHistoryArchive'
    AND idx.[type] <= 1
ORDER BY tbl.[name], pt.partition_number;
```

This query shows not only the partition number, which you need to switch partitions, but also shows the row counts and partition logics. For this table, Table 17-8 shows the results from this query.

Table 17-8. *CustomerOrderHistoryArchive Before Partition Switching*

Partition Number	Record Count	Boundary Value	Text Comparison
1	0	2022-01-01	>= Min Value and < Jan 1 2022 12:00AM
2	1	2022-02-01	>= Jan 1 2022 12:00AM and < Feb 1 2022 12:00AM
3	1	2022-03-01	>= Feb 1 2022 12:00AM and < Mar 1 2022 12:00AM
4	1	2022-04-01	>= Mar 1 2022 12:00AM and < Apr 1 2022 12:00AM
5	1	2022-05-01	>= Apr 1 2022 12:00AM and < May 1 2022 12:00AM
6	1	2022-06-01	>= May 1 2022 12:00AM and < Jun 1 2022 12:00AM
7	1	2022-07-01	>= Jun 1 2022 12:00AM and < Jul 1 2022 12:00AM
8	1	2022-08-01	>= Jul 1 2022 12:00AM and < Aug 1 2022 12:00AM
9	1	2022-09-01	>= Aug 1 2022 12:00AM and < Sep 1 2022 12:00AM
10	1	2022-10-01	>= Sep 1 2022 12:00AM and < Oct 1 2022 12:00AM
11	1	2022-11-01	>= Oct 1 2022 12:00AM and < Nov 1 2022 12:00AM
12	1	2022-12-01	>= Nov 1 2022 12:00AM and < Dec 1 2022 12:00AM
13	0		>= Dec 1 2022 12:00AM and < Max Value

This shows that you have two empty partitions. The first empty partition is for data before January 1, 2022. The last partition is for data on or after December 1, 2022.

The first step is to merge the partition for January 2022 into the partition for February 2022, as shown in Listing 17-24.

Listing 17-24. Merging Partitions for Customer Orders Over 15 Months Old

```
ALTER PARTITION FUNCTION CustomerOrderHistoryArchiveFunc()
MERGE RANGE ('2022-01-01');
```

This will take the oldest partition for data before January 1, 2022 and merge it into the partition for data before February 1, 2022. This will update the partitions as shown in Table 17-9.

Table 17-9. *CustomerOrderHistoryArchive After Merging Partitions*

Partition Number	Record Count	Boundary Value	Text Comparison
1	1	2022-01-01	>= Min Value and < Feb 1 2022 12:00AM
2	1	2022-02-01	>= Feb 1 2022 12:00AM and < Mar 1 2022 12:00AM
3	1	2022-03-01	>= Mar 1 2022 12:00AM and < Apr 1 2022 12:00AM
4	1	2022-04-01	>= Apr 1 2022 12:00AM and < May 1 2022 12:00AM
5	1	2022-05-01	>= May 1 2022 12:00AM and < Jun 1 2022 12:00AM
6	1	2022-06-01	>= Jun 1 2022 12:00AM and < Jul 1 2022 12:00AM
7	1	2022-07-01	>= Jul 1 2022 12:00AM and < Aug 1 2022 12:00AM
8	1	2022-08-01	>= Aug 1 2022 12:00AM and < Sep 1 2022 12:00AM
9	1	2022-09-01	>= Sep 1 2022 12:00AM and < Oct 1 2022 12:00AM
10	1	2022-10-01	>= Oct 1 2022 12:00AM and < Nov 1 2022 12:00AM
11	1	2022-11-01	>= Nov 1 2022 12:00AM and < Dec 1 2022 12:00AM
12	0		>= Dec 1 2022 12:00AM and < Max Value

The merge shows that that first partition is now for all data before February 1, 2022. This table also shows that there is one record in this partition. Based on Table 17-8 and Table 17-9, you can assume this one record is for some time in February 2022.

Now that you have merged the partitions, you can switch the last partition of dbo.CustomerOrderHistoryArchive to dbo.CustomerOrderPurge as shown in Listing 17-25.

Listing 17-25. Partition Switch Out of Customer Orders Over 60 Months Old

```
ALTER TABLE dbo.CustomerOrderHistoryArchive
SWITCH PARTITION 1 TO dbo.CustomerOrderPurge;
```

The expectation is that all of the data in partition 1 of dbo.CustomerOrderHistoryArchive is now in dbo.CustomerOrderPurge. You can verify this by getting the row counts of each table as you did before in Table 17-8. Querying the row counts for each table gets the results shown in Table 17-10.

Table 17-10. *Count of Records per Table for Managing Customer Orders*

Table Name	Record Count
dbo.CustomerOrderActive	1
dbo.CustomerOrderHistory	3
dbo.CustomerOrderHistoryArchive	11
dbo.CustomerOrderPurge	1

These record counts also indicate that the row for January 2022 in dbo.CustomerOrderHistoryArchive has been switched to dbo.CustomerOrderPurge. Before purging the data, you can again partition information for dbo.CustomerOrderHistoryArchive as shown in Table 17-11.

Table 17-11. *CustomerOrderHistoryArchive After Merging Partitions*

Partition Number	Record Count	Boundary Value	Text Comparison
1	0	2022-01-01	>= Min Value and < Feb 1 2022 12:00AM
2	1	2022-02-01	>= Feb 1 2022 12:00AM and < Mar 1 2022 12:00AM
3	1	2022-03-01	>= Mar 1 2022 12:00AM and < Apr 1 2022 12:00AM
4	1	2022-04-01	>= Apr 1 2022 12:00AM and < May 1 2022 12:00AM
5	1	2022-05-01	>= May 1 2022 12:00AM and < Jun 1 2022 12:00AM
6	1	2022-06-01	>= Jun 1 2022 12:00AM and < Jul 1 2022 12:00AM
7	1	2022-07-01	>= Jul 1 2022 12:00AM and < Aug 1 2022 12:00AM
8	1	2022-08-01	>= Aug 1 2022 12:00AM and < Sep 1 2022 12:00AM
9	1	2022-09-01	>= Sep 1 2022 12:00AM and < Oct 1 2022 12:00AM
10	1	2022-10-01	>= Oct 1 2022 12:00AM and < Nov 1 2022 12:00AM
11	1	2022-11-01	>= Nov 1 2022 12:00AM and < Dec 1 2022 12:00AM
12	0		>= Dec 1 2022 12:00AM and < Max Value

This also confirms that most of the data in the first partition has been switched out to dbo.CustomerOrderPurge.

Once the data has been switched from dbo.CustomerOrderHistoryArchive to dbo.CustomerOrderPurge, the data can be removed from dbo.CustomerOrderPurge. The quickest method to do this is to use truncate as shown in Listing 17-26.

Listing 17-26. Truncating a Table

```
TRUNCATE TABLE dbo.CustomerOrderPurge;
```

With the data purged out of dbo.CustomerOrderPurge, you can continue with the process of switching partitions between the remaining tables.

The next step is to update the partitions in dbo.CustomerOrderHistoryArchive. You need to prepare the table for the new data that will be switched out of dbo.CustomerOrderHistory. For your example, you need to split the last partition in dbo.CustomerOrderHistoryArchive to all for data from January 2023 to have its own partition. Listing 17-27 shows the T-SQL to split the most recent partition.

Listing 17-27. Split Partitions for Customer Orders Over Four Months Old

```
ALTER PARTITION FUNCTION CustomerOrderHistoryArchiveFunc()
SPLIT RANGE ('2023-01-01');
```

This partition split will create 13 available partitions in this table. This is similar to how the table was partitioned before you began your process. However, in your case, the partitions have been shifted by one month as shown in Table 17-12.

Table 17-12. *CustomerOrderHistoryArchive After Partition Switching*

Partition Number	Record Count	Boundary Value	Text Comparison
1	0	2022-02-01	>= Min Value and < Feb 1 2022 12:00AM
2	1	2022-03-01	>= Feb 1 2022 12:00AM and < Mar 1 2022 12:00AM
3	1	2022-04-01	>= Mar 1 2022 12:00AM and < Apr 1 2022 12:00AM
4	1	2022-05-01	>= Apr 1 2022 12:00AM and < May 1 2022 12:00AM
5	1	2022-06-01	>= May 1 2022 12:00AM and < Jun 1 2022 12:00AM
6	1	2022-07-01	>= Jun 1 2022 12:00AM and < Jul 1 2022 12:00AM
7	1	2022-08-01	>= Jul 1 2022 12:00AM and < Aug 1 2022 12:00AM
8	1	2022-09-01	>= Aug 1 2022 12:00AM and < Sep 1 2022 12:00AM
9	1	2022-10-01	>= Sep 1 2022 12:00AM and < Oct 1 2022 12:00AM
10	1	2022-11-01 00:00:00.000	>= Oct 1 2022 12:00AM and < Nov 1 2022 12:00AM
11	1	2022-12-01 00:00:00.000	>= Nov 1 2022 12:00AM and < Dec 1 2022 12:00AM
12	1	2023-01-01 00:00:00.000	>= Dec 1 2022 12:00AM and < Jan 1 2023 12:00AM
13	0		>= Jan 1 2023 12:00AM and < Max Value

You have successfully switched the January 2022 partition out of dbo.CustomerOrderHistoryArchive and switched in the January 2023 partition. You accomplished this by switching partitions from a partitioned table to a non-partitioned table.

The overall flow is that you switched one old partition out of dbo.CustomerOrderHistoryArchive, which is partitioned, to dbo.CustomerOrderHistoryPurge, which is not partitioned. You then truncated dbo.CustomerOrderHistoryPurge to remove the oldest data. After switching the partition out of dbo.CustomerOrderHistoryArchive, you were left with 11 partitions instead of 12. To get back to 12 partitions in dbo.CustomerOrderHistoryArchive, you split the newest partition. You then moved the oldest partition out of dbo. CustomerOrderHistory into dbo.CustomerOrderHistoryArchive. The oldest data from dbo.CustomerOrderHistoryArchive was moved into the partition that was split. Since dbo.CustomerOrderHistory now only has two partitions, you need to split the most recent partition so that the table will have three partitions again.

Now that the partition switching is complete, you can repeat the process for customer orders for the past one to three months. For this example, you will be switching partitions between two partitioned tables. Verifying your table counts in Table 17-13, there are only 11 records in dbo.CustomerOrderHistoryArchive.

Table 17-13. *Count of Records per Table for Managing Customer Orders*

Table Name	Record Count
dbo.CustomerOrderActive	1
dbo.CustomerOrderHistory	3
dbo.CustomerOrderHistoryArchive	11
dbo.CustomerOrderPurge	0

Since this table should have the past four to twelve months of data, you are missing data. From Table 17-12 above, you know that the last partition for data after January 2023 is empty. However, for this table partitioning to be complete, you need to switch the January 2023 data out of dbo.CustomerOrderHistory into the last partition of dbo. CustomerOrderHistoryArchive.

Since you are switching between two partitions, you need to identify which partition you are switching out from dbo.CustomerOrderHistory. Executing the query in Listing 17-28 will show the partition information for dbo.CustomerOrderHistory.

Listing 17-28. Merging Partitions for Customer Orders Over 15 Months Old

```
SELECT SCHEMA_NAME(tbl.[schema_id]) AS SchemaName,
    tbl.[name] AS TableName,
    pt.partition_number AS PartitionNumber,
    pt.[rows] AS NumberRecords,
    rv.[value] AS BoundaryValue,
    CASE WHEN ISNULL(rv.[value], rv2.[value]) IS NULL
```

```
                THEN 'N/A'
                ELSE
                        CASE WHEN fnc.boundary_value_on_right = 0
                                AND rv2.[value] IS NULL THEN '>='
                            WHEN fnc.boundary_value_on_right = 0
                                THEN '>'
                            ELSE '>='
                        END + ' '
                            + ISNULL(CONVERT(varchar(64), rv2.value),
                            'Min Value') + ' ' +
                        CASE fnc.boundary_value_on_right
                            WHEN 1 THEN 'and <'
                            ELSE 'and <='
                        END
                        + ' ' + ISNULL(CONVERT(varchar(64), rv.value),
                            'Max Value')
            END AS TextComparison
FROM sys.tables AS tbl
    INNER JOIN sys.indexes AS idx
    ON tbl.[object_id] = idx.[object_id]
    INNER JOIN sys.partitions AS pt
    ON idx.[object_id] = pt.[object_id]
        AND idx.index_id = pt.index_id
    INNER JOIN sys.partition_schemes AS pch
    ON idx.data_space_id = pch.data_space_id
    INNER JOIN sys.partition_functions AS fnc
    ON pch.function_id = fnc.function_id
    LEFT JOIN sys.partition_range_values AS rng
    ON fnc.function_id = rng.function_id
        AND rng.boundary_id = pt.partition_number
    LEFT JOIN sys.partition_range_values AS rv
    ON fnc.function_id = rv.function_id
        AND pt.partition_number = rv.boundary_id
    LEFT JOIN sys.partition_range_values AS rv2
```

```
        ON fnc.function_id = rv2.function_id
            AND pt.partition_number - 1= rv2.boundary_id
WHERE tbl.[name] = 'CustomerOrderHistory'
    AND idx.[type] <= 1
ORDER BY tbl.[name], pt.partition_number;
```

Running this query gets you the number of partitions, number of records, and boundary information for the table dbo.CustomerOrderHistory. The results from this query are in Table 17-14.

Table 17-14. *CustomerOrderHistory Before Partition Switching*

Partition Number	Record Count	Boundary Value	Text Comparison
1	0	2023-01-01	>= Min Value and < Jan 1 2023 12:00AM
2	1	2023-02-01	>= Jan 1 2023 12:00AM and < Feb 1 2023 12:00AM
3	1	2023-03-01	>= Feb 1 2023 12:00AM and < Mar 1 2023 12:00AM
4	1		>= Mar 1 2023 12:00AM and < Max Value

This table indicates that partition 2 has the records you need from dbo.CustomerOrderHistory. You can switch these records out using the T-SQL in Listing 17-29.

Listing 17-29. Partition Switch Out Customer Orders Over Four Months Old

```
ALTER TABLE dbo.CustomerOrderHistory SWITCH PARTITION 2
TO dbo.CustomerOrderHistoryArchive PARTITION 13;
```

You are taking the January 2023 data in the second partition of dbo.CustomerOrderHistory and switching this data into the last partition of dbo.CustomerOrderHistoryArchive, which allows for any records on or after January 2023. This is also a good time to verify the row counts for each table. Table 17-15 shows the row counts after you switched the data from dbo.CustomerOrderHistory to dbo.CustomerOrderHistoryArchive.

Table 17-15. *Count of Records per Table for Managing*
Customer Orders

Table Name	Record Count
dbo.CustomerOrderActive	1
dbo.CustomerOrderHistory	2
dbo.CustomerOrderHistoryArchive	12
dbo.CustomerOrderPurge	0

This confirms that you have successfully switched the January 2023 records between the two tables.

Now that you have switched the data out of dbo.CustomerOrderHistory, it is time to update the partitions for this table. Listing 17-30 shows the T-SQL needed to update the partitions so that the range begins with February 2023.

Listing 17-30. Merging the First Two Partitions for dbo.CustomerOrderHistory

```
ALTER PARTITION FUNCTION CustomerOrderHistoryFunc()
MERGE RANGE ('2023-01-01');
```

This code takes the first and second partitions in the table and merges them into one partition. This will reduce the total number of partitions from four to three. In your case, this will update the first partition so that it includes all data before February 2023. To finish preparing this table for the new month, you also need to split the last partition as shown in Listing 17-31.

Listing 17-31. Spliting the Last Partition for dbo.CustomerOrderHistory

```
ALTER PARTITION FUNCTION CustomerOrderHistoryFunc()
SPLIT RANGE ('2023-04-01');
```

After executing this T-SQL, there will be four partitions again in the table. The second-to-last partition will be for data in March 2023. The last partition will be for data on or after April 2023. The updated partitions are shown in Table 17-16.

Table 17-16. *CustomerOrderHistory Before Partition Switching*

Partition Number	Record Count	Boundary Value	Text Comparison
1	0	2023-02-01	>= Min Value and < Feb 1 2023 12:00AM
2	1	2023-03-01	>= Feb 1 2023 12:00AM and < Mar 1 2023 12:00AM
3	1	2023-04-01	>= Mar 1 2023 12:00AM and < Apr 1 2023 12:00AM
4	0		>= Apr 1 2023 12:00AM and < Max Value

You have successfully prepared the dbo.CustomerOrderHistory table to be ready to have the April 2023 data switched in from dbo.CustomerOrderActive.

Before you can switch data from the non-partitioned table of dbo.CustomerOrderActive, you need to add check constraints to the table. This allows SQL Server to ensure that the data being switched in from dbo.CustomerOrderActive to the fourth partition in dbo.CustomerOrderHistory can be successfully switched in. Listing 17-32 shows the T-SQL needed to create the check constraints needed.

Listing 17-32. Creating Check Constraints on the Non-Partitioned Table

```
ALTER TABLE dbo.CustomerOrderActive
WITH CHECK ADD CONSTRAINT CK_CustomerOrderActive3_MinDateCreated
CHECK (DateCreated IS NOT NULL AND DateCreated >= '2023-04-01');

ALTER TABLE dbo.CustomerOrderActive
WITH CHECK ADD CONSTRAINT CK_CustomerOrderActive3_MaxDateCreated
CHECK (DateCreated IS NOT NULL AND DateCreated < '2023-05-01');
```

This step assumes you have not previously created the check constraints. Due to the performance constraints, it is recommended to update the check constraint range instead of dropping the constraints. I will discuss that step after you finish switching the partitions.

Once these check constraints are added, you can switch out the data from dbo.CustomerOrderActive into dbo.CustomerOrderHistory as shown in Listing 17-33.

Listing 17-33. Partition Switch Out Last Month's Customer Orders

```
ALTER TABLE dbo.CustomerOrderActive
SWITCH TO dbo.CustomerOrderHistory PARTITION 4;
```

This T-SQL moves all of the data in dbo.CustomerOrderActive to the fourth partition in dbo.CustomerOrderHistory. Table 17-17 shows the record counts after switch the data out of dbo.CustomerOrderActive.

Table 17-17. *Count of Records per Table for Managing Customer Orders*

Table Name	Record Count
dbo.CustomerOrderActive	0
dbo.CustomerOrderHistory	3
dbo.CustomerOrderHistoryArchive	12
dbo.CustomerOrderPurge	0

You can verify the distribution of the rows in dbo.CustomerOrderHistory by executing the code from Listing 17-28. The partition distribution can be found in Table 17-18 below.

Table 17-18. *CustomerOrderHistory After Partition Switching*

Partition Number	Record Count	Boundary Value	Text Comparison
1	0	2023-02-01	>= Min Value and < Feb 1 2023 12:00AM
2	1	2023-03-01	>= Feb 1 2023 12:00AM and < Mar 1 2023 12:00AM
3	1	2023-04-01	>= Mar 1 2023 12:00AM and < Apr 1 2023 12:00AM
4	1		>= Apr 1 2023 12:00AM and < Max Value

The table dbo.CustomerOrderHistory has been updated to have the past three months of data. You have finished all of the necessary partition switching, but you still need to make some updates to the table dbo.CustomerOrderActive so that it can collect data for May 2023.

Since you are using T-SQL, you need to drop the existing check constraints on dbo. CustomerOrderActive and then create new constraints. Now that the table is empty, this process will be relatively quick. Listing 17-34 shows the code you can use to update the check constraint for May 2023.

Listing 17-34. Updating Check Constraints on dbo.CustomerOrderActive

```
ALTER TABLE dbo.CustomerOrderActive
DROP CONSTRAINT CK_CustomerOrderActive_MinDateCreated;

ALTER TABLE dbo.CustomerOrderActive
DROP CK_CustomerOrderActive_MaxDateCreated;

ALTER TABLE dbo.CustomerOrderActive
WITH CHECK ADD CONSTRAINT CK_CustomerOrderActive_MinDateCreated
CHECK (DateCreated IS NOT NULL AND DateCreated >= '2023-05-01');

ALTER TABLE dbo.CustomerOrderActive
WITH CHECK ADD CONSTRAINT CK_CustomerOrderActive_MaxDateCreated
CHECK (DateCreated IS NOT NULL AND DateCreated < '2023-06-01');
```

This code updates the table so that it will only allow records with a date created for May 2023 to be imported into the table. Add the constraint while the table is empty and don't try to add it during the window sliding code a month from now. This can save considerable time instead of adding the check constraint after the table it full.

Now that you have updated all of tables to have the correct data, you can also use partitioned views to access the data in these tables. There may be a business reason why an application or user would only want to access the current month of orders as well as the past three months. Refer to Listing 17-35.

Listing 17-35. Partitioned View for Recent Orders, Current Month, and Past Three Months

```
CREATE VIEW dbo.vwCustomerOrderHistoryRecent
AS
-- Select data from current read/write table
SELECT CustomerOrderHistoryID,
    CustomerOrderID,
    CustomerOrderHistoryStatusID,
```

```
        DateCreated,
        DateModified
FROM dbo.CustomerOrderActive
UNION ALL
-- Select data from historicial table
SELECT CustomerOrderHistoryID,
        CustomerOrderID,
        CustomerOrderHistoryStatusID,
        DateCreated,
        DateModified
FROM dbo.CustomerOrderHistory;
```

Now that you have updated the partitions, this view will return results for February 2023 through May 2023. If you find situations where access to all data is needed, then you can create another partitioned view to allow easy access to all available orders. In Listing 17-36, the view combines all order information from dbo.CustomerOrderActive, dbo.CustomerOrderHistory, and dbo.CustomerOrderHistoryArchive.

Listing 17-36. Partitioned View for All Orders

```
CREATE VIEW dbo.vwCustomerOrderHistoryAll
AS
-- Select data from current read/write table
SELECT CustomerOrderHistoryID,
        CustomerOrderID,
        CustomerOrderHistoryStatusID,
        DateCreated,
        DateModified
FROM dbo.CustomerOrderActive
UNION ALL
-- Select data from historicial table
SELECT CustomerOrderHistoryID,
        CustomerOrderID,
        CustomerOrderHistoryStatusID,
        DateCreated,
        DateModified
```

```
FROM dbo.CustomerOrderHistory
UNION ALL
-- Select data from archive table
SELECT CustomerOrderHistoryID,
     CustomerOrderID,
     CustomerOrderHistoryStatusID,
     DateCreated,
     DateModified
FROM dbo.CustomerOrderHistoryArchive;
```

This view shows any customer orders from February 2022 through May 2023. This is for any order that is in the database.

The intention for this example is to allow you to create a main table to hold data actively needed by the application. The history table is data needed for reporting, and the archive table is for data needed for archival purposes. This section covered how you can incorporate partition switching to manage data over an extended period of time. Often times our applications do not need access to the same data we need for other reporting purposes. Creating separate tables may be beneficial to allow you to manage data long-term.

This chapter continued on the concepts introduced into Chapter 18 about partitions. In this chapter, I covered how to switch partitions between non-partitioned tables, partitioned tables, and the combination of the two. You took this knowledge and used it to set up a method to manage archiving data. This allows you to manage access to data as well as potentially improve performance for your applications since they can use tables with smaller sets of data. This concludes the section on building scalable T-SQL that allows you to manage data effectively. The next section will cover how to enhance the security of your data.

CHAPTER 18

Implementing Security Features

It is becoming increasingly important to manage and control access to sensitive data within your database. This chapter goes through the various methods you can use to improve governance and access to sensitive data. The first section of this chapter explains how data discovery and classification can help you manage the sensitive data within your data estate. The next section uses dynamic data masking to prevent users from viewing sensitive data within specific columns. The third section covers how row-level security can be used to prevent users from accessing entire rows in a table. The chapter finishes with going through how you can use ledger to track changes to databases and tables.

Data Discovery and Classification

This section will walk you through how to search, categorize, and label sensitive data as well as show you how to view high-level information about all your sensitive data with built-in reports.

As data estates grow larger, it's become more difficult to manage all the different types of data within a company's databases. The focus on data governance has become an increasingly important part of managing data in an organization. This where SQL Server's built-in data discovery and classification can help you easily find data fields with sensitive data. Once identified, you can choose the information type and sensitivity label to give each column. If there are additional columns you want like to mark as sensitive, you have the option to add columns to the data classification. Using a built-in report, you can get a quick glance of what types of sensitive data you have as well as the significance of that sensitive data.

© Elizabeth Noble 2023
E. Noble, *Pro T-SQL 2022*, https://doi.org/10.1007/978-1-4842-9256-3_18

Data Discovery and Classification in SQL Server

Starting in SQL Server 2019 there are system catalog views you can use to review all columns. These views give you the ability to manage and review all sensitive data in one place.

If you are not certain how to begin using data discovery and classification, you can allow SQL Server to recommend columns that appear to have sensitive data. Figure 18-1 shows how you can use Object Explorer to begin the process of classifying your data.

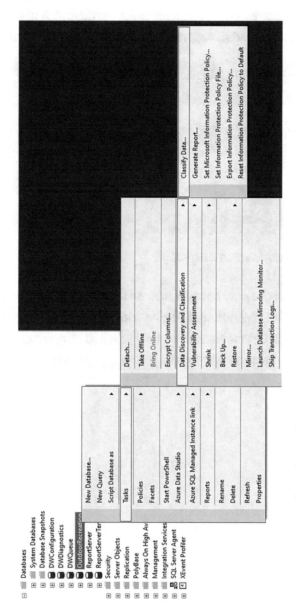

Figure 18-1. Classifying data on premises

You need to find the database where you want to classify data. Right-click the database name and select Tasks ➤ Data Discovery and Classification ➤ Classify Data. Once selected, SQL Server will scan through the database and open the Data Classification window. Figure 18-2 shows a message in the gray box indicating "We have found 6 columns with classification recommendations. Click here to view them."

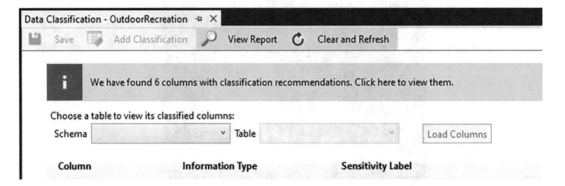

Figure 18-2. *Data classification output*

Clicking anywhere on the gray box will update the view in the Data Classification window. Now there is a new section that begins with a gray bar. The gray bar reads "6 columns with classification recommendations (click to minimize)." This additional section on the Data Classification window is shown in Figure 18-3.

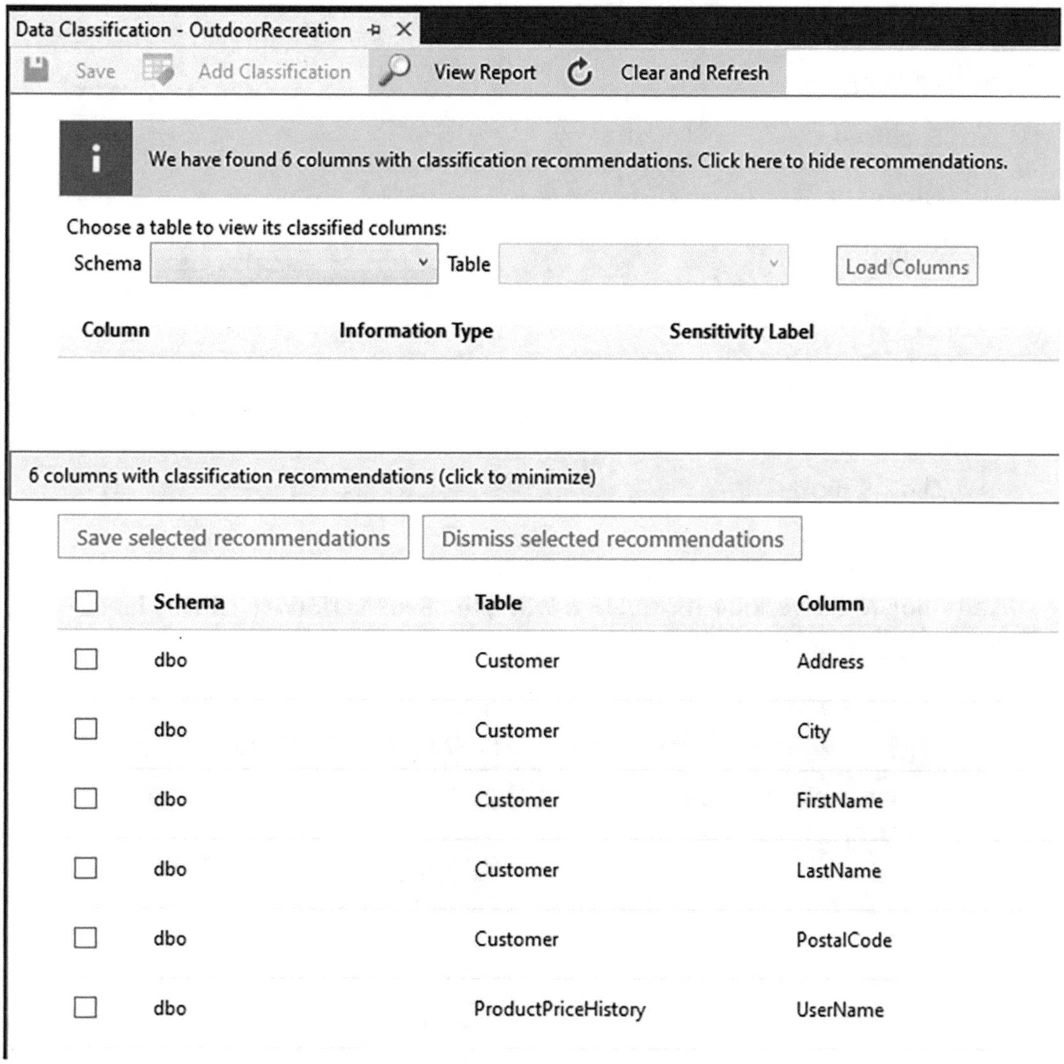

Figure 18-3. *Data classification results*

Figure 18-3 shows the six columns that have been identified as well as their schema and table where the columns can be found. The Data Classification window also has two columns with drop-down menus. The first column is for the Information Type. The available options are as follows:

- Networking

- Contact Info

- Credentials

- Credit Card

- Banking

- Financial

- Other

- Name

- National ID

- SSN

- Health

- Date of Birth

- [n/a]

In addition to the various information types, there are various sensitivity labels available as shown in Figure 18-4.

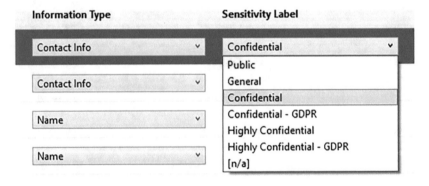

Figure 18-4. *Available sensitivity labels*

Once you have confirmed the information type and sensitivity label, you can select the check box on the left side of the table for as many columns as you want to update. Figure 18-5 shows a selected check box for the dbo.Customer.Address column.

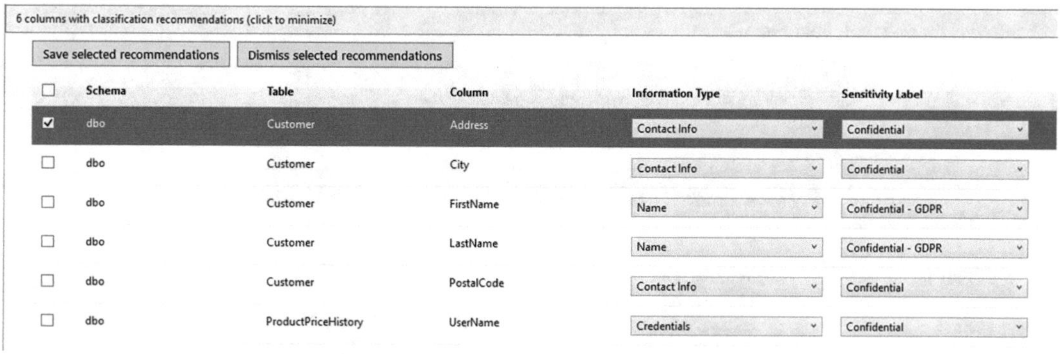

Figure 18-5. *Selecting to classify data on certain columns*

After the check box has been selected, you have the option to *Save selected recommendation* or *Dismiss selected recommendation*. In this example, save the recommendation for the first column, the Address in the dbo.Customer table. This is for example purposes only; you can choose to save one or more of the suggested columns.

Note   Sensitivity labels are managed in the Microsoft 365 compliance center. If you want different labels or your organization has different sensitivity labels already configured, you need to use the *Set Microsoft Information Protection Policy* option to access this configuration. However, using the Microsoft 365 compliance center is outside of the scope of this book.

Now that this information has been saved, the top portion of the Data Classification window will update. You can refer to Figure 18-6 that the column Address is now shown in the upper portion of the window.

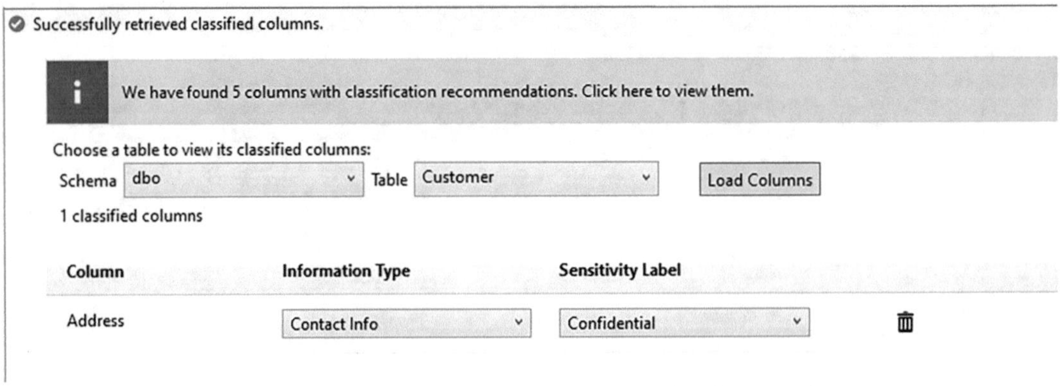

Figure 18-6. *Viewing classified data*

This indicates that the Address column in the dbo.Customer table is now tagged as sensitive data with an associated information type and label.

If you want to add a column to the data classification for the dbo.Customer table that was not recommended by SQL Server, you can select the Add Classification option near the upper left corner of the Data Classification window. The Add Classification button is highlighted in Figure 18-7.

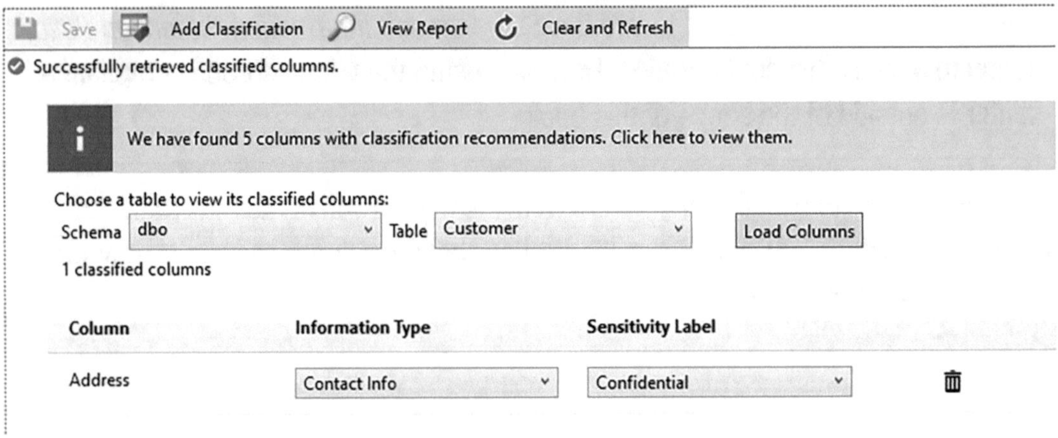

Figure 18-7. *Opening a window to add data classification*

Once you select the Add Classification, a new window opens on the right side of your screen. This is the Add Classification window, as shown in Figure 18-8.

Figure 18-8. *Adding a column to a classification*

This window inherits the schema and table referenced in the main Data Classification window. In this examples, this is the dbo schema and the `Customer` table. In the Add Classification window, you can select any column in the table as well as an information type and sensitivity label. Once you have confirmed these values, you can select the Add button at the bottom. This button will add the newly classified column into the main Data Classification window.

After adding columns to the data discovery and classification, you can review your sensitive data, the sensitivity labels, and information types in the SQL Data Classification Report, as shown in Figure 18-9.

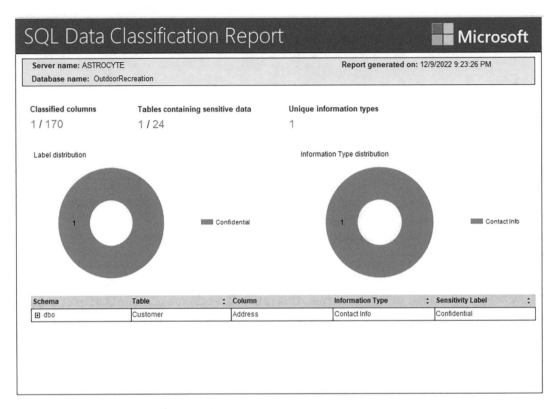

Figure 18-9. *The SQL Data Classification Report*

If you are unsure how to access this report, refer to Figure 18-1 above. This report can be accessed by right-clicking the database name and selecting Tasks ➤ Data Discovery and Classification ➤ Generate Report. The report shows the server name, database name, and report generation date.

The SQL Data Classification Report also shows the count of classified columns out of the total number of columns, the count of tables with sensitive data out of the total of all tables, and the count of the unique information types. Since you have only added one column, the count of classified columns is 1 column out of 170 total columns. Similarly, there is only 1 table out of 24 tables with sensitive data, and there is only one unique information type. There are also two charts showing a visual representation of the distribution of sensitivity labels and information types. For this example, both of these are green, showing only one label of Confidential and one sensitivity type of Contact Info. The last section of the report shows all columns that are classified as having sensitive data.

If you open up the column properties for the Address column in the dbo.Customer table, Figure 18-10 shows the sensitivity label for the Address column as Confidential.

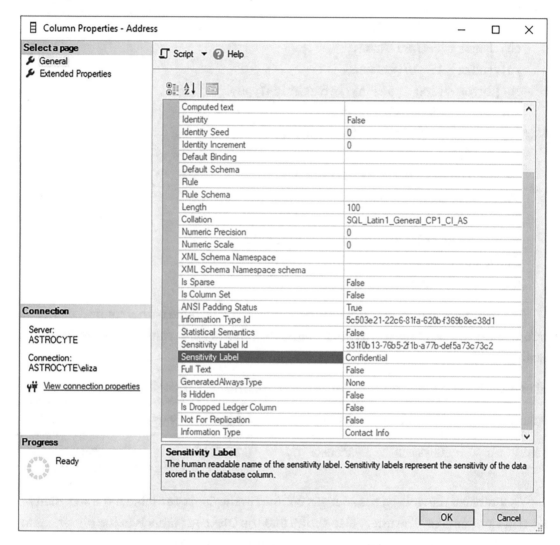

Figure 18-10. *Viewing Sensitivity in Column Properties*

The sensitivity label matches the same information you saw in the Data Classification window as well as the SQL Data Classification Report. You can also query the system catalog views to find all columns that have sensitivity labels as well as their information type. Listing 18-1 shows the query you can run to find all of the columns with sensitive data.

Listing 18-1. Finding Columns Identified as Sensitive Data

```
SELECT
    sch.[name] AS SchemaName,
    obj.[name] AS TableName,
    col.[name] AS ColumnName,
    sc.[information_type] AS InformationType,
    sc.[label] AS SensitivityLabel
FROM sys.sensitivity_classifications sc
    INNER JOIN sys.objects obj
    ON obj.[object_id] = sc.major_id
    INNER JOIN sys.columns col
    ON col.[object_id] = sc.major_id
            AND col.column_id = sc.minor_id
    INNER JOIN sys.schemas sch
    ON obj.[schema_id] = sch.[schema_id];
```

The results from this query include the schema name, table name, column name, information type, and sensitivity label. Table 18-1 shows these values for the query in Listing 18-1.

Table 18-1. *Viewing Columns Marked as Sensitive*

Schema Name	Table Name	Column Name	Information Type	Sensitivity Level
dbo	Customer	Address	Contact Info	Confidential

As indicated previously, the Address column in the Customer table has a sensitivity label of Confidential. The query also shows that the Customer table is in the dbo schema and the Address column has an information type of Contact Info.

Data Discovery and Classification in Azure

While data discovery and classification is also available in Azure SQL Database, Azure SQL Manager Instance, and Azure Synapse Analytics, the implementation and management is in the Azure portal.

To access or setup data discovery and classification, go to the SQL database (or other Azure SQL resource). Under Security, you will find a section for Data Discovery & Classification as shown in Figure 18-11.

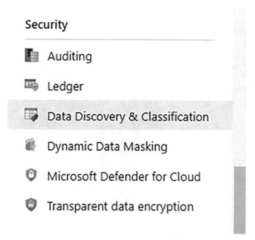

Figure 18-11. *Accessing the Data Discovery & Classification section in Azure*

SQL Server and Azure support the same two protection policies but choosing and managing the protection policies in Azure is easier than on SQL Server. Figure 18-12 shows how you can manage or change the protection policy by clicking Configure.

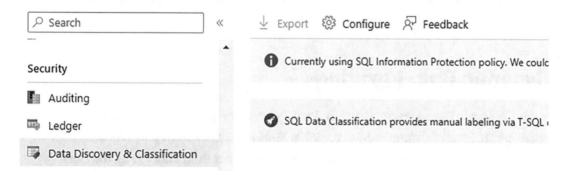

Figure 18-12. *Accessing the protection policy*

In addition to managing the protection policy, adding data classification labels is also managed on the Azure Portal. By selecting the Classification tab, as shown in Figure 18-13, you can classify and label your sensitive data.

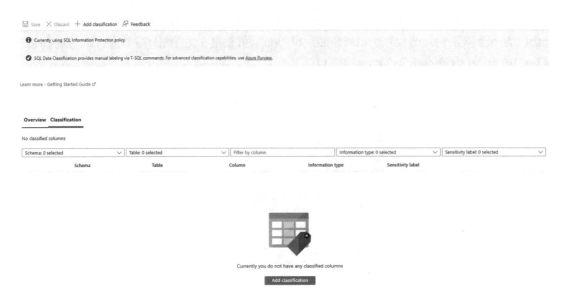

Figure 18-13. *Adding data classification*

Identifying, labeling, categorizing, and reporting on sensitive data can be an effective first step to improving data governance as it pertains to security. In addition, once you have identified all the sensitive columns, you can start making decisions about how you want to handle this data as it pertains to user access. In the following sections, I will discuss how you can obfuscate the columns or hide rows entirely based upon user permissions.

Dynamic Data Masking

In the Dynamic Data Masking section, I will go over the purpose, types, and implementations of dynamic data masking. Masking allows us to partially obfuscate data when we present it to certain users. This is different than encrypting the data. Masking an email address could turn ENoble@MyWebsite.com into EN***@**ite.com for users that aren't allowed to have access to actual email addresses. Those same users might only view the last four digits of a government ID number. I will also cover some challenges you may encounter when trying to implement dynamic data masking.

As discussed in the previous section, there may be data columns in your databases that contain information of varying levels of sensitivity. In many cases, you may not want all users to be able to access this data directly. There are situations when you can't limit access to the entire table because there are columns that the users need to be able to access. By using dynamic data masking, you can grant access to the entire table, but limit what can be returned in sensitive columns. Using a function on a column in a table, you can specify the type of masking you want to implement for any columns that have sensitive data. The types of masking available are as follows:

- Default: `default()`

- Email: `email()`

- Random: `random([start range], [end range])`

- Custom: `partial(prefix, [padding], suffix)`

- Datetime: `datetime("<time interval")`

With default data masking, SQL Server uses specific default values depending on the data type of the column. The email data masking function shows the first letter of the email address and the .com at the end for any string that ends in .com. The random data making function allows you to specify a range. The values displayed will be returned at random. If you want to create your own masking logic, you can use the custom masking function. The partial masking allows you to select how many characters of the original data type you would like unmasked for the beginning and the end of the mask. The padding in the middle is used to indicate your preferred mask to implement.

SQL Server 2022 introduces the ability to use the datatime masking function. This function is intended to mask the data to show the year, month, date, hour, minute, or second of the column selected. The supported data types for the datetime function include DATETIME, DATETIME2, DATE, TIME, DATETIMEOFFSET, or SMALLDATATIME. In order to specify the masking method for the column, you need to use the following values for the time interval in the datatime masking function:

- Year: Use "Y" as the time interval.

- Month: Use "M" as the time interval.

- Day: Use "D" as the time interval.

- Hour: Use "h" as the time interval.

- Minute: Use "m" as the time interval.

- Second: Use "s" as the time interval.

To create a table with dynamic data masking, Listing 18-2 includes the T-SQL to use a masking function on the Address column.

Listing 18-2. Creating a Table with Dynamic Data Masking

```
CREATE TABLE [dbo].[Vendor](
    [VendorID]         INT     IDENTITY(1,1)              NOT NULL,
    [CompanyName]      VARCHAR(100)                       NOT NULL,
    [Address]          VARCHAR(100)
        MASKED WITH (FUNCTION = 'partial(1, "xxxx", 2)')
                                                          NOT NULL,
    [City]             VARCHAR(100)                       NOT NULL,
    [PostalCode]       VARCHAR(20)                            NULL,
    [Country]          VARCHAR(75)                        NOT NULL,
    [EmailAddress]     VARCHAR(100)
        MASKED WITH (FUNCTION = 'email()')
                                                          NOT NULL,
    [IsActive]         BIT
        CONSTRAINT DF_Vendor_IsActive    DEFAULT 1    NOT NULL,
    [DateCreated]      DATETIME2(2)
        CONSTRAINT DF_Vendor_DateCreated DEFAULT GETDATE()
                                                          NOT NULL,
    [DateModified]     DATETIME2(2)
        CONSTRAINT DF_Vendor_DateModified DEFAULT GETDATE()
                                                          NOT NULL,
    [DateDisabled]     DATETIME2(2)                           NULL,
 CONSTRAINT [PK_Vendor] PRIMARY KEY CLUSTERED ([VendorID] ASC)
);
```

This table has two columns with masked data. The first column is the Address on the dbo.Vendor table. This column uses the partial function. The number 1 at the beginning indicates that the first character will be unmasked. The padding of xxxx will follow the first unmasked character. The end of the Address column, when masked, will show the last two unmasked characters.

In order to walk through an example of how dynamic data masking works, you should add some data to the dbo.Vendor table. If you have created the dbo.Vendor table, you can use the T-SQL code in Listing 18-3 to insert a new record into the table.

Listing 18-3. Adding Data to the Vendor Table

```
INSERT INTO dbo.Vendor
     (CompanyName, [Address], City, PostalCode, Country, EmailAddress)
VALUES
(
     'Kayak Unlimited',
     '567 3rd Street',
     'Somewhere',
     '10005',
     'United States',
     'sales@kayakutld.com'
);
```

Now that you have added the vendor Kayak Unlimited to the dbo.Vendor table, you can query the data to confirm the new vendor has been added. Executing the query in Listing 18-4 allows you to see the unmasked data.

Listing 18-4. Querying the Vendor Table

```
SELECT CompanyName,
     [Address],
     EmailAddress
FROM dbo.Vendor;
```

The results from Listing 18-4 are shown in Table 18-2.

Table 18-2. *Viewing Unmasked Vendor Information*

Company Name	Address	Email Address
Kayak Unlimited	567 3rd Street	sales@kayakutld.com

Referencing the table, you are able to identify that the address is 567 3rd Street and the email address is sales@kayakutld.com. Now that you've confirmed you the data is unmasked, you can test how a user with different permissions may see the data.

Listing 18-5 contains T-SQL code to create a new user, grant permissions, and execute a query as that user.

Listing 18-5. Creating a User to Test Dynamic Data Masking

```
CREATE USER TestDynamicMasking WITHOUT LOGIN;

GRANT SELECT ON SCHEMA::dbo TO TestDynamicMasking;

 -- impersonate for testing:
EXECUTE AS USER = 'TestDynamicMasking';

SELECT CompanyName,
       [Address],
       EmailAddress
FROM dbo.Vendor;

REVERT;
```

You created the user TestDynamicMasking, but you have not associated that user with a login. You have given the user the ability to select data on the dbo schema. After executing the query to access the Company Name, Address, and Email Address, you can see the results shown in Table 18-3.

Table 18-3. *Viewing Masked Vendor Information*

Company Name	Address	Email Address
Kayak Unlimited	5xxxxet	sXXX@XXXX.com

The table shows that Address as 5xxxxet and the email address as sXXX@XXXX. com. While this user has SELECT permissions, they do not have UNMASK permissions. Therefore, this confirms that the data as you expect. If you grant this login UNMASK permissions and rerun the example from Listing 18-5, the user will be able to see the unmasked data.

In SQL Server 2022, there is also the ability to have granular unmasking for a given user. This allows the user to view specific unmasked data as indicated in the GRANT UNMASK statement. The code in Listing 18-6 gives the UNMASK permission to the EmailAddress column for the TestGranularUnmasking user.

Listing 18-6. Creating a User to Test Granular Unmasking

```
CREATE USER TestGranularUnmasking WITHOUT LOGIN;

GRANT SELECT ON SCHEMA::dbo TO TestGranularUnmasking;

GRANT UNMASK ON dbo.Vendor(EmailAddress) TO TestGranularUnmasking;

  -- impersonate for testing:
EXECUTE AS USER = 'TestGranularUnmasking';

SELECT CompanyName,
     [Address],
     EmailAddress
FROM dbo.Vendor;

REVERT;
```

This T-SQL code indicates that the TestGranularUnmasking should be able to unmask the EmailAddress on the dbo.Vendor table. Table 18-4 shows the results returned from the query in Listing 18-6.

Table 18-4. *Viewing Granular Unmasked Vendor Information*

Company Name	Address	Email Address
Kayak Unlimited	5xxxxet	sales@kayakutld.com

The query results have sales@kayakutld.com as the EmailAddress, confirming that this column in unmasked. As expected, the Address column is still masked and has the value of 5xxxxet. In SQL Server 2022, you can use granular unmasking for databases, schemas, tables, or columns using the T-SQL code GRANT UNMASK ON.

Until now, I have only covered how to create a new table with dynamic data masking. However, it is far more likely that you will want to implement dynamic data masking when adding new columns in an existing table or on columns in existing tables. The T-SQL code to mask a customer's data of birth using the datetime masking function is available in Listing 18-7.

Listing 18-7. Adding a Column to a Table with Dynamic Data Masking

```
ALTER TABLE dbo.Customer
ADD DateOfBirth DATETIME2(2)
     MASKED WITH (FUNCTION = 'datetime("Y")')
     NULL;
```

This code will create a new column named `DateOfBirth` to the `dbo.Customer` table. As the same time, the column `DateOfBirth` will also be configured to use the datatime masking function. This T-SQL will cause any user that has not been granted UNMASK to the database, schema, table, or column to only have the year returned for the data of birth.

After you have used data discovery and classification to identify columns with sensitive data, you can decide how you may want to implement dynamic data masking on those columns. In addition, it is also possible to add a new column to an existing table where the new column is configured for dynamic data masking. Listing 18-8 has the T-SQL code needed to change an existing column to using dynamic data masking.

Listing 18-8. Altering an Existing Column to Have Dynamic Data Masking

```
ALTER TABLE dbo.CustomerOrder
ALTER COLUMN OrderNumber
     ADD MASKED WITH (FUNCTION = 'default()');
```

The existing column `OrderNumber` in the `dbo.CustomerOrder` table should be updated to use the default masking function. However, the column `OrderNumber` cannot be modified due to pre-existing dependencies on it. The error messages returned are indicated in Figure 18-14.

```
Msg 5074, Level 16, State 1, Line 83
The object 'vwCustomerOrderBound' is dependent on column 'OrderNumber'.
Msg 4922, Level 16, State 9, Line 83
ALTER TABLE ALTER COLUMN OrderNumber failed because one or more objects access this column.
```

Figure 18-14. *Error message: table has foreign key*

The error messages state that *The object 'viewCustomerOrderBound' is dependent on column 'OrderNumber'. ALTER TABLE ALTER COLUMN OrderNumber failed because one or more objects access this column.* The first error message is due to the schema binding on the view `dbo.vwCustomerOrderBound`. The second error message occurs any time the column has a dependency including non-clustered indexes. One possible solution is to temporarily remove the schema binding from the view dbo.vwCustomerOrderBound as shown in Listing 18-9.

Listing 18-9. Temporarily Removing Schema Binding

```
CREATE OR ALTER VIEW dbo.vwCustomerOrderBound
AS
SELECT cus.FirstName,
      cus.LastName,
      cus.FirstName + ' ' + cus.LastName AS FullName,
      ord.CustomerOrderID,
      ord.OrderNumber,
      ord.OrderDate,
      ord.ShipDate
FROM dbo.CustomerOrder ord
      INNER JOIN dbo.Customer cus
      ON ord.CustomerID = cus.CustomerID;
```

Once the schema binding has been removed, you can rerun the T-SQL code from Listing 18-8. The code will execute successfully, and the column OrderNumber will use default dynamic data masking going forward. Once the column has been updated, you can add schema binding back to the view dbo.vwCustomerOrderBound as shown in Listing 18-10.

Listing 18-10. Adding Schema Binding Back to the View

```
CREATE OR ALTER VIEW dbo.vwCustomerOrderBound
WITH SCHEMABINDING
AS
SELECT cus.FirstName,
      cus.LastName,
      cus.FirstName + ' ' + cus.LastName AS FullName,
      ord.CustomerOrderID,
      ord.OrderNumber,
      ord.OrderDate,
      ord.ShipDate
```

```
FROM dbo.CustomerOrder ord
    INNER JOIN dbo.Customer cus
    ON ord.CustomerID = cus.CustomerID;
```

This section showed how you can configure columns to use dynamic data masking. This includes the various types of functions available to mask your data. This section also included samples on how to create a table, add a column, or alter an existing column to use dynamic data masking. The next logical step is to consider what to do if you want to implement the concept of row-level encryption.

Row-Level Security

In this section, you will go over the definition of row-level security. You will also go through an example of how to set up row-level security and explore different types of functionality you can use when creating security policies.

SQL Server does not provide the ability to mask data at the column level. However, row-level security allows you to define who can see which rows beyond what the WHERE clause indicates.. Since this row limitation defined by row-level security will apply in addition to any WHERE clause that may be part of a query executed against the database, it will also limit a user's ability to modify data.

To start, let's check to see the results of a query before you implement row-level security. Listing 18-11 shows the count of all customers by country in the dbo.Customer table.

Listing 18-11. Viewing Current Customers by Country

```
SELECT Country, COUNT(*) AS CustomerCount
FROM dbo.Customer
GROUP BY Country;
```

The results from the query are shown in Figure 18-5.

Table 18-5. *Customer Count by Country*

Country	Customer Count
Egypt	1
India	200702
Mexico	200704
Portugal	1
United States	1

This query returns five countries with different customer counts per country. Now that you know the customer distribution before you implement row-level security, you can check to see what happens once you implement row-level security. A table-valued function can be used to determine if a row is eligible to be viewed by returning a one or a zero. A one indicates that the user can view the row, and a zero prevents the user from viewing the row. Listing 18-12 shows a function to manage row-level security based on the country provided.

Listing 18-12. Creating a Function for Row-Level Security

```
CREATE FUNCTION dbo.TVF_SecuritySalesIndia(@Country AS VARCHAR(25))
    RETURNS TABLE
WITH SCHEMABINDING
AS
    RETURN SELECT 1 AS tvf_region_result
    WHERE @Country = 'India' OR USER_NAME() = 'dbo';
```

This function will cause any use that is not in dbo to return a value of 1 only if the country is India. The dbo user will still be able to see all customers regardless of country.

Once you have created a table-valued function, you need a way to manage whether the row-level security is on or off. This is done by creating a security policy. When creating a security policy, there are three options. You can either indicate a FILTER PREDICATE, a BLOCK PREDICATE, or both. A filter predicate is used to determine what data can be accessed. This filter applies to SELECT, UPDATE, and DELETE operations. A block predicate can be used in combination with a function to block specific users from modifying the specified columns. An example of a BLOCK PREDICATE will be shown later in this chapter. In the example where you created the function in Listing 18-12, you can create a security policy on this function. Listing 18-13 shows a security policy using a filter predicate.

Listing 18-13. Creating a Filter Security Policy for Row-Level Security

```
CREATE SECURITY POLICY CountryFilter
ADD FILTER PREDICATE dbo.TVF_SecuritySalesIndia(Country)
     ON dbo.Customer
WITH (STATE=ON);
```

This security policy passes the country from the `dbo.Customer` table to the function creating in Listing 18-12. The dbo user will still be able see all customers as shown in Table 18-6 using the T-SQL code in Listing 18-11.

These results are the same as those in Table 18-5, as expected. This indicates that the current user is not affected by the new security policy.

Table 18-6. *Customer Count by Country for Current User*

Country	Customer Count
Egypt	1
India	200702
Mexico	200704
Portugal	1
United States	1

Once this security policy is in place, all other users will only be able to see customer information for the country of India. To test the new security policy for all other users, create a user and rerun the same query, as shown in Listing 18-14.

Listing 18-14. Viewing Current Customers by Country for a Test User

```
CREATE USER TestRowLevel WITHOUT LOGIN;

GRANT SELECT ON SCHEMA::dbo TO TestRowLevel;

  -- impersonate for testing:
EXECUTE AS USER = 'TestRowLevel';

SELECT Country, COUNT(*) AS CustomerCount
FROM dbo.Customer
GROUP BY Country;

REVERT;
```

The new user, TestRowLevel, is created but is not tied to a login. The only permission granted to the user is the ability to select data on objects in the dbo schema. The T-SQL code then executes the same query as in Listing 18-11. The results of that query are shown in Table 18-7.

Table 18-7. *Customer Count by Country for Current User*

Country	Customer Count
India	200702

The only result returned is for customers in the country of India. This confirms that the security policy is working as expected. Checking the execution plan for Listing 18-13, you saw an example of how to use a FILTER PREDICATE within a security policy to prevent a user from updating data. However, you may want to prevent certain users from being able to update data in the database, even if they can access the data. This is where you use a BLOCK PREDICATE.

Note   You will be unable to add a predicate to a table that already has a predicate unless you alter the existing security policy. Alternatively, you can have more than one predicate, including a filter and block, on the same table when you create security policy.

Listing 18-15 shows a BLOCK PREDICATE that will prevent the any user except dbo from updating any customer data that is not in the country of India.

Listing 18-15. Creating a Block Security Policy for Row-Level Security

```
CREATE SECURITY POLICY CountryBlock
ADD BLOCK PREDICATE dbo.TVF_SecuritySalesIndia(Country)
       ON dbo.Customer
WITH (STATE=ON);
```

The security policy will allow any non-dbo users to view all data in the dbo.Customer table. However, those same users will not be able to modify any data that has a country other than India. An example of how this block predicate works is shown in Listing 18-16.

Listing 18-16. Updating Data for a Test User

```
GRANT SELECT ON SCHEMA::dbo TO TestRowLevel;
GRANT UPDATE ON SCHEMA::dbo TO TestRowLevel;
  -- impersonate for testing:
EXECUTE AS USER = 'TestRowLevel';

UPDATE Customer
SET DateDisabled = GETDATE();

REVERT;
```

This query is attempting to update the DateDisabled for all records for the user TestRowLevel. This user has been granted the ability to update records. However, since there is a block predicate in place, the user will receive the error shown in Figure 18-15 when trying to update all the records.

```
Msg 33504, Level 16, State 1, Line 28
The attempted operation failed because the target object 'OutdoorRecreation.dbo.Customer'
has a block predicate that conflicts with this operation.
If the operation is performed on a view, the block predicate might be enforced on the underlying table.
Modify the operation to target only the rows that are allowed by the block predicate.
The statement has been terminated.
```

Figure 18-15. *Error message with block predicate*

The message indicates that this user cannot modify the data on the table dbo. Customer due to the block predicate security policy.

If you want to temporarily disable the security policy created in Listing 18-13, you can execute the T-SQL code in Listing 18-17.

Listing 18-17. Disabling a Security Policy

```
ALTER SECURITY POLICY CountryFilter
WITH (STATE=OFF);
```

This code disables the security policy. Identifying that the security policy can be disabled indicates that additional measures may need to put in place to confirm that someone has not tampered with the security policy.

Tip   If the security policy is disabled, the row-level security will not prevent users from viewing or updating data as expected.

As stated previously, you can only have one policy per table. However, that policy can have one filter and block predicate within it for the same table. Having more than one predicate that modifies data per table is not supported. These predicates can also use different table-valued functions. If a user is affected by a FILTER PREDICATE, they will be able to insert any data even if they are limited to the data they can SELECT, UPDATE, or DELETE. Similarly, if a user has a BLOCK PREDICATE but not a filter predicate, they will be able to see all data even if they cannot modify the data. However, these users are blocked from any change to the data including inserts, updates, and deletes. While you see a value of 1 for the RETURN in the table-valued function, any non-NULL value will produce the same result for row-level security. When there is no match, the function returns NULL and implements the security policy.

Always use some level of caution when using table-valued functions. For instance, you should avoid multiple table joins within the table-valued function. You also need to ensure that your query inside the function will not return a NULL due to conversion or calculation issues. It is also worth noting that the execution plan will not include an operator for the table-valued function. Instead, you will see a predicate listed on one of the operators, as shown in Figure 18-16.

Clustered Index Scan (Clustered)

Scanning a clustered index, entirely or only a range.

Physical Operation	Clustered Index Scan
Logical Operation	Clustered Index Scan
Actual Execution Mode	Row
Estimated Execution Mode	Row
Storage	RowStore
Number of Rows Read	401410
Actual Number of Rows for All Executions	200702
Actual Number of Batches	0
Estimated I/O Cost	7.00016
Estimated Operator Cost	7.07378 (98%)
Estimated Subtree Cost	7.07378
Estimated CPU Cost	0.073618
Estimated Number of Executions	1
Number of Executions	12
Estimated Number of Rows for All Executions	237057
Estimated Number of Rows Per Execution	237057
Estimated Number of Rows to be Read	401410
Estimated Row Size	16 B
Actual Rebinds	0
Actual Rewinds	0
Ordered	False
Node ID	2

Predicate

CONVERT_IMPLICIT(varchar(25),[OutdoorRecreation].[dbo].[Customer].
[Country],0)='India' OR user_name()=N'dbo'

Object

[OutdoorRecreation].[dbo].[Customer].[PK_Customer]

Output List

[OutdoorRecreation].[dbo].[Customer].Country

Figure 18-16. Predicate in an execution plan

This section covered the purpose of row-level security as well as an example of how to implement this type of security. The example also showed how the results are different when a filter predicate is in place for row-level security. There was also an example of how to disable row-level security, if needed.

Ledger

As mentioned, there are times when you want to monitor user behavior as it pertains to modifying data in the database. SQL Server 2022 introduces a way to confirm the integrity of the data stored in the database through ledger tables. These ledger table create a blockchain by hashing each transaction and using the hash for that transaction to has the next transaction. This method of hashing each transaction repeats for each successive transaction. This section will discuss the types of ledger tables available. You'll see examples of how you can set up either of these ledger tables, as well as the process to migrate an existing table to a ledger table. This section will finish with how you can verify if there has been tampering with the ledger tables.

The first type of ledger table is the append-only ledger table. This table functions in the same manner as its name; it only allow inserts to the table. It is not possible to update or delete data. This can be very helpful if you need a way to log user interactions like accessing an application, table, or badge readers. The T-SQL code in Listing 18-18 creates an append-only ledger table to record when a user accesses applications.

Listing 18-18. Creating an Append-Only Ledger Table

```
CREATE TABLE dbo.SystemAccess
(
        SystemAccessID        BIGINT       IDENTITY(1,1)       NOT NULL,
        UserID                INT                              NOT NULL,
        IsActive              BIT
            CONSTRAINT DF_SystemAccess_IsActive           DEFAULT 1
                                                          NOT NULL,
        DateCreated           DATETIME2(2)
            CONSTRAINT DF_SystemAccess_DateCreated DEFAULT
                SYSDATETIME()
                                                          NOT NULL
)
WITH (LEDGER = ON (APPEND_ONLY = ON));
```

The portion of the code that creates this table as an append-only ledger table is the last line of the CREATE TABLE statement. The last line enabled the ledger functionality with LEDGER = ON. The append-only portion of the table creation is specified in APPEND_ONLY = ON.

Now that you have created an append-only ledger table, you can insert some data to see how the ledger table functionality works. The T-SQL in Listing 18-19 simulates what would happen when a user attempts to log in to an application.

Listing 18-19. Adding Data to Append-Only Ledger Table

```
INSERT INTO dbo.SystemAccess (UserID)
VALUES (1001);
```

The query inserts a UserID into the dbo.SystemAccess table. Now that you have inserted a record, you can query how data is recorded in the dbo.SystemAccess table. Note that since the table dbo.SystemAccess is an append-only ledger table, there are two additional columns available in the table. The columns ledger_start_transaction_id and ledger_start_sequence_number are always generated for an append-only ledger table. The query in Listing 18-20 views the data in the dbo.SystemAccess table.

Listing 18-20. Viewing Data in the Append-Only Ledger Table

```
SELECT SystemAccessID,
       UserID,
       ledger_start_transaction_id,
       ledger_start_sequence_number
FROM dbo.SystemAccess;
```

The ledger_start_transaction_id column is system-generated with the transaction ID that inserted the record. The ledger_start_sequence_number is the sequence number within the transaction. The ledger information is in Table 18-8.

Table 18-8. *Viewing System Access*

System Access ID	User ID	Ledger Start Transaction ID	Ledger Start Sequence Number
1	1001	120017	0

The transaction ID for the insert is 120017. The sequence for the insert is 0.

Now that you have inserted a data record into dbo.SystemAccess, let's see what happens when you try to update a record in dbo.SystemAccess. Listing 18-21 shows the T-SQL code to update the DateCreated on dbo.SystemAccess.

Listing 18-21. Attempting to Update Append-Only Ledger Table

```
UPDATE dbo.SystemAccess
SET DateCreated = GETDATE()
WHERE SystemAccessID = 1;
```

When you try to update the record, you get the error message in Figure 18-17.

```
Msg 37359, Level 16, State 1, Line 173
Updates are not allowed for the append only Ledger table 'dbo.SystemAccess'.
```

Figure 18-17. *Error message when trying to update an append-only ledger table*

As expected, the dbo.SystemAccess table is not able to be updated by any user, including the dbo and sysadmin role members. When attempting the update in Listing 18-9, you get the error *Updates are not allowed for the append only Ledger table 'dbo. SystemAccess.'* Now that I have discussed the use of append-only ledger tables, I will go through setting up an updatable ledger table.The updatable ledger tables allow you to track when data is inserted, like the append-only ledger table. Both the append-only and updatable ledger tables are system-versioned tables. Since the updatable ledger table uses system-versioning, the prior version of any modified record is stored in history table. In addition, updatable ledger tables record when data is updated or deleted in the table. An update is recorded as a delete for the deletion of the existing data and an insert for the new value in the column. The T-SQL code to create an updatable table is in Listing 18-22.

Listing 18-22. Creating an Updatable Ledger Table

```
CREATE TABLE dbo.ApplicationRule(
    ApplicationRuleID                                    INT         NOT NULL,
    ApplicationRuleDescription                           VARCHAR(50) NOT NULL,
    IsActive BIT
        CONSTRAINT DF_ApplicationRule_IsActive           DEFAULT (1) NOT NULL,
    DateCreated [datetime]
        CONSTRAINT DF_ApplicationRule_DateCreated  DEFAULT (GETDATE())
                                                               NOT NULL,
    DateModified [datetime]
        CONSTRAINT DF_ApplicationRule_DateModified DEFAULT (GETDATE())
                                                                   NULL,
```

```
CONSTRAINT PK_ApplicationRule_ApplicationRuleID
     PRIMARY KEY CLUSTERED (ApplicationRuleID ASC)
)
WITH
(
 SYSTEM_VERSIONING = ON (HISTORY_TABLE =
     dbo.ApplicationRuleHistory),
 LEDGER = ON
);
```

In Listing 18-4, you specify a history table and the name for the history table. If you had not specified a name, SQL Server would still create a history table. This table is implicitly created as part of creating an updatable ledger table. The code to create an updatable ledger table is similar to the T-SQL in Listing 18-18. The last couple of lines in the query are the T-SQL code that is needed to create an updatable ledger table. The same command LEDGER = ON enables the ledger only functionality. The SYSTEM_ VERSIONING = (HISTORY_TABLE = dbo.ApplicatinRuleHistory) creates the table that will be used to record ledger history. Listing 18-23 has the T-SQL code to find the objects created when creating an updatable ledger table.

Listing 18-23. Viewing Updatable Ledger Objects

```
SELECT
       ts.[name] + '.' + t.[name] AS ledger_table_name,
       hs.[name] + '.' + h.[name] AS history_table_name,
       vs.[name] + '.' + v.[name] AS ledger_view_name
FROM sys.tables AS t
       INNER JOIN sys.tables AS h
       ON h.[object_id] = t.history_table_id
       INNER JOIN sys.views v
       ON v.[object_id] = t.ledger_view_id
       INNER JOIN sys.schemas ts
       ON ts.[schema_id] = t.[schema_id]
       INNER JOIN sys.schemas hs
       ON hs.[schema_id] = h.[schema_id]
```

```
    INNER JOIN sys.schemas vs
    ON vs.[schema_id] = v.[schema_id]
WHERE t.[name] = 'ApplicationRule';
```

This query gives the ledger table, history table, and ledger view for the updatable ledger table ApplicationRule. The ledger view is a system-created view that combines the data from the updatable ledger table and the history table. The names of the tables and views created are the following:

- dbo.ApplicationRule

- dbo.ApplicationRuleHistory

- dbo.ApplicationRule_Ledger

Since the table has been created, you can modify the data in the table dbo.ApplicationRule. In order to add and modify data, you can execute the queries in Listing 18-24.

Listing 18-24. Adding and Modifying Data in the ApplicationRule Table

```
INSERT INTO dbo.ApplicationRule (ApplicationRuleDescription)
VALUES ('Show only active customers');

UPDATE dbo.ApplicationRule
SET IsActive = 0,
    DateModified = GETDATE()
WHERE ApplicationRuleDescription = 'Show only active customers';
```

These queries create an entry in the dbo.ApplicationRule table and deactivate that application rule. To view the information recorded for the updatable ledger table, the query in Listing 18-25 has the T-SQL code you need.

Listing 18-25. Viewing Ledger History Information

```
SELECT trn.commit_time AS CommitTime,
    trn.principal_name AS UserName,
    app.ApplicationRuleDescription,
    app.IsActive,
```

```
    app.ledger_operation_type_desc AS ActionType
FROM dbo.ApplicationRule_Ledger app
    INNER JOIN sys.database_ledger_transactions trn
    ON app.ledger_transaction_id = trn.transaction_id
ORDER BY trn.commit_time;
```

This query uses the view dbo.ApplicationRule_Ledger to find the information that was recorded for the updatable ledger table. The query shows when the query was run, who executed the query, the columns from the dbo.ApplicationRule table, and the operator type performed. Since the updatable ledger table is system-versioned, users cannot modify data in the history table. Table 18-9 shows the results of Listing 18-23.

Table 18-9. *Viewing System Access*

Commit Time	Username	Application Rule Description	IsActive	Action Type
2023-05-01	Enoble	Show only active customers	1	INSERT
2023-05-01	Enoble	Show only active customers	1	DELETE
2023-05-01	Enoble	Show only active customers	0	INSERT

The first record in this table shows when the new application rule was inserted into the table. The Action Type shows the insert. The second and third rows are for when the IsActive column was updated from True (1) to False (0). The second row shows the delete since the IsActive of 1 is being deleted. The third row shows the inserted where the IsActive is set to False (0). The level of granularity record is similar some of the tracking discussed in Chapter 15.

Note that I have not given you an example of how to add ledger table functionality to an existing table. That is because it's not possible to add ledger functionality to an existing table. In order to implement ledger tables to an existing table, you need to make a new ledger table. Listing 18-26 shows the creation of a new updatable ledger table for the dbo.Product table.

Listing 18-26. Creating a New Updatable Ledger Table

```
CREATE TABLE dbo.Product_LedgerTable(
        ProductID           INT        IDENTITY(1,1)        NOT NULL,
        ProductName         VARCHAR(25)                     NOT NULL,
        ProductPrice        DECIMAL(6, 2)                   NOT NULL,
        IsActive            BIT
            CONSTRAINT DF_Product_LedgerTable_IsActive DEFAULT (1)
                                                            NOT NULL,
        DateCreated         DATETIME2(2)
            CONSTRAINT DF_Product_LedgerTable_DateCreated
                DEFAULT (GETDATE())
                                                            NOT NULL,
        DateModified        DATETIME2(2)
            CONSTRAINT DF_Product_LedgerTable_DateModified
                DEFAULT (SYSDATETIME())
                                                            NOT NULL,
        DateDisabled        DATETIME2(2)                    NULL,
 CONSTRAINT PK_Product_LedgerTable PRIMARY KEY CLUSTERED (ProductID ASC)
)
WITH
(
 SYSTEM_VERSIONING = ON,
 LEDGER = ON
);
```

Once the updatable ledger table has been created, you can use the system-stored procedure sys.sp_copy_data_in_batches to copy data from the original table to the new ledger table. An example of this code is in Listing 18-27.

Listing 18-27. Copying Data from Product to Product_Ledger

```
EXECUTE sp_copy_data_in_batches
    @source_table_name = N'Product' ,
    @target_table_name = N'Product_Ledger';
```

You specify the source table as the original table. The target table is the newly created updatable ledger table.

The benefit to using ledger tables is the ability to verify if someone has tampered with the ledger tables. To check for tampering, you first need to generate the ledger digest. Executing the T-SQL in Listing 18-28 will give you the JSON needed to verify tampering.

Listing 18-28. Finding the Ledger Digest

```
EXECUTE sp_generate_database_ledger_digest;
```

Once the JSON is executed, you need to copy the JSON to pass into the next system stored procedure. To check for tampering, you can execute the T-SQL code in Listing 18-29.

Listing 18-29. Checking Ledger Tables for Tampering

```
EXECUTE sp_verify_database_ledger N'
{
     "database_name":"OutdoorRecreation",
     "block_id":0,
     "hash":"0xE32AE537398CB3F1276C7BA16AF359C8E0365CB6AAE9617AEA40B54
     D61EAC865",
     "last_transaction_commit_time":"2022-12-09T23:40:44.9700000",
     "digest_time":"2022-12-11T22:24:06.7619426"
}';
```

If there has been no tampering, the query above with return the results *Ledger verification successfully verified up to block 0*. If you are using Azure SQL, you can use the query in Listing 18-30 to check for tampering.

Listing 18-30. Checking Azure SQL Database Ledger Tables for Tampering

```
DECLARE @digest_locations NVARCHAR(MAX) =
     (
          SELECT *
          FROM sys.database_ledger_digest_locations
          FOR JSON AUTO, INCLUDE_NULL_VALUES
     );

SELECT @digest_locations as digest_locations;
```

```
BEGIN TRY
    EXEC sys.sp_verify_database_ledger_from_digest_storage @digest_
    locations;
    SELECT 'Ledger verification succeeded.' AS Result;
END TRY
BEGIN CATCH
    THROW;
END CATCH
```

If you want to track the changes to the database over time, SQL Server 2022 introduces the ability to create a ledger database for SQL Server. The code to create a SQL Server ledger database is available in Listing 18-31.

Listing 18-31. Creating a SQL Server Ledger Database

```
CREATE DATABASE OutdoorRecreated_Ledger
WITH LEDGER = ON;
```

If you are using Azure SQL Database, you can configure the ledger in the Security table when creating the database in the Azure portal. Other options include PowerShell and Azure CLI. It is also possible using the T-SQL in Listing 18-32.

Listing 18-32. Creating a SQL Server Ledger Database

```
CREATE DATABASE OutdoorRecreated_Ledger
(
    EDITION = 'GeneralPurpose',
    SERVICE_OBJECTIVE='GP_Gen5_2',
    MAXSIZE = 2 GB
)
WITH LEDGER = ON;
```

Similar to the SQL Server ledger data, the Azure SQL Database ledger database must only contain ledger tables. If not specified, any table created will default to an updatable ledger table.

CHAPTER 19

Implementing Encryption

Continuing from Chapter 18, where I introduced methods to manage security features, this chapter will focus on how to implement encryption for your databases. The first section of the chapter will go over how you can use Always Encrypted to ensure that your most sensitive data remains encrypted at rest and in flight. The second section of the chapter will guide you through how to implement Transparent Data Encryption at rest for your databases. The goal of this chapter is to build on the concept of security access to data by also giving you the ability to encrypt data as needed.

Always Encrypted

In Chapter 18, I went over how you can use Dynamic Data Masking to prevent users from accessing sensitive data. This section covers how you can use Always Encrypted to ensure your sensitive data is encrypted at rest and in flight. I will discuss the types of encryption available and their associated limitations. This section will also include examples of how you can implement Always Encrypted and how to remove a column from Always Encrypted. Finally, this section will give a brief overview of how you can rotate the keys used for Always Encrypted.

Always Encrypted allows you to implement a separation of duties between the individuals maintaining the databases and the applications accessing the data. With Always Encrypted, applications can easily access encrypted data while the database administrators are unable to view this data, making this form of encryption especially appealing for the most sensitive data including credit card numbers, social security numbers, or national IDs.

Before implementing Always Encrypted, let's go over the two types of encryption available. The first type of encryption available is deterministic encryption. When using this encryption type, the same plain text value will have the same encrypted value. Therefore, deterministic encryption can be vulnerable to a brute force attack. The

E. Noble, *Pro T-SQL 2022*, https://doi.org/10.1007/978-1-4842-9256-3_19

advantages of deterministic encryption are that administrators can allow users to search, group, index, and join on encrypted columns. The other type of encryption available is randomized encryption. This type of encryption is more secure. However, you will not be able to use these columns in JOIN...ON, WHERE, or GROUP BY clauses or indexes.

Note   You will need to update connection strings to use `Column Encryption Setting = enabled` as part of the connection string.

Before enabling Always Encrypted, you should query the existing table to see how the data is returned from a query before Always Encrypted is implemented. Listing 19-1 has the query to find all customers in the United States as well as their social security number, abbreviated as SSN.

Listing 19-1. Creating the Master Key and Certificate

```
SELECT CustomerID, SSN
FROM dbo.Customer
WHERE Country = 'United States';
```

Once this query is executed, you can review the results in Table 19-1.

Table 19-1. *View Column Before Always Encrypted*

CustomerID	SSN
401405	123-45-6789

For this example, I created an entirely fictitious social security number, 123-45-6789. As Table 19-1 indicates, you can read the actual social security number.

To setup Always Encrypted, navigate to the database in Object Explorer. You can expand the `Tables` folder and navigate to the column you would like to encrypt. In this example, you will be encrypting the SSN column. By right-clicking the SSN column in the `dbo.Customer` table, you can select the Encrypt Column option, as shown in Figure 19-1.

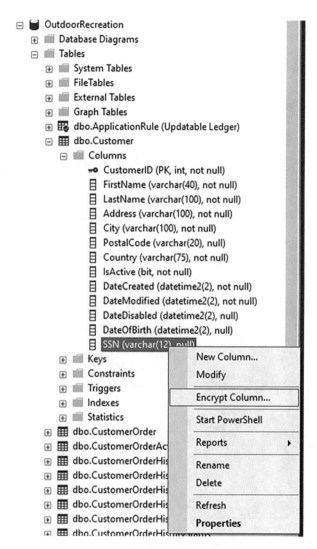

Figure 19-1. *Selecting the column to encrypt*

Selecting the Encrypt Column option will cause the Always Encrypted wizard to open. The first screen in the wizard is in the Introduction. The introduction step in the Always Encrypted wizard states "*Always Encrypted is designed to protect sensitive information - such as credit card numbers - stored in SQL Server databases. It enabled clients to encrypt data inside client applications and never reveal the encryption keys to SQL Server.*" Refer to Figure 19-2.

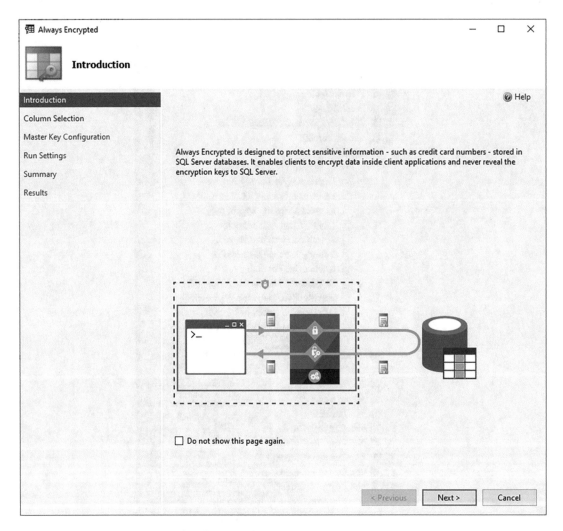

Figure 19-2. *Selecting the column to encrypt*

There is also a diagram on the Introduction screen displaying a graphical version of the statement above. Once you have reviewed this screen, you can select Next. The Column Selection is the second screen in the wizard. As shown in Figure 19-3, you can use this screen to select the column name, encryption type, and encryption key.

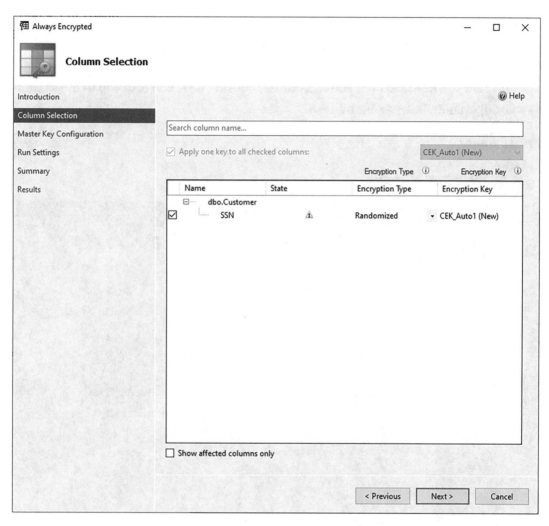

Figure 19-3. *Select the column(s) and encryption type*

As shown in Figure 19-3, select the column SSN. The options for encryption type are plaintext, deterministic, or randomized. Choose to use randomized for the social security number. Since this is the first column you are encrypting, you only have the option to make the new encryption key CEK_Auto1. The warning message in Figure 19-3 is shown in Figure 19-4.

The collation will be changed from SQL_Latin1_General_CP1_CI_AS to Latin1_General_BIN2.

Figure 19-4. *Warning for collation change*

This warning message indicates that Always Encrypted will change the collation method of the SSN column from SQL_Latin1_General_CP1_CI_AS to Latin1_General_BIN2.

Now that you have selected your columns, choosing Next will take you to the Master Key Configuration. Refer to Figure 19-5.

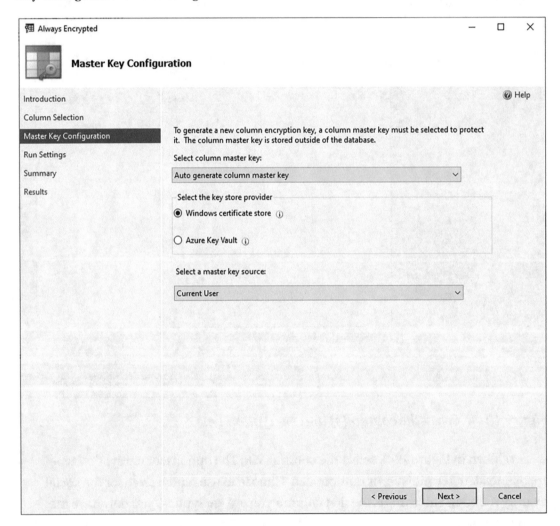

Figure 19-5. *Master Key Configuration screen*

On this screen, you can specify the column master key, key store provider, and master key source. For this example, choose Auto generate column master key, Windows certificate store, and Current User. Choose the Windows certificate store here but note that I recommend using the Azure Key Vault for your Production environment.

Now that you have configured the master key for Always Encrypted, you can select Next to go to the Run Settings screen. As shown in Figure 19-6, you can choose to either generate a PowerShell script to run later or implement Always Encrypted now.

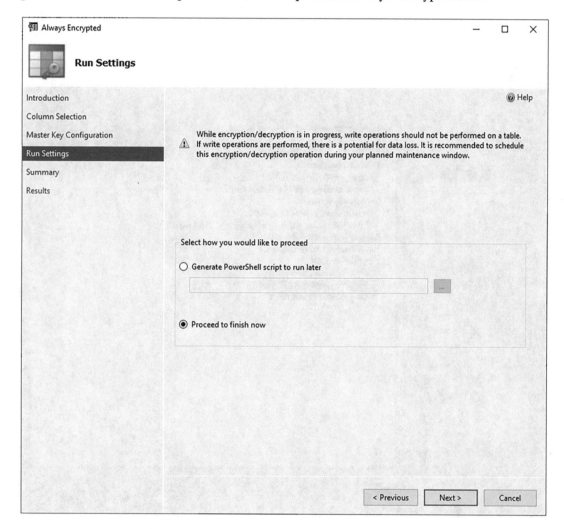

Figure 19-6. *Run settings*

There is a warning stating that *While encryption/decryption is in progress, write operations should not be performed on a table. If write operations are performed, there is a potential for data loss. It is recommended to schedule the encryption/decryption operation during your planned maintenance window*. As I am running this in my development environment, I can choose to run this now.

After selecting Next, you will have the option to verify the Always Encrypted configuration on the Summary screen in the Always Encrypted wizard. Figure 19-7 shows the summary for the current setup.

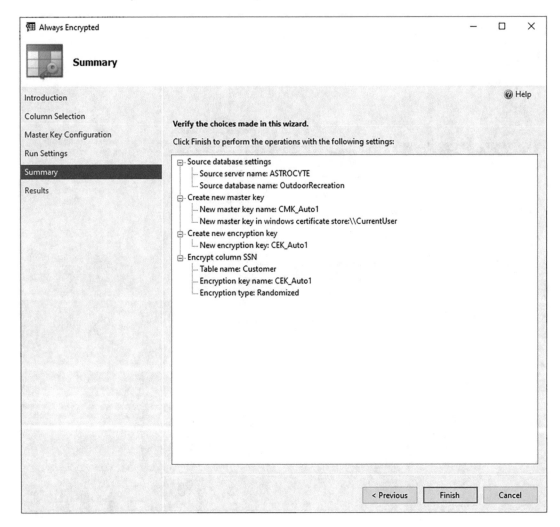

Figure 19-7. *Summary for Always Encrypted*

Once you have reviewed the summary configuration, you can select Next. However, Figure 19-8 shows the error message I saw when I tried to finish implementing Always Encrypted.

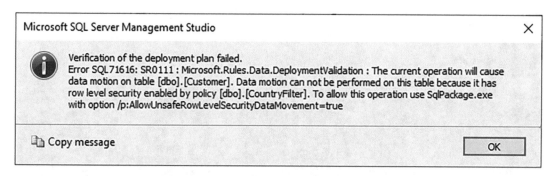

Figure 19-8. *Error for table with row-level security*

The error message indicates that the *data motion cannot be performed on this table because it has row-level security enabled by policy [dbo].[CountryFilter].* This is referencing the row-level security that was set up in Chapter 18. I dropped row-level security from the table and retried adding Always Encrypted to the SSN column, as show in Figure 19-9.

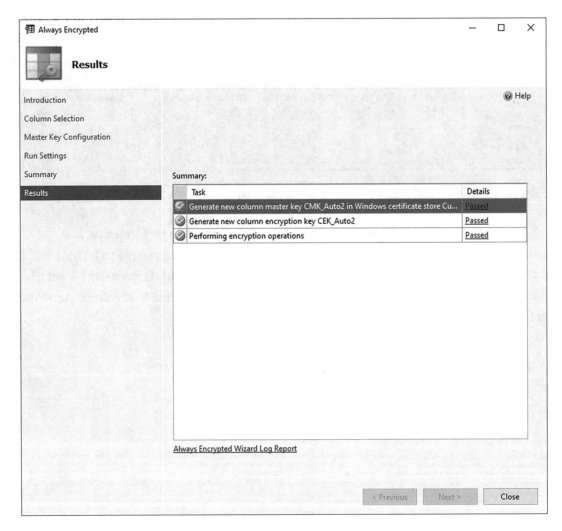

Figure 19-9. *Successful Always Encrypted column*

After Always Encrypted is added, the Results screen displays the status. For this example you have successfully generated a new column master key, generated a new column encryption key, and performed the encryption operations.

You can now execute the same query from Listing 19-1. The results of this query using the current connection are shown in Table 19-2.

Table 19-2. *View Column After Always Encrypted*

Customer ID	SSN
401405	0x01C0716043E1D97311AA2A0C456CA358359B9A4882D2B80FC1A 95718BB31066F165150E252F3582003B543F4B37A7C3DE7A9310F 487CFDDD3969DC05AC76B0B2BE

It is evident that the SSN column is now encrypted. As indicated previously, it is still possible to access the data using an updated connection string as long as you have access to the encryption key previously generated. Figure 19-10 shows the Always Encrypted option that can be configured in SSMS.

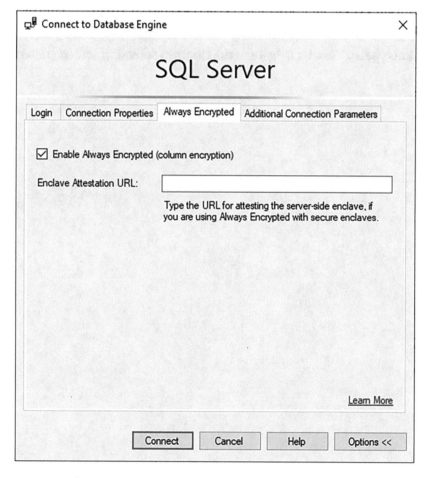

Figure 19-10. *Configuring the Always Encrypted connection*

After you have connected to the SQL Server instance with the Always Encrypted enabled, you can rerun the query in Listing 19-1. The results of running this query are shown in Table 19-3.

Table 19-3. *View Column With Always Encrypted Enabled*

CustomerID	SSN
401405	XXX-XXX-XXXX

As indicated in the table, enabling Always Encrypted allows you to access the data in the SSN column unencrypted.

If you find that you no longer want or need to use Always Encrypted on a column, you can navigate to column encryption as shown in Figure 19-1. Once you open the Always Encrypted wizard, navigate to the Column Selection screen shown in Figure 19-11.

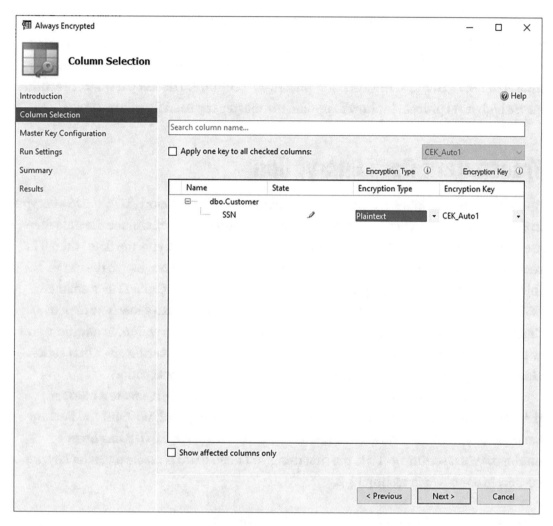

Figure 19-11. *Removing an encryption key*

By selecting the encryption type of plaintext, the column will no longer be affected by Always Encrypted.

Another consideration of using Always Encrypted is the need to rotate encryption keys. Here is a brief overview of the steps to rotate the master key:

1. Create a new column master key.

2. Use the new column master key to encrypt an existing column's encryption keys.

3. Update applications with the new column master key.

4. Clean up the old column master key.

This section covered the purpose of Always Encrypted. The deterministic and randomized encryption keys have been explained. You set up Always Encrypted for a column and confirmed that the encryption is working as expected. This section also indicated how to remove Always Encrypted from a column. The last part of this section gave a high level process for how to update the master key used for encryption.

Transparent Data Encryption

Another option for data encryption is Transparent Data Encryption (TDE). TDE encrypts the entire database on disk, not just a column or group of columns. Since the data files are encrypted, the backups are also encrypted. SQL Server decrypts the data when it is read into the buffer pool so the users have no idea this is going on, hence the name. In this section, you will implement Transparent Data Encryption. Once TDE is enabled, SQL Server will attempt to encrypt the data. This section will also show how to pause that encryption and view the current status of the database encryption. In addition, you will learn how to verify the certificate backups and back up the certificate. This section closes with instructions on how to remove Transparent Data Encryption.

Before you begin implementing Transaction Data Encryption, create a plan for managing certificate. This is a critical part of implementing TDE. **Without the backup certificate, you will not be able to restore a database backup if TDE has been enabled.** When setting up TDE, the first thing you need to do is create a master key and certificate as shown in Listing 19-2.

Listing 19-2. Creating a Master Key and Certificate

```
USE master;

CREATE MASTER KEY ENCRYPTION BY PASSWORD = 'oUtd@or*R3cre&tion!';

CREATE CERTIFICATE DataEncryption
WITH SUBJECT = 'OutdoorRecreation Certificate';
```

The master key and certificate should be created in the master database. After creating the master key and certificate, you need to create a database encryption key. As shown in Listing 19-3, make sure you create the key in the OutdoorRecreation database.

Listing 19-3. Creating a Database Encryption Key

```
USE OutdoorRecreation;
GO

CREATE DATABASE ENCRYPTION KEY
WITH ALGORITHM = AES_256
ENCRYPTION BY SERVER CERTIFICATE DataEncryption;
```

The encryption is created using the server certificate from Listing 19-2. The algorithm for the encryption key can be AES 128, AES 192, or AES 256. If you have not backed up your encryption key, you will get the following message:

Warning   The certificate used for encrypting the database encryption key has not been backed up. You should immediately back up the certificate and the private key associated with the certificate. If the certificate ever becomes unavailable or if you must restore or attach the database on another server, you must have backups of both the certificate and the private key or you will not be able to open the database.

The database is now ready to have Transparent Data Encryption enabled as written in Listing 19-4.

Listing 19-4. Enabling Transparent Data Encryption

```
ALTER DATABASE OutdoorRecreation
SET ENCRYPTION ON;
```

Once you enable TDE on the database, the background encryption operation will run in the background.

Note   Enabling TDE for any user database will also enable TDE on `tempdb`.

If you want to suspend this process, Listing 19-5 has the T-SQL code you can run.

Listing 19-5. Suspending a Background Encryption Operation

```
ALTER DATABASE OutdoorRecreation
SET ENCRYPTION SUSPEND;
```

Learning how to manage the encryption status for the database can be helpful. It may be even more helpful to know how to monitor the status of the database encryption. The query in Listing 19-6 can be used to find information about the state of database encryption.

Listing 19-6. Finding the Encryption Status

```
SELECT db.[name] AS DatabaseName,
      encryptor_type,
      encryption_state_desc,
      encryption_scan_state_desc
FROM sys.dm_database_encryption_keys ky
      INNER JOIN sys.databases db
      ON ky.database_id = db.database_id;
```

This query provides the database name, type of encryption, description of the encryption status, and the encryption scan description. When the encryption is in progress, you should have results similar to those in Table 19-4.

Table 19-4. *Encryption Status Suspended*

Database Name	Encryptor Type	Encryption State Description	Encryption Scan State Description
tempdb	ASYMMETRIC KEY	ENCRYPTED	COMPLETE
OutdoorRecreation	CERTIFICATE	ENCRYPTION_IN _PROGRESS	SUSPENDED

In the scenario for the OutdoorRecreation database, the encryption is in progress. This query was run after I ran the code in Listing 19-5, so the scan state of suspended is expected.

To resume TDE encryption, you can execute the code in Listing 19-7.

Listing 19-7. Suspending a Data EncryptionScan

```
ALTER DATABASE OutdoorRecreation
SET ENCRYPTION RESUME;
```

This will allow the encryption process to continue on the `OutdoorRecreation` database. Table 19-5 shows the results from running the code in Listing 19-6 after resuming the encryption scan.

Table 19-5. *Encryption Status in Progress*

Database Name	Encryptor Type	Encryption State Description	Encryption Scan State Description
tempdb	ASYMMETRIC KEY	ENCRYPTED	COMPLETE
OutdoorRecreation	CERTIFICATE	ENCRYPTION_IN _PROGRESS	RUNNING

The `OutdoorRecreation` database is relatively small so the encryption process should not take too long. If you execute the T-SQL in Listing 19-6 again, you get the results in Table 19-6.

Table 19-6. *Encryption Status Completed*

Database Name	Encryptor Type	Encryption State Description	Encryption Scan State Description
tempdb	ASYMMETRIC KEY	ENCRYPTED	COMPLETE
OutdoorRecreation	CERTIFICATE	ENCRYPTED	COMPLETE

Table 19-6 indicates that the database `OutdoorRecreation` has been encrypted. Now that TDE has been enabled on your database, make sure to have your certificate backed up in a secure location.

Caution   If you are accustomed to encrypted your certificates with a password, do not do this to the certificate enabling TDE. Your database will be inaccessible after the instance is restarted.

The query in Listing 19-8 indicates how you can find the most recent backup date for the certificate.

Listing 19-8. Checking the Last Backup Date for a Certificate

```
USE master;
GO

SELECT crt.pvt_key_last_backup_date AS LastBackupDate,
      DB_NAME(dky.database_id) AS EncryptedDatabase,
      crt.[name] AS CertificateName
FROM sys.certificates crt
      INNER JOIN sys.dm_database_encryption_keys dky
      ON crt.thumbprint = dky.encryptor_thumbprint;
```

Executing this query will return the last backup date for all certificates with the associated database. The results for this query are Table 19-7.

Table 19-7. *Result for the Last Backup Date for a Certificate*

Last Backup Date	Encrypted Database	Certificate Name
NULL	OutdoorRecreation	DataEncryption

This table indicates that the DataEncryption certificate for the OutdoorRecreation database has not been backed up. To back up the certificate, you can execute the T-SQL in Listing 19-9.

Listing 19-9. Backing Up Encryption Certificates

```
BACKUP CERTIFICATE DataEncryption
TO FILE = N'C:\Certificates\DataEncryption.cer'
   WITH PRIVATE KEY (
   FILE = N'C:\Certificates\DataEncryption.pvk',
     ENCRYPTION BY PASSWORD = 'pRO!5Ql#'
  );
```

For this example, this certificate has been backed up to the Certificates folder on the C drive.

Note   As of the writing of this book, you need to specify the private key in order for the certificate last backup date to be updated.

After backing up the certificate, you can rerun the query in Listing 19-8. The results of this query are in Table 19-8.

Table 19-8. *Result for the Last Backup Date for a Certificate*

Last Backup Date	Encrypted Database	Certificate Name
2023-04-01	OutdoorRecreation	DataEncryption

The results above indicate that the certificate has been backed up recently.

Caution   Once TDE is enabled, backup files will also be encrypted with the database encryption key.

Now that you have a backup of the certificate saved, you should save the certificate backup to a secure location. You should also make sure you have the password that was used to back up the certificate. Both of these will be needed if you need to restore the database encrypted with TDE to a new server. If I want to restore this database to a new server, I need to copy the backup of the certificate to the new server. For this example, I will copy DataEncryption.cer and DataEncryption.pvk to D:\Certificates on the new server. I can then execute the code from Listing 19-10 to create a new certificate using the previous certificate and encryption key.

Listing 19-10. Backup Encryption Certificates

```
USE master;

CREATE MASTER KEY ENCRYPTION BY PASSWORD = 'oUtd@or*R3cre&tion#';

CREATE CERTIFICATE DataEncryption
FROM FILE = N'D:\Certificates\DataEncryption.cer'
  WITH PRIVATE KEY (
      FILE = N'D:\Certificates\DataEncryption.pvk',
      DENCRYPTION BY PASSWORD = 'pRO!5Ql#'
  );
```

After creating a new master key and certificate, you will be able to restore the database encrypted with TDE.

If you find that you want to remove TDE, you first need to disable the encryption by executing the T-SQL code in Listing 19-11.

Listing 19-11. Removing TDE

```
ALTER DATABASE OutdoorRecreationTDE
SET ENCRYPTION OFF;
```

This will cause the background decryption process to run so it is advisable to perform this action during a maintenance window. Before continuing, you must confirm that the decryption process is complete by executing the query in Listing 19-8. Once the decryption process is complete, you can drop the database encryption key using the code in Listing 19-12.

Listing 19-12. Dropping the Database Encryption Key

```
DROP DATABASE ENCRYPTION KEY;
```

After the encryption key is dropped, TDE has been removed from the database.

This section covered the purpose of Transparent Data Encryption. You also learned the steps needed to implement TDE. This section also provided instructions on how you can suspend or resume the encryption or decryption process and view the status of the background process. You also learned how to back up and restore the certificate and find that most recent backup date for the certificates. Finally, this section covered how to remove TDE.

Index

Printed in the United States
by Baker & Taylor Publisher Services